6 lines to an inch

12 spaces to an inch Elite

10 spaces to an inch Pica

CONTENTS

DIVISION 1
LEVEL ONE

LEVEL TWO

DIVISION 2
LEVEL THREE

INTENSIVE COURSE

COLLEGE KEYBOARDING/TYPEWRITING
11th Edition

Charles H. Duncan
Professor of Business Education
Eastern Michigan University

S. Elvon Warner
Head, Department of Information Management
University of Northern Iowa

Thomas E. Langford
President, Bay State Junior College
Boston, Massachusetts

Susie H. VanHuss
Professor of Management
University of South Carolina

ISBN: 0-538-20270-X

1 2 3 4 5 6 7 8 9 10 11 12 13 14 H 2 1 0 9 8 7 6 5

Printed in U.S.A.

COVER PHOTO: Aetna Life and Casualty Company

PHOTO, p. 6: Location courtesy of Public Library of Hamilton County, Mt. Washington Branch

PHOTO, p. 57: Location courtesy of American Express Travel Related Services Co., Inc., Cincinnati Office

Published by

T27 SOUTH-WESTERN PUBLISHING CO.

CINCINNATI   WEST CHICAGO, IL   DALLAS   PELHAM MANOR, NY   LIVERMORE, CA

PREFACE

College Keyboarding/Typewriting, Intensive Course, 11th edition, is the latest revision of a series of learning materials that were first designed specifically for college students over fifty years ago. Since 1930, the various editions of the book have established a reputation for providing college students with those skills and knowledges required for efficient operation of keyboard-activated equipment. In keeping with this tradition, the 11th edition aims specifically at helping students achieve the following personal and professional goals:

1 to operate keyboard-activated equipment rapidly and accurately;
2 to improve their written communication skills;
3 to learn to format rapidly and accurately the kinds of documents most often used in business, professional, and government offices;
4 to develop high-level document production skill;
5 to learn to work and to evaluate their work with little supervision;
6 to become acquainted with terminology, equipment, and procedures of modern offices.

ORGANIZATION

College Keyboarding/Typewriting is divided into three main divisions and six levels of learning structured to correspond with student skill-growth patterns. Division 1 introduces students to keyboarding and formatting techniques, teaches them to proofread and make corrections, and develops their basic keystroking speed and accuracy skills. Division 2 builds directly on the competencies developed in Division 1, leading students toward greater speed, improved accuracy, and greater refinement of formatting ability. Division 3 emphasizes vocational application of keyboarding/formatting/editing skills in sections that portray realistic office-like settings that encourage students to perform as if they were at work in real job situations.

SPECIAL FEATURES

Content. The scientifically structured lessons in College Keyboarding/Typewriting are built on the findings of scholars who have researched the areas of keyboarding learning and application.

The lessons, therefore, have a sound psychological as well as topical base that leads to practical achievement.

Goals. To orient and motivate students, learning goals are stated at the beginning of each section of lessons. Intermediate goals are stated periodically throughout the sections to identify purpose of practice, to indicate how to practice, and to identify expected outcomes.

Skill building. Special sections devoted exclusively to the development and improvement of basic skills are interspersed among application sections. Instructors may use these sections in order of occurrence, group them for intensive emphasis, or select from them to tailor instruction to individual student needs.

Measurement. Sections of lessons that focus on measurement of achievement in basic skill and production power are set midway through each division and again at its end. Thus, ample opportunities are provided to evaluate each student's growth.

Controlled copy. Basic skill-building and measurement paragraph copy is triple-controlled to insure uniformity of difficulty. Three factors—syllable intensity, average word length, and percentage of high-frequency words—are simultaneously controlled in each paragraph to assure valid and reliable measures of skill growth. Special keyboarding drills are controlled in other ways to assure "loading" of the factors to be emphasized. Even application problems are controlled so that they progress in length, in complexity, and in vocabulary.

Cycled learning. Each operational presentation (letters, reports, tables, and others) is repeated in cycles of emphasis that provide ample practice, assure longer and better retention, and maximize opportunities for transfer.

Input skills. To provide realism and promote transfer of learning, emphasis is placed on preparing final copy from script and rough-draft source documents.

Directions/illustrations. Complete directions and visual models are used liberally in presenting new learning. The directions-left/copy-right format helps students distinguish operational directions from copy to be typed. As soon as appropriate, students are given a sense of direction, but fewer directions, so that they learn to make necessary decisions about format, spacing, and placement.

Communication skills. Periodic instruction and review to help students develop basic written communication skills are included in supplementary sections of each division. In addition, selected document preparation jobs require students to apply the language skills they have developed. Further, this new edition includes the most up-to-date business terminology and gives specific attention to new procedures and equipment of electronic offices.

ACKNOWLEDGMENTS

The authors gratefully acknowledge the helpful contributions made by instructors who used prior editions of the text, especially those who responded to the national user survey made just prior to the preparation of this new edition. Special recognition is given, also, to Dr. D. D. Lessenberry, the original author of College Typewriting, who for over fifty years set the pattern and pace of typewriting instruction in the United States.

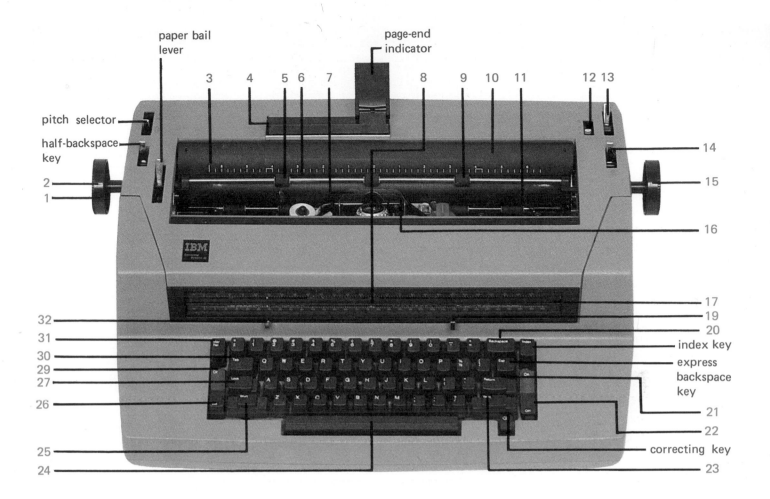

The diagram above shows the parts of an electric typewriter. Since typewriters have similar parts, you should be able to locate the parts of your machine from this diagram. However, if you have the instructional booklet that comes with your machine, use it to identify exact locations of these parts.

If you are learning on a non-electric (manual) typewriter, refer to page 3 for those machine parts and keys that differ in location from an electric machine.

Illustrated on page 2 is an array of data/word processing machines to which your keyboarding skills will transfer.

1 Left platen knob: used to activate variable line spacer

2 Variable line spacer: used to change writing line setting permanently

3 Paper guide scale: used to set paper edge guide at desired position

4 Paper edge guide: used to position paper for insertion

5/9 Paper bail rolls: used to hold paper against platen

6 Paper bail: used to hold paper against platen

7 Card/envelope holder: used to hold cards, labels, and envelopes against platen

8 Printing point indicator: used to position element carrier at desired point

9 (See 5)

10 Paper table: supports paper when it is in typewriter

11 Platen (cylinder): provides a hard surface against which type element strikes

12 Line–space selector: sets typewriter to advance the paper (using carrier return key) 1, 2, or (on some machines) 3 lines for single, double, or triple spacing

13 Paper release lever: used to allow paper to be removed or aligned

14 Automatic line finder: used to change line spacing temporarily, then refind the line

15 Right platen knob: used to turn platen as paper is being inserted

16 Aligning scale: used to align copy that has been reinserted

17 Line–of–writing (margin) scale: used when setting margins, tab stops, and in horizontal centering

18 Ribbon carrier: positions and controls ribbon at printing point (not shown—under the cover)

19 Right margin set: used to set right margin stop

20 Backspace key: used to move printing point to left one space at a time

21 Carrier return key: used to return element carrier to left margin and to advance paper up

22 ON/OFF control: used to turn electric typewriters on or off

23 Right shift key: used to type capitals of letter keys controlled by left hand

24 Space bar: used to move printing point to right one space at a time

25 Left shift key: used to type capitals of letter keys controlled by right hand

26 Tab set: used to set tab stops

27 Shift lock: used to lock shift mechanism so that all letters are capitalized

28 Ribbon control: used to select ribbon typing position (not shown—under cover)

29 Tab clear: used to clear tab stops

30 Tabulator: used to move element carrier to tab stops

31 Margin release key: used to move element carrier beyond margin stops

32 Left margin set: used to set left margin stop

On most electric and electronic machines, certain parts may be used for automatic repeat, such as:

    20—backspace key
    21—carrier return key
    24—space bar

maximum range of options. Even though computer-aided instruction cannot 449

take the place of a good teacher, it will provide an excellent supplement to the 466

efforts of the classroom teacher. 473

Job 2
Unbound report (plain sheet)
Prepare this notice as an unbound report.

Job 3
Topbound report (plain sheet)
Prepare this notice as a topbound report.

FLEXITIME WORK SCHEDULE 5

Effective July 1, our company will initiate a flexi- 15

time work scheduling procedure. It is a voluntary pro- 27

gram, and those who wish to remain on their current work 40

schedule should indicate tis preference to their depart- 52

ment manager. 55

Rules and Regulations 64

The following rules and regulations will goven the 71

new flextime program: , including 30 minutes of breaktime 75

a. All employees must work an 8-hour day. All 92

employees must work between the hours of 10:00 and 2:00 104

p.m., the core working period. 110

b. An employee may start work as ealy as 7:00 a.m. and 122

work as late as 6:00 p.m. 127

c. An employee must schedule one hour for lunch. 137

The cafeteria will be open from 11:30 a.m. to 1:30 p.m. 148

to serve those who wish to take an earlier lunch hour. 162

d. Over time rate and distribution of overtime 172

will be governed by the same regulations as recently 183

used in a department. 188

Work Scheduling 195

Each manager will distribute to all employees a 201

flextime scheduling form for each employees to complete. 212

One a daily routine schedule has been agreed upon 223

between the department manager and the employee, any 233

variation from that schedule should happen only for 243

reasons which have been discussed and approved by the 248

department manager. 252

150a ▶ 5
Preparatory Practice

each line 3 times SS (slowly, faster, slowly); DS between 3-line groups; retype selected lines as time permits

alphabet 1 Elizabeth Coxe vowed to make a journey to present a gift to the queen.

fig/sym 2 The room rates are $514.79/double and $268.30/single (plus sales tax).

direct reach 3 My younger brother, who is often hungry, wants rum cake and ice cream.

fluency 4 The city may end the downtown bicycle problem with a sign and penalty.

| 1 | 2 | 3 | 4 | 5 | 6 | 7 | 8 | 9 | 10 | 11 | 12 | 13 | 14 |

150b ▶ 45
Production measurement: reports

Time schedule

Assembling materials ... 2′
Timed production ...... 35′
Final check; compute
  n–pram .... 8′

Job 1
Two-page leftbound report
(plain sheets)

words

COMPUTER-AIDED INSTRUCTION
5

Computer-aided instruction is the process of having a student interact 20
with an instructional program that is controlled by a computer. Basically, the 36
computer presents the information and/or questions about the subject matter to 51
the student in a systematic manner, usually in small steps from simple to com- 67
plex. After the computer has supplied the information or question, the student 83
will study and analyze the material and then will make a response via the 98
keyboard. At times, the student is permitted an inquiry concerning a specific 114
question he or she may have about the topic being studied. 126

Instructional Software
135

The program which leads the student through the instructional process 149
may be simple in design or very complex. Most software, however, generally 164
accepts student responses, checks the responses for accuracy, and then pro- 179
vides the student with immediate feedback as to the accuracy of his or her 194
response. The more sophisticated instructional package monitors the student's 210
progress and may even provide various levels of instruction based upon the 225
student's understanding of the subject. Most instructional software packages 240
can be classified into two basic areas: drill and practice or tutorial. 255

Drill and practice. These types of instructional software packages put the 274
student through a series of repetitive exercises. One major advantage of these 290
software programs is that they allow the computer to monitor a student's 305
progress and provide immediate feedback. One major disadvantage, however, 320
is that they are usually very structured and provide little deviation from the 336
step-by-step sequence of the program. 343

Tutorial. These instructional programs are designed to present new ma- 359
terial to the student. A good tutorial program will provide for a variety of 375
responses from the student and then will branch to one of the several different 391
levels based upon the achievement of the student. 401

Conclusion
406

Computer-aided instruction can be a very useful tool in the classroom if 420
the programs have been carefully developed to provide the student with a 435

(Job 1 continued on next page)

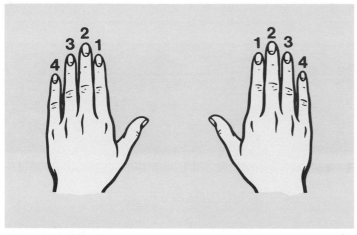

Finger Identification

If you are using a nonelectric (manual) typewriter to learn to keyboard, several of the reaches shown on subsequent pages may be different because of differences in location of the machine part on manual and electric machines. Refer to this page for help in locating these reaches.

Apostrophe

The ' (apostrophe) is the shift of 8. Shift with the left little (fourth) finger; then reach for ' with the right second finger.

k'k k'k k'k it's

Asterisk

The * (asterisk) is the shift of – (hyphen). Depress left shift; then strike * with the right fourth (;) finger.

;–; ;*; ;*; ;*;
*See page 190.

Backspacer

Reach to the backspace key with the appropriate little (fourth) finger. Depress the key firmly for each backspace desired.

Carriage return

Move the left hand, fingers bracing one another, to the carriage return lever.

Move the lever inward to take up the slack; then return the carriage with a quick inward flick-of-the-hand motion.

Drop the hand quickly to typing position without letting it follow the carriage across the page.

Carriage release

If your typewriter has a movable carriage, depress the right carriage release to move it freely. When you have finished keyboarding for the day, leave the carriage approximately centered.

Exclamation mark

On most manual typewriters (and some electrics), there is no exclamation mark key. To *make* an exclamation mark, strike ' (apostrophe); then backspace and strike . (period).

Oh!   I just won!

Quotation marks

The " (quotation mark) is the shift of 2. Shift with the right little (fourth) finger; then reach for " with the left third finger.

s"s s"s s"s "so"

Tabulator bar

Depress and hold down the tabulator bar with the right first finger until the carriage has stopped.

Tabulator key

Depress and hold down the tabulator key with the nearest little (fourth) finger until the carriage has stopped.

Underline

The — (underline) is the shift of 6. Shift with the left little (fourth) finger; then reach for — with the right first finger.

<u>j j j To Yes</u>

Special procedures for nonelectric typewriters

Job 2
Bill of sale
(LM p. 173)

BILL OF SALE

ANN H. TIMMS, in consideration of the re- 13
ceipt by ~~his/~~her~~/them~~ from KIM D. FOX of 19
Three Thousand Dollars, ($3,000), the receipt of 29
which is hereby acknowledged, has~~/have~~ transferred and hereby 40
convey(s) to KIM D. FOX the following interest, 49
to have and to hold the same unto KIM D. FOX , 58
her successors and assigns forever: 66

Diamond necklace and matching 72
brooch. 74

ANN H. TIMMS , for *herself* , *her* heirs, 81
executors, and administrators, warrant(s) and agree(s) to defend 93
the title to such assets subject to all liabilities for the bene- 106
fit of KIM D. FOX , *her* successors and assigns, 116
against all persons. 120

IN WITNESS WHEREOF, ANN H. TIMMS , has~~/have~~ 128
signed this Bill of Sale the 14th day of *March* , 19 -- , to 139
be effective as of the 25th day of *March* , 19 -- . 149

_____ 156
Ann H. Timms 158

Job 3
Table with horizontal and vertical rulings and a braced heading

Center in exact vertical center on a full sheet. DS body and leave 4 spaces between columns.

Job 4
Table

Repeat Job 3 making these changes: half sheet; SS body; 6 spaces between columns; delete all rules and the braced heading **Membership.** Change the main heading to **Membership in Metropolitan Professional Organizations.**

Job 5

If time permits, retype Job 1 on plain paper. Do not type printed headings. Use same margins and tab settings as in Job 1.

Job 3   Job 4

METROPOLITAN PROFESSIONAL BUSINESS ORGANIZATIONS   10 | 11

Organization	Membership		
	Females	*Males*	*Total*
Administrative Management Society	65	82	147
American Accounting Association	40	110	150
American Marketing Association	20	55	75
Association for Computing Machinery	19	62	81
Association for Systems Management	13	38	51
National Association of Accountants	30	45	75
Professional Secretaries International	85	10	95

① Adjust paper guide

Line up paper edge guide (4) with zero on the line–of–writing scale (17).

② Insert typing paper

Take a sheet of paper in your left hand and follow the directions and illustrations at the right and below.

1 Pull paper bail (6) forward (or up on some machines).

2 Place paper against paper edge guide (4), behind the platen (11).

3 Turn paper into machine, using right platen knob (15) or index key.

4 Stop when paper is about 1½ inches above aligning scale (16).

5 If paper is not straight, pull paper release lever (13) forward.

6 Straighten paper, then push paper release lever back.

7 Push paper bail back so that it holds paper against platen.

8 Slide paper bail rolls (5/9) into position, dividing paper into thirds.

9 Properly inserted paper.

③ Set line-space selector

Many machines offer 3 choices for line spacing—1, 1½, and 2 indicated by bars or numbers on the line–space selector (12).

Set the line–space selector on (—) or 1 to single–space (SS) or on (=) or on 2 to double–space (DS) as directed for lines in Level 1.

```
1 Lines 1 and 2 are single-spaced (SS).
2 A double space (DS) separates Lines 2 and 4.
3                          1 blank line space
4 A triple space (TS) separates Lines 4 and 7.
5
6                          2 blank line spaces
7 Set the selector on "1" for single spacing.
```

④ Determine type size

Most machines are equipped with pica (10 spaces to a horizontal inch) or elite (12 spaces to a horizontal inch) type size.

Marked intervals on the line–of–writing scale (17) match the spacing of letters on the machine. This scale reads from 0 to 110 or more for machines with elite type, from 0 to 90 or more for machines with pica type.

```
This is elite (12-pitch) type, 12 spaces to an inch.

This is pica (10-pitch) type, 10 spaces to an inch.
```

inches		1		2		3		4		5		6
centimeters	1	2	3	4	5	6	7	8	9	10	11	12	13	14	15

149a ▶ 5

Preparatory practice

each line 3 times SS (slowly, faster, still faster); DS between 3-line groups; repeat selected lines as time permits

alphabet	1	Major Weavers shipped by rail express the quick-frozen fruit packages.
fig/sym	2	Sanders & Johnson (P.O. #3128479) ordered 560 boxes of our #2 pencils.
double letter	3	Her business success occurred suddenly when it hardly seemed possible.
fluency	4	The duty of an auditor is to visit a city and do a formal field audit.

| 1 | 2 | 3 | 4 | 5 | 6 | 7 | 8 | 9 | 10 | 11 | 12 | 13 | 14 |

149b ▶ 45

Production measurement: medical and legal reports and tables

(LM pp. 171–173)

Time schedule
Assembling materials ... 2'
Timed production ...... 36'
Final check; compute
   n–pram .... 7'

Job 1
Medical report
(LM p. 171)

words

E.N.T. Medical Services

OPERATIVE REPORT

Name:	*Harold D. Washington* Case No.: *63241*	5
Date of Surgery:	*February 21, 19--*	9
Preoperative Diagnosis:	*Pilonidal cyst*	12
Postoperative Diagnosis:	*Pilonidal cyst*	15
Operation:	*Excision of cyst*	18
Surgeon:	*Roberta M. Cunningham, M.D.*	24

PROCEDURE: An elliptical incision was made | 33
around the cyst. Also, an incision was made | 42
in the midline over the sacrum. The cyst was | 51
removed totally. Catgut ligatures were used to | 61
control the bleeding. Four interrupted | 69
chromic catgut sutures were used to close the | 78
subcutaneous tissue. The skin was closed | 86
with dermal sutures. For drainage, a small | 95
plastic tube was inserted into the wound. A | 104
sterile dressing was applied. The patient left | 114
the operating room in good condition. | 121

⑤ Plan margin settings

When 8 ½– by 11-inch paper is inserted into the typewriter (8½–inch end first) with left edge at 0 on the line–of–writing scale (17), center point is 51 (elite) or 42½ (pica). Use 42 for pica center.

To center typed lines, set left and right margin stops the same number of spaces left and right from center point. Diagrams at the right show margin settings for 50–, 60–, and 70–space lines. When you begin to use the warning bell, 5 or 6 spaces may be added to the right margin.

Elite center   Pica center

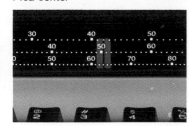

Elite (12-pitch)

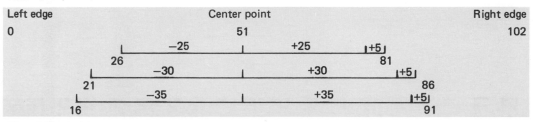

Pica (10-pitch)

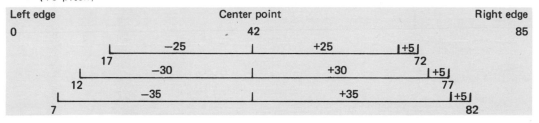

---

⑥ Set margin stops

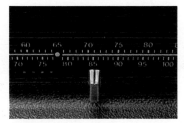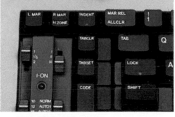

Type A
Push-button set

Adler, Olympia, Remington, Royal 700/870 manuals, Smith-Corona

1 Press down on the left margin set button.

2 Slide it to desired position on the line–of–writing (margin) scale.

3 Release the margin set button.

4 Using the right margin set button, set the right margin stop in the same way.

Type B
Push-lever set

Single element typewriters, such as Adler, Olivetti, Remington Rand, Royal, Selectric

1 Push in on the left margin set lever.

2 Slide it to desired position on the line–of–writing (margin) scale.

3 Release the margin set lever.

4 Using the right margin set lever, set the right margin stop in the same way.

Type C
Key set

IBM typebar, Olivetti electric

1 Move carriage to the left margin stop by depressing the return key.

2 Depress and hold down the margin set (IBM reset) key as you move carriage to desired left margin stop position.

3 Release the margin set (IBM reset) key.

4 Move carriage to the right margin stop.

5 Depress and hold down the margin set (IBM reset) key as you move carriage to desired right margin stop position.

6 Release the margin set (IBM reset) key.

Type D
Electronic set

To set margins on some electronic machines, such as Xerox and Silver–Reed, space to the desired margin position and strike the appropriate (left or right) margin key.

On other machines, such as IBM, space to the desired margin position and strike the CODE key and the appropriate (left or right) margin key *at the same time*.

> General information for setting margin stops is given here. If you have the manufacturer's booklet for your typewriter, however, use it; the procedure for your particular model may be slightly different.

Job 3
Letter (LM p. 169)

Use block style with open
punctuation.

October 18, 19--   3

Mr. Leonard I. Owens, President   10
Owens Office Discount Center   16
7500 East McDowell Road   20
Scottsdale, AZ 85257-2229   26

Dear Mr. Owens   29

    We have completed our review of your application for   36
a franchise Distributorship. We are pleased to welcome you   48
as our large family of distributors. Within a few days you will   61
recieve the the sample display kits and a temporary sup-   72
ply of our special ball-point pens. Please submit your   83
order within 30 dyas in order to take advantage of our   94
special "new" distributor discount.   101

    The new WINGMATIC series (Stock #6B-3) is the top of our   113
ball-point pen line. It features a patented clip mechanism   125
and a carbide ultrafine ball-point cartridge. In order   136
to continue to qualify for the special 20 percent discount, however,   150
you must sell a minimum of 1000 pens per year.   160

    You will be receiving a complete advertising kit   168
which will include newspaper advertisements, window   179
dispalys, and a very attractive counter display unit.   190
If you need additial help, our advertising department   201
will be happy to assist you.   207

Sincerly   228

Richard V. Turnbull   232
Vice President, Marketing   237

Enclosure: Franchise agreement   243

Job 4
Letter (plain sheet)

Retype Job 3 in modified
block style with paragraphs
indented and mixed punctuation.

¶ If you have any questions relating to the   215
franchise agreement or our products,   223
please call us.   226/248

LEVEL ONE

Learning to keyboard and to format copy

Your decision to learn to keyboard is a wise one. Just as the 1960's were the decade of the computer and data processing, the 1980's are the decade of microcomputers, text editors, and word or information processing. In business, industry, and the professions, the use of electronic input/output devices is growing at lightning speed. Whether you learn to keyboard on a typewriter or a microcomputer, your keyboarding skill will transfer directly to other data/word processing machines because all use the same standard arrangement of the letter and number keys. In addition, some machines have a 10-key numeric pad arrangement which is the same as that on electronic calculators.

Learning to keyboard with speed and accuracy is only the first step, however. To be able to *use* your skill productively, you must also learn the features of frequently prepared documents (such as letters, reports, and tables) and develop skill in arranging and typing them in their conventional formats.

The purpose of Level 1 (Lessons 1-29), therefore, is to help you develop keyboarding efficiency and to begin teaching you how to format and type documents for personal use. The textbook, like your keyboarding instrument, is only a partner in learning. For your textbook and your machine to help you effectively to learn, you as the third partner must *intend* to learn and must practice intensively to reach your goals.

Production measurement procedure

1 Remove the appropriate materials from the laboratory manual (LM); have a supply of carbon sheets and plain sheets available.

2 Arrange laboratory materials and plain sheets in the order of need for completing the jobs.

3 Place your correction supplies in a convenient place next to your machine.

4 When you are signaled to begin, make all necessary machine adjustments, insert paper, and begin the first job. Make 1 cc for each job.

5 Before removing your paper from the machine, be sure to proofread and make all necessary corrections.

6 After the time is called to end the measurement, proofread the final job and circle any uncorrected errors.

7 Compute *n–pram* for this measurement.

148c ▶ 37
Production measurement: letters and memos
(LM pp. 167–169)

Time schedule
Assembling materials ...... 2'
Timed production .... 30'
Final check; compute
  n–pram .... 5'

Job 1
Simplified memo
(plain full sheet)
To: **All Managers**
Date: **June 15, 19--**
Subject: **MICROCOMPUTER TRAINING PROGRAM**
From: **Susan Wipple, Training Director**

words

opening lines   12

(¶) The results of our recent training survey indicated that 85 percent of the company's managers felt a strong desire to have a training seminar devoted entirely to the use of the microcomputer as a business tool.

21
31
40
51
54

(¶) We have scheduled a one-day training seminar for August 25. It will be held in the Training Center beginning at 8:30 a.m. The morning will be devoted to basic information about the microcomputer, and the afternoon will be a practical approach to the varied uses of the microcomputer within our organization. You will also be given an opportunity to have some limited hands-on experience at the microcomputer.

63
74
85
95
105
113
124
134
137

(¶) Please notify me by July 1 if you plan to attend this one-day training seminar.

145
153

closing lines   159

Job 2
Informal government letter (LM p. 167; no envelope needed)
Date: **September 10, 19--**
Reply to
Attn of: **AFAW**
Subject: **Annual supplies inventory**
To: **U.S. Services Agency**
ATTN: **Miss Ai-ling Fu**
7539 Baltimore Drive
Dallas, TX 75225-2331
Signed by: **Anita R. Sanchez, Deputy Chief, U.S. Services Agency**
cc for Official File—AFAW and Ms. Winifred G. Rothchild—AFAX

opening lines   28

Your annual supplies inventory report is due on October 10; therefore, will you please make the necessary arrangements to have a physical inventory taken on September 30 so that our counts will be accurate.

44
59
69

After you have taken the inventory, please complete the necessary forms and submit them to your Agency Deputy Director for approval prior to forwarding them to Washington, D.C.

85
100
105

closing lines   131

Learning goals

1 To master alphabetic reaches.

2 To operate keyboard without looking at your fingers or the keys—"by touch."

3 To type easy paragraph copy.

4 To type or keyboard at a rate of 14 or more gross words a minute (*gwam*).

Machine adjustments

1 Set paper guide at 0.

2 Set ribbon control to type on upper half of ribbon.

3 Set left margin stop for a 50–space line (center − 25); set right margin stop at end of line–of–writing scale.

4 Set line–space selector for single spacing (SS).

Prepare for Lesson 1

1 Acquire a supply of 8½″ by 11″ typing paper of good quality.

2 If your chair is adjustable, raise or lower it to a height that is comfortable for you.

3 If your desk is adjustable, raise or lower it until your forearms parallel the slant of the keyboard when your fingers are placed over asdf jkl;.

4 Follow carefully all directions, both oral and written. Therein lies much of the secret for gaining keyboarding skill.

1a
Get ready to keyboard

1 Clear work area and chair of un–needed books and clothing.

2 Place textbook at right of machine, the top elevated for easy reading; stack paper supply at left of machine.

3 Refer briefly to page 1 of this book where typewriter parts are named, illustrated, and described. In these early lessons, frequent reference is made to these parts; you will need to refer to the illus–trated typewriter on page 1 at those times.

4 Locate on page 5 the type of margin sets that match those on your machine. Set the left margin stop for a 50–space line (center − 25); move the right stop to the ex–treme right end of the line–of–writing scale.

5 Study pages 4 and 5 carefully. If necessary, adjust the paper edge guide (at 0) on your machine. In–sert paper as illustrated.

6 Set line–space selector for single spacing (SS) as directed on page 4.

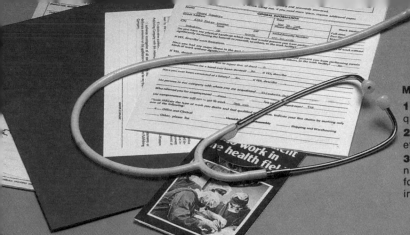

Measurement goals

1 To select and organize all re–quired materials and supplies.
2 To plan your work carefully and efficiently.
3 To complete a maximum number of jobs in satisfactory form (all errors corrected properly) in the time allowed.

Machine adjustments

1 Set paper guide at *0*.
2 Set ribbon control to use upper half of ribbon.
3 Margins: 70–space line for drills and timed writings; as directed (or appropriate) for jobs.
4 Spacing: SS for drills; as ap–propriate for jobs.

148a ▶ 5
Preparatory practice

each line 3 times SS (slowly, faster, slowly); DS between 3-line groups; repeat selected lines as time permits

alphabet 1 A black taxi quickly moved from a parking zone just as a man whistled.

fig/sym 2 Please ship 25 pieces of Stock #3067 (list price $4.98 each) by May 1.

direct reach 3 Barb, my niece, brought many musicians to hear my first cello recital.

fluency 4 The eighty authentic ivory emblems may be downtown in the antique box.

| 1 | 2 | 3 | 4 | 5 | 6 | 7 | 8 | 9 | 10 | 11 | 12 | 13 | 14 |

148b ▶ 8
Measure straight-copy skill

one 5' writing on ¶s combined

Difficulty index

| all letters used | A | 1.5 si | 5.7 awl | 80% hfw |

gwam 1'   5'

Business organizations now have a new system called electronic mail   14 | 3 | 51
for the distribution of documents. With this new system, a letter or   28 | 5 | 54
report can be prepared on a word processor and then forwarded within a   42 | 8 | 57
few seconds to the addressee. All of this is done without preparing a   56 | 11 | 60
hard copy of the document. This new delivery system uses data communica-   71 | 14 | 63
tion technology to transmit and receive mail. After a letter or report   85 | 17 | 66
is keyed into the system and a file copy saved, the document is then sent   100 | 20 | 68
to the addressee's location where it is stored in a computer system.   113 | 23 | 71
Then, with just the touch of a key on the terminal, the addressee is   127 | 26 | 74
able to see the document on a video screen.   136 | 27 | 76

Yet another application of this advanced technology is the use of an   14 | 30 | 78
electronic message system within a firm. Much like electronic mail, this   29 | 33 | 81
type of message system permits all internal communication, such as memos,   43 | 36 | 84
to take place electronically. For example, rather than prepare a memo   58 | 39 | 87
on a sheet of paper, a person can enter the message with her or his key-   72 | 41 | 90
board and then quickly send it to another person's terminal within the   86 | 44 | 93
firm. By using this method, much time and effort is saved, since hard   100 | 47 | 96
copy does not need to be prepared.   107 | 49 | 97

gwam 1' | 1 | 2 | 3 | 4 | 5 | 6 | 7 | 8 | 9 | 10 | 11 | 12 | 13 | 14 |
5'   1   2   3

1b
Take keyboarding position

1 Sit back in chair, body erect.

2 Place both feet on floor to maintain proper balance.

3 Let your hands hang relaxed at your sides. Your fingers will relax in curved position.

4 From this position, raise the left hand and lightly place the fingertips of your left hand on **a s d f** (home keys). Study the location of these keys.

5 Similarly, lightly place the fingertips of your right hand on **j k l ;** (home keys). Study the location of these keys.

6 Your fingers should be curved and upright; wrists should be low, but they should not touch the frame of the machine.

1 Keep fingers curved and upright, wrists low.

2 Keep forearms parallel to slant of keyboard.

3 Keep eyes on copy.

4 Sit back in chair, body erect.

5 Place textbook at right of machine, top raised for easy reading.

6 Keep table free of unneeded books.

7 Keep feet on floor for balance.

1c
Strike home keys, space bar, and return

1 Strike each key with a quick, sharp finger stroke; snap the fingertip toward the palm as the stroke is made.

Type (keyboard):

ffjjffjjfj

2 Strike the space bar with a down-and-in motion of the right thumb.

Type (on same line):

dd kk dd kk dk
<u>space once</u>

3 Keep the fingers well-curved. Concentrate on proper finger action as you keyboard.

Type (on same line):

ss ll ss ll aa ;;
<u>space once</u>

4 Reach with the little finger of the right hand to the return key and tap it. Then quickly return the little finger to its home position. *Refer to page 3 if your machine is nonelectric.*

Build rough-draft skill

1 Two 1' writings on each ¶ (1 for accuracy, 1 for control).
2 One 3' writing; proofread and circle errors; determine *gwam*.

Difficulty index

all letters used	A	1.5 si	5.7 awl	80% hfw

gwam 1' 3'

Every body has goals, no matter how unclearly these goals maybe de- 13 | 4 | 57

fined. For example, we understand that all in but a few excep- 25 | 9 | 61

tional cases, the main objective of most individuals is happiness. 39 | 13 | 65

In order So, to reach this objective, we set various goals. A goal may 53 | 18 | 70

be to complete college or to find the right job or to re- 64 | 21 | 73

dieve a salary increase or to head an organization. 74 | 25 | 77

Another known fact is that most people change their goals 12 | 29 | 81

from time to time. In fact, experts who specialize in helping 25 | 33 | 85

others to plan for the future often urge that goals should be 37 | 37 | 89

made for the short, intermediate, and long term, and that these 50 | 41 | 93

goals should be revised often. We usually modify our goals 62 | 45 | 97

when we acquire new confidence about our own capabilities or new information 77 | 50 | 102

about the world around us. 82 | 52 | 104

Build statistical-copy skill

1 One 1' writing for accuracy on each ¶.
2 Two 3' writings for accuracy on both ¶s combined. Record *gwam* and number of errors for more accurate 3' writing (LM p. 3).

Difficulty index

all letters used	HA	1.7 si	6 awl	75% hfw

gwam 1' 3'

The Area Micro Store, Limited, sold 1,031 personal computers during 14 | 5 | 67

the second quarter of 1985. The hardware sales (including all peripheral 28 | 9 | 72

kits) were $1,870,947, or 78% of the total sales; and software sales were 43 | 14 | 77

$527,703, or 22% of the total sales. Total revenues for the second per- 58 | 19 | 82

iod were $2,398,650; sales are up over 23% over the 1984 second quarter 72 | 24 | 86

period. 73 | 25 | 87

The major reason for the extremely large increase in total revenues 14 | 29 | 91

was that the organization, during the 1984 fourth quarter, had expanded 28 | 34 | 96

into 11 states and had increased the number of retail outlets from 12 42 | 39 | 101

to 21. The average gross revenue per retail outlet during this second 56 | 43 | 106

quarter was $113,220, up 35.4% over the previous second quarter. The 70 | 48 | 110

exceptional growth was due in part to the establishment of five new re- 84 | 53 | 115

tail outlets in large metropolitan areas. These five new outlets pro- 98 | 57 | 120

duced an average of $160,840 per outlet or 58% of the total increased 112 | 62 | 124

sales. 114 | 62 | 125

gwam 1' | 1 | 2 | 3 | 4 | 5 | 6 | 7 | 8 | 9 | 10 | 11 | 12 | 13 | 14 |
3' | 1 | 2 | 3 | 4 | 5 |

1d
Learn the home row

1 Strike the return key twice more to leave extra space between the line you have just typed and the lines you will now type.

2 Practice once each line shown at the right. Strike the return key once to single–space (SS) be–tween the two lines of a pair.

3 Strike the return key twice to double–space (DS) between pairs of lines.

4 Strike the return key 3 times to triple–space (TS) after completing Line 6.

5 Repeat the drill.

Fingers curved

Fingers upright

```
1  fj fj fj dk dk dk sl sl sl a; a; a; fj dk sl a; a;
2  jf kd ls ;a al ak aj sl sk sj dl dk dj fj fk fl f;
                                         Return twice to double–space (DS)
3  as as ask ask sad sad jak jak fad fad lad lad lass
4  ad ad ads ads jak jak dad dad all all add add fall
                                                              DS
5  a lad; a lass; a jak; all ads; all fall; ask a lad
6  ask dad; all ads; a jak ad; a sad lad; a jak falls
                                    Return 3 times to triple–space (TS)
```

1e
Learn new keyreach: E

1 Find new key on illustrated keyboard; then find it on your keyboard.

2 Study carefully the "Reach technique for **e**."

3 Watch your finger make the *reach* to **e** and back to **d** a few times *without striking the keys.* Keep your fingers curved.

4 Practice the lines once as shown. Keep your eyes on the copy as you keyboard; look only when you "feel lost."

5 If time permits, repeat the drill.

Reach technique for e

Reach *up* with *left second* finger.

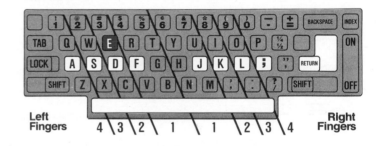
Left Fingers   4 \ 3 \ 2 \ 1 \ 1 \ 2 \ 3 \ 4   Right Fingers

all reaches learned

```
1  e ed ed led led lea lea ale ale elk elf eke els ed
2  ed fed fed fled fled kale kale self self lake lake
                                         Return twice to double–space (DS)
3  e elk ekes leek leak sale dale kale lake fake self
4  sell fell jell sale sake jade sled seek leal deal;
                                                              DS
5  a sled sale; a fake jade; see a lake; a kale leaf;
6  sell a safe; a leaf fell; see a leaf; sell a desk;
```

1f
End the lesson
(standard procedure for all lessons)

1 Raise the paper bail (6) or pull it toward you. Pull the paper release lever (13) toward you.

2 Remove paper with your left hand. Push paper release lever back to its normal position.

3 Turn off the power on an electric or electronic machine. See page 3 if you have a movable carriage typewriter.

Build keystroking precision

each line at least 3 times without error

long words 1   A northwestern congressional representative announced the appointment.

double letters 2   William will cooperate by assigning a room that will accommodate them.

hyphen 3   We hope your mother-in-law and father-in-law have first-class tickets.

word response 4   The busy man may halt work on eight of my maps to visit the city lake.

| 1 | 2 | 3 | 4 | 5 | 6 | 7 | 8 | 9 | 10 | 11 | 12 | 13 | 14 |

Build straight-copy skill

1 Two 1' writings for accuracy on each ¶.
2 Two 5' writings for accuracy on all ¶s combined. Record *gwam* (LM p. 3).

Difficulty index

all letters used	A	1.5 si	5.7 awl	80% hfw

gwam 1'   5'

Each year the cost of operating a business normally rises. Because   14 | 3 | 69
of this, a good business manager must seek constantly for ways to reduce   28 | 6 | 72
his or her firm's operating costs so that there is no need to raise the   43 | 9 | 74
price of goods or services. Many managers look to their expenditure   56 | 11 | 77
accounts to find ways to lower costs. One item often costing more than   71 | 14 | 80
needed is postage. By keeping the following simple guides in mind, post-   85 | 17 | 83
age costs often can be cut significantly.   94 | 19 | 85

Use express mail only for urgent long-distance mailings. First-   13 | 21 | 87
class mail is delivered promptly in most major cities, and a significant   27 | 24 | 90
cost savings will result if the majority of a firm's mail is delivered   42 | 27 | 93
by regular first-class postal service. If first-class mail is deposited   56 | 30 | 96
at the post office prior to noon each day, it is normally delivered   70 | 33 | 99
within a day or two as long as there is frequent air service between   84 | 36 | 101
the point of origin and the destination. When in doubt, check before   98 | 38 | 104
posting an item to be certain that the item sent by express mail will   112 | 41 | 107
actually be delivered faster than if posted by first-class mail.   124 | 44 | 110

Remember also that mail sent on the fifth workday will not be re-   13 | 46 | 112
ceived by the addressee any faster by express mail than by first-class   27 | 49 | 115
mail if the addressee is not at the office on the weekend. Registered   41 | 52 | 118
mail should be used only if the contents have insurable value; otherwise,   56 | 55 | 121
certified mail will give the same service at lower cost. Do not over-   70 | 58 | 124
insure packages; any repayment for a loss is for actual value and not   84 | 61 | 127
for the insured amount. Also, you may realize a notable cost reduction   99 | 63 | 129
in the postage account if you eliminate unnecessary letters.   111 | 66 | 132

gwam 1' | 1 | 2 | 3 | 4 | 5 | 6 | 7 | 8 | 9 | 10 | 11 | 12 | 13 | 14 |
5' | 1 | 2 | 3 |

2a
Prepare to keyboard
Reread procedures described in
1b, 1c, and 1d, pages 8 and 9.

2b
Preparatory practice
each line twice SS
(slowly, then faster);
DS between 2-line groups

home row 1 `ff jj ff jj dd kk dd kk ss ll ss ll aa ;; aa ;; a;`

e 2 `e el els led ale lea eke lee elf elk eel lake kale`

all reaches
learned 3 `as all ask; a jak ad; ask a lad; a fall fad; a fee`
TS

2c
Learn new keyreaches:
T and O
Use the standard procedure at the
right to learn each new keyreach
in this lesson and in lessons that
follow.

Standard procedure for learning new keyreaches

1 Find new key on illustrated keyboard;
then find it on your keyboard.

2 Study carefully the reach technique illustrated for the key.

3 Watch your finger make the reach to the
new key a few times. Keep other fingers
curved on home keys. Straighten the finger slightly for an upward reach; curve it a
bit more for a downward reach.

4 Practice twice SS the two lines in which
the new reach is emphasized. Keep your
eyes on the book copy as you keyboard.

5 DS; then learn and practice the next new
keyreach according to Steps 1-4.

6 Finally, DS; then practice Lines 5-8 once
as shown. If time permits, repeat them.
Work for continuity. Avoid pauses.

Reach technique for t

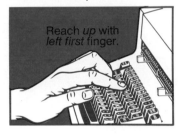

Reach *up* with
left first finger.

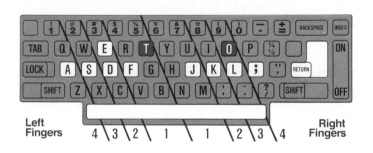

Left
Fingers 4 \ 3 \ 2 \ 1 \ 1 \ 2 \ 3 \ 4 Right
Fingers

Reach technique for o

Reach *up* with
right third finger.

t 1 `t tf tf aft aft tall tall talk talk tale tale task`
2 `tf at at aft jet let take tell felt flat slat salt`
DS

o 3 `o ol ol sol sol sold sold of of off off fold folds`
4 `ol old sold sole dole do doe does lo loll sol solo`

t/o 5 `to tot tote told dolt toe toes load toad foal soak`
6 `to too toot lot slot do dot oft loft soft jot jolt`

all letters
learned 7 `to do | to do a lot | take a jet | to let a | to do a task`
8 `so to | so to do | to take a | to tell a joke | left off a`
TS

To complete your work assignments for Information Processing Services, Inc., Mr. O'Mariety asks you to prepare form letters for Mathas Equipment Company.

CUSTOMER INSTRUCTIONS:

Please prepare form letters for the individuals listed. Use the variable information which is listed after the name and address. Date the letters March 18, 19—.

Dear

It is a pleasure to confirm your order for a new Model (VI--insert number) **Mathas** (Electronic Printer/Word Processor/Copier). It is scheduled to be installed on (V2--insert date).

Our representative, (V3--insert name), will contact you soon to schedule an appointment to site clear the area for the machine. (He/She) will also check to see that you have adequate supplies for the first month of operation. (She/He) will also be able to answer any questions you may have about the installation.

Our training coordinator, Martha Miller, will schedule operator training for your employees as soon as the equipment is installed. We will be happy to train as many employees as you would like to have trained.

You have selected an excellent (printer/word processor/copier) that will give you many years of dependable service.

Sincerely | Miss Leslie Willis | Customer Service Representative

---

Ms. Amanda Kupier
Dutch Industries, Inc.
2104 Oak Creek Street
Sherman, TX 75090-5310
VI 9051 - Electronic Printer
V2 March 26, 19--
V3 Betsy Jung

Miss Carolyn Luke
Acadiana Rice Company
194 Colonial Drive
Terre Haute, IN 47805-3337
VI 5410 - Word Processor
V2 April 6, 19--
V3 Felix Bernard

Mr. Robert Gregory
Circle R Company
2155 Warren Avenue
Joliet, IL 60162-3330
VI 9401 - Electronic Printer
V2 April 3, 19--
V3 Ken Bishop

Mr. Peter Sheppard
South-West Print Shop
5300 Kenwood Avenue, South
Chicago, IL 60615-3221
VI 9510 - Electronic Printer
V2 March 27, 19--
V3 Rodrigo Gonzalez

Mrs. Mary Thomas
3629 Sunny Lane
Indianapolis, IN 46220-4511
VI 5610 - Word Processor
V2 March 28, 19--
V3 Celia Castillo

Mr. John Burleson
T. J.'s Accounting Service
200 University Place
Evanston, IL 60201-4422
VI 3410 - Copier
V2 April 10, 19--
V3 Lucy Dunlap

2d
Practice keystroking technique

each line twice SS; DS between 2-line groups

home row 1 `as ask asks ad ads add jak jaks all fall lass dads`

e 2 `led lead fee feel ell ells elk elks fee fees leads`

t 3 `at kat sat tall talk last fast salt slat task tall`

o 4 `so sol old do ado odd sod of off oaf oak loaf load`

all letters learned 5 `of a | to do | do so | a joke | to lead | odd leaf | ask a lad`

TS

2e
Practice words/phrases

1 Practice the Level 1 lines once SS at an easy pace.

2 DS; then practice the Level 2 lines in the same way.

3 DS; then practice the Level 2 lines again at a faster pace.

4 If time permits, practice the Level 3 lines once, trying to keep the carrier (carriage) moving steadily.

Note: The 3 sets of lines progress gradually in diffi–culty.

Goal: *At least* 1 line per minute (10 *gwam*).

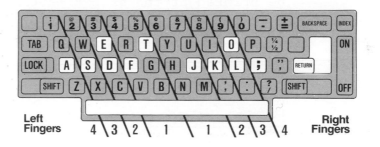

Left Fingers   4 3 2 1   1 2 3 4   Right Fingers

all reaches learned

```
       1 a as ask to too foe doe jot jet jak so do sod does
Level 1 2 ale ask ode old oak let led ade a at kat take told
       3 to see; to a set; ask a lad; lot of tea; ate a jak

       4 ale oak jet lot all jak doe too off oft odd dot to
Level 2 5 led doe eat let sol ask add eel sad eke see old of
       6 do a loaf; a leaf fell; tell a joke; a lot of talk

       7 elf self ask asks jet jets lot lots led lead takes
Level 3 8 elk elks add adds joke jokes feel feels talk talks
       9 to a lake; eat a salad; ask a lass; sell oak desks
```

2f
End the lesson
(See page 9 if necessary.)

Remove paper

Turn electric off

printers have been approved for the administrative offices of all departments. The electronic printer will facilitate the forms management program that was piloted and approved for general use. All forms have been stored on an 8-inch floppy disk, and each form can now be printed at the same time the information typed on the form is printed. The Vogel printer has type-font flexibility and prints 12 pages per minute.

<u>Photocomposition</u>. Photocomposition equipment has not been approved for general use. The pilot study on computer-based type-setting supported the installation of a small centralized operation. Final management decision is pending.

<u>Purchasing Authority</u>

Final authority for purchasing all office technology rests with the Information Resource Management Committee. Users requesting technology must conduct a thorough needs analysis, provide complete cost justification, and obtain approval of the department manager prior to submitting the request to the IRMC.

The Senior Management Committee has the power to overrule any decisions made at Hudson Advertising Agency. Only in rare circumstances will the Senior Management Committee agree to consider appeals to the decisions made by the IRMC.

3a
Prepare-to-keyboard checklist

Before you begin to keyboard, check your readiness to begin the lesson.

- ✔ Work area cleared of unneeded clothing and books
- ✔ Book elevated at right of machine

- ✔ Left margin set for 50–space line (center − 25)
- ✔ Right margin set at extreme right end of scale

- ✔ Ribbon control set to type on upper half of ribbon
- ✔ Paper edge guide on correct setting
- ✔ Paper inserted expertly, straightened if necessary

3b
Preparatory practice

each line 3 times SS (slowly, faster, still faster); DS between 3-line groups

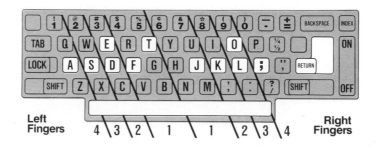

Left Fingers 4 3 2 1 1 2 3 4 Right Fingers

home row 1 a; sl dk fj a;sl dkfj all lad as ask fall lass add

e/o/t 2 ol old sold ed fed led ft oft at dot doe let of to

all reaches learned 3 to fold; take a loaf; a lot of; as a joke; at last
TS

3c
Check position and techniques

As you complete the remainder of the lesson, observe the points of good keyboarding position and techniques listed at the right.

- ✔ Seated erect in chair
- ✔ Both feet on floor
- ✔ Fingers relaxed, curved, upright
- ✔ Fingertips touching home keys
- ✔ Wrists low but not touching the machine

- ✔ Slant of forearms parallel to slant of the keyboard
- ✔ Each key struck with a quick stroke of the fingertip
- ✔ Space bar struck with inward motion of the thumb

3d
Practice keystroking technique

each pair of lines SS as shown; DS between 2-line groups; repeat if time permits

Technique hint:
Strike keys at a smooth pace; avoid pauses.

home row 1 a jak; ask dad; as a lad; as a lass; add a fall ad
2 a fad; as a dad; a fall ad; as all ask; a sad fall

e 3 a doe; led a doe; a sea eel; see a lake; jade sale
4 a sea; a joke; tell tales; a doe fled; seal a deal

o 5 do so; to do so; odd load; lot of old; sold a sofa
6 a foe; old oak; jot off a; does a lot; a soft sofa

t 7 to let; to talk; tall tale; eat a lot; told a tale
8 a tea; to salt; at a late; take a lot; took a seat
TS

Word) Processors. The Vogel 8~~9~~0 [8] Word Processor ~~and~~ or the Vogel

890 Information Processor can be purchased by departments∧ that
∧ can
justify~~ing~~ the need and cost of the unit. The Vogel 890 ~~may~~ should
ing
be used by the account∧ staff who ~~need to~~ communicate with

major accounts which have devises that use binary syn~~c~~chron- [s]

ous communications. Both the 8~~69~~ 80 and 890 use the Adsearch

~~/~~Modem to access the Adsearch data base. The Management
made a
Committee∧ commitment to continue the subscription to this

computer-assisted research system.
DS
Personal Computers. The personal computer will be the profes-

sional workstation at Hudson Advertising. Any personal com-
i
puter compat~~a~~ble with our Spreadnet network can be purchased

if justified by need and cost; however, Vogel personal com-
recommended
puters are ~~suggested~~. The Vogel is a 16-bit processor with
256,000 bytes of random access memory.
~~256K RAM~~. The duel disk drive uses 8-inch double-density∧ floppy

disks or rigid disks. The personal computer supports a wide

range of software including word processing, data-base manage-
financial
ment, and electronic spreadsheet ~~type~~ analysis as well as

several programming languages.
required
    Printers. Letter-quality printers are ~~necessary~~ for all

work which goes out from Hudson Advertising. Dot-matrix
v
printers (including those with strike over and multistrike
only
features) may ~~not~~ be used ~~except~~ for graphics, rough∧-draft

work, and for documents used internally. Daisy∧-wheel∧-type

printers with a minimum speed of 40 characters per second

can be purchased by microcomputer users. Distributed ~~image~~ electronic

(Job 2 continued on page 298)

3e
Practice special reach combinations

each line twice SS;
DS between 2-line groups

Technique hint:
Do not push for speed; work for smooth, fluid keystroking.

as/sa 1 as ask task fast last lass asks sad salt sale sake

lo/ol 2 lo lot lots lode load loaf old fold sold told sole

ed/de 3 led fed deed seed sled fled ode lode ade deal desk

el/le 4 el els sell felt jell self let leak dale dole lest
TS

3f
Practice phrases

1 Practice the Level 1 lines once SS at an easy pace.

2 DS; then practice the Level 2 lines in the same way.

3 DS; then practice the Level 2 lines again at a faster pace.

4 If time permits, practice the Level 3 lines once, trying to keep the carrier (carriage) moving steadily.

Note: The 3 sets of lines progress gradually in diffi–culty.

Goal: *At least* 1 line per minute (10 *gwam*).

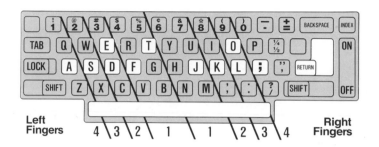

all reaches learned

Level 1
1 to let; to set; a jak; to do all of; to a sad lad;
2 to set; to do a; fed a doe; ask a fee; ask a lass;
3 ask a lad; a sad ode; to see a foe; a sad old oak;
DS

Level 2
4 to last a; take a jet; tell a tale; take a lot of;
5 fall ad; as a set; take a deed; to sell a loaf of;
6 old jade; to see a; of a sad doll; to seek a deal;

Level 3
7 of a flake; to take a salad; to lose a sales deal;
8 too stale; to float a; add a total; of a sad tale;
9 to a; told jokes; soaks a lot; see a lot of lakes;

3g
End the lesson

(See page 9 if necessary.)

Mr. O'Mariety also re-
quests that this report be
prepared in final form. He
asks you to follow the
customer's instructions.

CUSTOMER'S INSTRUCTIONS:

This technology procurement
policy must be prepared in
the same format as our Policy
Manual because it will be incorporated as part of the
manual. Please follow these
directions carefully.

1 Single–space the body of
the report; DS between ¶s.

2 Use 1″ side and bottom
margins.

3 Place the page number on
Line 4 at the right margin;
then triple–space. Number
the first page 2.3, the second
page, 2.4, etc.

4 Please correct any undetected errors which may have
been overlooked.

STANDARDS FOR PROCUREMENT OF OFFICE TECHNOLOGY

TS

Hudson Advertising ~~plans to~~ *has* standardize*d* the purchase of
all office technology so that ~~all of the~~ office opera*t*ions ~~may~~ *can*
be integrated into one comprehensive system. All purchase*s of*
office technology ~~automation~~ must ~~conform~~ *adhere* to the standards described in this
policy and ~~should~~ *must* be approved by the information resource
management committee.

TS

Technology

Typewriters. The only typewriter*s* which may be purchased is an electronic typewriter with a thin-window display
or partial screen, a minimum *memory* capacity of ~~12~~ *15* pages, and ~~also~~
a communi*c*ations protocol option. Department needs must be
analyzed carefully; and, if justified, an electronic typewriter with a 5 1/4-inch disk should be purchase*d* to provide
unlimited ~~greater~~ memory. Up-to-date ~~data~~ *information* on products compatable with
the current Hudson system are available from the Information
Resource Management Committee

Communication Network. ~~All~~ word and information processing equipment must ~~tie in~~ *interface* with the Spreadnet Network which
have been installed. This network allows point-to-point data
communications with out the use of a mainframe computer. Communications software operates as a back ground function allowing text editing functions and communications to occur *simultaneously*.
Applications *include terminal-to-terminal communications* for electronic document distribution and multi-
function interfaces. The network is ~~able to~~ *capable of* support*ing* ~~some~~
photocomposition, high-speed printers, micrographics, and
optical character recognition devices.

(Job 2 continued on page 297)

4a
Prepare-to-keyboard checklist

Check your readiness to begin Lesson 4.

- ✔ Work area cleared of unneeded clothing and books
- ✔ Book elevated at right of machine
- ✔ Left margin set for 50–space line (center − 25)
- ✔ Right margin set at extreme right end of scale
- ✔ Ribbon control set to type on upper half of ribbon
- ✔ Paper edge guide on correct setting
- ✔ Paper inserted expertly, straightened if necessary

4b
Preparatory practice

each line twice SS (slowly, then faster); DS between 2-line groups

home row 1 `fj dk sl a; jk fd kl ds l; sa as all fad jak dads;`

e/o/t 2 `ed ol tf led old oft ode dot toe doe foe jets fold`

space bar 3 `to do | do so | a foe | to add | a lot | as a joke | to do so;`

all reaches learned 4 `a jak fell; tell a tale; sold a desk; to a sole ad`
                                                                    TS

4c
Learn new keyreaches: C and H

Reach technique for c

Reach technique for h

Left Fingers 4 \ 3 \ 2 \ 1 \ 1 \ 2 \ 3 \ 4 Right Fingers

Follow the "Standard procedure for learning new keyreaches" on page 10 (Lines 1–4 twice; Lines 5–8 once; repeat 5–8 if time permits).

Technique hint:

Strike the space bar with a down–and–in motion of the thumb.

c 1 `c cd cd cod cod cot cot call call code codes tacks`
c 2 `cold clod clad coal cola lack lock dock cool cakes`
                                                        DS

h 3 `h hj hj he he she she ah ah ha ha lash dash flash;`
h 4 `oh ho aha the has had hoe that josh shad hall halt`

c/h 5 `ache echo each cash chat chef hack hock tech check`
c/h 6 `a chef; a chat; the ache; all cash; check the hack`

all letters learned 7 `had a look | took the jet | josh the chef | cash a check`
all letters learned 8 `to teach | had the jack | he took half | a cache of food`
                                                        TS

144a-147a ▶ 5
Preparatory practice

each line 3 times SS (slowly, faster, slowly); DS between 3-line groups; repeat selected lines as time permits

alphabet	1	Jack quoted five experts who were trying to formalize a building plan.
fig/sym	2	I ordered 24 blinds (Rx-475/93), but I received 36 shades (Rx-208/16).
combi-nation	3	A bottle with a cork in it rested on the sand at the edge of the lake.
fluency	4	They own the land, and they work in the field when they wish to do so.

| 1 | 2 | 3 | 4 | 5 | 6 | 7 | 8 | 9 | 10 | 11 | 12 | 13 | 14 |

144b-147b ▶ 45
Office job simulation
(LM pp. 139–149)

Job 1
Prepare tables from computer printout (full sheets)

Mr. O'Mariety gives you the first order form from Mathas Equipment Company and asks you to prepare two tables from the computer printout.

CUSTOMER'S INSTRUCTIONS:

Please prepare two tables from the computer printout. Use "Current Orders" as the main heading for the first table and "Equipment Cancellation Orders" for the main heading of the second table. Double-space the columnar items; use full headings instead of abbreviations above the columns in the tables. The abbreviations stand for:

Customer Number
CODE Number
Billing Code
Machine Code
Data Unit

CUST. NO.	CODE NO.	B/C	MC	D.U.
ORDERS TAKEN THIS MONTH				
641001193	092723	23632	8221	1574
087992319	092741	20212	8211	V117
641012448	092670	20333	9999	1574
641013735	092695	28201	9999	1571
641003710	092701	21961	9741	1571
641008529	092746	21923	8221	1574
857225825	092679	18221	9032	1581
093024511	092855	23222	8231	1574
	092855	23222	8231	1574
641012554	092653	23222	9999	1574
	092653	23222	9999	1574
***EQUIPMENT CANCELLATION ORDERS				
087992319	0927411	20212		V117
642231104	2400871	59021		V117
092844414	0928851	55722		V117
087926713	0928921	20212		H823
	0928921	20212		H823
641001193	092723	23632	8221	1574

4d
Learn new keyreaches:
R and Right Shift

Reach technique for r

Reach *up* with *left first* finger.

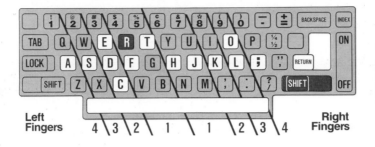

Left Fingers 4 3 2 1 1 2 3 4 Right Fingers

Control of right shift key

Reach *down* with *right little* finger; shift, type, release.

Follow the "Standard procedure for learning new keyreaches" on page 10 (Lines 1–4 twice; Lines 5–8 once; repeat 5–8 if time permits).

r

```
1 r rf rf or or for for fro fro ore ore her her ford
2 roe for oar are fork role tore oral soar rode fort
```
DS

right shift
```
3 A; A; Al Al Alf Alf Flo Flo Ed Ed Ted Ted Del Del;
4 Flo Dole; Chad Alte; Alf Slak; Ella Todd; Sol Ekas
```

r/right shift
```
5 Alf Roe; Elke or Rolf Dorr; Rose Salk or Dora Ford
6 Sol Ross asked for Ella; Carl Alda rode for Rhoda;
```

all reaches learned
```
7 Rose Ford told Cora the joke Ross had told to her;
8 Dot Roe has the oar here; Al left the oar for her;
```
TS

4e
Practice words/phrases

1 Practice the Level 1 lines once SS at an easy pace.

2 DS; then practice the Level 2 lines in the same way.

3 DS; then practice the Level 2 lines again at a faster pace.

4 If time permits, practice the Level 3 lines once, trying to keep the carrier (carriage) moving steadily.

Note: The 3 sets of lines progress gradually in diffi-culty.

Goal: *At least* 1 line per minute (10 *gwam*).

all reaches learned

```
            1 or to do so of he for the she roe toe cod cot coal
Level 1     2 jak jet hat hot lot jar her car ask lad lass chose
            3 Cal had a jar; Rod has a cat; Della has a red hat;

            4 cod code jet jets for fore ash cash old hold holds
Level 2     5 are hare ere here car card ale kale rod rode check
            6 Al left; Theo has roe; Flo ate cake; Doc had half;

            7 elf self shelf led sled sleds fed feed feeds chose
Level 3     8 old fold folds she shed sheds hot shot shots jokes
            9 Rolf added a cash ad; Flora called here for Chloe;
```

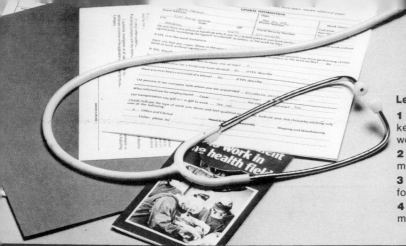

Learning goals

1 To become familiar with the keyboarding/formatting tasks of a word processing office.

2 To learn to produce long docu–ments efficiently.

3 To improve skill in working with form letters.

4 To improve ability to work with minimum instructions.

Machine adjustments

1 Set paper guide at *0.*

2 Set ribbon control to use upper half of ribbon.

3 70–space line for drill lines.

4 Follow customer's instructions for problems.

Office Job Simulation

Read carefully the material at the right before you begin the work in Section 37. Note any standard procedures that you think will save you time in the completion of the word processing activities.

Daily practice plan:

Preparatory practice .... 5'
Work on simulation .... 45'

Work Assignments

You have been assigned by Office Services Temporaries, Inc., to work as a keyboard specialist at Information Processing Services, Inc., a company which provides typing and other office services for a variety of businesses in the Chicago metropolitan area. The company is located at 944 Adella Avenue, Joliet, IL 60433-2212.

Customers can either place their orders via telephone, or they can request pick up and delivery service. You have been assigned to work with materials which have been picked up from the different businesses. Each order will have attached to it instructions stating the procedures that the particular company wishes to have followed. Mr. O'Mariety, your supervisor, will be handing to you these in-structions with the material(s) to be prepared, and you are to follow carefully the procedures indicated.

The procedures manual at Information Processing Services, Inc., specifies that all let-ters are to be formatted with block style and open punctuation unless otherwise indicated by the customer. Closing lines of all letters are to include the typed name of the person for whom the letters are prepared followed on the next line by the person's business title. An en-velope is addressed for each letter unless otherwise stated.

Information Processing Services, Inc., has based its procedures manual on COLLEGE KEYBOARDING/TYPEWRITING, so use your textbook to look up matters of style when in doubt. When a job requires unusual or definite specifications, Information Processing Serv-ices provides them in "Excerpts from the In-formation Processing Manual."

Excerpts from the Information Processing Manual

Information Processing Services, Inc., often uses form letters to reply to orders and corre-spondence. Slightly different procedures are used to prepare form letters on an electric typewriter than on a word processor.

If you are using an electric typewriter, always type a form letter from the letter you have just typed, so that the previous letter will be proofread while you are typing the subsequent letter. All materials prepared should be proofread at least twice to make sure the ma-terial is error free.

On a word processor, if the copy is stored correctly, then you have to proofread only the variable material to make certain that it is error free.

Several different types of form letters may be used. Complete forms are usually printed in bulk. This type of form letter is very imper-sonal. Most companies prefer to use form let-ters which are personalized. The same letter could be prepared on a word processor with only the variable information being the date, letter address, and salutation. Other letters may have one or more items of variable infor-mation in the body of the letter.

Some form letters are prepared from form paragraphs. The date, letter address, and salutation are usually variable information; then the proper form paragraphs are selected. To proofread letters from form paragraphs, proof any variable information and check to make certain that the proper paragraphs were selected.

5a
Prepare-to-keyboard checklist

Are you ready to keyboard? Check the items listed at the right before you begin. Review 4a, page 14, if you are unsure about any of the items.

- ✔ Work area
- ✔ Book placement
- ✔ Margin stops
- ✔ Ribbon control
- ✔ Paper guide
- ✔ Paper insertion

5b
Preparatory practice

each line twice SS (slowly, then faster); DS between 2-line groups

home row 1 a; as all lad ask add ash fad jak sad has had lash

c/r 2 or ore core jar jars ark lark rock cord lack cross

h/t 3 a hat ate hate the that oath heat halt sloth loath

all reaches learned 4 Ro has a fake jade; ask Cal to let her do the lot;
TS

5c
Learn new keyreaches: W and U

Reach technique for w

Reach *up* with *left third* finger.

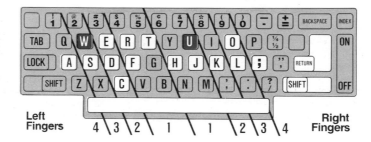

Left Fingers 4 3 2 1 1 2 3 4 Right Fingers

Reach technique for u

Reach *up* with *right first* finger.

Follow the "Standard procedure for learning new keyreaches" on page 10 (Lines 1–4 twice; Lines 5–8 once; repeat 5–8 if time permits).

w 1 w ws ws was was sow sows law laws jaw jaws wow wow
2 ow how owl owe woes cow cows row rows sow sows low
DS

u 3 u uj uj jut jut cut cut us us use use due due fuse
4 cue sue hue rut rude just jute sure lure loud cute

w/u 5 how we do; just a duck; we work out our four cues;
6 we row; use a wok; our used fuse; Sue wore a tutu;

all reaches learned 7 two or four; the cut hurt Wu; a hut for us to use;
8 cut two; Duke had a cake; we just saw Dale at two;
TS

Job 7
Memorandum of loan and promissory note
(LM p. 137)

You are asked by Ms. Adams to complete this document today because the clients will be in the office tomorrow at 8:30 a.m. This document does not require a notary statement.

MEMORANDUM OF LOAN AND PROMISSORY NOTE

IT IS AGREED between the parties hereto that

JAMES R. DOYLE has loaned the sum of

Ten Thousand Dollars ($ 10,000.00)

to PATRICIA V. LYON , and that the

borrower intends to use said sums for the following:

as a down payment on purchase of the house at 310 South Grove Avenue, Oak Park, IL 60302-3331.

THE BORROWER, namely PATRICIA V. LYON

, hereby agrees to pay to the lender,

namely JAMES R. DOYLE , the full amount of

the sum loaned as set forth above, together with annual

simple/compound interest at the rate of 12 % no later

than the 14th day of March , 19 94 .

SHOULD THE BORROWER default, either in whole or in part, on this note, the lender shall have the option of claiming an interest in the asset or property purchased with the money in proportion that said money was expended thereon, or to sue for money judgment.

In case suit or action is instituted to collect this note or the asset, the borrower promises to pay to the lender such reasonable attorney's fees and costs as may be fixed by the court.

Dated the 14th day of March , 19 -- .

_____
Patricia V. Lyon--Borrower

_____
James R. Doyle--Lender

5d
Learn new keyreaches:
Left Shift and . (period)

Control of left shift key

Reach *down* with *left little* finger; shift, type, release.

Left Fingers   4 3 2 1   1 2 3 4   Right Fingers

Reach technique for . (period)

Reach *down* with *right third* finger; space twice after . at end of sentence.

Follow the "Standard procedure for learning new keyreaches" on page 10 (Lines 1–4 twice; Lines 5–8 once; repeat 5–8 if time permits).

Period: Space once after a period that fol–lows an abbreviation or an initial, twice after a period that ends a sentence. Do not, however, space after a period at the end of a line.

left shift	1	L La La Lars Lake Ladd Jae Jake Karl Kate Hal Harl
	2	Jae or Jake Kale or Lara Karl or Lars Hart or Ladd

DS

. (period)	3	. .l .l l.l fl. fl. Dr. E. F. Roe asked for a lot.
	4	Dale has left for Soho. Dr. Sorel saw her at two.

left shift and .	5	Hal saw us. He also saw Joe. He was at the lake.
	6	J. J. does work for us; he used to work for Laura.

all reaches learned	7	Kae used to read to Joe; she works for the Roe Co.
	8	Sr. Jude left for Tulsa; her car was full of food.

TS

5e
Practice words/sentences

1 Practice the Level 1 lines once SS at an easy pace.

2 DS; then practice the Level 2 lines in the same way.

3 DS; then practice the Level 2 lines again at a faster pace.

4 If time permits, practice the Level 3 lines once, trying to keep the carrier (carriage) moving steadily.

Note: The 3 sets of lines progress gradually in diffi-culty.

Goal: *At least* 1 line per minute (10 *gwam*).

all reaches learned

	1	rf or of uj us sue use ws ow sow cow ol lo low old
Level 1	2	ed led eke tf to lot dot cd cod doc hj hut hue wok
	3	Jeff used the old wok to cook; Lu added the sauce.

	4	we woe awl cow sow led low for fur let cut our hut
Level 2	5	for fat law saw how use jet jut the work chew fake
	6	Aldo took the saw; Ed has to cut the old jak tree.

	7	we our was wore were just jade josh take sake hour
Level 3	8	that lurk wash four keel chew walk crow talk would
	9	Suella saw the letter that Cora wrote at the lake.

Mr. Fong has just completed a marriage contract, or ante-nuptial agreement, for Rex V. Rose and Lea K. Miller. Ms. Adams asks you to review the fill–in form and prepare it in final form. She tells you to include two signature lines on which the parties may sign. Remember to type the signer's name centered below the line. Use a spread heading.

A N T E N U P T I A L   A G R E E M E N T

THIS AGREEMENT is made on the 12th day of March _____, 19 --, between REX V. ROSE , party of the first part, and LEA K. MILLER , party of the second part,

WHEREAS, a marriage is intended to be entered in-to and solemnized in the near future between the said

REX V. ROSE and LEA K. MILLER ;

AND WHEREAS, each of the parties hereto is pos-sessed of considerable property, as set forth in Schedules A and B, annexed hereto, and has made a full and frank disclosure to the other in relation to its character and amount, and each of them has been fully advised as to their respective rights therein in the event of their marriage and in the absence of any agreement between them;

NOW, THIS AGREEMENT WITNESSETH that each of them, the said REX V. ROSE and LEA K. MILLER , hereby declares it to be his or her intention and desire that during their marriage each of them shall be and continue completely independent of the other in regard to the enjoyment and disposal of all property whether owned by either of them at the commencement of the marriage or coming to either of them during the marriage; and each of them hereby agrees with the other, in view and in consider-ation of the said proposed marriage, that so far as is legally possible, by their private act, declaration, and agreement, all property belonging to either of them at the commencement of the marriage or coming to either of them during the marriage shall be and is enjoyed by him or her, and be subject to the dispositions of him or her as his or her separate property, and after the death of either it shall be free from any claim by the other on account of dower, courtesy, or other statutory right in the same man-ner as if the said proposed marriage had never been cele-brated.

AND WHEREAS, it is further agreed by and between the parties hereto that in the event either one of them desires to sell or mortgage any real or personal property owned by either of them respectively, then the other shall sign and join in such deed or mortgage as the case may be in order to make the same legal and effectual.

IT IS FURTHER MUTUALLY AGREED that the terms of this contract shall be binding on the heirs, personal repre-sentatives, executors and/or administrators of the parties hereto.

IN WITNESS WHEREOF, the parties have hereunto set their hands and seals this 12th day of March , 19--.

6a
Prepare-to-keyboard checklist

Are you ready? Check the list at the right.

✔ Desk and chair
✔ Work area
✔ Book placement

✔ Paper guide
✔ Line–space selector (SS)
✔ Margin stops

6b
Preparatory practice

each line twice SS (slowly, then faster); DS between 2-line groups

home row	1	a jak lad as ash ad had add has all fall hash dash
e/o/t/c	2	ed ol tf cd led old cot toe eke due lot colt docks
w/h/r/u	3	ws hj rf uj we raw hut war who haul hawk rule what
all reaches learned	4	Rosela had to cut her rate; Jeff took a weak lead.

TS

6c
Check keystroking technique

each set of lines twice SS; DS between 3-line groups

> **Technique hint:**
> Check the list of techniques at the right; use them as you do the drill lines.

✔ Seated erect in chair
✔ Both feet on floor
✔ Fingertips lightly touching home keys
✔ Wrists low, but not touching the machine

✔ Slant of forearms parallel to slant of keyboard
✔ Each key struck with a quick stroke of the fingertip
✔ Space bar struck with inward motion of the thumb

all reaches learned

words	1	or do he so of el la ow to she for the fur due row
	2	cue jak foc sod cut doe sow sue all too wood would
	3	alto also hall fall tall rust dust lark dark jowls
phrases	4	to do so | he or she | to do the | of all our | as the doe
	5	had to do | ask the lad | ate the jak | has the fur coat
	6	do the work | saw the show | just as she | take the test
sentences	7	Drew saw the late show. She had to cut law class.
	8	Walt was at Olde Lake at two; Joel also was there.
	9	Kate was at the dock at four to see all of us off.

TS

6d
Check spacing/shifting technique

each set of lines twice SS; DS between 3-line groups

> **Technique hint:**
> Check the techniques above right; use them as you do the drill.

✔ Space with down–and–in motion of the thumb
✔ Shift with quick, 1–2–3/ shift–type–release motions
✔ Quiet hands; no pauses before or after spacing or shifting

✔ Space once after abbreviation period
✔ Space twice after a sentence period
✔ Space once after a semicolon

all reaches learned

spacing	1	ah so he do la of el us to ha for she due cot work
	2	to do of us do so a jak the fur for the of all the
	3	Ask the lad for the oak. He cut the wood at work.
shifting	4	Ask for Dr. Lor. She took a call. Jae heard her.
	5	Todd has to work. Talk to Jewel; she has the ads.
	6	Laura left for Duluth. She took the jet at three.

Job 5
Certificate of limited partnership (LM pp. 129–131)

Mr. Fong met with the general partners of The Pottery Shed this morning to draft a certificate of limited partnership. The general partners are returning with their limited partners tomorrow at 2 p.m. to sign the document. Ms. Adams asks you to prepare this document for Mr. Fong. She reminds you to note the three sections that are to be indented to paragraph point and single-spaced. Also, an acknowledgment (notary statement) needs to be included. (See page 289 for sample.)

CERTIFICATE OF LIMITED PARTNERSHIP

THE UNDERSIGNED, desiring to form a Limited Partnership under the Uniform Limited Partnership Act of the State of Illinois, make this certificate for that purpose.

1. The name of the Partnership shall be _The Pottery Shed_ .

2. The purpose of the Parnership shall be to _sell hand-crafted pottery articles and pottery supplies_ .

3. The location of the Partnership's principal place of business is _Cook_ County, Illinois.

4. The names of the members, and their designation as General or Limited Partners are:

DS→
Gary R. Trotter	General/~~Limited~~ Partner
Caroline J. Knutzen	General/~~Limited~~ Partner
Nadine C. Rhiner	~~General~~/Limited Partner
Dennis K. Bascom	~~General~~/Limited Partner

SS

DS→ 5. The term for which the partnership is to exist is indefinite.

6. The amount of cash and a description of the agreed value of the other property contributed by each Limited Partner are:

SS
| _Nadine C. Rhiner,_ | _$5,000.00_ |
| _Dennis K. Bascom,_ | _$10,000.00_ |

7. Each Limited Partner may (but shall not be obliged to) make such additional contributions to the capital of the Partnership as may from time to time be agreed upon by the General Partners.

8. The share of the profits which each Limited Partner shall receive by reason of his or her contribution is:

SS
Nadine C. Rhiner	. . . .	_10_ %
Dennis K. Bascom	. . . .	_20_ %
	. . . .	%

Signed _March 12_ , 19-- .

_____
Gary R. Trotter
_____
Caroline J. Knutzen
_____
Nadine C. Rhiner
_____
Dennis K. Bascom

(Include a notary statement.)

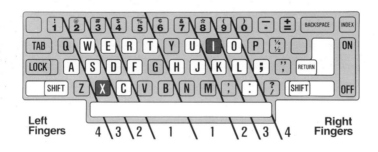

7a ▶ 8
Preparatory practice

each line twice SS
(slowly, then faster);
DS between 2-line groups

Note: Beginning with Les–
son 7, each lesson part will
include in its headings a
suggested number of min–
utes for practicing that
activity.

all letters learned	1 Doc took just four hours to row to the south lake.
c/u/r	2 Lou cut the rate cost of our letters to the coast.
w/h	3 Ask Walt Howe to heat the water to wash the shelf.
all reaches learned	4 We saw Jack a lot later; he worked for four hours.

TS

7b ▶ 6
Develop keyboarding fluency

two 30″ writings on each line

Goal: To complete each line in 30″ (14 *gwam*).

all letters learned

1 Do the oak shelf for the lake dock.
2 She cut half the fuel for the auto.
3 Throw the kale to the cow for Jake.
4 The autos do the work of the world.

TS

7c ▶ 12
Learn new keyreaches: X and I

Reach technique for x

Reach *down* with *left third* finger.

Reach technique for i

Reach *up* with *right second* finger.

Follow the "Standard procedure for learning new keyreaches" on page 10 (Lines 1–4 twice; Lines 5–8 once; repeat 5–8 if time permits).

x
1 x xs xs ox ox axe axe sox sox fox fox hex hex axle
2 xs ax ox tux lox lax sax flex flax flux crux taxed

i
3 i ik ik if if is is it it did did kid kid aid aids
4 ik kit sit fit wit sir lid its side cite kick wick

x/i
5 Felix fixed the six tax rules I asked Exie to fix.
6 I will fix tea for Dixie if she will wax the taxi.

all reaches learned
7 Sid Cox said it was a lax law; Roxie also said so.
8 Jackie will fix the cut foot of the old fox I saw.

TS

Jobs 3 and 4
Letter and promissory note (LM pp. 125–127)

Mr. Fong has edited a draft copy of a letter that is to accompany the promissory note (*shown below*). Ms. Adams asks that you prepare the letter in final form for Mr. Fong's signature. You are also to prepare the promissory note that will be enclosed with the letter. Although the promissory note is very short, you should still prepare it as a full–page legal document. Date the letter **March 11** and address it to:

**Mr. and Mrs. Jeffery T. Hall
1239 North Jackson Avenue
Oak Park, IL   60305-3511**

Mr. Fong's signature block should be:

**Mr. Y. R. Fong
Attorney-at-Law**

Use a spread heading and no acknowledgment for the promissory note. Also correct any undetected errors you may find in the draft letter.

Dear Mr. and Mrs. Hall:

I am enclosing a promissory note for the $80,000 ~~that must~~ to be signed by your son, William, upon advanching the funds. As we discussed the funds will be advanced upon an interest-fee basis to be used to produce necessary income. while he attends college

You have both indicated to me that you understand the potential tax savings form this type of ~~loss~~ advance. If, however, either of you ~~have~~ has additional questions please call me before your consummating ~~of the~~ this transaction.

Several aspects of ~~this~~ the loan are ~~quite~~ important. It First, must be a demand note; and the note attached is such a note. Secondly, the loan must be bonafide; that is, it must be, in truth, an actual a loan. I have stressed to both of you that you must allow william complete discretion in the way he invests the money. It would be wise ~~sie~~, however, to recomend to him the types of investments which you think most appropriate in view of the fact that he will need to produce ~~the~~ income during the current year. I have discussed with you the major advantages and disadvantages of money market funds. The majer advantage of this type of investment is that it would give William the flexibility of making withdrals whenever a need occurs ~~needed~~.

Sincerely,

PROMISSORY   NOTE

$80,000

1239 North Jackson Avenue
Oak Park, IL   60305-3511

March 11, 19--

FOR VALUE RECEIVED, on demand, the undersigned promises to pay to the order of Mr. and Mrs. Jeffery T. Hall the principal sum of Eighty Thousand Dollars ($80,000) without interest.

William J. Hall

7d ▶ 12
Learn new keyreaches:
G and N

Reach technique for g

Reach to *right* with *left first* finger.

Left Fingers 4 \ 3 \ 2 \ 1 \ 1 \ 2 \ 3 \ 4 Right Fingers

Reach technique for n

Reach *down* with *right first* finger.

Follow the "Standard procedure for learning new keyreaches" on page 10 (Lines 1–4 twice; Lines 5–8 once; repeat 5–8 if time permits).

g   1 g gf gf go go fog fog got got rug rug dog dog frog
    2 gf log dug fig wig dig lag tog leg keg jig cog got
                                                         DS
n   3 n nj nj an an and and end end hen hen ran ran lend
    4 nj on won wan den tan ten can land want rent sends

g/n 5 Gwen longs to sing a grand song she knew in Genoa.
    6 Gig noted that one swan wing was green with algae.

all reaches   7 Leonor left the show to take a cruise to Calcutta.
learned   8 Just set a fair goal; then work hard to extend it.
                                                              TS

7e ▶ 12
Build keyboarding continuity

1 Practice the Level 1 lines once SS at an easy pace.

2 DS; then practice the Level 2 lines in the same way.

3 DS; then practice the Level 2 lines again at a faster pace.

4 If time permits, practice the Level 3 lines once, trying to keep the carrier (carriage) moving steadily.

Note: The 3 sets of lines progress gradually in difficulty.

Goal: *At least* 1 line per minute (10 *gwam*).

Count typewritten words:
Five characters and spaces are counted as one standard typewritten word. The figures in the scale under the copy show the word-by-word count (5 strokes a word) for each line.

all reaches learned

         1 I will need four to six weeks to work out the act.
Level 1 2 Janet can ask six of the girls to guide the tours.
         3 Ask Nellie to sing one alto aria in our next show.

         4 He will fix a snack; he will also fix fruit juice.
Level 2 5 The four girls will use their auto or hire a taxi.
         6 Gil has asked six girls to a light lunch in Akron.

         7 Luann wore a ring and long necklace of green jade.
Level 3 8 Dixie will send her tax check to the local office.
         9 Lex is an officer of high rank in Jackson Tool Co.

         | 1 | 2 | 3 | 4 | 5 | 6 | 7 | 8 | 9 | 10 |

To determine words-a-minute rate:

1 List the figure 10 for each line completed during a writing.

2 For a partial line, note from the scale the figure directly below the point at which you stopped.

3 Add these figures to determine the total gross words typed (the same as *gwam* for a 1′ writing).

Another client has an appointment with Mr. Fong tomorrow to complete a stock certificate transfer. Ms. Adams asks that you prepare this document with an appropriate acknowledgment (notary statement). Most legal firms have one of their employees as a Notary Public. In this office, Ms. Adams is a Notary Public and is able to execute the notary statements for Mr. Fong's clients. Place an appropriate endorsement on the back of the page.

(Indent 9½s 10 spaces)

ASSIGNMENT OF SHARE CERTIFICATE

Share Certificate dated: *October 15*, 19*75*

Issued to: *Rosemary E. Stone*

FOR VALUE RECEIVED, ROSEMARY E. STONE does hereby sell, assign, and transfer unto JARED Q. McGARVEY, *15* shares of the common shares of *Longmont Oil Company* represented by the within certificate numbered *235*, and standing in the name of ROSEMARY E. STONE _____ on the books of said Corporation, and does hereby irrevocably constitute and appoint Y. R. Fong, attorney, to transfer the said shares on the books of the within named Corporation, with full power of substitution.

Dated this the *10th* day of *March*, 19--.

_____
Rosemary E. Stone

STATE OF ILLINOIS)
                                    : SS.
County of Cook   )

    On this *10th* day of *March*, 19-- , before me personally appeared the above-named individual(s), to me known to be the person(s) described in and who executed the foregoing instrument and acknowledged that he/ she/they executed the same as his/her/their own free act and deed.

    In testimony whereof, I have hereunto subscribed my name at Oak Park, Illinois, this day.

_____
Notary Public

My commission expires on October 28, 19--.

8a ▶ 8
Preparatory practice

each line twice SS
(slowly, then faster);
DS between 2-line
groups

all letters
learned

1 Alexi Garcia had gone to San Juan for three weeks.

x/i 2 I next fixed the axle; then I waxed the six taxis.

g/n 3 Ginger is going to England to sing for Jonah King.

all reaches
learned

4 Lex and Rolf saw Luan Ling; Jack had not seen her.

Recall: TS between
lesson parts.

| 1 | 2 | 3 | 4 | 5 | 6 | 7 | 8 | 9 | 10 |

8b ▶ 8
Improve keyboarding technique

each line once as shown;
if time permits, repeat the
drill

keystroking
and spacing

all reaches learned

1 ws ik ed ol nj rf uj tf cd .l xs gf hj ec un rg tf
2 if so is do it of an go he el ha ox ah or eh to us
3 as to | we go | at an | we do | as he | see us | get it | ate an

spacing
and shifting

4 Ken can win if he will set a goal and work for it.
5 Dorn is now in Rio; Janice is to go there in June.
6 Ann and J. D. Fox had seen Lt. Green at the dance.

| 1 | 2 | 3 | 4 | 5 | 6 | 7 | 8 | 9 | 10 |

8c ▶ 12
Learn new keyreaches: V and , (comma)

Reach technique for v

Reach *down* with
left first finger.

Left
Fingers   4 \ 3 \ 2 \ 1   1 / 2 / 3 / 4   Right
Fingers

Reach technique
for , (comma)

Reach *down* with
right second finger;
space once after ,
used as punctuation.

Follow the "Standard procedure
for learning new keyreaches" on
page 10 (Lines 1–4 twice; Lines
5–8 once; repeat 5–8 if time
permits).

v

1 v vf vf vie vie vow vow van van via via five fives
2 vf vf live have dive love vane vain vile view viva

DS

'

3 , ,k ,k kit, kit, Dick, Jane, Nate, and I read it.
4 a rug, a jig, a ski, an igloo, the ring, two songs

Comma: Space once after a
comma.
---

v/,

5 Vic, Iva, and Viv dived over and over to save Van.
6 Val, Reva, and Vi voted for Eva; even so, Iva won.

all reaches
learned

7 Kevin Nix was a judge at the garden show in Flint.
8 Joan, not Vi, took the jet; Vic also tried for it.

| 1 | 2 | 3 | 4 | 5 | 6 | 7 | 8 | 9 | 10 |

Preparatory practice

each line 3 times SS (slowly, faster, slowly); DS between 3-line groups; repeat selected lines as time permits

alphabet	1	An expert must move quickly to adjust a water gauge before the freeze.
fig/sym	2	The net due on $3,987.46 after a 5.2% discount ($207.35) is $3,780.11.
outside reach	3	A small quail at the local zoo was looking at six gorillas plus a fox.
fluency	4	The sorority girls may go to the island to dig for the ancient emblem.

| 1 | 2 | 3 | 4 | 5 | 6 | 7 | 8 | 9 | 10 | 11 | 12 | 13 | 14 |

140b-143b ▶ 45

Office job simulation

(LM pp. 121–137)

Ms. Adams welcomes you to the office and explains the basic office procedures to you. She suggests that you study carefully the *Legal Office Manual*. She indicates to you that the majority of the jobs in Mr. Fong's office involve the preparation of legal documents. She further informs you that most of the legal documents prepared in this office will be prepared by Mr. Fong on fill-in forms; however, Mr. Fong does not use the preprinted forms as the final legal document. Ms. Adams reminds you to delete the underlining from under the filled-in elements on the preprinted forms when you are preparing final legal documents. For those cases where a fill-in form is not available, Mr. Fong will write out the document in long-hand.

Mr. Fong's letters are usually dictated and draft copies are prepared for him to edit. He requests the modified block style with mixed punctuation and indented paragraphs for all his letters. Prepare an envelope for each letter. You begin work today, March 8.

Job 1
Joint purchase agreement
(LM p. 121)

Ms. Adams asks you to prepare this legal document for Mr. Fong. His client will be coming to the office tomorrow to sign the document. You are reminded that the date placed on the legal document is the date the instrument is signed; therefore, you note that Mr. Fong has tomorrow's date on the document. This document does not require an acknowledgment (notary statement).

TS >

JOINT PURCHASE AGREEMENT

RUTH A. FISK and CAROL G. BROWN, who are living in the same house, agree to purchase jointly a car from CENTRAL AUTO COMPANY for a total price, including tax, of $6,543.52.

IT IS AGREED that RUTH A. FISK shall pay toward the down payment the sum of $1,000.00, and CAROL G. BROWN shall pay toward the down payment the sum of $1,000.00. The monthly payments are $212.00. Of this, RUTH A. FISK agrees to pay $106.00 per month, and CAROL G. BROWN agrees to pay $106.00 per month.

IT IS AGREED that this automobile shall be owned by each party equally on a fifty-fifty basis.

IT IS AGREED that should litigation or the use of an attorney be required to enforce this agreement, the defaulting or losing party agrees to pay to the prevailing party such reasonable attorney's fees and costs as may be fixed by the court.

Dated: March 9, 19--

_____
Ruth A. Fisk
_____
Carol G. Brown

8d ▶ 12
Learn new keyreaches:
Q and Y

Reach technique for q

Reach *up* with *left little* finger.

Left Fingers 4 \ 3 \ 2 \ 1 / 1 / 2 / 3 / 4 Right Fingers

Reach technique for y

Reach *up* with *right first* finger.

Follow the "Standard procedure for learning new keyreaches" on page 10 (Lines 1–4 twice; Lines 5–8 once; repeat 5–8 if time permits).

q

1 q qa qa qu qu quo quo quit quits quad quads quotes
2 qa qu quo quit quad quick quite equal quilt quarts
DS

y

3 y yj yj jay jay you you yet yet day day yell yells
4 yj eye yes rye dye sky cry sly try joy soy yen toy

q/y

5 Jay says Quay is quite young; he is quiet and shy.
6 Troy, Quent, and I are quite glad that Quinn quit.

all reaches learned

7 Frank Cage enjoyed the novel; Jo can read it next.
8 Next, Jacky Quire will leave; she can go in a day.

| 1 | 2 | 3 | 4 | 5 | 6 | 7 | 8 | 9 | 10 |

8e ▶ 10
Build sustained keyboarding power

1 Practice Paragraph (¶) 1 once SS.
2 DS and practice ¶ 2 in the same way.

Technique hints:

1 Keep your eyes on the book copy as you keyboard.
2 Do not pause or look up as you return the carrier or car–riage (or cursor on a personal computer).

all reaches learned

¶ 1 We often need to choose, and yet it is never easy
to know which of two roads to take. One can look
exactly like another, yet we are never quite sure
what is involved with each journey or each choice.

¶ 2 However, we do have to choose; and, since we will
not know where the unchosen road would have taken
us, we have to trust that we chose the right road.

| 1 | 2 | 3 | 4 | 5 | 6 | 7 | 8 | 9 | 10 |

Approx. 2" top margin

Heading centered between ruled lines

ASSIGNMENT OF SHARE CERTIFICATE

Share Certificate dated: October 15, 1975

Issued to: Rosemary E. Stone

    FOR VALUE RECEIVED, ROSEMARY E. STONE does hereby sell, assign, and transfer unto JARED Q. McGARVEY, 15 shares of the common shares of Longmont Oil Company represented by the within certificate numbered 235, and standing in the name of ROSEMARY E. STONE on the books of said Corporation, and does hereby irrevocably constitute and appoint Y. R. Fong, attorney, to transfer the said shares on the books of the within named Corporation, with full power of substitution.

    Dated this the 10th day of March, 19--.

                           _____
                                Rosemary E. Stone

STATE OF ILLINOIS)
             : ss.
County of Cook)

Acknowledgment SS

    On this 10th day of March, 19--, before me personally appeared the above-named individual, to me known to be the person described in and who executed the foregoing instrument and acknowledged that she executed the same as her own free act and deed.

    In testimony whereof, I have hereunto subscribed my name at Oak Park, Illinois, this day.

                           _____
                                  Notary Public

One-page instrument does not need a page number

My commission expires on October 28, 19--.

Assignment of Share Certificate

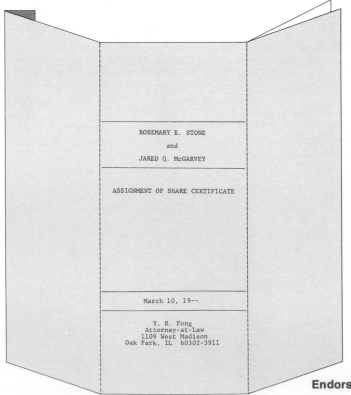

ROSEMARY E. STONE
and
JARED Q. McGARVEY

ASSIGNMENT OF SHARE CERTIFICATE

March 10, 19--

Y. R. Fong
Attorney-at-Law
1109 West Madison
Oak Park, IL 60302-3911

Endorsement on a legal back

Titles on Legal Documents. The title should be in all capital letters, centered between the side margins (vertical rulings). Often a title is s p r e a d. To spread a title or heading, follow these procedures:

1. Backspace from horizontal center point one *backspace for* each stroke in the title or heading (letters, numbers, symbols, and spaces) *except* the last stroke.

2. Enter the title (in all capital letters) with one blank space between characters (letters, numbers, or symbols) and with 3 blank spaces between words in the title.

Example:

center point
↓
PROMISSORY NOTE
└ backspace

P R O M I S S O R Y   N O T E
3 spaces ─┘

Signature Lines. The page on which the signatures of the maker(s) and any witness appear must contain at least 2 lines of the body of the document.

Place the signature lines for the maker or makers of the legal document on the right side of the page. Place the witness' signature, if any, on the left side of the page. Type the first signature line on the third or fourth line below the last line of the document. The actual line upon which the signature is written is about 3" long. If more than one signature is needed, leave 2 or 3 blank lines between them.

Latin Abbreviations. When a legal document is "under seal," the signature on the document is followed by "L.S." which refers to the Latin phrase *locus sigilli*. Use the abbreviation "ss" for the Latin word *scilicet*, meaning "to wit."

Proofreading. Use the verifying method to proofread all legal documents. In this method, one person reads from the originating material while the other person checks the newly prepared copy. Tricky or unfamiliar words are spelled, and all punctuation marks are also indicated by the person reading aloud.

Endorsements and Legal Backs. The names of the parties, the title of the legal document, the date, and the name and address of the attorney or legal firm appear on the back of legal documents. This information is called the *endorsement*. It may be typed either directly on the back of the last page of the document or on a *legal back* (a heavier and larger paper used to cover the document). If typing the endorsement directly on the back of the legal document, fold the document into thirds and type the endorsement in the middle fold for 8½" × 11" paper; fold the document into fourths and type the endorsement on the outer fold for longer, legal-sized paper. If a legal back is used to cover the legal document, prepare it in the following manner for 8½" × 11" paper:

1. Fold down the top ½" and crease it; this fold will later be used to bind the legal document.

2. Fold the remainder into equal thirds (as in folding a business letter).

3. Place the endorsement within the middle section.

Note that most preprinted legal forms have the title of the legal document preprinted on the back and additional information for the endorsement needs only to be typed in the proper place.

9a ▶ 8

Preparatory practice

each line twice SS (slowly, then faster); DS between 2-line groups

all letters learned	1	Work quickly, and we can fix the van Janet got us.
v/q/,/y	2	Standing on the quay, Dave, too, felt very queasy.
space bar	3	if it| to do| or he| an ox| for us| to do the| a yen for
easy	4	The city got a quantity of fish for the town lake.

| 1 | 2 | 3 | 4 | 5 | 6 | 7 | 8 | 9 | 10 |

Recall: TS between lesson parts.

9b ▶ 14

Practice keyreaches

1 Practice each line twice SS; DS between 2–line groups.
2 Repeat lines that seem most troublesome.

x	1	Lex next sent six yards of flax to Roxy in a taxi.
g	2	Gwen sang a song as George raised the ragged flag.
y	3	I say Ayn is shy; yet I did enjoy her story a lot.
n	4	For Nana, France was a land of sun, sand, and tan.
v	5	Van ran to visit the levee to view the vast river.
q	6	Quay quickly quoted Queen Arqua. Quent was quiet.

| 1 | 2 | 3 | 4 | 5 | 6 | 7 | 8 | 9 | 10 |

9c ▶ 14

Develop machine parts control

twice as shown; repeat as time permits

Lines 1-4: Practice each short line and return without pausing or looking up.
Lines 5-7: Use space bar efficiently and maintain typing fluency.
Lines 8-10: Shift smoothly and rhythmically.

	1	Finish final stroke in the line.
return	2	Reach quickly to the return key.
	3	Hold your eyes down on the text.
	4	Return; start next line at once.
	5	an key fox van vie own hay can jay coy lay rug any
space bar	6	Vote for Gin; Lu is not a good choice. Tell Quin.
	7	Lex, not Tay, has a wagon; he will hang the signs.
	8	Owen Hays and Lil Young will see Neil in New York.
shift keys	9	Cyd, Rod, Susi, and Don will go on to Vienna soon.
	10	J. C. Wert will see Nel Foyt at the Old City Hall.

| 1 | 2 | 3 | 4 | 5 | 6 | 7 | 8 | 9 | 10 |

9d ▶ 14

Build sustained keyboarding power

1 Practice Paragraph (¶) 1 once.
2 DS and practice ¶2 in the same way.

Technique hint:
Keystroke smoothly, continuously; avoid pauses.

all reaches learned

¶ 1 There are certain things that each of us wants to own, and we know there are ways to acquire things we want. However, there is a flaw in this design.

¶ 2 As soon as we get the thing we want, it loses its value; so we exchange one want for another. Then we find that just having does not satisfy wanting.

| 1 | 2 | 3 | 4 | 5 | 6 | 7 | 8 | 9 | 10 |

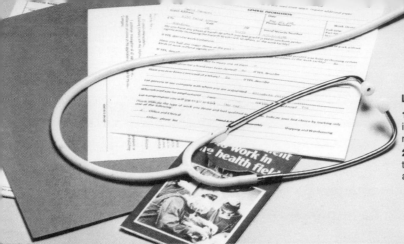

Learning goals

1 To develop knowledge and skill in the preparation of legal documents.

2 To plan your work carefully and to complete your work correctly and efficiently.

Machine adjustments

1 Set paper guide at *0*.

2 Set ribbon control to use upper half of ribbon.

3 Set line–space selector for SS.

4 Set 70–space line for drills.

5 Margins: 2″ top, 1½″ left, ½″ right, and 1″ bottom for legal documents. Other jobs as directed.

Office Job Simulation

Read carefully the material at the right and on page 287 before you begin the work of Section 36. Note any standard procedures that you think will save you time during the completion of the legal office jobs.

Daily practice plan:

Preparatory practice .... 5′
Work on simulation .... 45′

Work Assignment

You have been assigned by Office Service Temporaries, Inc., to work as a legal office assistant for Mr. Y. R. Fong, Attorney-at-Law, 1109 West Madison, Oak Park, IL 60302-3911. One of Mr. Fong's office assistants is on vacation, and you have been hired as a temporary replacement. Ms. Joyce Adams is in charge of office operations and will instruct you on your work assignments.

Mr. Fong has prepared a *Legal Office Manual* that contains both office procedures and examples of document formats. Some of the basic information from this manual has been provided in the "Excerpts from the Legal Office Manual." Mr. Fong has based his office procedures on COLLEGE KEYBOARDING/ TYPEWRITING; therefore, use your textbook as a reference guide for all matters of style and placement. Remember to proofread and correct all errors before removing your paper from the machine.

Excerpts from the Legal Office Manual— Preparation of Legal Documents

Top and Bottom Margins. The top margin is usually 2″ (12 blank lines) on each page. The bottom margin should be at least 1″. It is sometimes necessary to leave more than a 1″ bottom margin because the page on which the signature of the maker(s) or any witness appears must contain at least 2 lines of the body of the document.

Side Margins. When using plain paper, set the margin stops for a 1½″ left margin and a ½″ right margin. When using ruled paper, leave one or two spaces between the ruling at the left and the beginning of the line of writing. End the line of writing no closer than one space before the right marginal ruling. In deciding where to end a line, try to avoid hyphenation and to create an overall good appearance.

Spacing. Indent paragraphs 10 spaces. DS the body of the legal document *except* when typing quoted material and land descriptions. Single-space and indent this material 10

spaces from both margins. Also, when used, the witness statement and notary statement should be single-spaced.

Paper. Legal documents may be prepared on preprinted forms, marginal ruled paper, or plain paper. The paper may be either standard-size (8½″ × 11″) or special legal-size paper (8½″ × 13″ or 14″).

Paper with marginal rulings has a double vertical ruling down the left side 1⅜″ from the left edge of the paper, and a single vertical ruling down the right side ⅜″ from the right edge of the paper.

Multiple Copies of Legal Document. Prepare all copies in this office on a photocopy machine. If any corrections have been made on the document, use a photocopy as the "original" document (see *Correcting Errors* below).

Verification of Numbers. Type any important number or sum of money in both numbers and words to provide positive identification of the correct amounts. No legal question would arise if a single digit or letter were corrected provided verification of the amount could be made by the double typing.

Page Numbers. *Except* in a will, do not number the first page of a legal document. Center the numbers on all subsequent pages between the margins 3 blank lines from the bottom of the page. Type a hyphen before and after the page number; for example, -8-.

Correcting Errors. Correct carefully all important items such as names, sums of money, and numbers. Any obvious corrections on an original legal document should be initialed by all parties concerned to verify agreement of the change or correction. However, if a photocopy of the document is used as the signed "original," neat corrections made with lift-off tape or liquid coverup material would not show on the photocopies; therefore, initialing of corrections would not be necessary on the photocopy.

10a ▶ 8
Preparatory practice
each line twice SS
(slowly, then faster);
DS between 2-line
groups

all reaches learned   1 Yes, Clive took a few quarts; Jan had six gallons.

shift keys   2 The Fortune Five will sing at our Lake Youth Hall.

v/y   3 Every year, I have given Yves five heavy old keys.

easy   4 Diane owns the oak shanty; she also owns the land.

Recall: TS between lesson parts.

| 1 | 2 | 3 | 4 | 5 | 6 | 7 | 8 | 9 | 10 |

10b ▶ 8
Reach for new goals

1 Take a 30–second (30") writing on Line 4 of 10a above; determine *gwam* (total words typed × 2).

2 From the sentences at the right, choose one that will cause you to aim for 2–3 *gwam* more than your rate in Step 1. (30" *gwam* for each sentence is shown in Column 2 at the right.)

3 Take two 30" guided writings on the chosen sentence; try to reach the end of the line each time "Return" is called.

4 If you reach your goal in both 30" writings, take two 30" writings on the next sentence. (A total of eight 30" writings will be given.)

5 Take another 30" writing on Line 4 of 10a above; determine *gwam* (total words typed × 2).

Goal: An increase of *at least* 2 *gwam* from Step 1 to Step 5.

		words in line	gwam 30'	gwam 20'
1 Nan lent the auto to the girl.		6	12	18
2 Iris did throw a rock at the signs.		7	14	21
3 He did work with vigor to land the fish.		8	16	24
4 Hang the keys to the shanty on the oak chair.		9	18	27
5 The girls wish to visit the city to fix the signs.		10	20	30

| 1 | 2 | 3 | 4 | 5 | 6 | 7 | 8 | 9 | 10 |

10c ▶ 12
Learn new keyreaches: Z and M

Reach technique for z

Reach *down* with *left little* finger.

Left Fingers   4 \ 3 \ 2 \ 1 \ 1 / 2 / 3 / 4   Right Fingers

Reach technique for m

Reach *down* with *right first* finger.

Follow the "Standard procedure for learning new keyreaches" on page 10 (Lines 1–4 twice; Lines 5–8 once; repeat 5–8 if time permits).

z   1 z za za az az zoo zoo zed zed jazz jazz lazy crazy

  2 za za haze doze zone cozy zany zing zinc size raze

m   3 m mj mj jam jam ham ham may may yam yam make makes

  4 mj am me ma man men made must fame dome fume major

z/m   5 Zack was amazed when Mazie came home from the zoo.

  6 Lazy Mr. Zym dozed at home in the dim haze of May.

all reaches learned   7 Craving quiet, Jeff mildly dozed; he awoke at six.

  8 Zed will move as quickly next June; why, I forget.

| 1 | 2 | 3 | 4 | 5 | 6 | 7 | 8 | 9 | 10 |

Job 7
Information sheet
(plain sheet)

Dr. Rosenbloom has just made the final changes on the new postoperative nasal surgery information sheet. Mr. Moss has asked you to prepare it in final form. The format of this information sheet should follow the un-bound manuscript style as far as margins and second–page numbers are concerned. Mr. Moss asks you to use in-verted paragraphs for the body of the information sheet. Show the paragraph headings in ALL CAPS flush with the left margin. Indent all lines except the first in each paragraph 10 spaces from the left margin. Remember, each paragraph should be single–spaced with double spacing between paragraphs. The main heading is:

POSTOPERATIVE NASAL SURGERY INFORMATION

Job 8
Composing a memorandum
(LM p. 115)

Dr. Rosenbloom wants all staff physicians to be in-formed about the new post-operative nasal surgery in-formation sheet. Therefore, Mr. Moss asks you to prepare a memorandum from Dr. Rosenbloom to the staff physicians informing them of this new information sheet. Tell them that it will be avail-able for distribution and use by March 10. Also, inform the staff that they may see a copy in Dr. Rosenbloom's office before next week's distribu-tion. Date the memo March 5.

SWELLING. Most of the swelling is gone within two weeks in the majority of patients. The avoidance of lift-ing and bending will help to minimize the swelling. Swelling may also be reduced if you sleep with your head propped up at a 45-degree angle. The swelling around the eyes is often worse on the second day, especially if you lie flat during the night.

DISCOLORATION. You must remember discoloration is tem-porary. The amount of discoloration will vary from patient to patient and is dependent mostly on the amount of surgery needed, the thinness of your skin, and also your tendency to small vessel bleeding.

NOSEBLEEDS AND DISCHARGE. Blood will not likely come from your nose in the postoperative healing period if you avoid all strenuous physical activity inside or outside the home for ten days. This includes such items as exercise and lifting that tend to increase body temperature and blood pressure. There is, however, a bloody mucous discharge that comes from the nose. You must not dab the bottom of the nose, since this may produce a poorer functional and cosmetic result. If you do have a nosebleed, put chipped ice--in a plastic bag--on the bridge of your nose for 15 minutes. If the nosebleed does not stop, please telephone my office or go directly to the hospital where you had the operation.

NASAL BLOCKAGE. Your nose is not usually packed; but if it is, the packing will be removed in the early post-operative period as soon as medically advisable. Inside your nose is a surgical swelling which pro-duces nasal obstruction forcing you to mouth-breathe. Mouth-breathing may give you a dry mouth and throat and cause discomfort. Sips of fluids, hard candies, and mouthwash will be helpful. The nasal blockage usually starts to resolve in two weeks. You should not use any vasoconstrictive spray unless especially instructed to do so.

PAIN. Although there is little pain associated with nasal surgery, there may be pressure and discomfort occasionally that require some medication. A non-prescription drug is useful; but if a stronger drug is required, it will be given to you at the time of hospital discharge.

WEAKNESS. Lightheadedness and cold sweats are quite com-mon in the early postoperative course. These condi-tions will usually clear up without medication.

10d ▶ 12
Learn new keyreaches:
B and P

Reach technique for b

Reach *down* with *left first* finger.

Left Fingers   4 \ 3 \ 2 \ 1 \ \ 1 \ 2 \ 3 \ 4   Right Fingers

Reach technique for p

Reach *up* with *right little* finger.

Follow the "Standard procedure for learning new keyreaches" on page 10 (Lines 1–4 twice; Lines 5–8 once; repeat 5–8 if time permits).

b 1 b bf bf by by fib fib fob fob bit bit jib jib buff
   2 bf by fib fob but rub job rib rob buy tub bid boff
DS

p 3 ; p; p; pa pa pan pan pen pen pad pad pep pep paid
   4 up up; cup cup; sip sip; nap nap; map map; ape ape

b/p 5 Pepe bobbed for an apple; Bo jumped rope; I boxed.
    6 Pablo Paz paid Barb to probe deeply for old bulbs.

all reaches learned 7 Caleb sipped a cup of pink juice at the Boise Zoo.
      8 Five quiet zebus walk up; yet, Drex Marsh jogs on.

| 1 | 2 | 3 | 4 | 5 | 6 | 7 | 8 | 9 | 10 |

10e ▶ 10
Review keyboarding techniques

each line once SS; repeat as time permits

Lines 1-3: Keep wrists low; do not rest palms on machine.

Lines 4-6: Keep unused fingers in home-row position.

Lines 7-9: Move quickly and smoothly from letter to letter and word to word (no pauses).

Spacing review: Strike the space bar with a down-and-in motion of the thumb.

all letters 1 Alice is to speak for the group at the next forum.
      2 Dan joined the squad for spring drills last month.
      3 Denzyl took a short, fast hike; Bev went with him.
DS

spacing and shifting 4 If it were up to me, I would go for the top prize.
      5 Vi, Don, and Jo have yet to win a set in the meet.
      6 Ask Dr. Su. She knows O. J.; she once taught him.

easy sentences 7 It is the duty of the firm to fix the eight signs.
      8 This land is held by the city to make into a park.
      9 If you wish to make a big profit, work with vigor.

| 1 | 2 | 3 | 4 | 5 | 6 | 7 | 8 | 9 | 10 |

Job 5
Consultation report
(LM p. 117)

Mr. Moss gave you a dictation disk and asked you to transcribe Dr. Rosenbloom's consultation report. You have transcribed the report at draft speed and submitted it to Mr. Moss for correction. Dr. Rosenbloom checked the draft and Ok'd it to be finalized without any further corrections. Prepare the report in final form for the patient's file.

CONSULTATION REPORT

Name: Rowena C. Thompson   Case No.: 283761

Date: March 4, 19--   Sex: Female   Age: 2

Attending Physician: David E. Randolph, M.D.

Consultative Physician: Susan T. Rosenbloom, M.D.

PRESENT ILLNESS: The child was born with a very unusual midline cleft of the lip with some degree of bifid nose.

PHYSICAL EXAMINATION: A notching effect of the mucous membrane in the midline of the upper lip is apparent. Also, there is a thinning of the musculature with a very slight depression that extends up near the midline. Her lip is near normal in other respects. Each alar cartilage has separation, and there is a wide depressed cleft tip of the nose; columella is short and wide. A little midline sulcus is apparent, and there is a very small pocket in the mucous membrane between the incisor teeth. An alveolar margin is connected in the midline.

DIAGNOSIS: The bifid nose as well as the upper lip midline cleft is congenital.

CONCLUSION: Recommend surgery to correct the midline cleft lip and the bifid nose. Dermal skin graft techniques should be used.

Job 6
X-ray report
(LM p. 119)

Mr. Moss hands you this handwritten X-ray report to be finalized. Prepare the final copy for the patient's file.

X-RAY REPORT

Name: Arthur W. Brockbank   Case No.: 289877

Date: March 5, 19--   Sex: Male   Age: 35

Attending Physician: Susan T. Rosenbloom, M.D.

Radiologist: Elizabeth M. Mehmen, M.D.

Examination Requested: Paranasal sinuses

There is a moderate degree of thickening of the mucous membrane in the left frontal area. The left antrum is rather uniformly opaque. The ethmoid on the left is probably involved. Both the maxillary and ethmoid sinuses on the right side appear to be clear.

IMPRESSION: A chronic hyperplastic bilateral frontal and left ethmoid sinusitis exists. There is also a left maxillary sinusitis with a dense unaerated left antrum. A pansinusitis on the left may exist. All other sinuses are essentially clear and unremarkable.

11a ▶ 8
Preparatory practice

each line twice SS
(slowly, then faster);
DS between 2-line
groups

Recall: TS between
lesson parts.

all letters	1	Have Jeff Pim quickly walk the bridge zone at six.
z/p	2	Pat puzzled Zora; he played a happy piece of jazz.
m/b	3	Bob may remember he was a member of my brass band.
easy	4	The big map firm may make the usual profit for us.

| 1 | 2 | 3 | 4 | 5 | 6 | 7 | 8 | 9 | 10 |

11b ▶ 10
Practice difficult reaches

1 Practice each line once. Place a
check mark on your paper next to
lines that seem difficult for you.
2 Practice at least twice each line
that you checkmarked.

q	1	Quay made a quiet quip to quell a quarrel quickly.
x	2	Knox can relax; Alex gets a box of flax next week.
y	3	Ty Clay may envy you for any zany plays you write.
v	4	Eve and Vera drive the heavy vans every five days.
n	5	Nan danced many a dance, often with Nick and Donn.

| 1 | 2 | 3 | 4 | 5 | 6 | 7 | 6 | 7 | 8 | 9 | 10 |

11c ▶ 12
Learn new keyreaches:
: (colon) and ? (question mark)

Reach technique for : (colon)

Left shift and strike ; key;
space twice after : used
as punctuation.

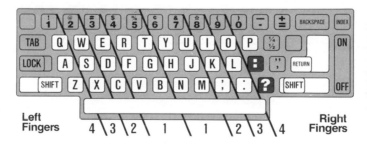

Left
Fingers   4   3   2   1   1   2   3   4   Right
Fingers

Reach technique
for ? (question)

Left shift; reach *down* with
right little finger;
space twice after ? at
end of sentence.

Follow the "Standard procedure
for learning new keyreaches" on
page 10 (Lines 1–4 twice; Lines
5–9 once; repeat 5–9 if time
permits).

Colon, Question mark:

Hold the left shift key down as
you strike ? and : keys. Except in
rare instances, they are followed
by 2 blank spaces.

| : | 1 | ; ;: :; : : To wit: Date: Name: Address: From: |
| | 2 | Space twice after a colon, thus: To: No.:   Time: |

DS

| ? | 3 | ; ?; ?; ? ? Who? When? Where? Who is? Why not? |
| | 4 | Did he go? Is she ill? Do I see it? Is it here? |

| :/? | 5 | Who is here? I see the following: Joe, Lee, Ray. |
| | 6 | Have you a pen? Copy these two words: tier, rye. |

	7	When you are puzzled, ask yourself some questions;
all letters	8	for example: Do I have facts? Can I judge? What
	9	options do I have? Who else may be of help to me?

| 1 | 2 | 3 | 4 | 5 | 6 | 7 | 8 | 9 | 10 |

DS→ 6. I consent to the photographing or televising of the operations or procedures to be performed, including appropriate portions of my body, for medical, scientific, or educational purposes, provided my identity is not revealed by the pictures or by descriptive texts accompanying them.

DS→ 7. For the purpose of advancing medical education, I consent to the admittance of observers to the operating room.

DS→ 8. I consent to the disposal by hospital authorities of any tissues or body parts which may be removed.

(Center)

TS

(CROSS OUT ANY PARAGRAPHS NOT APPLICABLE)

TS

(Begin at center point) → Signed _____
(Patient or authorized person)

SS

Witness _____

DS Date _____

SS

Check hospital

Move to left margin →

_____ Community

_____ Evanston

_____ Saint Francis

Job 4
Composing a memorandum
(LM p. 115)

Mr. Moss asks you to compose a memo from Dr. Rosenbloom to all staff physicians. Notify them that the new patient consent form will be available after March 10. Ask them to use only the new form after March 10. They should destroy all copies of the old form after they receive the new ones. Date the memo March 4.

11d ▶ 10
Learn to operate the tabulator mechanism

① Clear all tab stops

1 Move carrier to extreme right (or carriage to extreme left).
2 Depress tab clear (29) and hold it down as you return carrier to extreme left (or move carriage to extreme right).

② Set tab stops

Move the carrier (or carriage) to the desired position; then depress the tab set (26). Repeat this proce‒dure for each stop needed.

③ Tabulate (tab)*

Tap lightly the tab key (30), using the nearer little finger; or bar, using the right index finger, and return the finger to home position at once.

* If you are using a nonelectric typewriter, refer to page 3 for tabulating technique.

1 Clear all tab stops as directed.
2 Beginning at the left margin, set 3 tab stops at 5‒space intervals from the margin stop.
3 Practice the drill once DS as shown. Begin Line 1 at left mar‒gin; tab once for Line 2; twice for Line 3; 3 times for Line 4.

1 It is now time for me to learn to use the tab key.

2 $\frac{tab}{once}$ ⟶ Every tab stop now set must first be cleared.

3 $\frac{tab}{twice}$ ⟶ After that, I set tab stops that I need.

4 $\frac{tab}{three\ times}$ ⟶ Then I touch the tab key to indent.

11e ▶ 10
Check keyboarding skill

1 Practice the two ¶s once DS. Try to type without looking up, especially at the end of lines.
2 Take two 1' writings on each ¶; determine *gwam*.

Goal: At least 14 *gwam*.

Difficulty index

all letters	E	1.2 si	5.1 awl	90% hfw

gwam 1'

¶ 1   Some people like their music fast; some of us   9
do not. Some people have a taste for certain food   19
that others abhor. Some like flying; some do not.   29

¶ 2   Just why we differ should be quite clear. We   9
set our own example. We try a thing, then we make   19
a choice. Decisions others make need not faze us.   29

| 1 | 2 | 3 | 4 | 5 | 6 | 7 | 8 | 9 | 10 |

Key to difficulty index of timed writings

E   = easy
LA = low average difficulty
A   = average difficulty
si = syllable intensity
awl = average word length
hfw = high‒frequency words

To determine words-a-minute rate

1 Note the figure at the end of the last line of the writing that you completed.

2 For a partial line, note the figure on the scale directly below the point at which you stopped keyboarding.

3 Add these two figures to deter‒mine the total gross words a minute (*gwam*) you typed.

Mr. Moss has just received a handwritten draft of the new consent form from Dr. Rosenbloom. She wants this form to be prepared in final form today. You are asked to prepare this form on one page; use 1" margins for top and sides so that the form will fit on one page. Follow Mr. Moss's notations on the draft copy.

CONSENT TO OPERATION, ANESTHETICS, AND OTHER MEDICAL SERVICES

DS {
1. I authorize the performance upon
← 24 spaces
_____ of the following operation
(myself or patient)
← 39 spaces
_____ to be per-
(state nature and extent of operation)
formed by Dr. _____. ← 25 spaces
}

DS → 2. I consent to the performance of operations and procedures in addition to or different from those now contemplated arising from presently unforeseen conditions which the above-named doctor may consider necessary or advisable in the course of the operation.

DS → 3. I consent to the administration of such anesthetics as may be considered necessary or advisable by the physician responsible for this service.

DS → 4. The nature and purpose of the operation, possible alternative methods of treatment, the risks involved, the possible consequences, and the possibility of complications have been explained to me.

DS → 5. I acknowledge that no guarantee or assurance has been given by anyone as to the results that may be obtained.

(Job 3 continued on page 283)

12a ▶ 8
Preparatory practice
each line twice SS
(slowly, then faster);
DS between 2-line
groups

Recall: TS between
lesson parts.

alphabet	1	Biff was to give the major prize quickly to Dixon.
space bar	2	is it me of he an by do go to us if or so am ah el
shift keys	3	Pam was in Spain in May; Roy Bo met her in Madrid.
easy	4	He may sign the form with the name of the auditor.

| 1 | 2 | 3 | 4 | 5 | 6 | 7 | 8 | 9 | 10 |

12b ▶ 15
Develop keystroking technique
1 Practice each line 3
times SS; DS between
3–line groups; place a
check mark on your
paper next to each line
that was difficult for
you.

2 If time permits, repeat each line that was
difficult.

home row	1	Dallas sadly had a salad as Hal had a large steak.
bottom row	2	Can my cook, Mrs. Zockman, carve the big ox roast?
third row	3	The purple quilt is quite pretty where you put it.
1st/2d fingers	4	I took the main route by the river for five miles.
3d/4th fingers	5	Pam saw Roz wax an aqua auto as Lex sipped a cola.
double letters	6	Ann took some apples to school; Dee, a cherry pie.

| 1 | 2 | 3 | 4 | 5 | 6 | 7 | 8 | 9 | 10 |

12c ▶ 15
Reach for new goals
1 Take a 1' writing on Line 4
of 12a above; determine
gwam (total words typed).

2 From the second column
at the right (*gwam* 30"),
choose a goal that will cause
you to aim for 2–3 *gwam*
more than your rate in Step 1.
Note the sentence that accompanies that goal.

3 Take two 1' writings on
the chosen sentence; try
to reach the end of the
line each time "Return" is
called (each 30").

4 If you reach your goal on both 1'
writings, take two 1' writings on
the next sentence. (A total of eight
1' writings will be given.)

5 Take another 1' writing on Line 4
of 12a above; determine *gwam*
(total words typed).

Goals:
12–14 *gwam*, acceptable
15–17 *gwam*, good
18–20 *gwam*, very good
21+ *gwam*, excellent

		words in line	gwam 30"	gwam 20"
1	I paid for six bushels of rye.	6	12	18
2	Risk a penalty; this is a big down.	7	14	21
3	Did their form entitle them to the land?	8	16	24
4	Did the men in the field signal for us to go?	9	18	27
5	Did she enamel a sign on the auto body with a pen?	10	20	30
6	The ivory emblem is on a shelf in the town chapel.	10	20	30

| 1 | 2 | 3 | 4 | 5 | 6 | 7 | 8 | 9 | 10 |

12d ▶ 12
Check/develop keyboarding continuity
1 Clear tab stops; set a tab for
5–space ¶ indention.

2 Practice ¶1 once DS for orientation.

3 Take two 1' writings on ¶1; determine *gwam* on each writing.

4 Use ¶2 as directed in Steps 2
and 3.

Goal: *At least* 14 *gwam*.

Difficulty index

all letters	E	1.2 si	5.1 awl	90% hfw

gwam 1'

¶ 1   What is time? Time is the standard needed to   9
fix in sequence each event that makes up the whole   19
fabric of this effort that we like to call living.   29

¶ 2   Time, we realize, means constant pressure for   9
each of us; it must be used. Our minutes are just   19
tiny sums in a book of account. We are the total.   29

| 1 | 2 | 3 | 4 | 5 | 6 | 7 | 8 | 9 | 10 |

E.N.T. MEDICAL SERVICES

EAR, NOSE, AND THROAT EXAMINATION

NAME: *Carlos X. Biaz* CASE NO.: 283763

DATE: *March 2, 19--* SEX: *Male* AGE: 27

EXAMINING PHYSICIAN: *Susan T. Rosenbloom, M.D.*

RIGHT EAR: *External canal clear. Drum membrane intact. No evidence of suppuration. Hearing, 20/20. Eustachian tube patent.*

LEFT EAR: *External canal clear. Drum membrane intact. No evidence of suppuration. Hearing, 20/20. Eustachian tube patent.*

NOSE: *No evidence of obstruction, discharge, or polyps. Nasal septum approximately .5 cm to the right of midline. Turbinate bones normal in size and color.*

THROAT: *No tonsils. Mucous membrane abnormal in color and size. Evidence of pathology noted.*

LARYNX: *Epiglottis and ventricular bands normal. Both vocal cords appeared normal in size and color.*

DIAGNOSIS: *Esophageal web*

COMMENT: *Recommend an esophagoscopy and dilation procedure be performed.*

Learning goals

1 To achieve smoother keystrok–ing.

2 To improve use of special machine parts.

3 To develop a relaxed, confident attitude.

4 To increase keystroking speed.

Machine adjustments

1 Set paper guide at 0.

2 Set ribbon control to type on upper half of ribbon.

3 Set left margin for a 50–space line (center point − 25); move right stop to end of scale.

4 Single–space (SS) drills; double–space (DS) paragraphs (¶).

13a ▶ 8
Preparatory practice

each line twice SS (slowly, then faster); DS between 2-line groups

Recall: TS between lesson parts.

alphabet	1	Jacques Lopez might fix the wrecked navy tugboats.
z	2	Liz drove hazardous, zigzag Zaire roads with zeal.
y	3	Kay said you should stay with Mary for sixty days.
easy	4	Their form may entitle a visitor to fish the lake.

| 1 | 2 | 3 | 4 | 5 | 6 | 7 | 8 | 9 | 10 |

13b ▶ 12
Develop keyboarding technique

once as shown; repeat if time permits

Lines 1-2: Reach with fingers; keep hand movement to a mini–mum.

Lines 3-4: Curve fingers over home row.

Lines 5-6: Reach fingers to third–row keys without moving hands.

bottom row	1	Did Cam, the cabby, have extra puzzles? Yes, one.
	2	Do they, Mr. Zack, expect a number of brave women?
home row	3	Gayla Halls had a sale; Jake had a sale last fall.
	4	Gladys had half a flask of soda; Josh had a salad.
third row	5	There were two or three quiet people at our party.
	6	Trudy Perry quietly sewed the four pretty dresses.

| 1 | 2 | 3 | 4 | 5 | 6 | 7 | 8 | 9 | 10 |

13c ▶ 8
Practice difficult reaches

1 Each line once; checkmark any line that you do not keystroke fluently.

2 Repeat each checkmarked line as time permits.

Technique hint:
Work for smoothness and continuity.

v	1	Eva visited every vivid event for twelve evenings.
m	2	A drummer drummed for a moment, and Mimi came out.
p	3	Pat appears happy to pay for any supper I prepare.
x	4	Tex Cox waxed the next box for Xenia and Rex Knox.
b	5	My rubber boat bobbed about in the bubbling brook.

| 1 | 2 | 3 | 4 | 5 | 6 | 7 | 8 | 9 | 10 |

Preparatory practice

each line 3 times SS, DS between 3-line groups

alphabet	1	Jorge Willman said to be here at five or six to take the physics quiz.
fig/sym	2	The 8 saucers were $28.56 ($3.57 ea.); 9 cups were $12.60 ($1.40 ea.).
shift key	3	Pamela, Mim, Nancy, and Lacy ate at Tooele's Club Fourteen Restaurant.
fluency	4	The man paid my neighbor for eight turkeys and eighty bushels of corn.

| 1 | 2 | 3 | 4 | 5 | 6 | 7 | 8 | 9 | 10 | 11 | 12 | 13 | 14 |

136b-139b ▶ 45

Office job simulation

(LM pp. 113–119)

Mr. Moss, the Office Manager, orients you to your new job. He explains that a typical day in a medical office requires an office assistant to perform a variety of jobs. He also informs you that the completion of assigned tasks promptly and accurately is particularly important in any health care service field. A patient's record must be up to date in order to provide the physician with all pertinent information needed to make health care decisions.

Most of the medical reports are either completed by the physician in handwriting or dictated on voice recording equipment. The normal procedure is to prepare in final form any handwritten reports; however, prepare a draft copy of any dictated material and then have the physician make any desired corrections before the final copy is prepared.

Mr. Moss will assign you one job at a time. Upon completion of each job, he will give you another job to do.

Job 1
Operative report
(LM p. 113)

One of the other medical assistants prepared a draft copy of an operative report last Friday. Dr. Rosenbloom made the final corrections on it this morning, and Mr. Moss asks you to prepare it in final form for the patient's file.

E.N.T. Medical Services

OPERATIVE REPORT

Name: Carols X. Biaz   Case No.: 283763

Date of Surgery: March 3, 19--

Preoperative Diagnosis: Esophageal web

Postoperative Diagnosis: Esophageal web with ~~and~~ cardiospasm

Operation: esophagoscopy and dialation

Surgeon: S. T. Rosenbloom, M.D.

PROCEDURE: A general endotracheal anesthesia was given to ~~Mr. Biaz~~ the patient. A 9-mm. esophagoscope was passed into ~~his~~ the esophagus. A slight fibrous constriction of the cervical esophagus was noted. The passage of the esophagoscope ~~rectified~~ corrected this ~~quite~~ very easily. Otherwise, The esophagus appeared to be normal until about ~~ten~~ 10 to 15 cm. below the incisor line. The lower esophageal musculature at ~~this~~ the cardioesophageal juncture appeared to have a fairly marked spasm. A No. 10 bougie was able to pass through this juncture but The esophagoscope did not enter the stomach. A ~~small~~ nominal amount of bleeding occurred after bougienage. After removal of the 9-mm. esophagoscope ~~was removed~~, an 8-mm. esophagoscope was used with similar results. No additional lesions were ~~found~~ seen. The esophagoscope was ~~taken~~ removed from the patient, and he left the operating room in good condition.

13d ▶ 10
Control machine parts

once as shown; repeat if time permits

Lines 1-3: From left margin, set two tab stops at 20–space intervals; tab for second and third sentences in each line.

Lines 4-6: Use space bar with down–and–in motion; space correctly after punctuation marks.

Lines 7-8: Use shift–type–release motions.

tab/return	1 Why not us?	Did she ask?	Is it not?
	2 Who was it?	Will he bid?	Why is it?
	3 Can he see?	Is she well?	Was it he?

space bar
4 an any many am ham them by buy bouy ha ah bah bath
5 to buy | for any | the man | did both | by them | the theory
6 I went; Bo did, too. Is it true? To: Ms. Dudley

shift keys
7 Sofie Lamas visits Al and Mae in Denver, Colorado.
8 Tony lives on Elm Court; he works for K. L. Hains.

| 1 | 2 | 3 | 4 | 5 | 6 | 7 | 8 | 9 | 10 |

13e ▶ 12
Develop keyboarding continuity

1 Clear tab stops; set tab stop for 5-space indention.

2 Practice each ¶ once as shown for orientation.

3 Take three 1' writings on each ¶.

Goal: At least 16 *gwam*.

Difficulty index			
all letters used	E	1.2 si	5.1 awl	90% hfw

gwam 1'

¶ 1   If we exert great efforts to do something, it   9
could be true that our effort will bring us higher   19
quality returns to match the work that we put out.   29

¶ 2   Is zeal worth the cost? Some people say that   9
maximum efforts will pay off in real results; even   19
others say the joy of hard work is its own reward.   29

| 1 | 2 | 3 | 4 | 5 | 6 | 7 | 8 | 9 | 10 |

Technique hint:
Work for smooth, continuous typing, not for high speed.

14

14a ▶ 8
Preparatory practice

each line twice SS (slowly, then faster); DS between 2-line groups

alphabet 1 Kim Janby gave six prizes to qualified white cats.
shift keys 2 Jay Nadler, a Rotary Club member, wrote Mr. Coles.
y 3 Why do you say that today, Thursday, is my payday?
easy 4 Did the girl also fix the cowl of the formal gown?

| 1 | 2 | 3 | 4 | 5 | 6 | 7 | 8 | 9 | 10 |

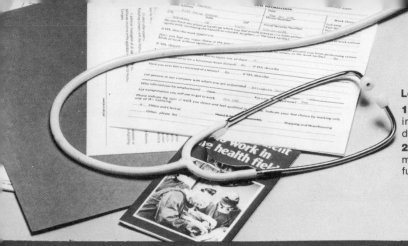

136-139

Learning goals

1 To develop knowledge and skill in preparing medical reports and documents.

2 To become familiar with the many administrative support functions within a medical office.

Machine adjustments

1 Set paper guide at *0*.

2 Set ribbon control to use upper half of ribbon.

3 Set line–space selector for SS.

4 Margins: 70–space line for drills; 1″ top and side margins for medi–cal reports; as directed for other jobs.

Office Job Simulation

Read carefully the material at the right before you begin the work of Section 35. Note any standard procedures that you think will save you time during the completion of the medical office jobs.

Daily practice plan:

Preparatory practice .... 5′
Work on simulation .... 45′

Work Assignment

You have been assigned by Office Service Temporaries, Inc., to work as a medical office assistant at E.N.T. Medical Services, 1059 Sheridan Road, Evanston, IL 60202-3338. This medical office specializes in ear, nose, and throat cases. E.N.T. Medical Services is a large partnership of 15 physicians, including a pathologist and radiologist. Dr. Susan T. Rosenbloom is the Director of the firm; her regular office assistant is on vacation this week, and you have been hired as a temporary replacement. Most of your work will be for Dr. Rosenbloom; however, all your work will be assigned to you by Reginald R. Moss, the Office Manager.

When a job requires unusual specifications, E.N.T. Medical Services provides them in the "Excerpts from the Medical Office Manual." E.N.T. Medical Services has based its office procedures on COLLEGE KEYBOARDING/TYPE-WRITING; therefore, use your textbook as a reference guide for all matters of style and placement. Proofread and correct all errors before removing the paper from the machine.

Excerpts from the Medical Office Manual

Medical Reports. Most medical reports are prepared on preprinted forms.

If a preprinted form is not available, prepare the medical report on plain sheets; follow the illustration below as a general style guide. For medical reports prepared on plain sheets, leave 1″ top and side margins on all pages. Leave *at least* a 1″ bottom margin for all pages. Center and type the main heading in ALL CAPS and triple-space to the pertinent summary in-formation concerning the patient. Double-space the patient summary information, in-cluding the title of the examination, the pa-tient's name, case number, date, sex, age, and name(s) of appropriate physician(s). Triple-space below the patient summary information to the body of the report.

The body of all medical reports should be single-spaced with a double space between paragraphs. Captioned headings in ALL CAPS followed by a colon introduce general topics or areas of examination.

Other Reports. Prepare all other reports as you would a regular business report, following the basic format of an unbound, topbound, or leftbound report.

Letters. Use modified block style with mixed punctuation and indented paragraphs. Close all letters with the name of the person signing the letter, followed on the next line by the per-son's official title. Prepare *one* carbon copy for the file. Address an envelope for each letter.

```
                              1″


                    E.N.T. MEDICAL SERVICES
                                 TS

          EAR, NOSE, AND THROAT EXAMINATION

          NAME:  Carlos X. Biaz                CASE NO.:  283763

     1″   DATE:  March 2, 19--      SEX:  Male          AGE:  27      1″

          EXAMINING PHYSICIAN:  Susan T. Rosenbloom, M.D.
                                         TS

          RIGHT EAR:  External canal clear.  Drum membrane intact.  No evi-
          dence of suppuration.  Hearing, 20/20.  Eustachian tube patent.
```

Medical report on plain sheet

14b ▶ 9
Improve response patterns

once as shown; then repeat

Lines 1-2: *Say* and type each word as a unit.

Lines 3-4: *Spell* each word as you type it; work at a steady pace.

Lines 5-6: *Say* and type short, easy words as units; spell and type longer words letter by letter.

word response	1	he of to if ah or by do so am is go us it an me ox
	2	The corps may pay for the land when they visit us.
stroke response	3	was pop saw ink art oil gas kin are hip read lymph
	4	Sara erected extra seats; Jimmy sat in only a few.
combination response	5	is best | an area | to pump | to join | an acre | he read it
	6	My act forms a base for a tax case with the state.

| 1 | 2 | 3 | 4 | 5 | 6 | 7 | 8 | 9 | 10 |

14c ▶ 9
Control machine parts

once as shown; repeat if time permits

Lines 1-4: Clear tabs; set tab at center point. Tab where indicated.

Line 5: Use correct spacing after each punctuation mark.

Line 6: Depress shift key firmly; avoid pauses.

tab and return	1	—————————tab————▶ Can you work the parts of
	2	your machine?————tab————▶ Can you work them without
	3	looking at them?————tab————▶ Do you trust your fingers
	4	to do the work you have taught them to do?
space bar	5	We did. Was it here? I saw it; Lois saw it, too.
shift keys	6	Jena visited Washington, D.C., to see Kay and Pat.

| 1 | 2 | 3 | 4 | 5 | 6 | 7 | 8 | 9 | 10 |

14d ▶ 10
Improve keyboarding technique

1 Once as shown; checkmark each line that you do not keystroke fluently.

2 Repeat any line that caused you difficulty.

adjacent reaches	1	Bert read where she could stop to buy gas and oil.
	2	We three are a trio to join the Yun Oil operation.
direct reaches	3	My uncle and my brother have run many great races.
	4	Grace Nurva hunted my canyon for unique specimens.
double letters	5	Jeanne took a day off to see a book show in Hobbs.
	6	Jerry has planned a small party for all the troop.

| 1 | 2 | 3 | 4 | 5 | 6 | 7 | 8 | 9 | 10 |

14e ▶ 14
Reach for new goals

1 Take a 1' writing on Line 2 of 14b above; determine *gwam* (total words typed).

2 From the second column at the right (*gwam* 30"), choose a goal that will cause you to aim for 2–3 *gwam* more than your rate in Step 1. Note the sentence that accompanies that goal.

3 Take two 1' writings on the chosen sentence; try to reach the end of the line each time "Return" is called (each 30").

4 If you reach your goal on either 1' writing, take two 1' writings on the next sentence. (A total of eight 1' writings will be given.)

5 Take another 1' writing on Line 2 of 14b above; de–termine *gwam* (total words typed).

Goals:
13–15 *gwam*, acceptable
16–18 *gwam*, good
19–21 *gwam*, very good
22+   *gwam*, excellent

		words in line	gwam 30"	gwam 20"
1	The six girls work with vigor.	6	12	18
2	He got the right title to the land.	7	14	21
3	He works a field of corn and rye for us.	8	16	24
4	Row to the big island at the end of the lake.	9	18	27
5	They do their duty when they turn the dials right.	10	20	30

| 1 | 2 | 3 | 4 | 5 | 6 | 7 | 8 | 9 | 10 |

135c ▶ 15
Build rough-draft skill

1 Two 1' writings for accuracy on each ¶.

2 Two 3' writings for accuracy on both ¶s combined. Record *gwam* (LM p. 3).

Difficulty index

all letters used	A	1.5 si	5.7 awl	80% hfw

	gwam 1'	3'
~~How~~ would you like to be a *good* leader? If so, you must ~~know~~ *learn*	12	4	60
how to influence another ~~person~~ *the behavior of*. How do you do this? First,	26	9	64
communicate your ideas clearly *in a manner*. Second, coordinate all ~~of the~~	39	13	69
activities around ~~the~~ *whatever is* goal to be achieved. Third, ~~also~~ coop-	52	17	73
erate with the other person *in order* to achieve the goal ~~wanted~~. Fourth,	65	22	78
correlate any result with the ~~end~~ *goal*. And fifth, correct ~~all the~~ *any*	77	26	82
mistaeks you or the other person ~~makes~~ *may have made*.	87	29	85
By adhering to these steps, you will ~~also~~ discover that	10	32	88
~~the other person~~ *your co-worker* will always be up to date on all project	21	36	92
developments. If ~~some~~ *a* change in ~~your~~ *the* plans is expected *or required*,	34	40	96
your ~~friend~~ *co-worker* will know about it *well* in advance and will accept the	47	45	101
change with the proper atitude. This ~~type of~~ approach to	57	48	104
leadership will not eliminate all ~~of the~~ difficulties, but It	68	52	108
will minimize the number ~~fo~~ *of* conflicts *that can arise*.	79	56	111

135d ▶ 15
Build statistical-copy skill

1 Two 1' writings for accuracy on each ¶.

2 Two 3' writings for accuracy on both ¶s combined. Record *gwam* and number of errors (LM p. 3).

Difficulty index

all letters/figures used	A	1.5 si	5.7 awl	80% hfw

	gwam 1'	3'
Our revenue from earned interest was approximately 25% higher than	13	4	66
last fiscal year. This year we invested $1,675,000 in 6-month treasury	28	9	71
bills at 8.79%; $2,535,500 in 180-day certificates of deposit at 9.25%;	42	14	75
and $895,000 in a money-market fund at 9.12% for the last 9 months of	56	19	80
the year. The total earned revenue this year from these sources is	70	23	85
$445,984.25; last year's total interest revenue was only $354,387.50.	84	28	89
As we plan for next fiscal year's revenues, our projections indicate	14	33	94
that we should have a sizable increase (17.68%) in earned interest reve-	28	37	99
nue. We will request that a majority of our surplus fund ($3,500,000)	42	42	103
be invested in 180-day certificates of deposit at about 9.35% for the	56	47	108
first 6 months and 9.43% for the last 6 months. The balance of the fund	71	52	113
($2,000,000) will be invested in money-market funds for about 9.3%. The	86	57	118
expected earned interest revenue for next year will be about $521,304.	100	61	123

gwam 1'	1	2	3	4	5	6	7	8	9	10	11	12	13	14
3'		1			2			3			4			5	

15a ▶ 8
Preparatory practice

each line twice SS (slowly, then faster); DS between 2-line groups

alphabet	1	Max Jewel picked up five history quizzes to begin.
space bar	2	Did she say she may copy the form in a day or two?
z	3	Liz Zahl saw Zoe feed the zebra in an Arizona zoo.
easy	4	They risk a penalty if he signs their usual forms.

| 1 | 2 | 3 | 4 | 5 | 6 | 7 | 8 | 9 | 10 |

15b ▶ 14
Improve response patterns

1 Once as shown; checkmark three most difficult lines.

2 Repeat the lines you checked as difficult.

3 Take a 1' writing on Line 2, next on Line 4, and then on Line 6. Determine *gwam* on each writing.

word response	1	with they them make than when also work such right
	2	Diana did key work for the city dock for half pay.
stroke response	3	were only date upon ever join fact milk care nylon
	4	Milo acted on only a few tax rebate cases in July.
combination response	5	with were they only them upon than ever when plump
	6	Julio paid the tax on six acres of rich lake land.

| 1 | 2 | 3 | 4 | 5 | 6 | 7 | 8 | 9 | 10 |

15c ▶ 14
Reach for new goals

1 Using your best rate in 15b as a base, choose from the sentences at the right one that will raise your goal by 2–3 *gwam*.

2 Beginning with that sentence, take a series of 1' writings as directed in 14e, page 31.

Goals:

13–15 *gwam*, acceptable
16–18 *gwam*, good
19–21 *gwam*, very good
22+ *gwam*, excellent

		words in line	gwam 30"	gwam 20"
1	This is an authentic ivory antique.	7	14	21
2	Did the cowhand dismantle the worn auto?	8	16	24
3	Is the body of the ancient dirigible visible?	9	18	27
4	If they wish, she may make the form for the disks.	10	20	30
5	Did they mend the torn right half of their ensign?	10	20	30

| 1 | 2 | 3 | 4 | 5 | 6 | 7 | 8 | 9 | 10 |

15d ▶ 14
Check/develop keyboarding continuity

1 Clear tab stops; set a tab for 5-space ¶ indention.

2 Practice ¶1 once DS for orientation.

3 Take two 1' writings on ¶1; determine *gwam* on each writing.

4 Use ¶2 as directed in Steps 2 and 3.

Goal: At least 15 *gwam*.

Technique hints:
Keep the carrier moving at a fairly steady pace. Avoid looking up, especially at line endings.

Difficulty index

all letters used	E	1.2 si	5.1 awl	90% hfw

gwam 1'

¶1   To learn to keyboard requires that you simply   9
allow the skill to form day by day. You may often   19
be concerned as a result of doubt that the fingers   29
will do just what you have been told they will do.   39

¶2   So the secret is revealed. Typing is not the   9
hard job it once may have seemed. Now you realize   19
that what you must do is simply relax and read the   29
copy carefully; your hands should do all the rest.   39

| 1 | 2 | 3 | 4 | 5 | 6 | 7 | 8 | 9 | 10 |

135a ▶ 5
Preparatory practice

each line 3 times SS (slowly, faster, slowly); DS between 3-line groups; repeat selected lines as time permits

alphabet	1	My quest in Luvungi will be to find an oryx, zebra, hippo, and jackal.
fig/sym	2	We sold consignments #136 for $298 less 5% and #470 for $375 less 10%.
double letter	3	If you succeed in applying the wood filler, you will see good effects.
fluency	4	The panel may blame the firm for toxic clay by the quay on the island.

| 1 | 2 | 3 | 4 | 5 | 6 | 7 | 8 | 9 | 10 | 11 | 12 | 13 | 14 |

135b ▶ 15
Measure straight-copy skill

1 Two 1' writings on each ¶ for accuracy; circle errors; determine *gwam*.

2 One 5' control writing on all ¶s; circle errors; record *gwam* and number of errors (LM p. 3).

Difficulty index

all letters used	A	1.5 si	5.7 awl	80% hfw

gwam 1' | 5'

Have you lately attempted to express a significant point, and the — 13 | 3 | 64

person to whom you were talking was not paying attention? This behavior — 28 | 6 | 67

is not only frustrating for the speaker, but it is also damaging to the — 42 | 8 | 69

person listening. Much of our daily time is spent listening to what — 57 | 11 | 72

others are saying, and most of the knowledge we gain comes from this — 71 | 14 | 75

form of communication. Yet, most of us either do not listen well or — 84 | 17 | 78

are passive listeners. It is important that we learn to become good — 98 | 20 | 81

listeners. In order to do this, we must become active listeners. — 111 | 22 | 83

Important to one becoming an active listener is to show the speaker — 14 | 25 | 86

that you are interested in what is being said. Look directly at the — 27 | 28 | 89

person who is speaking. Once eye contact has been established, be re- — 41 | 30 | 92

sponsive to what the speaker is saying. A nod of the head or a smile — 55 | 33 | 94

of agreement can illustrate to the speaker that you are interested. An- — 70 | 36 | 97

other way of becoming an active listener is to ask questions that refer — 84 | 39 | 100

to the particular topic at hand. Try to avoid asking questions that — 98 | 42 | 103

might lead the speaker into areas that have no relationship to the topic — 112 | 45 | 106

of discussion. — 115 | 45 | 106

Last, it is important to keep an open mind about what the speaker — 13 | 48 | 109

is attempting to communicate. Do not interrupt; allow the speaker an — 27 | 51 | 112

opportunity to completely make his or her point. Then analyze thoroughly — 42 | 54 | 115

the point made before rejecting what has been said or offering an argu- — 56 | 57 | 118

ment against it. Being an active listener is a key to knowledge, and — 71 | 60 | 120

it is a courtesy we can give to others. — 79 | 61 | 122

gwam 1' | 1 | 2 | 3 | 4 | 5 | 6 | 7 | 8 | 9 | 10 | 11 | 12 | 13 | 14 |
5' | 1 | 2 | 3 |

Learning goals

1 To learn figure keyreaches.
2 To proofread/revise copy.
3 To type statistical copy.
4 To type handwritten copy.
5 To improve stroking continuity.

Machine adjustments

1 Set paper edge guide at 0.
2 Set ribbon control to type on upper half of ribbon.
3 Set left margin for a 50–space line (center point − 25); move right stop to end of scale.
4 SS drills; DS paragraphs.

16

16a ▶ 7

Preparatory practice

each line twice SS (slowly, then faster); DS between 2-line groups; repeat selected lines if time permits

alphabet	1	We got six quaint bronze cups from heavy old junk.
q/?	2	Did Marq Quin go? Did Quent Quin go? Did Quincy?
z/:	3	To: Zane Mozel, Tempe, AZ From: Ezra A. Lazzaro
easy	4	She may do the work when she signs the right form.

| 1 | 2 | 3 | 4 | 5 | 6 | 7 | 8 | 9 | 10 |

16b ▶ 16

Learn new keyreaches: 3 7 1

Follow the "Standard procedure for learning new keyreaches" on page 10 (Lines 1–6 twice; Lines 7–10 once; repeat 7–10 if time permits).

Under certain circumstances, the small letter l can be used to type the figure 1. Your instructor will tell you which reach to use for daily work.

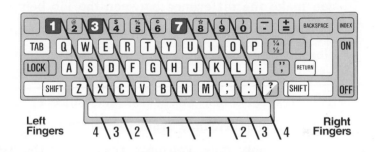

Left Fingers 4 \ 3 \ 2 \ 1 \ 1 \ 2 \ 3 \ 4 **Right Fingers**

Reach technique for 3

Reach *up* with *left second* finger.

Reach technique for 7

Reach *up* with *right first* finger.

Reach technique for 1

Reach *up* with *left little* finger.

NOTES ON ABBREVIATIONS

Space once after a period (.) following an initial. Abbreviations such as M.D., B.C., Ph.D., U.S., N.Y., C.O.D., a.m., and p.m. may be typed solid (without internal spacing).

Abbreviations such as mph, rpm, and mg are usually expressed without caps, periods, or internal spacing.

Abbreviations such as ERA, AMA, and TVA are typed in ALL CAPS (without internal spacing).

3	1	d 3d 3d 3 3; 3 did, 3 days, 3 deals, 3 dozen, 3 33
	2	The 33 girls and 3 boys met at 3 p.m. near Gate 3.
7	3	j 7j 7j 7 7; 7 jobs, 7 jets, 7 jacks, 7 jeeps, 7 7
	4	She wrote 7, 7, 7, not 777. She wrote it 7 times.
1	5	a la la l l lla; 1 arm, 1 aide, 1 awl, 11 ayes, 11
	6	He bought 11 tons of No. 1 coal on May 1 at 1 p.m.
3/7/1	7	Page 371 of Volume 31 states the date as 1737 B.C.
	8	Flight 173, a 737 jet, left on May 31 at 1:31 p.m.
all figures learned	9	Only 3 of the 7 cars clock 71 to 73 mph or better.
	10	Read pages 7, 17, and 37; copy Lines 3, 7, and 31.

| 1 | 2 | 3 | 4 | 5 | 6 | 7 | 8 | 9 | 10 |

134c ▶ 10
Improve keystroking precision

each line at least twice without error

left hand 1 The best rewards at a drag race are for the fast cars and eager crews.

right hand 2 I may lend you only my pink pumps, nylon kimono, jumper, or mink muff.

one hand 3 Only Edward Linny saw Lou Street win the awards at the bazaar in Lyon.

long words 4 On examination, an increase in polymorphonuclear leukocytes was shown.

| 1 | 2 | 3 | 4 | 5 | 6 | 7 | 8 | 9 | 10 | 11 | 12 | 13 | 14 |

134d ▶ 20
Build straight-copy skill

1 Two 1' writings for speed on each ¶.
2 Two 5' writings for speed on all ¶s combined. Record *gwam* (LM p. 3).

Difficulty index

all letters used | A | 1.5 si | 5.7 awl | 80% hfw

gwam 1' | 5'

The way in which you assign a task to a worker in your organization   14 3 | 64
can make the difference between the job being accomplished correctly and   28 6 | 67
on time or incorrectly and late. An assignment must be delivered in   42 8 | 70
clear, simple language; and the deadline should be very carefully stated.   57 11 | 73
Also, be sure that the worker feels you have respect for her or him.   71 14 | 75
This respect must be honest and sincere; if it is, you will receive ex-   85 17 | 78
ceptional performance from the worker.   93 19 | 80

Not only must you have respect for the worker, but you must be cer-   13 21 | 82
tain that your expectations are reasonable and that the amount of time   28 24 | 85
allotted is sufficient to perform the assignment. Another technique to   42 27 | 88
create a good attitude on the part of the employee is to present all di-   56 30 | 91
rections in such a way that they appear to be suggestions or requests.   71 33 | 94
Also, follow up on each assigned task. You can be certain that most   85 36 | 97
individuals will feel a job is very important if a routine progress check   99 39 | 99
is made.   101 40 | 100

Another important policy that will help to insure the successful   13 42 | 103
completion of an assigned job is to limit the job to a single goal or   27 44 | 105
objective whenever possible. If a job is to have multiple goals and   41 47 | 108
objectives, however, be sure that all instructions are given in writing   55 50 | 111
to avoid confusion and misunderstanding by the worker. In any case, you   70 53 | 114
should always have the directions repeated to you to make certain they   84 56 | 117
are clear both to you and the employee. If you follow these basic pro-   98 59 | 120
cedures, your employee will do very well on nearly every job.   111 61 | 122

gwam | 1 | 2 | 3 | 4 | 5 | 6 | 7 | 8 | 9 | 10 | 11 | 12 | 13 | 14 |
5' | 1 | 2 | 3 |

17

16c ▶ 12
Reach for new goals

Follow the directions given for 12c on page 28. Use Line 4 of 16a to determine beginning and ending *gwam*.

Goals:

12–14 *gwam*, acceptable
15–17 *gwam*, good
18–19 *gwam*, very good
20+   *gwam*, excellent

all figures learned

		words in line	gwam 30"	gwam 20"
1	Did the girl hang the 37 maps?	6	12	18
2	She paid Jane to turn the 71 dials.	7	14	21
3	I got 73 burlap panels to make the form.	8	16	24
4	Kent kept 17 worn keys to work the 17 panels.	9	18	27
5	Did they augment the 371 bushels of corn with rye?	10	20	30
6	I did visit a neighbor at 1737 Iris Lane on May 7.	10	20	30
7	Dismantle the 37 chairs in the shanty at 173 Palm.	10	20	30

| 1 | 2 | 3 | 4 | 5 | 6 | 7 | 8 | 9 | 10 |

16d ▶ 7
Improve figure response patterns

each line once DS; repeat Lines 2, 4, and 6

Technique hint:
Control your reading speed. Read only slightly ahead of what you are typing.

all figures learned

1 Flight 371 left Miami at 3:17 on Monday, March 31.

2 *Bill 731 was for 71 boxes of No. 33 bailing brads.*

3 Rico counted 3,711 cartons containing 7,317 tools.

4 *Send Nan 731 No. 3 nails for her home at 771 Anne.*

5 On May 31, Eva drove 373 miles to Denver in Van 7.

6 *Max put 71 extra boxes in the annex at 3731 Parks.*

16e ▶ 8
Improve keystroking technique

once as shown; repeat if time permits

1st finger
1 Bob Mugho hunted for five minutes for your number.
2 Juan hit the bright green turf with his five iron.

2d finger
3 Kind, decent acts can decidedly reduce skepticism.
4 Kim, not Mickey, had rice with chicken for dinner.

3d/4th fingers
5 You will write quickly: Zeus, Apollo, and Xerxes.
6 Who saw Polly? Max Voe saw her; she is quiet now.

| 1 | 2 | 3 | 4 | 5 | 6 | 7 | 8 | 9 | 10 |

17a ▶ 7
Preparatory practice

each line twice SS (slowly, then faster); DS between 2-line groups; repeat selected lines if time permits

alphabet 1 Roz Groves just now packed my box with five quail.

b 2 Barb, not Bob, will buy the new bonds at the bank.

figures 3 Try Model 3717 with 7 panels or Model 1733 with 3.

easy 4 Their problems may end when they audit the profit.

| 1 | 2 | 3 | 4 | 5 | 6 | 7 | 8 | 9 | 10 |

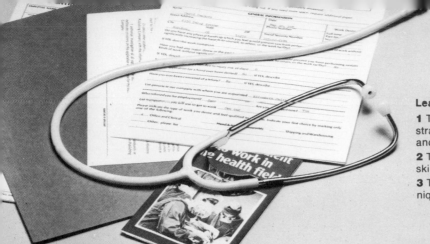

Learning goals

1 To increase basic skill on straight, rough–draft, statistical, and script copy.

2 To improve communication skills.

3 To refine keyboarding tech–nique.

Machine adjustments

1 Set paper guide at *0*.

2 Set ribbon control to use upper half of ribbon.

3 Margins: 70–space line for drills and ¶ writings.

4 SS drill lines; DS ¶s.

134a ▶ 5
Preparatory practice

each line 3 times SS (slowly, faster, slowly); DS between 3-line groups; repeat selected lines as time permits

alphabet	1	We have had Jack itemize and ship by air the exact quantity of grills.
fig/sym	2	The discount may be $1,250 (8.36% of $14,950) when paid within 7 days.
third row	3	Roy Roper reported to Pru Tow after the territory dispute was stopped.
fluency	4	A visitor paid the girl for a mantle and a pair of antique ivory pens.

| 1 | 2 | 3 | 4 | 5 | 6 | 7 | 8 | 9 | 10 | 11 | 12 | 13 | 14 |

134b ▶ 15
Build script-copy skill

1 Two 1' writings for speed on each ¶.

2 Two 3' writings for speed on both ¶s com–bined. Record *gwam* (LM p. 3).

Difficulty index

all letters used	A	1.5 si	5.7 awl	80% hfw

gwam 1' 3'

A computer can only run a program that is written in *11 | 4 | 60*
binary code; this program language is known as machine *22 | 7 | 63*
language. Because this language is very hard to learn, only *34 | 11 | 67*
those persons who work directly with the creation of the *45 | 15 | 71*
hardware use it. Almost all other programmers will use either *58 | 19 | 75*
an assembly or high-level language to program their jobs. *69 | 23 | 79*

A program written in machine language can be executed *11 | 27 | 83*
faster by the computer than can a program that must be *22 | 30 | 87*
translated from either an assembly or high-level language *33 | 34 | 90*
into a machine-language program. The use of a translator *45 | 38 | 94*
to change a program will not result in an object program *57 | 42 | 98*
that is as unique or as customized as a program written *68 | 46 | 102*
directly in machine language. However, the small differ- *79 | 50 | 106*
ence in speed and efficiency is more than made up *89 | 53 | 109*
by the ease of learning a nonmachine language. *98 | 56 | 112*

17b ▶ 16
Learn new keyreaches: 8 4 0

Follow the "Standard procedure for learning new keyreaches" on page 10 (Lines 1–6 twice; Lines 7–10 once; repeat 7–10 if time permits).

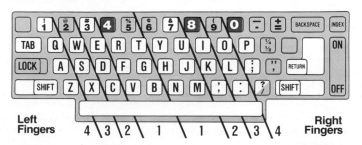

Left Fingers 4 3 2 1 1 2 3 4 **Right Fingers**

Reach technique for 8	Reach technique for 4	Reach technique for 0
 Reach *up* with *right second* finger.	 Reach *up* with *left first* finger.	 Reach *up* with *right little* finger.

Note: Capitalize nouns that are identified by a number except for certain ones such as *page* and *verse* with*in* a sentence.

```
     8    1  k 8k 8k 8 8; 88 keys, 8 kegs, 8 kits, 888 kwh, 8 8
          2  I took 8 keys to lock 8 kits in Truck 8 on Dock 8.

     4    3  f 4f 4f 4 4; 4 fans, 4 fobs, 44 folk, 4 forks, 4 4
          4  Tour 44 leaves at 4 p.m. to see 4 bays in 4 lakes.

     0    5  ; 0; 0; 0 0; 30 paid, 70 posts, 30 pages, 10 plays
          6  Send 30 palms to 30730 East 30th Street on May 30.

  8/4/0   7  Page 10 of the program listed 48, not 84, members.
          8  In 1840, the 84 men and 80 women walked to Toledo.

all figures  9  On June 30, we sent Check 184 to pay Invoice 7403.
 learned 10  In 1830, 14 feet of snow fell; in 1831, almost 18.
          |  1  |  2  |  3  |  4  |  5  |  6  |  7  |  8  |  9  |  10  |
```

17c ▶ 7
Improve figure response patterns

each line once DS; repeat Lines 2, 4, and 6

all figures learned

1 I live at 418 East Street, not at 418 Easy Street.

2 *Memorize pages 137 to 148; omit pages 140 and 141.*

3 Tours 478 and 4781 travel to 10 cities in 30 days.

4 *Cy will be 18 on May 30; Jo, 17 on May 4 or May 7.*

5 English 348 meets in Room 710 at 10 a.m. each day.

6 *Memo 7481 says 7 pads and 8 pens were sent May 30.*

17d ▶ 8
Improve keystroking technique

each line twice SS; DS between 3-line groups; repeat if time permits

adjacent reaches 1 Teresa knew well that her opinion of art was good.

direct reaches 2 Herb Brice must hunt for my checks; he is in debt.

double letters 3 Anne stopped off at school to see Bill Wiggs cook.

long words 4 Debate concerned parochialism versus universalism.

| 1 | 2 | 3 | 4 | 5 | 6 | 7 | 8 | 9 | 10 |

THE OFFICE ENVIRONMENT--THE SPENCER COMPANY

Job 5
Report (full sheet):

As Bradley Hubbard is leav—ing the office to meet his last client of the day, he hands you this report and says to you: *I roughed out this staff report very rapidly without correcting errors. You may need to type a draft before typing the final report. Also, please single-space this report because it will accompany other single-spaced documents. DS between paragraphs.*

project team VI ma*d*ke the initial visit to assess the

present ~~current~~ office facilities *of the Spencer Company*. The present ~~condition of the~~

office environment leaves a great deal to be desired but the poten-

tial for i*m*proving the ~~situation are great~~ *facility is tremendous.* A The open-

office conce*I*pt ~~supposedly~~ was used in ~~layingout~~ *designing* the office*s*;

but *little* ~~no~~ consideration was given to territoriality aesthe*t*ic

facters, acoustics, lighting, workstation design, or layout.

Worker *complained* ~~griped~~ most aboyt lack of accoustical privacy. *we*

extimated the articulation index to be over ~~sixty~~ *60* per cent.

The noise *problem* can be *resolved* ~~elimated~~ by *using* ~~installi~~ng sound-aborbent

materials, minimizing sound-reflective serfaces, and by

workstation arrang ~~ement~~ *ing* so that sound*s* are channelled ~~to~~ *in*

directions that cause ~~little~~ *the least* disturbance.

an excessive amount of ~~A lot of people~~ movement *by people* was observed ~~in the workplace~~. ~~None~~

~~of the~~ workers *did not* complain about workflow, but it ~~is~~ *seems to be* a major

problem. Task analyses need to be made and work flow *must* ~~will~~

~~have to~~ be carefully charted.

Two ~~The~~ cost proposal has been drafted. The first pro-

posal ~~will~~ reconfigure*s* the office and *provides for* ~~makes~~ minor *design* changes

~~in design~~ too improve workflow to control noise and to make

the ofice more aesthetically pleasing. The *second* ~~2nd~~ proposal

provide*s* for *completely* ~~the total~~ redesigning the interir of the building.

A Redesigning the *in* ~~ex~~terior of the building would produce *far* ~~for~~ s

better results. The cost however is significantly high*er* ~~cost~~.

Cost justifications are attached. *A final* ~~The ultimate~~ decision on *which* ~~what~~

proposal to present *the Spencer Company* must be made soon,

17e ▶ 12
Improve keyboarding continuity

1 Practice the ¶ once for orientation.
2 Take three 30″ writings (30″ *gwam* = words typed × 2).
3 Take three 1′ writings.
4 Determine *gwam*.
Goal: *At least* 14 *gwam*.

Difficulty index

| all letters/figures learned | E | 1.2 si | 5.1 awl | 90% hfw |

```
        .      2      .      4      .      6      .      8      .
Why did we not all realize that July 17 was a
       10      .     12      .     14      .     16      .     18      .
hot day?  For 30 days, still summer air had closed
   20      .     22      .     24      .     26      .     28      .
in on us.  Just to move was an effort; but here we
   30      .     32      .     34      .     36      .     38      .
stood, 48 quite excited people, planning our trek.
```

18

18a ▶ 7
Preparatory practice

each line twice SS (slowly, then faster); DS between 2-line groups; repeat selected lines if time permits

alphabet 1 One judge saw five boys quickly fix the prize elm.
p/x 2 Dixie, please have Pam fix the tax forms Hope has.
figures 3 Is it Channel 3, 8, or 10? Was the score 14 to 7?
easy 4 The girl may enamel the chair for the town chapel.
```
 |  1  |  2  |  3  |  4  |  5  |  6  |  7  |  8  |  9  | 10  |
```

18b ▶ 16
Learn new keyreaches: 6 2 / (diagonal)

Follow the "Standard procedure for learning new keyreaches" on page 10 (Lines 1–6 twice; Lines 7–10 once; repeat 7–10 if time permits).

Left Fingers   4 \ 3 \ 2 \ 1 \ 1 / 2 / 3 / 4   Right Fingers

Reach technique for 6

Reach *up* with *right first* finger.

Reach technique for 2

Reach *up* with *left third* finger.

Reach technique for /

Reach *down* to / with *right little* finger.

```
6   1 j 6j 6j 6 6; 6 jobs, 6 jugs, 66 jays, 6 jokes, 6 6
    2 On July 6, 66 jumpers made 6 jumps of over 6 feet.

2   3 s 2s 2s 2 2; 2 skis, 2 sons, 22 sites, has 2 signs
    4 On May 2, Car 222 delivered 22 tons of No. 2 sand.

/   5 ; /; /; / /; 1/3; and/or; 4/7/84; 4/14; 8 1/3; / /
    6 Type these mixed fractions:  1 3/8; 4 4/7; 1 3/14.

6/2/diag.  7 On May 26, I ordered 2 2/6 yards, not 6 2/6 yards.
           8 The recorder, Model 226/62, Serial 626/A, is mine.

all figures  9 Aida was 21 on 3/7/80.  Bill will be 21 on 4/6/87.
learned    10 The terms for Invoice 7867/3 are 4/10, 2/30, n/60.
 |  1  |  2  |  3  |  4  |  5  |  6  |  7  |  8  |  9  | 10  |
```

Job 4
Memorandum
(LM p. 101)

After handing you this memo to prepare for distribution to the project teams, Bradley Hubbard instructs you: *Please single-space the memo and double-space above and below listed items. Date the memo February 24, 19--.*

Project teams

Willis DESIGN PROGRAM *SUMMARY*

An *final* agreement has been reached on the first *phase* ~~part~~ of the Willis Project. Summary information ~~includes the s~~ following:

Floors: 3

Floor space: 145,000 sq. ft. *Average area/floor: 48,000 sq. ft.*

Lighting: Task/ambient

Closed/open office ratio: 8:90

Construction cost: $34/sq. ft.

Design/furnishings cost: $25/sq. ft.

HVAC system: Nine 100-ton air cooler chillers

Communication and power: access floor for all cables

We hope to finalize ~~by~~ next week the selections *of* ~~for~~ the suppliers for the following items:

alphabetize columnar items

Accessories	General furniture	Shelving
Ceiling	Carpet	Partitions
Lighting	Workstations	Upholstery fabrics

The design team coordinators for the Willis Project have been selected. They are Barbara Romero (Interior Design), Ken Davis (Lighting Design), and Joseph Wayne (Landscape).

Tom *Fox* has *developed* ~~formulated~~ a new *program* ~~way~~ to predict acoustic noise and will try it on the Willis project. He *measures* ~~calculates~~ present noise *and* ~~then~~ calculates the difference between the acoustics of the present environment and *that* of the proposed environment.

**Compare skill:
sentences**

1 Take a 1′ writing on Line 1; de—termine *gwam* and use this score for your goal as you take two 1′ writings on Line 2 and two on Line 3.

2 Take a 1′ writing on Line 4; de—termine *gwam* and use this score for your goal as you take two 1′ writings on Line 5 and two on Line 6.

Goal: To have rates on Lines 2 and 3 and Lines 5 and 6 equal those on Lines 1 and 4.

words in line

1 Did the men enamel emblems on big panels downtown? 10

2 Pay the men to fix a pen for 38 ducks and 47 hens. 10

3 *They blame the chaos in the city on the big quake.* 10

4 Did the amendment name a city auditor to the firm? 10

5 He owns 20 maps of the 16 towns on the big island. 10

6 *Dian may make cocoa for the girls when they visit.* 10

18d ▶ 5
**Proofread/revise
as you keyboard**

each line once DS; correct circled errors as you keyboard; read carefully

1 Court will not (ve) in session again until (august) 6.

2 Put more grass (sede) on the lawn at 307 Elm (Strett).

3 A team is (madeup) of 11 men; 12 were on (t he) field.

4 Liza and/or Dion (willldirect) the choir on (Tuseday).

5 (Theer) were (abuot) 10 or 11 pictures in the gallery.

18e ▶ 9
**Improve keyboarding
continuity**

1 Practice the ¶ once for orienta—tion.

2 Take three 30″ writings.

3 Take three 1′ writings.

4 Determine *gwam*.

Goal: *At least* 14 *gwam*.

Difficulty index

all letters/figures learned	E	1.2 si	5.1 awl	90% hfw

Volume 27 is quite heavy. Its weight must be
in excess of 10 pounds; yet I realize the only way
to complete this type of job is to study 164 pages
of Chapter 183 and all of the art in the big book.

NB:01 Thank you for giving us the opportunity to provide you with information about the design services we offer. We are committed to developing a total office environment which contributes to the productivity, comfort, job satisfaction, and motivation of the employees who work in the environments we design.

NB:02 One of our clients indicated that you are considering moving to new office space soon. If so, you will be interested in the services we can provide for you. Ergonomic Consultants, Inc., is committed to developing a total office environment which contributes to the productivity, comfort, job satisfaction, and motivation of the employees who work in the environments we design.

NB:03 One of our clients indicated you are considering renovating your present office space and may be interested in the services we can provide for you. Ergonomic Consultants, Inc., is committed to developing a total office environment which will contribute to the productivity, comfort, job satisfaction, and motivation of the employees who work in the environments we design.

NB:04 The enclosed booklet describes our approach to helping you design and build new office facilities. It explains how we work with your employees and how we coordinate the activities of other professionals involved in the total building project.

NB:05 The enclosed booklet describes our approach to helping you renovate your present office facilities. It explains how we work with your employees and how we coordinate the activities of other professionals involved in the total renovation project.

NB:06 One of our design specialists will call you in a few days to arrange an appointment at a mutually convenient time. You will be pleased to learn that our services are very cost effective.

NB:07 One of our design specialists would be pleased to visit your office and prepare a proposal for designing your office facilities. You would, of course, be under no obligation. Just return the enclosed card or call us, and a design specialist will arrange an appointment at a mutually convenient time.

19a ▶ 7
Preparatory practice

each line twice SS (slowly, then faster); DS between 2-line groups; repeat selected lines if time permits

Space once after a question mark when the question is incomplete.

alphabet	1	Mavis Zeff worked quickly on the next big project.
q/?	2	Can you spell queue? quay? aqua? quavered? acquit?
figures	3	If 24 of the 87 boys go on May 10, 63 will remain.
easy	4	Fit the lens at a right angle and fix the problem.

| 1 | 2 | 3 | 4 | 5 | 6 | 7 | 8 | 9 | 10 |

19b ▶ 16
Learn new keyreaches: 9 5 - (hyphen) -- (dash)

Follow the "Standard procedure for learning new keyreaches" on page 10 (Lines 1–6 twice; Lines 7–11 once; repeat 7–11 if time permits).

Hyphen, dash: The hyphen is used to join closely related words or word parts. Striking the hyphen twice results in a dash--a symbol that shows sharp separation or interruption of thought.

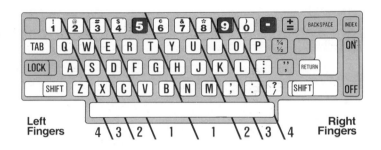

Left Fingers 4 3 2 1 1 2 3 4 Right Fingers

Reach technique for 9
Reach *up* with *right third* finger.

Reach technique for 5
Reach *up* with *left first* finger.

Reach technique for –
Reach *up* to - with *right little* finger.

9	1	l 9l 9l 9 9; 9 left, 9 lost, 9 loans, sell 99 lots
	2	On May 9, 99 buyers offered 99 bids for 999 lambs.
5	3	f 5f 5f 5 5; 5 fish, 5 fans, 5 forms, for 55 firms
	4	At 5 p.m., the 55 cars, 55 vans, and 5 jeeps left.
-	5	; -; -; - -- co-op; top-rate; in-depth; up-to-date
	6	Use a 5-inch line--50 pica spaces--for lines 1-10.
9/5/-	7	We--all 59 of us--have read pages 59, 95, and 595.
	8	All 95 girls--5 did not attend--voted on Item 599.
all figures/ symbols learned	9	Of 13,687 ex-workers, 2,481--or 9/50--had retired.
	10	Invoice 347/8--it is dated 2/9, not 2/10--is here.
	11	Do Problems 2-27, 8-35, and/or 16-42 before May 9.

| 1 | 2 | 3 | 4 | 5 | 6 | 7 | 8 | 9 | 10 |

Job 2
Prepare tables from computer printout (full sheets)

Roberta Tassin gives you the two tables at right, which resulted from a recent research study at Ergonomic Consultants, Inc. She tells you to make the following amendments to the computer printouts: *Do not use abbreviations for column headings. Substitute the following information for the Code Column on both tables:*

Rating

Very frequently
Frequently
Occasionally
Seldom
Never
No answer

Table 1. Eye Strain Experienced By VDT Operators.

CODE	ABSOLUTE FREQ	RELATIVE FREQ (PCT)	ADJUSTED FREQ (PCT)	CUM FREQ (PCT)
1.	124	51.7	58.5	58.5
2.	23	9.6	10.8	69.3
3.	17	7.0	8.0	77.4
4.	15	6.3	7.1	84.4
5.	33	13.7	15.6	100.0
0.	28	11.7	MISSING	100.0
	--------	--------	--------	
TOTAL	240	100.0	100.0	

Table 2. Back Problems Experienced By VDT Operators.

CODE	ABSOLUTE FREQ	RELATIVE FREQ (PCT)	ADJUSTED FREQ (PCT)	CUM FREQ (PCT)
1.	72	30.0	33.6	33.6
2.	15	6.3	7.0	40.7
3.	13	5.4	6.1	46.7
4.	18	7.5	8.4	55.1
5.	96	40.0	44.9	100.0
0.	26	10.8	MISSING	100.0
	--------	--------	--------	
TOTAL	240	100.0	100.0	

Job 3
Prepare letters by using standard form paragraphs (LM pp. 89–99)

You receive through company mail a note from Scott Cockrell requesting that you send form letters to potential clients. Attached to his note is the list of form paragraphs you will need to complete the task (see page 272). Date each letter **February 25, 19--**.

(form paragraphs on next page)

From the desk of ...　　**SCOTT COCKRELL**

Please send form letters to:

Ms. Connie Bogner, Manager
Bogner Distributors, Inc.
200 Austin Avenue
Skokie, IL 60077-8221

Ps NB:03; NB:05; NB:07

Ms. Mary Fox, Manager
Fox and Associates
1801 Calumet Avenue
Chicago, IL 60616-8541

Ps NB:02; NB:04; NB:07

Mr. Jack Rutcosky
Rutcosky Enterprises
933 Star Lane
Joliet, IL 60435-8610

Ps NB:02; NB:04; NB:07

Mr. Mike Goings, Manager
Great Lakes Glass Company
403 Sheridan Road
Evanston, IL 60202-8520

Ps NB:01; NB:05; NB:06

Miss Annie Cox, Office Manager
Corbett Medical Center
1030 Jackson Avenue
Evanston, IL 60201-8522

Ps NB:01; NB:04; NB:06

Mr. John Smith, Vice President
The Teakwood Company
5629 Fargo Avenue
Skokie, IL 60077-8211

Ps NB:03; NB:05; NB:06

19c ▶ 7

Improve figure response patterns

each line twice SS; DS between 2-line groups

all figures used

1 Send immediately 30 Solex cubes, Catalog No. 2748.

2 As of 6/28, your new extension number will be 375.

3 Reserve for me Tape 640. My identification: 819 .

4 Date of call: 2/7 . Time: 3:30 p.m. No message.

5 Top individual score: 87 . Top team average: 46 .

19d ▶ 5

Proofread/revise as you keyboard

each line once DS; correct circled errors as you keyboard; read carefully

1 Erin had (s) size 11/12 dress, but it was (two) large.

2 The figure he wrote--475-0(is) not a correct answer(o)

3 All that snow--(mroe) than 5 (feat)--kept her at home.

4 Edna says 936 Valley (Rode) is (here) new home address.

5 He scored 80 on the first (test;hc) must do (bet ter).

19e ▶ 5

Improve keystroking technique

each line twice SS; DS between 2-line groups

bottom row 1 Zach, check the menu; next, beckon the lazy valet.

home row 2 Sal was glad she had a flashlight; Al was as glad.

third row 3 Powell quit their outfit to try out for our troop.

| 1 | 2 | 3 | 4 | 5 | 6 | 7 | 8 | 9 | 10 |

19f ▶ 10

Improve keyboarding continuity

1 Practice the ¶ once for orientation.
2 Take three 30″ writings.
3 Take three 1′ writings.
Goal: *At least* 14 *gwam.*

Difficulty index

| all letters/figures used | E | 1.2 si | 5.1 awl | 90% hfw |

Think with me back to a quite cold morning in
1984. It was just 7:50; I opened my door to leave
for work. Little did I realize that snow had been
expected--2/3 foot of it. I live at 6 Summer Way.

Several factors must be considered before we begin with the preliminary design of the new facilities for Atlas. The following paragraphs summarize the important factors which need to be considered and suggest how to attain desired results.

<u>Access floors</u>. All floors, excluding the executive floor, should be raised a minimum of four inches off the slab to accommodate cables and conduits. Flooring should consist of modular, removable floor panels. Squares of carpet should be laid over the two-foot panels. The power system must be readily accessible to provide flexibility in installing electronic equipment in the workstations.

<u>Energy</u>. The entire building must be energy efficient. Recovering heat generated by office equipment and lighting as well as environmental control is an important factor to consider in the attempt to conserve energy. The influence of technology on ventilation, heat, and air conditioning is another factor which must be determined and controlled.

<u>Office design</u>. All interior office space should be designed with movable wall partitions except the executive office area. Floor-to-ceiling partitions can be used for selected offices.

<u>Lighting</u>. Task/ambient lighting should be used throughout the office area to control glare. The ceiling fixtures should be recessed and should provide soft ambient illumination.

<u>Workstations</u>. Ergonomic design of workstations is crucial. Components must be flexible and must have an effective wire management system. The components must accommodate a wide range of office functions and a wide range of user needs.

Complete documentation for these recommendations will be provided at the initial design planning session.

20

Learning goals

1 To set margins.
2 To determine line endings using the warning bell.
3 To center copy horizontally and vertically.
4 To divide words at line endings.
5 To type short reports and an‑nouncements.

Machine adjustments

1 Set paper guide at 0.
2 Set ribbon control to type on upper half of ribbon.
3 Use a 60–space line (center point −30; center point +30).
4 SS drills; DS paragraphs; indent first line of ¶ 5 spaces.
5 Insert half sheets long side first, unless otherwise directed.

20a ▶ 7
Preparatory practice

each line twice SS (slowly, then faster); DS between 2-line groups; repeat selected lines if time permits

alphabet	1	Freda Jencks will have money to buy six quite large topazes.
o/i	2	We take action from our position to avoid spoiling our soil.
figures	3	The 26 clerks checked Items 37 and 189 on pages 145 and 150.
easy	4	She bid by proxy for eighty bushels of a corn and rye blend.

| 1 | 2 | 3 | 4 | 5 | 6 | 7 | 8 | 9 | 10 | 11 | 12 |

20b ▶ 15
Learn to establish margin widths

study copy at right; then do the drills below

Margin release (31)
If the carrier locks, depress the margin release key with the little finger and complete the line.

Know your machine: margin stops

Typewriters (and other keyboarding machines) are usually equipped with one of two type sizes: pica or elite (some with both). Pica (10-pitch) is the larger—10 pica spaces fill a horizontal inch. Paper 8½ inches wide will accommodate 85 pica characters and spaces. Center point for pica type is 42 when left edge of paper is inserted at 0 on line-of-writing scale.

Elite (12-pitch) type is smaller—12 elite spaces fill a horizontal inch. Paper 8½ inches wide will accommodate 102 elite characters and spaces. Center point for elite type is 51 when left edge of paper is at 0 on line-of-writing scale.

Equal margin widths can be had either by (1) setting margin stops an equal distance in inches or spaces from extreme right and left edges of paper or by (2) setting the margin stops an equal distance right and left from center point. In lessons that follow, the second procedure will be used.

Drill 1

exact 60–space line (center − 30; center + 30); DS; make one copy, line for line

Note: A warning bell will sound as you approach the end of each line; listen for it.

If the margins are set correctly, if the paper guide is set at 0, and if you have made no mistakes which affect line length, each of these paragraphs can be typed with right and left margins which are exactly equal in width to each other.

| 1 | 2 | 3 | 4 | 5 | 6 | 7 | 8 | 9 | 10 | 11 | 12 |

Drill 2

exact 50–space line (center − 25; center + 25); DS; make one copy, line for line

If it is not already obvious to you, you will soon find that, while the left edge of a paragraph is even, the evenness on the right edge depends on your ability to decide where and how to end lines.

| 1 | 2 | 3 | 4 | 5 | 6 | 7 | 8 | 9 | 10 |

Preparatory practice

each line 3 times SS; DS between 3-line groups; retype selected lines as time permits

alphabet 1 Alex Wajorski apologized for being ill and left the room very quickly.

fig/sym 2 The bill of $1,427.61 ($1,389.40 plus 2.75% interest) is due on May 9.

double letter 3 Jerry and Lynnette will meet at noon to discuss the accounting errors.

fluency 4 A neighbor paid me to go to the island to dig up the bush and burn it.

| 1 | 2 | 3 | 4 | 5 | 6 | 7 | 8 | 9 | 10 | 11 | 12 | 13 | 14 |

Office job simulation

(LM pp. 89–101)

Job 1
Report (full sheets)

Roberta Tassin, Vice President for Ergonomic Consultants, Inc., stops by your desk and tells you: *Please type this report as soon as possible to accompany a transmittal to Atlas, Inc. I think side headings would look better than the paragraph headings I used.*

PRELIMINARY DESIGN CONSIDERATIONS
Atlas, Inc.

The project team recommends, on the basis of its assessment of current Atlas facilities and growth projections of Atlas management, that the new building contain 50,000 square feet. This figure was based on the projected increase in the number of employees, the projected increase in the amount of automation at Atlas, and the 10 percent expansion cushion mandated by the Senior Management Committee.

PRESENT FACILITIES AND FIVE-YEAR PROJECTIONS

Floor	No. of Employees Current	Projected	% Using Terminals Current	Projected	Sq. Ft. Space Current	Projected
1	50	65	40	70	6,200	10,000
2	55	60	60	85	6,800	9,500
3	60	80	45	80	6,500	14,000
4	40	50	20	40	6,000	10,000

The design of the facilities will be impacted heavily by the projected increase in the amount of automation over the next five years. The current facility simply is not designed to accommodate automation. The new facility must reflect the current needs and must be flexible to accommodate future needs.

(Job 1 continued on next page)

20c ▶ 5
Learn to use the backspacer and the margin release

exact 50-space line

Backspacer (20)

Use a quick, light stroke with the little finger. Depress the key firmly for repeated backspace action on an electric or electronic type-writer.

1 At the left margin of your paper, type the first word as it appears in the list at the right.

2 After typing the word, back-space and fill in the missing letter v.

3 Return, then repeat the proce-dure with each of the remaining words on the list.

lea e

har est

o ens

oli es

sa ings

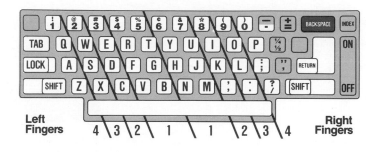

Margin Release (31)

1 Before typing the sentence be-low, depress the margin release with the little finger and back-space 5 spaces into the left margin.

2 Type the sentence. When the carrier locks, depress the margin release and complete the line.

My typed work should be done neatly, correctly, and quickly.

20d ▶ 13
Learn to end lines

study copy at right; then do Drills 1 and 2

Know your machine: line ending warning bell

Margin stops cause the machine to lock at the point at which they are set. To bypass the lock, you must use the margin release (31), a time-consuming operation if used often.

Lines of a paragraph automatically align at the left margin, but they do not automatically align at the right margin. It is necessary, therefore, that the operator or typist ends lines at the right as evenly as possible.

To help you know when to end a line, a warning bell sounds 7 to 12 spaces before the margin stop is reached. Most typists find that a warning of 5 or 6 spaces (a half inch) is adequate to maintain a fairly even righthand margin. Thus, after setting margins for an exact line length, they move the right margin set 5 or 6 spaces farther to the right.

To use this procedure, set margin stops for an exact line length (50, 60, or 70 spaces); then move the right margin set another 5 or 6 spaces to the right. Doing so allows you to: (1) end a short word or (2) divide a longer one within 5 or 6 spaces after the bell rings.

Drill 1

full sheet; begin on Line 10; DS copy

1 Set exact 60-space line.

2 Move right margin stop 5 or 6 spaces farther to the right.

3 Read the ¶ at the bottom of this page. Then, as you type it, listen for the bell. When it sounds, com-plete the word you are typing; re-turn immediately. If the machine locks on a long word, operate the margin release, complete the word, and return.

Your typed line endings will not match those in the textbook.

Drill 2

1 After typing Drill 1, return twice.

2 Set machine for a 50-space line with appropriate right margin bell adjustment.

3 Retype the ¶; follow the di-rections in Step 3 of Drill 1.

When the bell sounds, you must decide just where to end that line and begin a new one. If the word you are typing as the bell rings can be finished within 5 letters, finish it. If it takes more, you may need to divide it. You will learn soon how and when to divide words.

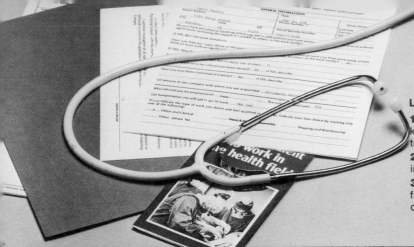

Learning goals

1 To become familiar with keyboarding/formatting tasks in a technical office.

2 To learn to work with minimum instructions.

3 To improve your ability to work from differing copy sources and to detect and correct errors.

Machine adjustments

1 Paper guide at *0*.

2 Set ribbon control to use upper half of ribbon.

3 Margins: 70–space line and single spacing for drill lines; 6–inch line for copy.

Office Job Simulation

Before you begin the jobs of Sec–tion 33, read carefully the infor–mation at the right.

Make notes of any standard procedures that you think will save you time during the completion of the production activities in this section.

Daily practice plan:

Preparatory practice .... 5'
Work on simulation .... 45'

Work Assignment

You have been assigned by Office Service Temporaries, Inc., to work for Ergonomic Con-sultants, Inc., a consulting firm specializing in designing office environments with major em-phasis on human factors engineering. In your position, you will be working for: Roberta Tassin, Vice President; Scott Cockrell, Busi-ness Manager; and Bradley Hubbard, Design Engineer. The company is located at 300 Simpson Avenue, Chicago, IL 62526-3302.

The Office Procedures Manual for Er-gonomic Consultants, Inc., specifies the fol-lowing standard procedures:

1. A standard 6-inch line is used for all communications unless otherwise noted.

2. Letters are prepared in block style with open punctuation.

3. Reports are double-spaced unless otherwise noted.

4. Copies are made on a photocopy machine.

Because you are regarded as both com-petent and professional, you are not always provided with explicit and detailed instruc-tions. You are expected to use good judg-ment in setting up communications and in making decisions where detailed instructions are not given.

Because the consultants you are working for are frequently out of the office visiting clients, you will be given instructions primarily by either short, handwritten memos or verbally. A transcript of all verbal communications is pro-vided in italics in the left margin.

Ergonomic Consultants, Inc., has based its Office Procedures Manual and job instructions on COLLEGE KEYBOARDING/TYPEWRITING, so use your textbook to look up matters of style and placement when in doubt. When a job re-quires unusual specifications or procedures, Ergonomic Consultants, Inc., provides special guides in "Excerpts from the Office Proce-dures Manual."

Excerpt from the Office Procedures Manual

Standard placement. For all communications, use a 6-inch line length (60 pica spaces; 72 elite spaces) to increase office efficiency. For letters, place the date on a standard dateline, regardless of letter length: Place dateline on Line 13 and leave 3 blank line spaces between the date and the letter address. For memos, use the simplified memo style: Use 1" top mar-gin for half-page memos and 1½" top margin for full-page memos. For reports, use 1½" top margin.

Block style letter with standard placement

20e ▶ 10
Learn to divide words

half sheet; insert (with long side up) to Line 9

1 Read the ¶; it explains basic rules for dividing words.

2 Use a 60–space line, ad–justed for bell warning.

3 As you type, listen for the bell. Complete or divide words as appropriate for a fairly even right margin.

As long as certain guides are observed, words may be divided in order to keep line lengths nearly even. For example, always divide a word between its syllables; as, care-less. Words of one syllable, however long, may not be divided, nor should short words --such as often--of five or fewer letters. The separation of a one- or two-letter syllable, as in likely or across, from the rest of a word must also be avoided.

21a ▶ 7
Preparatory practice

60-space line; each line twice SS (slowly, then faster)

Note: Line 3 has two ALL–CAP items. To type them, find the shift lock (27); depress the key with the left little finger; type the item; release the lock by striking either shift key.

alphabet	1	Jessie Quick believed the campaign frenzy would be exciting.
figures	2	The 2 buyers checked Items 10, 15, 27, 36, and 48 on page 9.
shift/lock	3	Titles of reports are shown in ALL CAPS; as, DIVIDING WORDS.
easy	4	Did they fix the problem of the torn panel and worn element?

| 1 | 2 | 3 | 4 | 5 | 6 | 7 | 8 | 9 | 10 | 11 | 12 |

21b ▶ 9
Learn to use the warning bell

half sheet; DS; begin on Line 9; 60-space line

Listen for the bell as you type. Make decisions about line endings. Avoid looking at the paper or typewriter as you type.

Learning to use a keyboard is worth our efforts. Few of us do so for the sheer joy of it. When most people type, they have a goal in mind--they want something in return. If we send a letter, we expect a reply--at least a reaction. If it is a job that we are doing for someone, we want approval--maybe payment. If it is for school, we hope for a top grade. What we get, though, will depend on what we give.

21c ▶ 9
Learn to center lines horizontally (side to side)

Drill 1

half sheet; DS; begin on Line 16

1 Insert paper (long side up) with left edge at 0.

2 Move each margin stop to its end of the scale. Clear all tab stops; set a new stop at center point of the page (elite, 51; pica, 42).

3 From center point, backspace once for each two letters, figures, spaces, or punctuation marks in the line.

4 Do not backspace for an odd or leftover stroke at the end of the line.

5 Begin to type where you com–plete the backspacing.

6 Complete the line; return; tab to center point. Type subsequent line in the same way.

Drill 2

half sheet; DS; begin on Line 14; center each line

Drill 1

LEARN TO CENTER LINES

Horizontally--Side to Side

Drill 2

You are invited

to attend the opening

of the new

JONES PUBLIC LIBRARY

Monday, May 3, 10 a.m.

Job 5, continued

Job 6
Title page
(full sheet)

Mr. Rutledge has asked that the report prepared in Job 5 be finished by preparing an appropriate title page.

The title page should contain the following:

INFORMAL GOVERNMENT
LETTER STYLE
Mr. Terence J. Rutledge
U.S. Services Agency
February 19, 19—

Job 7
Composing an informal government letter (LM p. 85)

Ms. Sanchez asks that you prepare a letter for distribution to the office staff informing them of the decision to adopt the new letter style. A copy of the report will accompany each copy of the letter. Provide whatever information that you feel is appropriate. Ms. Sanchez will sign the letter. Date the letter **February 20.** Prepare the rough draft on plain paper and the final draft on letterhead.

Job 8
Informal government letter with window envelope
(LM p. 87)

Ms. Sanchez has drafted a letter to the Los Angeles branch office informing the staff about the adoption by the Chicago branch of the government letter style. Prepare a letter to the Deputy Director in Los Angeles. Date the letter **February 20.** Use as a subject line: **Adoption of new letter style.** Correct any undetected errors.

---

must be divided, indent the second line 2 spaces from the left margin. After the adress has been completed, space down to the 20th line to begin the body of the letter.

Special Style Characteristics

DS body of report

Style. The informal government letter uses block style with necessary headings to the right of the preprinted captions. Exclude the salutation and the complementary close.

Sender's reference. Place the official symbol of the sender (e.g., AFAW) flush with the left margin in line with the "Reply to Attn of:" caption.

Special mailing instructions. place mailing notations on the same lien as the sender's reference, starting at the horizontal center.

Subject line. Place the subject on the 11th lien.

Address. The address begins on the same line as the "To:" caption.

The chicago Branch office will adopt on February 28 the informal government letter style recommended by the Gen. Services Adm. Pehaps your branch will want too consider adopting this letter style as well. I am enclosing a brief report that we prepared for our office staff to familiarize them with the informal letter style. Also, I am sending to you under separate cover, a copy of the U.S. Government Correspondence Manual. Arnold, I am confident you will appreciate the simplicity of this letter style. If you would like to have a copy of our new correspondnece training materials, please let me no, and I will send a copy to you.

Format a short report on dividing words

full sheet; 60-space line; DS body; begin on Line 10; TS below heading; proofread and circle errors

To TS when machine is set for DS: DS, then by hand turn cylinder (platen) forward one space.

1 Read the report carefully.

2 Center heading on Line 10; then type the report.

3 Listen for the warning bell; decide quickly about line endings. Avoid looking up.

4 When finished, examine the margins critically; proofread your copy and circle errors.

Proofreading. Conscientious keyboard operators always check carefully what they have keyboarded before they remove the paper from the machine. They *proofread* paragraphs; that is, they read them for *meaning*, as if they had not read them before. They double–check figures, proper names, and uncertain spellings against the original or some other source.

---

words

DIVIDING WORDS   3
TS

A word may be divided at the end of a line in order to keep   15
the margins as nearly equal in width as possible. Divided words,   28
of course, tend to be more difficult to read than undivided words;   41
so good judgment is needed. The following guides can help you   54
make sound decisions about word division.   62

Words that contain double consonants are usually divided be   74
tween consonants; as, bal-lots. However, if a word that ends in   87
double letters has a suffix attached, divide after the double let   100
ters; as, dress-ing or stuff-ing.   107

Words that contain an internal single-vowel syllable should   119
be divided after that syllable; as, miti-gate. If two internal   132
one-letter syllables occur consecutively in a word, divide between   145
them; as, situ-ation or gradu-ation.   153

Compound words that contain a hyphen should be divided only   165
at the hyphen; as, second-class. Compound words written without a   178
hyphen are best divided between the elements of the compound; as,   191
super-market.   194

Two final suggestions: Once you have decided to divide a   205
word, leave as much of that word as you can on the first linc; that 219
way, a minimum of guesswork is required of the reader. Further,   232
when in doubt about how to divide a word, remember that a dictio   245
nary is still the best friend a writer can have.   254

22

Preparatory practice

60-space line; each line twice SS (slowly, then faster); DS between 2-line groups

alphabet 1 Roxy waved as she did quick flying jumps on the trapeze bar.

shift keys 2 Yang Woerman hopes Zoe Quigley can leave for Maine in March.

figures 3 Buy 25 boxes, 147 bags, 39 sacks, 68 cartons, and 10 crates.

easy 4 Did the girl make the ornament with fur, duck down, or hair?

| 1 | 2 | 3 | 4 | 5 | 6 | 7 | 8 | 9 | 10 | 11 | 12 |

Attention line. An attention line, when needed, is placed lc as the second line of the address. The caption "attn:" should preceed the name of the person to whose attention the letter is called

Body. Begin the body or message of the letter at least two or message lines below the last line of the address or on the twentieth line if a window envelope is used. Begin the main paragraphs flush with the left margin, and single-space the lines of the paragraphs. Double-space between the paragraphs in the body. Number or letter all subparagraphs, and indent the first line of each subparagraph five spaces; begin all succeeding lines in the subparagraph flush with the left margin. If the body of the letter consists of a single paragraph of fewer than ten lines, double-space the body.

Enclosure(s). Place the work "Enclosure(s)" a double space below the signature element, if needed. If no specific reference to an enclosure is made in the body, a listing of all enclosures--single-spaced and each one flush with the left margin--should be made below the word "Enclosure(s)."

Signature element. Place the signers name flush with the left margin in ALL CAPS on the fourth line space below the last line fo the body or complmentary close. Place the signers title flush with the left margin on the next line.

Material sent Under Separate Cover. If any material is to be sent under separate cover, list each item each item--single-spaced and flush with the left margin--below the words "Separate cover."

Copy and identification notations. These Notations are not shown on the original; they appear copy only on the file copies.

Window envelopes. If a window envelope is used, the address should not contain more than five lines. Each line of the address should not be no longer than ④ inches. -sp If any part of an address

(Job 5 continued on next page)

22b ▶ 13

Review procedure for horizontal centering

half sheet (long side up); begin on Line 13; DS body; TS below heading; proofread and circle errors

1 Review steps for centering lines horizontally (see 21c).
2 Center each line of the announcement shown at right.

EASTERN HILLS GOLF CLUB
TS
Annual Awards Banquet

The Nineteenth Hole

October 10, 6:30 p.m.

22c ▶ 30

Learn to center copy vertically

half sheet

Study the guides for vertical centering given at the right; then format and type Problem 1 below and Problem 2 on p. 45.

Guides for vertical centering

1 Count all lines and blank line spaces required by the problem (1 blank line space between DS lines; 2 blank line spaces between TS lines).

Note. Both pica and elite type require 1″ for 6 lines of copy.

2 Subtract the total lines required by the problem from the number of lines on the paper (33, half sheet; 66, full sheet).

3 Divide the resulting number by 2 to determine number of lines to be left in top margin. *Disregard any fraction that may result from the division.*

4 From the top edge of the paper, space down 1 more than the number of lines figured for the top margin; begin typing on that line.

5 Center each line of the problem horizontally.

Calculation check

Lines available:	33
Lines required:	12
Lines remaining:	21
Top margin: (20 ÷ 2)	10
	(Begin on Line 11)

This procedure places copy in what is called "exact center."

Problem 1

```
 1
 2
 3
 4                              Center
 5
 6
 7
 8
 9
10
11          HISAKO GIBSON HARROW
12                              TS
13
14      will read selections from her book
15                              DS
16          ONE GRAY MORNING
17
18      on Friday evening, August 9, at eight
19
20              in Benjamin Court
21
22      The Art Institute of Jersey City
23
24
25
26
27
28
29
30
31
32
33
```

Job 3
Composing an informal government letter (LM p. 81)

Ms. Sanchez asks that you compose an informal letter for her signature that will be duplicated and distributed to the Chicago branch office staff.

The subject is: **Out-of-town schedule for February 23-28.**

For future reference, remember that the office symbol for the Chicago branch is AFAW.

Ms. Sanchez wants you to include the following information in the letter:

1 The purpose of her trip.
2 The dates and places she will visit.
3 The fact that Mr. Terence J. Rutledge, Assistant Deputy Director, will be directing the office while she is away.

Two copy notations should be made, one for the Official File—AFAW, and one for Mr. Terence J. Rutledge—AFAW.

Note: All correspondence should have 1 cc for the Official File—AFAW.

Date the letter **February 16, 19--.**

Because you are composing a letter for Ms. Sanchez' signature, place your initials and surname in the identification line.

Prepare a rough draft on plain paper, final copy on letterhead.

Job 4
Informal government letter (LM p. 83)

Prepare the following informal letter to be sent to the purchasing agent from Ms. Sanchez. Mr. Rutledge wrote the letter for Ms. Sanchez. Send the letter by Express Mail.

The subject of the letter is: **Immediate order for correspondence manuals.** Date the letter **February 17, 19--;** address the letter to:

Mr. Anthony Thomaswick
Purchasing Agent
U.S. Services Agency
Washington, DC 20469-5514

(¶) A decision has been made to adopt a new letter style for all written communications within our branch office. The decision also was made to implement the new written communication procedures on February 28.

(¶) We do not have very much time to inform our personnel and to provide our keyboard specialists with the necessary training materials and correspondence manuals. Therefore, will you please expedite the preparation of the purchase order for these correspondence manuals. I am confident we can receive the manuals within seven days if the purchase order is sent immediately.

(¶) Order the manuals from the Superintendent of Documents, U.S. Government Printing Office, Washington, DC 20402-5541. The title of the manual is: U.S. Government Correspondence Manual (U.S. Printing Office Stock Number 022-000-00129-9). Please order 25 copies at $3.80 each.

Job 5
Three-page report (full sheets)

Mr. Rutledge has been assigned to draft a report about the government letter styles that the branch will adopt on February 28. He asks that you prepare this report in final form as an unbound manuscript.

Copies of this report will be distributed to all branch office personnel and to the other agency branches.

Heading for the report is:
INFORMAL GOVERNMENT LETTER STYLE. Correct any undetected errors that Mr. Rutledge may have overlooked.

The General Services Administration has developed the U.S. Government correspondence Manual which includes the basic informal letter format. The basic style characteristics of the format are presented first, and then its special style characteristics are noted.

Basic Style Characteristics

Stationery. Official agency letterhead should be printed on the standard 8½" × 11" paper.

Subject line. The first letter of the first word and all proper nouns capitalized in the subject line. If more than one line is needed for the subject, single-space and place the succeeding line flush with the left margin.

Margins. The side margins on all government correspondence should be 1 inch. The bottom margin should not be less than 1 inch on any page

(Job 5 continued on next page)

22c, continued

Problem 2

half sheet; DS; center each line
horizontally and the entire an–
nouncement vertically; proofread;
circle errors

Calculation check

Lines on half sheet	33
Lines in announcement	12
Unused lines	21
Top margin	10
(Begin on Line 11)	

THE RUGBY SHOP
TS

invites you to attend

a special unadvertised sale

of sweaters, slacks, and shirts

one day only

Saturday, March 13, from 9 to 9

23a ▶ 7

Preparatory practice

60-space line; each line
once DS; two 1' writings on
Line 4

alphabet	1	Merry will have picked out a dozen quarts of jam for boxing.
d/s	2	Eddie Deeds sold daisy seeds to a student from East Dresden.
figures	3	Your 3:15 p.m. show drew 49 men, 72 women, and 680 children.
easy	4	As usual, Len bid and paid for a quantity of big world maps.

| 1 | 2 | 3 | 4 | 5 | 6 | 7 | 8 | 9 | 10 | 11 | 12 |

23b ▶ 10

Measure straight-copy skill

two 1' writings
two 3' writings

Difficulty index

| all letters used | E | 1.2 si | 5.1 awl | 90% hfw |

gwam 3'

By this time, you must realize that there are many rules 4

you should learn about line endings and word division. Add 8

to your store of rules those that explain when you ought to 12

avoid dividing a word at the end of a line. Unless you must, 16

for example, you should not divide a figure, a proper name, a 20

date, or the last word on a page. If you learn these rules 24

and combine them with just a little common sense, you will be 28

able to handle problems of word division quickly and wisely. 32

| 1 | 2 | 3 | 4 |

Preparatory practice

each line 3 times SS (slowly, faster, slowly); retype selected lines as time permits

alphabet	1	Both judges gave my wax sculpture of a quail the coveted king's prize.
fig/sym	2	Please pay Invoice #1937 for $26,450 (less 8% discount) by November 3.
bottom row	3	Seven members of the city zoning council have condemned six buildings.
fluency	4	The name of the neighbor also may be on the title of the antique auto.

| 1 | 2 | 3 | 4 | 5 | 6 | 7 | 8 | 9 | 10 | 11 | 12 | 13 | 14 |

126b-129b ▶ 45

Office job simulation

(LM pp. 77–87)

Job 1
Itinerary with braced headings (full sheet)

Ms. Sanchez received her flight confirmations yesterday for her upcoming trips to the agency branch offices in New Orleans and Los Angeles. She will also go to Washington, D.C. in order to report to Ms. Jean Carson, Chief of the U.S. Services Agency, and discuss with her the visits to the branch offices.

She requests that you prepare her itinerary as a boxed table, DS. Center the table horizontally and vertically in reading position. Leave 2 spaces between the columns. Add heading: **ANITA R. SANCHEZ**; Add subheading: **Itinerary for February 23-28, 19—**.

Job 2
Informal government letters
(LM pp. 77–79)

Ms. Sanchez asks that you prepare the following letter for the branch Deputy Directors in the New Orleans and Los Angeles offices informing them of her on-site visits at the end of the month. To insure fast mail service, be sure to send the letters by Express Mail.

The address for the Los Angeles Deputy Director is:

Mr. Arnold V. Stucki
Deputy Director
U.S. Service Agency
11000 Wilshire Blvd.
Los Angeles, CA 90024-3105

If you were using information word processing equipment, you would need to key the data only once, and then change only the variable data (name and address) for each subsequent letter printed.

	Departure			Arrival	
Date	City	Time	Flight	City	Time
23	Chicago	10:45 a.m.	EA 925	New Orleans	12:50 p.m.
25	New Orleans	1:38 p.m.	DL 132	Los Angeles	5:05 p.m.
27	Los Angeles	7:28 a.m.	TW 630	Washington	2:05 p.m.
28	Washington	6:45 p.m.	UA 496	Chicago	7:09 p.m.

Date: February 15, 19-- | Sender's reference: AFAW | Special Mailing Instructions: EXPRESS MAIL | Subject: Confirmation of on-site visit | Address: Ms. Nicole Goulet | Deputy Director | U.S. Services Agency | 569 Loyola Avenue | New Orleans, LA 70113-2211

(¶) Ms. Jean Carson, Chief of the U.S. Services Agency, has assigned me to visit each branch office for the following purposes:

a. Audit the branch's affirmative action records for the past year to verify compliance with the Agency's Affirmative Action Plan.

b. Audit the employee attendance records to verify that proper documentation was obtained to support all sick leaves, personal leaves, and vacation periods.

c. Deliver and discuss with you the Agency's budget plans for the next fiscal year.

(¶) Please have all documentation readily available and the necessary records up to date prior to my arrival.

(¶) A copy of my itinerary is enclosed. Please have someone meet me at the airport when I arrive. Also, will you please make a hotel reservation for me at the most convenient location.

ANITA R. SANCHEZ | Deputy Chief, U.S. Services Agency | Enclosure | cc: Official File--AFAW | Ms. Jean Carson--AFAC | AFAW:ARSanchez:xx 2-15---

23c ▶ 15

Center announcements

Problem 1

half sheet; DS; use exact vertical center; center each line hori-zontally (not aligned as shown); proofread/circle errors

Problem 2

full sheet; DS; use directions for Problem 1, but center in *reading position*

Reading position

Reading position places data slightly higher on a page than exact vertical center. Find top margin for exact center, then sub-tract 2 lines. Reading position is generally used only for full sheets (or half sheets with short side up—long edge at the left).

THE ELMIRA CONCERT SOCIETY

TS

proudly presents

the eminent Latin American pianist

Jorge Cabrara

in concert

Saturday afternoon, April 30, at 4:00

Carteret Auditorium

23d ▶ 9

Center data on special-size paper

half sheet, short side inserted first; DS; begin on Line 22; center information requested for each line

---

Finding horizontal center

To find the horizontal center of special-size paper or cards

1 Insert the paper or card into the machine. From the line-of-writing scale, add the numbers at the left and right edges of the paper.

2 Divide this sum by 2. The result is the horizontal center point for that size paper or card.

Your name

Your street address

Your city and state

The name of your college

Current date

23e ▶ 9

Center on a card

use a 5″ × 3″ card or paper cut to size; insert to type on 5″ width; center the data verti-cally and horizontally DS; proofread/circle errors

Calculation checks

There are 6 horizontal lines to a vertical inch. A 3″ card, therefore, holds 18 lines.

Lines available	18
Lines required	9
Lines remaining	9
Top margin	4
(Begin on Line)	5

John and Mary Dexter

DS

announce the arrival of

Meredith Anne

Born December 8

7 pounds 8 ounces

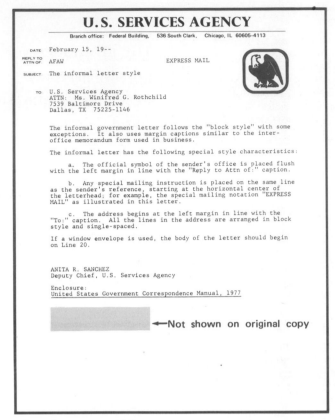

U.S. SERVICES AGENCY

Branch office: Federal Building, 536 South Clark, Chicago, IL 60605-4113

DATE February 15, 19--

REPLY TO ATTN OF AFAW EXPRESS MAIL

SUBJECT The informal letter style

TO U.S. Services Agency
ATTN: Ms. Winifred G. Rothchild
7539 Baltimore Drive
Dallas, TX 75225-1146

The informal government letter follows the "block style" with some exceptions. It also uses margin captions similar to the interoffice memorandum form used in business.

The informal letter has the following special style characteristics:

  a. The official symbol of the sender's office is placed flush with the left margin in line with the "Reply to Attn of:" caption.

  b. Any special mailing instruction is placed on the same line as the sender's reference, starting at the horizontal center of the letterhead; for example, the special mailing notation "EXPRESS MAIL" as illustrated in this letter.

  c. The address begins at the left margin in line with the "To:" caption. All the lines in the address are arranged in block style and single-spaced.

If a window envelope is used, the body of the letter should begin on Line 20.

ANITA R. SANCHEZ
Deputy Chief, U.S. Services Agency

Enclosure:
United States Government Correspondence Manual, 1977

←Not shown on original copy

Informal government letter

Address begins at the left margin in line with the "To:" caption. Arrange the lines in block style single-spaced. (See **Window Envelopes** for further directions.)

Attention Line. If needed, place the attention line as the second line of the address. Precede the name of the person to whose attention the letter is called with the "ATTN:" caption.

Body (Message). Begin the message of the letter at least 2 lines below the last line of the address. Begin the main paragraphs flush with the left margin single-spaced; double-space between paragraphs. Indent the first line of numbered or lettered subparagraphs 5 spaces; begin all succeeding lines in subparagraphs flush with the left margin. If a letter consists of a single paragraph of fewer than 10 lines, double-space the body.

Signature Element. Place the name of the signer flush with the left margin in all capital letters on the 4th line space below the last line of the body. Place the signer's title on the next line, flush with the left margin. If more than 1 line is needed for the signer's title, place the succeeding lines flush with the left margin. The entire signature element (name and title) should be 4 lines or fewer.

Enclosures. When needed, place the word "Enclosure " a double space below the signature element. If more than 1 item is enclosed, use the plural form and indicate the number of enclosures; for example: "3 enclosures." When specific references to all enclosures are not made in the body of the letter, list each enclosure on a separate line below the word "Enclosure:"; single-space enclosure lines flush with the left margin.

Material Sent Under Separate Cover. If material that is to be sent under separate cover is mentioned in the letter, place the words "Separate cover:" flush with the left margin, a double space below the signature element or the enclosure notation (if there is an enclosure notation). List the material to be sent under separate cover, whether or not it is identified in the body, below the words "Separate cover:", single-spaced, and flush with the left margin. For example:

Separate cover:
Copy of bid form
Bidding packet

Information Not Shown on Original Copy. *The Distribution of Copies* and *Identification of Office, Writer, and Keyboard Specialist* elements are shown *only* on file copies.

Distribution of Copies. This notation is shown only on the file copies. Place the *Distribution of Copies* notation a double space below the signature element or enclosure notation or the separate cover listing. List the names of all recipients one below the other with their corresponding office symbol when appropriate:

cc:
Official File--AFAW
Reading File--AFAW
RTBrown--AFAX

Identification of Office, Writer, and Keyboard Specialist. This notation is shown only on the file copies. Place the office symbol of the preparing office, the writer's initials and surname, the keyboard specialist's initials, and the date on this line a double space below the last line used and flush with the left margin. For example:

AFAW:RJFranz:cv 4-19-85

Note: In some cases the writer of the letter is not the signer of the letter; therefore, the writer's name should be placed in the identification line instead of signer's name.

Window Envelopes. When a window envelope is used, the address should be 5 lines or fewer, and no address should be more than 4 inches wide. If a line must be divided, begin the second line 2 spaces from the left margin. The body (message) of the letter should start on Line 20.

Learning goals

1 To learn symbol keystrokes.

2 To improve facility on figure keyreaches.

3 To improve proofreading and revision skills.

4 To learn proofreader's marks and their uses.

5 To improve keyboarding continuity.

Machine adjustments

1 Set paper edge guide at 0.

2 Set ribbon control to type on upper half of ribbon.

3 Use a 60–space line (adjusted for bell) unless otherwise directed.

4 SS drills; DS paragraphs.

5 Space problems as directed.

24a ▶ 6

Preparatory practice

each line twice SS (slowly, then faster); DS between 2-line groups; repeat selected lines as time permits

alphabet 1 John Quigley packed the zinnias in twelve large, firm boxes.

n/m 2 Call a woman or a man who will manage Minerva Manor in Nome.

figures 3 Of the 13 numbers, there were 4 chosen: 29, 56, 78, and 90.

easy 4 An auditor may handle the fuel problems of the ancient city.

| 1 | 2 | 3 | 4 | 5 | 6 | 7 | 8 | 9 | 10 | 11 | 12 |

24b ▶ 12

Learn new keyreaches: $ &

$ = dollars
& = ampersand (and)

Technique hint

Pace your shift–type–release technique when practicing the symbol reaches. Straighten the appropriate finger; avoid as much as you can moving the hands and arms forward.

Reach technique for $

Shift; then reach *up* to $ with *left first* finger.

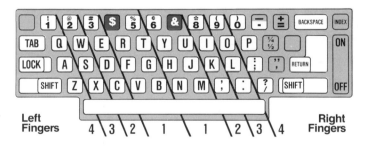

Reach technique for &

Shift; then reach *up* to & with *right first* finger.

Follow the "Standard procedure for learning new keyreaches" on page 10 (Lines 1–4 twice; Lines 5–7 once; repeat 5–7 if time permits).

$ 1 $ $ $4 $4, if $4, 4 for $44, her $444 fur, per $4, $4 tariff
    2 The items cost them $174, $184, and $54. They paid $14 tax.

&   3 & & J & J, Jory & Jones, Bern & James, H & U Co., Foy & Hope
    4 We buy pipe from Smith & Jones, Li & Hume, and Clay & Young.

all fingers/ new symbols
    5 The $185 check is from J & J. The $192 check is from B & B.
    6 Send $274 to Fish & Heath; deposit $300 with Booth & Hughes.
    7 Hecot & Ryne charged us $165; Carver & Hunt charged us $340.

| 1 | 2 | 3 | 4 | 5 | 6 | 7 | 8 | 9 | 10 | 11 | 12 |

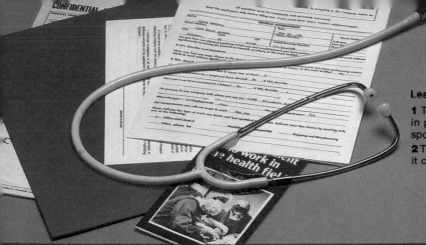

Learning goals

1 To develop knowledge and skill in preparing government correspondence.

2 To plan your work and complete it correctly and efficiently.

Machine adjustments

1 Set paper guide at *0*.

2 Set ribbon control to use upper half of ribbon.

3 Set line–space selector for SS.

4 Margins: 70–space line for drills; 1″ side margins for government letters.

126-129

Office Job Simulation

Read carefully the material at the right and on page 263 before you begin the work in Section 32. Note any standard procedures that you think will save you time during the completion of the government office activities.

Daily practice plan:

Preparatory practice .... 5′
Work on simulation .... 45′

New Location

Your parents recently moved to Chicago, and you decided to relocate with them. You asked Ms. DeSoto if you could be reassigned to work through the Chicago office of Office Service Temporaries, Inc. She has agreed and has transferred your file to the Chicago office. You are requested by the Office Manager of the Chicago office to report to work for a first assignment on February 15.

Work Assignment

You have been assigned by Office Service Temporaries, Inc., to work as a keyboard specialist with the U.S. Services Agency, an agency of the U.S. Government. You will work directly for Ms. Anita R. Sanchez, Deputy Chief, Chicago Branch, U.S. Services Agency, Federal Building, 536 South Clark Street, Chicago, IL 60605-4113.

Ms. Sanchez orients you to your work assignment the morning you arrive. She informs you of the decision to adopt the informal government letter style recommended by the General Services Administration. Although the Chicago branch will not officially adopt the new letter style until February 28, she has requested that all of her correspondence be prepared using this new format. She also requires that 1 carbon copy of each government letter be prepared, unless otherwise instructed.

The U.S. Services Agency bases most of its keyboarding and formatting preparation on COLLEGE KEYBOARDING/TYPEWRITING; therefore, if you have questions regarding style or format, refer to your textbook. Ms. Sanchez has a copy of the *U.S. Government Correspondence Manual* for you to use as a reference. Excerpts from the manual are given at the right and on page 263 for quick reference.

Basic Style Characteristics for Informal Government Letters

Style. The informal letter format is a combination of the block letter style and an interoffice memorandum.

Stationery. Stationery for the informal government letter is 8½″ × 11″ and will have the following captions preprinted in the left margin: ''Date:'', ''Reply to Attn of:'', ''Subject:'', and ''To:'' (see illustration on page 263).

Margins. Side margins on all government correspondence are 1″. A 1″ left margin in the informal government letter should leave about 2 spaces between preprinted captions and the typed headings. The bottom margin should not be less than 1″.

Sender's Reference is the official symbol of the sender (e.g., AFAW). Place the official symbol flush with the left margin in line with the ''Reply to Attn of:'' caption (placed a double space below the dateline). An office that does not have an official symbol uses an abbreviation of the office name.

Special Mailing Instructions such as SPECIAL DELIVERY, REGISTERED, CERTIFIED, or EXPRESS MAIL should be placed on the same line as the sender's reference, starting at the horizontal center of the letterhead. If the sender's reference line extends to or beyond the center of the line, begin the special mailing notation 3 spaces to the right of it. Note: Special mailing instructions are placed on the letter *only* if the keyboard specialist does not prepare the envelope.

Subject Line. Capitalize only the first letter of the first word and all proper nouns. When more than 1 line is needed for the subject, single-space and begin each succeeding line flush with the left margin.

24c ▶ 8
Reach for new goals

1 Two 30" writings on each line; try to pace yourself to end each writing just as time is called.
2 Three 1' writings on Line 4; de–termine *gwam* on each writing.

gwam 30"

1	The six girls paid $81 to visit the old city.	18
2	Lana paid the man the $94 due for the work he did.	20
3	Coe & Wu may sign the form for the auditor of the firm.	22
4	If Torke & Rush paid $730, then Corlan and Aldorn paid $637.	24

| 1 | 2 | 3 | 4 | 5 | 6 | 7 | 8 | 9 | 10 | 11 | 12 |

24d ▶ 7
Use the warning bell/ divide words

two half sheets; begin on Line 12; once with 70-space line, once with 60-space line

Take time to evaluate your completed work. Look carefully at what you have done. Would you be impressed with it if you were a reader? Is it attractive in form and accurate in content? If it does not impress you, it will not impress anyone else.

24e ▶ 9
Proofread/revise as you keyboard

each line twice SS; DS be-tween 2-line groups; identify and correct the circled errors *as you keyboard*

1 He chose 12 to 14 dozen (carda) for my all-(prupose) card shelf.
2 The expert (quick ly) listed 23 sources of information (forher).
3 I drove my new jeep at an average (ratt) of 56 miles per hour(?)
4 Minimum (spedd) on that part of Route 789 is 35 miles an (horu).
5 The (whit) pine frame is 15 x 20 inches; (○) there is no picture.

24f ▶ 8
Improve keyboarding continuity

1 Practice the ¶ once for orienta–tion.
2 Take three 30" practice writings on the ¶. Determine *gwam*: words typed × 2.
3 Take three 1' speed writings on the ¶. Determine *gwam*: total words typed = 1' *gwam*.

Goal: 20 or more *gwam*.

Difficulty index

all letters used	E	1.2 si	5.1 awl	90% hfw

We purchased our computer from the Jeff & Zorne Company for $500. That is quite a lot of money; but I think it will be a good investment if I can use the machine and all of the parts--figures and symbols, for example--in the correct way.

25a ▶ 7
Preparatory practice

each line twice SS (slowly, then faster); DS between 2-line groups; repeat selected lines if time per-mits

25

alphabet	1	Why did the judge quiz poor Victor about his blank tax form?
t/r	2	Bart had trouble starting his truck for a trip to Terrytown.
figure/ symbol	3	Buy 103 ribbons and 45 erasers from May & Muntz for $289.67.
easy	4	Did she rush to cut six bushels of corn for the civic corps?

| 1 | 2 | 3 | 4 | 5 | 6 | 7 | 8 | 9 | 10 | 11 | 12 |

LEVEL SIX
Processing information (service office simulations)

This level of Advanced Keyboarding/Formatting Skills is designed to provide you with the opportunity to develop your production skills in a variety of simulations that are commonly found in government, medical, legal, consulting, and information processing offices.

A secondary purpose of this level is to help you continue to improve your basic speed and accuracy skills. In addition to the daily Preparatory Practice, Section 34 and supplemental skill-building practices are devoted almost entirely to speed and accuracy development.

The final section of Level 6 is a measurement section that tests both your basic speed and accuracy skills and your production skills. Your two major performance goals in Level 6 are the same as those for Level 5. They are:

- To develop a keen responsibility for high-quality work.
- To develop the ability to make decisions without direct supervision.

This level provides for about 15 percent of your classroom time to be devoted to basic speed and accuracy development and 85 percent to simulated production activities.

25b ▶ 12
Learn new keyreaches
( )

Follow the "Standard procedure for learning new keyreaches" on page 10 (Lines 1–4 twice; Lines 5–8 once; repeat 5–8 if time per–mits.)

= number/pounds
( ) = parentheses

Reach technique for #

Shift; then reach *up* to # with *left second* finger.

Reach technique for (

Shift; then reach *up* to (with *right third* finger.

Reach technique for)

Shift; then reach *up* to) with *right little* finger

#	1	# # #3 #33 Card #3, File #3, Car #33, #3 grade. Try #3 now.
	2	Memo #169 says to load Car #3758 with 470# of #2 grade sand.
( )	3	(1 (1);); (90) two (2); type (1) and (2); see (8) and (9).
	4	He (John) and his cousin (Lynne) are both the same age (17).
#/( )	5	Pay the May (#34) and June (#54) bills soon (before July 1).
	6	We lease Car #84 (a white sedan) and Car #86 (a blue coupe).
all figures/ new symbols	7	Our Check #230 for $259 paid Owen & Cobb (auditors) in full.
	8	Deliver the $78 order (collect) to Fox & Tucker (Room #416).

| 1 | 2 | 3 | 4 | 5 | 6 | 7 | 8 | 9 | 10 | 11 | 12 |

25c ▶ 8
Proofread/revise
as you keyboard

each line twice SS; DS be–tween 2-line groups; correct circled errors as you type

1 I saw them fill the (Baskets) full of (appels) (form) the orchard.

2 None of (use) took that (specal) train to Cincinnati (adn) Dayton.

3 They (paln) an intensive (campaing) for television and/or (raido).

4 (Teh) two leaders (Betty and Luis) left at 2--not 1:30 today.

5 (put) a fork, knife, and (sppon) at each informal place setting.

Job 3
Balance sheet
(full sheet)

Format and type the bal-
ance sheet. Leave a 1″ top
margin; leave 8 spaces between Columns 1 and 2 and
2 spaces between Columns
2 and 3.

words

COLEMAN REAL ESTATE COMPANY   6

Balance sheet   8

June 30, 19--   11

Assets   14

Current assets:			17
Cash		$ 45,650	20
Accounts receivable	$ 42,000		26
Less reserve for bad debts	1,500	40,500	34
Office supplies		3,500	38
Fixed assets:		175,000	41
Land		~~176,300~~	44
Building	$150,000		47
Less *accumulated* depreciation	75,000	75,000	59
Office equipment	$ 85,000		64
Less accumulated depreciation	25,000	60,000	75
Total assets		#399,650	81

TS → ### Liabilites   85

Current liabilites:			89
Accounts payable	$ 20,000		94
Notes payable	35,000	$ 55,000	102
Long-term liabilities:			107
Mortgage payable		50,000	113
Total liabilities		$105,000	119

Job 4

Repeat Job 3 leaving 10
spaces between Columns 1
and 2 and 6 spaces between
Columns 2 and 3.

Owner's Equity   125

Capital:			127
Capital stock	$280,000		131
Retained earnings	14,650	$294,650	142
Total liabilities and			146
owner's equity		$399,650	154

25d ▶ 8
Improve keyboarding continuity

1 Practice the ¶ once for orienta–tion.

2 Take three 30″ writings and three 1′ writings.

Goal: At least 14 *gwam*.

all letters/
figures/
symbols learned

Difficulty index

| E | 1.2 si | 5.1 awl | 90% hfw |

  .   2   .   4   .   6   .   8   .   10   .

Issue #27 of a recent (1/9/85) magazine told how an ex-

 12   .   14   .   16   .   18   .   20   .   22

ecutive got her first job with a top-level firm (Roe & Roe):

 24   .   26   .   28   .   30   .   32   .   34   .

She knew how to keyboard. Paid merely $140 a week at first,

 36   .   38   .   40   .   42   .   44   .   46   .

she moved up quickly; now she is making about $1,360 a week.

25e ▶ 15
Review centering an announcement on special-size paper

half sheet; insert short side first; DS; center vertically in reading position; center each line horizontally; proofread/circle errors

Calculation checks:

The page is 8½″ long. There are 6 lines in one vertical inch. 8½ × 6 = 51 available lines.

Lines in problem: 14
Exact top margin: 18
Reading position
    top margin: 16

Add right paper edge reading to left paper edge reading; divide by 2. The result is the center point of the page.

Members of THE CHORALIERS
                     TS

Arvid Badger

Muriel Ann Bressuyt

Bertram Garrett, Jr.

Wayne L. Jewell

Phillip R. Runyun

Bette Lee Yamasake

26a ▶ 7
Preparatory practice

each line twice SS (slowly, faster); as many 30″ writings on Line 4 as time permits

Goal: Complete Line 4 in 30″.

alphabet 1 Jewel quickly explained to me the big fire hazards involved.

space bar 2 is by it do in be of am my go me an us so if to or ad on and

figure symbol 3 Silva & Stuart checked Items #2346 and 789 (for a $150 fee).

easy 4 The auditor did the rush work right, so he risks no penalty.

  | 1 | 2 | 3 | 4 | 5 | 6 | 7 | 8 | 9 | 10 | 11 | 12 |

125a ▶ 5
Preparatory practice

each line 3 times SS (slowly, faster, top speed); DS between 3-line groups; repeat selected lines as time permits

alphabet	1	An expert adjustment by Virge was made quickly before the pipes froze.
fig/sym	2	In the fall (9/20/86), we purchased 357.4 metric tons of #1 red wheat.
shift lock	3	A mailing notation--REGISTERED or HOLD FOR ARRIVAL--should be in caps.
fluency	4	She may sight a whale if she pays a visit to the downtown island dock.

| 1 | 2 | 3 | 4 | 5 | 6 | 7 | 8 | 9 | 10 | 11 | 12 | 13 | 14 |

125b ▶ 45
Production measurement

(LM p. 75; full sheets)

Time schedule

Assembling materials . 2'
Timed production ..... 38'
Final check; compute
  n-pram .... 5'

Job 1
Invoice (LM p. 75)

Format and type the invoice given at the right; prepare 1 cc on plain half sheet; proofread carefully; correct errors neatly.

words

Invoice

		words
Brown & Row Publishers	Date July 12, 1986	7
200 Malvern Avenue	Our Order No. M-3211-005	13
Cleveland, OH 44116-0032	Cust. Order No. Z-511-250	23
Terms Net 30 days	Shipped Via UPS	26

Quantity	Description	Unit Price	Total	
25	File folders (9⅜" × 11¾") -- A1593	.40	10.00	37
2	MLZ microfiche readers -- M-7821	304.20	608.40	47
3	Computer terminal tables (oak finish) -- S-5502	56.20	168.60	55 / 60
1	Portable changeable letterboard (with color panel) -- Z-4559	84.65	84.65	68 / 76
			871.65	77

Job 2
Agenda (full sheet)

Prepare for left binding the agenda shown at the right. Leave a 2" top margin.

```
                 RUSSELL DISTRIBUTORS, INC.                    }  DS      5
          Agenda for Meeting of the Board of Directors                   14
                      November 13, 19--   TS                             18

      1.  Call to order . . . . . . . . . . . . . Percy Kolstad          30
                                                  Raymond Kofer
      2.  Minutes of Last meeting . . . . . . . . Fred Kuker             42

      3.  Special reports                                                46
             Manufacturer's Liaison  . . . . . .  Carol Sixes           57
             Retailer's Division . . . . . . . .  Tim Rathe  }          67
             Special Promotions  . . . . . . . .  Renee High            76
             Land Acquisition Committee . . . .  Martha Seely           87

      4.  Discussion of Special reports . . . . .  Percy Kolstad         99

      5.  Declaration of Dividend . . . . . . . .  Rebecca Nettle       111

      6.  Other business . . . . . . . . . . . .  Percy Kolstad        123

      7.  Adjournment                                                  126
```

Learn new keyreaches: % ' !

% = percent
' = apostrophe/single quote
! = exclamation point

Note: If you are using a nonelectric machine, refer to page 3; see directions for reach to '.

Reach technique for %

Shift; then reach *up* to % with *left first* finger.

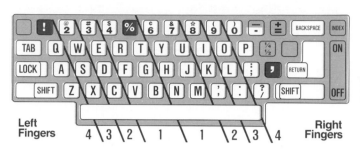

Left Fingers   4 3 2 1 1 2 3 4   Right Fingers

Apostrophe (')

Reach to ' with *right little* finger.

Follow the "Standard procedure for learning new keyreaches" on page 10 (Lines 1–4 twice; Lines 5–8 once; repeat 5–8 if time permits).

Exclamation point:

If your machine has an exclamation point key, strike it with the nearest little finger. If it does not, refer to page 3. Space twice after an exclamation point when used after an emphatic interjection or as end–of–sentence punctuation.

%
1 % % 5%, off 5%, if 5%, save 15%, ask 15%, less 50%, 5% force
2 Mark prices down 15% on coats, 5% on hats, and 10% on shoes.

'
3 ' ' 10's, it's, Bob's, Sec'y, Ok'd; It's summer. I'm going.
4 It's time for Ann's party. I don't have Melanie's notebook.

!
5 Fire! Ouch! Oh wow! Keep out! They offer a big discount!
6 Their slogan reads THINK! They used the headline OOPS SALE!

%/'/!
7 Don't give up! Keep on! We're over the top! We have $950!
8 Uhl & Co. had a 16% profit! Their third quarter showed 20%!

| 1 | 2 | 3 | 4 | 5 | 6 | 7 | 8 | 9 | 10 | 11 | 12 |

Proofread/revise as you keyboard

Errors are often circled in copy that is to be retyped. More frequently, perhaps, the copy is marked with special symbols called "proofreader's marks" which indicate changes desired by an editor.

Some commonly used proofreader's marks are shown at the right. Study them; then type each drill line at least twice, SS; DS between 2–line groups.

Concentrate on copy content as you keyboard.

Proofreader's marks

Symbol	Meaning	Symbol	Meaning
Cap or ≡	Capitalize	#	Add horizontal space
^	Insert	/ or lc	Lowercase letters
ℓ	Delete (remove)	⊂	Close up space
⊏	Move to left	⌣	Transpose
⊐	Move to right	stet	Leave as originally written

1 patience pays; the espert's goalis 1% every day improvement.

2 do today's work today; tommorrow's work will be 100% lighter.

3 One's best isusually enough; Few are expect ed to give 101%.

4 It's easier to risk 10%, but return depedns on risk.

5 We miss life's pleasures I know because we refuse to sample.

6 I'll be lucky if at anytime I can solve 50% of my problems.

124a ▶ 5
Preparatory practice

each line 3 times SS (slowly, faster, slowly); DS between 3-line groups; repeat selected lines as time permits

alphabet 1 Ask Quincy Janze if he expects good work to be accomplished every day.

fig/sym 2 My building sold for $157,363, 14% less than its valuation ($182,980).

shift–key 3 Nathan will go to Spain from Italy; Larry will go to Egypt from India.

fluency 4 Due to the virus problem, it is their civic duty to suspend the visit.

| 1 | 2 | 3 | 4 | 5 | 6 | 7 | 8 | 9 | 10 | 11 | 12 | 13 | 14 |

124b ▶ 45
Production measurement: tables

(2 half sheets and full sheet)

Time schedule

Assembling materials .... 2′
Timed production .... 38′
Final check; compute
  n–pram .... 5′

Job 1
Unruled table

half sheet, long side up; SS body of table; 6 spaces between columns

words

MICROELECTRONICS, INC. 5
(Annual Sales Comparison by District) 12

District	1987	1986	
			16 21
Eastern	$2,138,265	$2,022,035	27
Central	1,962,820	1,826,250	33
Northern	862,210	851,928	38
Southern	432,025	425,632	43
Western	2,041,632	1,989,281	49 53
Totals	$7,436,952	$7,115,126	55 57 59

Job 2
Ruled table

full sheet, reading position; DS body of table; 4 spaces between columns

Job 3
Boxed table

Retype Job 1 as a boxed table on a half sheet, long side up. Center the following braced heading above Columns 2 & 3: **June 30.** SS columnar mate–rial; leave 6 spaces between columns. (Add 36 words for braced heading and rules.)

words

PETERSON-BROWN EQUIPMENT COMPANY 7

(Summary of Female/Male Employees) 14

Year	Number of Men Employees	Percentage of Total Employees	Number of Women Employees	Percentage of Total Employees	Total Number of Employees	
						28 42 51 60 71 85
1981	64	40	96	60	160	89
1982	67	40	99	60	166	93
1983	75	43	98	57	173	98
1984	70	37	120	63	190	102
1985	70	37	120	63	190	106
						120

26d ▶ 11
Reach for new goals

1 Take a 1′ writing on Line 1.

2 Take a 1′ writing on Line 2, trying to type as many lines as on Line 1.

3 Practice each of the other pairs of lines in the same way to improve figure/symbol keyboarding speed.

		words in line
1	Did the girls make soap in a handy clay bowl?	9
2	They spent $85 on a visit to Field & Co.	8
3	Did the men visit the dismal shanty on the island?	10
4	Form #72 is title to the island (their half).	9
5	I turn the dials on the panel a half turn to the right.	11
6	She may pay me for my work, and I make 40% profit.	10
7	It is a shame he spent the endowment on a visit to the city.	12
8	She paid 20% down for the $18 formal tie; it's apricot.	11

| 1 | 2 | 3 | 4 | 5 | 6 | 7 | 8 | 9 | 10 | 11 | 12 |

26e ▶ 10
Improve keyboarding continuity

1 Practice the ¶ for orientation.

2 Take three 30″ writings and three 1′ writings.

3 Proofread/circle errors after each writing.

Goal: At least 14 *gwam*.

Avoid looking at the keyboard when you encounter figures and symbols.

Difficulty index

| all letters/symbols learned | E | 1.2 si | 5.1 awl | 90% hfw |

Sales Report #38/39 of the modern firm of Wenz & Jelkes states that, if they are to remain in business, they are required to clear a profit of 10% on all sales (net)--or $1 on each $10. They don't expect the figure to change very soon.

27

27a ▶ 7
Preparatory practice

each line twice SS (slowly, then faster); DS between 2-line groups; take a 1′ writing on Line 4 if time permits

alphabet	1	Jacky Few's strange, quiet behavior amazed and perplexed us.
shift	2	Lily read BLITHE SPIRIT by Noel Coward. I read VANITY FAIR.
fig/sym	3	Invoice #38 went from $102.74 to $97.60 after a 5% discount.
easy	4	They may go to a town social when they visit the big island.

| 1 | 2 | 3 | 4 | 5 | 6 | 7 | 8 | 9 | 10 | 11 | 12 |

27b ▶ 8
Practice long reaches

each line twice SS; DS between 2-line groups; repeat lines you find most difficult

Keep eyes on copy as you strike figures and symbols.

$	1	He spent $25 for gifts, $13 for dinner, and $7 for cab fare.
( )	2	We (my uncle and I) watched his sons (my cousins) play golf.
%	3	If I add 3% to the company discount of 8%, I can deduct 11%.
&	4	Send the posters to Bow & Held, Mans & Tow, and Wick & Jens.
'	5	It's time to send Hale's credit application to Land's Store.

| 1 | 2 | 3 | 4 | 5 | 6 | 7 | 8 | 9 | 10 | 11 | 12 |

Time schedule

Assembling materials .... 2'
Timed production .... 30'
Final check; compute
n–pram .... 5'

**Job 1
Leftbound
manuscript**

Prepare the report shown at the right in leftbound style. The report is to be photocopied, so make corrections very neatly.

**Job 2
Unbound
manuscript**

Using the leftbound report you have just typed, prepare it un–bound style. Copying from your leftbound manuscript will provide you with an additional opportunity to detect errors.

words

INFORMATION PROCESSING SYSTEM — 6

Introduction — 11

When a decision was reached last year to install information processing — 25
equipment in our home office, a target date of July 1 was established to have the — 42
system in full operation. The following report summarizes the changes and — 57
results of this new system. — 63

History — 66

Before the installation of the information processing equipment last — 79
March, the word processing department consisted of one supervisor, five cor- — 95
respondence secretaries, one administrative secretary, and a clerk-typist. The — 110
workload was provided mainly by middle-management personnel. — 123

The same workload is now performed in our home office by four infor- — 136
mation processing employees. Supervision is now handled by the information — 152
processing supervisor. — 156

New Information Processing System — 170

The new system operates with three text-editors connected directly with — 184
our mainframe computer. The text-editor consoles allow the operators to — 199
keyboard copy at increased speeds and to make necessary corrections when — 213
needed. As the information is keyboarded, it is recorded on the auxiliary stor- — 229
age device at our central computer center. Once the information has been — 244
saved on disk storage, it can be retrieved for future reference. The stored — 260
information can be used with information from other departments to produce — 275
letters or reports. The ability of this system to store and to integrate various — 291
data from different departments provides many new and exciting applications — 306
that before installation were too difficult to achieve. — 317

Future Applications — 325

We are now beginning to install information processing input equipment — 339
in all departments so that the collection of critical data from the various — 354
departments can be achieved with a minimum of time and effort. As soon as — 369
this phase of the system has been fully implemented, the information process- — 384
ing system will have the capacity to retrieve, sort, and merge information from — 400
all departments within our company. Also, with the upgrading of our data base — 416
management system, we shall have all information stored and updated con- — 430
tinuously to provide a base for timely management decisions and reports. — 445

Long-Range Goal — 452

The private consulting firm that we hired to design and install our present — 467
information processing system has been retained to provide us with an evalua- — 482
tion of ongoing information processing needs. Twice a year, the consultants — 498
will review our system and make recommendations of needed changes within — 512
the system. We anticipate that our system will continue to change with our — 528
company's growth. — 531

27c ▶ 20
Learn new keyreaches:
" __

" = quotation marks
__ = underline

Quotation (")

Shift; then reach to " with *right little* finger.

Left Fingers 4 \ 3 \ 2 \ 1 \ 1 \ 2 \ 3 \ 4 Right Fingers

Underline (__)

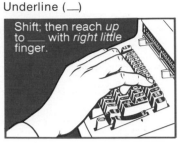

Shift; then reach *up* to __ with *right little* finger.

Follow the "Standard procedure for learning new keyreaches" on page 10 (Lines 1–6 twice; the ¶ once, then again if time permits).

Note: If you are using a non-electric machine, see page 3 directions for reach to ".

To underline: Type the word, backspace to first letter, then strike underline once for each letter in the word.

" __
1 ; "; "; James was "Jim"; Mary was "Mo"; and Janis was "Jan."
2 "We are," he said, "alone." "Wrong," said I, "Lee is here."

__
3 There is a <u>right</u> way and a <u>wrong</u> way; then there is <u>her</u> way.
4 I ordered <u>hose</u>, not hoes, and soda for <u>baking</u>, not <u>drinking</u>.

"/ __
5 "This," she stated, "is the <u>antique</u>; <u>that</u> is the facsimile."
6 She said, "I know that I <u>should</u> go, but I cannot do it <u>now</u>."

Wenz & Jelkes tell us too (in their Report #3) that the margin figure, 10%, is not "very high" for what a major firm makes. The profit this year ($1.5 million) isn't so high as it could have been, but the firm hopes to improve <u>next</u> year.

| 1 | 2 | 3 | 4 | 5 | 6 | 7 | 8 | 9 | 10 | 11 | 12 |

27d ▶ 15
Type a short report

full sheet; DS; 60-space line; 2" top margin; make corrections as you type; proofread/circle errors

SOME FACTS TO REMEMBER (Center)

words
4

TS
one horizontal

There are 10 pica and 12 elite spaces to ~~an~~ inch. With   18
size
either ^ ~~style~~ of type, six lines comprise a vertical inch.   30
horizontal   *sheet,*
To find the ^ center point of a given ~~area~~ add the readings   44
its   *edges*
for ~~the~~ left and right ^ ~~limits~~ from the line ^ of writing scale;   56
sum
divide the ~~total~~ by 2.   61
determine   *for vertical centering*
to ~~set~~ top and bottom margins, subtract the number of   79
to format
lines needed ~~for~~ the problem from the number available ~~of~~ the   91
the remaining lines
page; divide by 2 to find exact top margin. Subtract ~~12~~ if   107
you desire <u>reading position</u>. After computing lines to be left   120
one line
in the margin, space down ~~once~~ more and begin the first   133
line of the problem.   137

123a ▶ 5
Preparatory practice
each line 3 times SS (slowly, faster, slowly); DS between 3-line groups; repeat selected lines as time permits

alphabet	1	Jack Weylan received inquiries about a zoological exhibit performance.
fig/sym	2	Yung & Marx, Inc., 3168 Oak Ave. (Suite #97) paid $2,450 for the vase.
outside reaches	3	Last, he hopes people will analyze all quizzes and express an opinion.
fluency	4	Firms may make the profit they wish if they handle the city's problem.

| 1 | 2 | 3 | 4 | 5 | 6 | 7 | 8 | 9 | 10 | 11 | 12 | 13 | 14 |

123b ▶ 8
Measure straight-copy skill
one 5' writing on ¶s combined; record *gwam* and number of errors (LM p. 3)

Difficulty index

all letters used	A	1.5 si	5.7 awl	80% hfw

gwam 1' | 5'

	1'	5'
Data processing can be divided into three basic steps. First, data	14	3	76
must be obtained or collected. The collected data are called source	27	6	79
documents. Although a source document can vary depending on the needs	42	8	81
of the collector of the data, a common source document may be a cash	55	11	84
register tape, a sales slip, a purchase order, or a time card. Once	69	14	87
the data are obtained, they must be loaded or entered into a data pro-	83	17	90
cessing system (usually a computer). The usual manner of entry into the	98	20	93
system is through a keyboard.	104	21	94
The second basic step is manipulation of the data. Many procedures	14	23	97
may be required to produce an end result, depending on the information	28	26	99
desired and the source documents that have been obtained. The data may	42	29	102
have to be sorted into some logical order, such as a numeric or alpha-	56	32	105
betic list. They may also have to be adjusted into classifications, such	71	35	108
as grouping employee time cards by last name. Calculations using one or	86	38	111
more of the arithmetic functions may have to be performed on the data.	100	41	114
Results may have to be stored temporarily for later use, such as storing	115	44	117
data of an employee's gross pay, retirement deduction, and various taxes	129	47	120
to be used later to compute his or her net pay. Last, the data must be	144	49	123
reduced to a size that can be easily handled.	153	51	124
The third and final operation includes output and storage of the	13	54	127
data. After the data have been manipulated and processed, the results	27	57	130
must be presented in a form that is easily understood. For example, a	41	59	133
printed report of an employee's gross pay with various amounts deducted	56	62	136
for taxes and other deductions may be given to the employee with his or	70	65	138
her paycheck. This printed report is called hard copy. If the results	85	68	141
of the data processing need to be kept for future reference, they may	99	71	144
be stored on tapes, disks, or in the form of hard copy.	110	73	146

gwam 1' | 1 | 2 | 3 | 4 | 5 | 6 | 7 | 8 | 9 | 10 | 11 | 12 | 13 | 14 |
5' | 1 | 2 | 3 |

28

Learning goals

1 To achieve smooth, continuous keystroking.
2 To improve ability to concentrate on copy.
3 To improve proofreading skills.
4 To improve facility with figure and symbol reaches.
5 To type script and rough-draft copy smoothly.

Machine adjustments

1 Set paper guide at 0.
2 Set ribbon control to type on upper half of ribbon.
3 Use 60-space line throughout.
4 SS drills; DS paragraphs.

28a ▶ 7
Preparatory practice

each line three times SS (slowly, faster, still faster); DS between 3-line groups; repeat selected lines if time permits

alphabet 1 My wife helped fix a frozen lock on Jacque's vegetable bins.

difficult reaches 2 Beverly sneezed even though she ate a dozen square lozenges.

figures 3 Do Problems 6 to 19 on page 275 before class at 8:30, May 4.

easy 4 Did the form entitle Jay to the land at the end of the lane?

| 1 | 2 | 3 | 4 | 5 | 6 | 7 | 8 | 9 | 10 | 11 | 12 |

28b ▶ 10
Control machine parts

once as shown DS; repeat if time permits

Lines 1-4: Clear all tabs; set tab at center point; tab and type. Keep eyes on book copy.
Line 5: Supply appropriate spacing after punctuation.
Line 6: Release margin; backspace 5 spaces into left margin to begin.
Line 7: Depress shift/lock keys firmly.

center

1 ⟶ The tab key should be operated

tab and return 2 quickly. ⟶ One quick flick of your finger

3 should suffice. ⟶ Avoid pauses; do not slow down

4 or look up when you tab.

space bar 5 Was it Mary? Judy? Pam? It was a woman; she wore a big hat.

margin release/ backspacer 6 When you type from copy, elevate the copy to make reading easier.

shift/lock 7 Al read A TALE OF TWO CITIES; Vi read THE MILL ON THE FLOSS.

28c ▶ 10
Improve response patterns

1 Once as shown; checkmark the three most difficult lines.
2 Repeat the lines you checked as difficult.
3 Take a 1' writing on Line 2, next on Line 4, and then on Line 6. Determine *gwam* on each writing.

word 1 Did the antique map of the world also hang by the oak shelf?
2 Did they pay the auditor the duty on eighty bushels of corn?

stroke 3 Holly tests fast race cars; we get oil at my garage in Juno.
4 Johnny erected a vast water cascade on my acreage in Joplin.

combination 5 She paid the extra debt and the taxes on their land in Ohio.
6 Lynn sewed the nylon flaps on the six burlap bags with care.

| 1 | 2 | 3 | 4 | 5 | 6 | 7 | 8 | 9 | 10 | 11 | 12 |

Production measurement procedure

For each production measure-ment activity in this section, follow the procedures at the right.

1 Remove whatever stationery is supplied in the laboratory materials (LM); have plain full sheets avail-able, also.

2 Arrange stationery and plain paper in the order of need for completing the jobs.

3 Place correction supplies in a convenient location.

4 When the signal to begin is given, insert paper and make machine adjustments for the first job. Type as many jobs as you can in the time allowed.

5 Proofread each job and make needed corrections before remov-ing it from the typewriter.

6 When time is called, proofread the final job and circle any uncor-rected errors.

7 Compute *n-pram*.

122c ▶ 37
Production measurement: letters and memo

(LM pp. 71–75)

Time schedule

Assembling materials	2'
Timed production	30'
Final check; compute *n-pram*	5'

Job 1
Rough-draft letter (LM p. 71)

AMS style; 1cc; address envelope. Use current date; address the letter to:

Columbia Computers, Inc.
Attention Ms. Karen T. Gammill
7504 Oak Street, N.E.
St. Petersburg, FL 33702-7714

Send the letter **SPECIAL DELIVERY**

Enclosures
CP/M Product List
CP/M Order Forms

cc to **Mr. Roland V. Upchurch**

Job 2
Letter (LM p. 73)

Use the finished copy of Job 1, and retype it in Modified Block style with indented ¶s and mixed punc-tuation. Use subject line and ap-propriate salutation and com-plimentary close; address en-velope. (Add 6 words for salutation and complimentary close.)

words
opening lines 36
43

NEW CP/M SOFTWARE FOR MICROCOMPUTERS

¶ Our company ^*has* recently ~~ly~~ acquired, ^*through a merger,* the ~~good and~~ well-established   58

Joplin Micro Software Company. ~~Because~~ ^*As a result* of the merger, we ^*is*   70
^*now in a position to* offer ~~able~~ to offer ^*our dealers* a much broader range of software packages   88

for nearly all makes and models of microcomputers on the   99

market. ^*today*   102

¶ ^*Now that* Most of the microcomputers have a CP/M based operating system   116

available, we are ^*discovering* ~~finding~~ that more computer users are asking   129

for CP/m based software. As a further advantage of our mer-   141

ger, we are able to offer some very exciting new CP/M programs   154

to meet these requests. ^*Because you are* ~~As~~ one of our preferred ^*dealers* ~~customers~~,   168

we can offer to you--for a 30-day period--^*only* the opportunity to   181

order any CP/M package at an additional 20 percent discount.   193

Our new CP/M product list and special CP/M order forms are   205

enclosed for your convenience ^*in placing your order.*   215

¶ We are ^*confident* ~~sure~~ that you will be ^*completely* satisfied with this new line of   231

CP/M software. ^*As always,* We will ~~continue to~~ appreciate your input as   245

to how we can improve ^*or change a* ~~the~~ product line to better serve our   257

users.   258

CARLOS J. FERNANDES, SALES MANAGER   265

closing lines 280/**305**

Job 3
Memorandum

(LM p. 75)

Prepare the memorandum at the right; address a company mail envelope. (Add 5 words if prepared on plain paper.)

TO: Sylvester Throckmorton, Accounting Supervisor FROM: Virginia Ashton,   13
Director of Training DATE: Current date SUBJECT: Information Processing   24
Seminar   25

(¶) The information processing seminar planned for Friday at 3 p.m. will be held   41
in the Training Room rather than in the Main Floor Seminar Room. Please   55
announce this change to those employees in your department who are planning   71
to attend. xx   73/85

Improve keyboarding continuity

full sheet; DS; 60-space line; 1½″ top margin

1 Prepare the report once, making the corrections designated by the proofreading symbols.

2 Correct any new errors using proofreader's marks.

3 Prepare a final copy from your marked paragraphs; proofread; circle errors.

words

my ARIZONA HIDEAWAY   4

TS

In arizona, there is a small hotel that is locatd near   15
six high green and white mountains. I like it there, for I   27
enjoy the quite of that palce. The morningview is special,   40
and each day there i feel better that I fell the day before.   52

The six mountains are quite high, green just so far up;   63
then they turn white. They reach into the azure beyond like   75
human hands; and when a cloud appears, it seems as if one of   88
the hands has flung a small piece of vapor into the heavens.   100

Rates are excellent. The hotel provides two (2) large-   111
size rooms and a tasty dinner for just $65 daily. The hotel   123
has only 134 rooms; therefore, I call early for reservations   136
when I visit this area--as I did last April 7, 8, 9, and 10.   148

29

Preparatory practice

each line twice SS (slowly, then faster); DS between 2-line groups; 1′ writings on Line 4 as time permits

alphabet	1	Bob realized very quickly that jumping was excellent for us.
fig/sym	2	Ann's 7% note (dated May 23, 1985) was paid at 4690 J Drive.
double letters	3	Will Buzz and Lee carry the supplies across the street soon?
easy	4	He paid for the endowment, and he owns the giant coal field.

| 1 | 2 | 3 | 4 | 5 | 6 | 7 | 8 | 9 | 10 | 11 | 12 |

Improve symbol keyreaches

each line twice SS; DS between 2-line groups; repeat lines that seemed difficult

Keep eyes on copy; keep keystrok-ing smooth and continuous.

'	1	Ray's brother didn't plan for the day's work; it's not done.
-	2	A pay-freeze plan on so-called full-time jobs is well-known.
( )	3	All of us (including Vera) went to the game (and it rained).
"	4	They read the poems "September Rain" and "The Lower Branch."
$	5	His weekly checks totaled $128.35, $96.20, $114.80, and $77.
/	6	The Sr/C Club walked and/or ran 15 1/2 miles in 6 3/4 hours.

Measurement goals

1 To select and organize all needed materials and supplies quickly for efficient use.

2 To plan your work and make machine adjustments efficiently.

3 To complete a maximum number of jobs acceptably (errors neatly corrected) in the production time allowed.

Machine adjustments

1 Set paper guide at *0*.

2 Set ribbon control to use upper half of ribbon.

3 Margins: 70–space line for drills and ¶ writings; as directed (or appropriate) for problems.

4 SS drills lines; DS ¶s; space jobs as directed (or appropriate).

122a ▶ 5

Preparatory practice

each line 3 times SS (slowly, faster, slowly); DS between 3-line groups; repeat selected lines as time permits

alphabet	1	My objectives were analyzed quickly during the corporate proxy fights.
fig/sym	2	June sales for Model #243 are $1,348,602 (15,395 units at $87.60 ea.).
bottom row	3	Mountain climbers examined unexpected phenomena in an amazing crevice.
fluency	4	The visit to the ancient map in the town chapel may amend the problem.

| 1 | 2 | 3 | 4 | 5 | 6 | 7 | 8 | 9 | 10 | 11 | 12 | 13 | 14 |

122b ▶ 8

Measure straight-copy skill

one 5' writing on ¶s combined; record *gwam* and number of errors (LM p. 3)

Difficulty index

all letters used	A	1.5 si	5.7 awl	80% hfw

gwam 1' | 5'

Our modern-day computers are less than forty years old. In this — 13 | 3 | 55
short period of time, three generations of computers have been devel- — 27 | 5 | 58
oped. The first computers were large in size, often filling a whole — 41 | 8 | 61
room; they were hard to run, and if compared to computers today, they — 55 | 11 | 64
were also very slow. Made up of thousands of vacuum tubes, these ma- — 68 | 14 | 66
chines often overheated; and this caused many systems to fail. As a — 82 | 16 | 69
result of these traits, the first computers were not very effective. — 96 | 19 | 72

The next generation of computers was more reliable because of the — 13 | 22 | 75
use of the transistor. These very small and low-heat-producing units — 27 | 25 | 77
took the place of the large vacuum tubes. Because of the transistors, — 42 | 27 | 80
the actual size of the machine was smaller; and more data could be stored — 56 | 30 | 83
in the main storage area. These computers were small, fast, and reli- — 70 | 33 | 86
able; yet, there were still some jobs that would need an even greater — 84 | 36 | 89
reduction in the size of the central processing unit. — 95 | 38 | 91

As a result of our space-age needs, the silicon chip was developed; — 14 | 41 | 94
and the modern-day computer was ushered into being. Thousands of tran- — 28 | 44 | 96
sistors were put in a single one-fourth-inch-square chip, and millions — 42 | 47 | 99
of data items could be held in the central unit. The third generation — 56 | 49 | 102
machines were very small, very fast, and more reliable than the previous — 71 | 52 | 105
generations. — 73 | 53 | 106

gwam 1' | 1 | 2 | 3 | 4 | 5 | 6 | 7 | 8 | 9 | 10 | 11 | 12 | 13 | 14 |
5' | 1 | | 2 | | 3 |

**Develop concentration
with fill-ins**

each line once DS; proofread
and mark with proofreader's
marks any errors you make;
retype from your edited copy

1 Rent in the amount of $185 is payable the 5th of each month.

2 In response, refer to Invoice #187-3 and the date, April 21.

3 Plant seedlings 3 inches deep, 12 inches apart, after May 1.

4 On 3-17-85 Bands 7746-7789 were used to band Canadian geese.

5 Shipments left Dock 15 via Atlantic Express May 29 at 3 p. m.

**Improve response
patterns**

once as shown; repeat if
time permits

Lines 1-2: Say and type each
word as a unit.

Lines 3-4: Spell each word as
you type it letter by letter at a
steady pace.

Lines 5-6: Say and type short,
easy words as units; spell and
type longer words letter by
letter.

word
1 Their goal is to do social work downtown for a city auditor.
2 Did the men cut the eight bushels of corn down by the field?

stroke
3 He acts, in my opinion, as if my cards gave him greater joy.
4 Jimmy deserves my extra reward; few cars ever tested better.

combination
5 Based on my theory, she decreased that quantity of protozoa.
6 They sign with great care several of their formal abstracts.

| 1 | 2 | 3 | 4 | 5 | 6 | 7 | 8 | 9 | 10 | 11 | 12 |

**Improve keystroking
technique**

each line twice SS; DS between 2-line groups; keep
wrists low, eyes on copy

bottom row
1 Did six brave, zany exhibitors and/or bakers climb Mt. Zemb?

home row
2 Sada and Jake had a dish of salad; Gail had a glass of soda.

3d row
3 At her party, a quiet waiter poured tea as I wrote a letter.

figures
4 On June 24, Flight 89 left at 1:30 with 47 men and 65 women.

| 1 | 2 | 3 | 4 | 5 | 6 | 7 | 8 | 9 | 10 | 11 | 12 |

**Measure skill growth:
straight copy**

60-space line; DS

three 1' writings
three 3' writings

Goal:

1'—25 or more *gwam*
3'—21 or more *gwam*

Difficulty index

all letters used	E	1.2 si	5.1 awl	90% hfw

gwam 3'

Do we care about how people judge us? Most of us do. 4 | 26

We hope and expect that other people will recognize quality 8 | 30

in what we do, what we say, and the way we act. Is it not 12 | 34

true, though, that what others think of us results from some 16 | 38

image that we have created in their minds? In other words, 20 | 42

are we not really our own creation? 22 | 44

gwam 3' | 1 | 2 | 3 | 4 |

Supplemental communication activities

Active/passive voice

Each sentence is identified by the voice in which it appears; type each sentence, changing the voice from active to passive or passive to active.

Note: A passive verb is a form of *be* and a past participle. All other verbs are active.

active   1   The First National Bank of Reno, Nevada, employs Ms. Jessica Goldberg.

passive   2   The amounts reported in the report were thoroughly checked by Phillip.

active   3   The students studied the major modern authors in the literature class.

passive   4   The company's annual report was approved by the senior vice president.

passive   5   The new customer was asked by the store manager to return later today.

| 1 | 2 | 3 | 4 | 5 | 6 | 7 | 8 | 9 | 10 | 11 | 12 | 13 | 14 |

Functional punctuation

1 Study the 3 groups of sentences and note the punctuation that is used in each sentence.

2 Type each sentence twice; DS between 4–line groups.

3 Compose 3 sentences, using one of the types of functional punctuation in each sentence.

separate ideas   1   Your instructions were correct, but they were not very well presented.

2   You should plan to leave by six o'clock, and they should leave by ten.

enclose parenthetic expressions   3   The new accounting instructor, Dr. Wilma Williamson, arrives tomorrow.

4   Our letter of June 1 (a copy is attached) should answer the questions.

give special emphasis   5   They need to leave--right now--before another accident happens to her.

6   This textbook--newly revised--is now available at the local bookstore.

Proofreading for meaning

1 Read the paragraphs at the right carefully, noting changes that must be made to correct the material.

2 Type the paragraphs, making the necessary changes as you type.

3 Remove the paper from your machine and proofread, making any additional corrections with proofreader's marks.

4 If necessary, retype the paragraphs, making all corrections.

words

Most of us want to make sure are own well fair is being taken care   13
of properly. This need embraces such items as job security, fringe bene-   28
fits, and final retiremint. Their are dozens of other items that could   42
be listed under personal well fair, but we can cope with these other   55
items if the basic three are covered. Four individuals, personal well   69
fair means more than acquiring the mirror basics of life--food, clothing,   84
and shelter; we also want two be able to afford a few luxuries.   96

Job security, two some, is thought to be the single most criticle   109
item of all on the list. If your do not possess good job security, you   123
may not have adiquate fringe benifits nor a sufficient retiremint pack-   137
age. If you are like mose people, you expect a job that is pleasent and   151
financially rewarding as will; but a good environment is oftimes of more   166
importance than wages too some people. Your hole outlook on life   179
cam be more positive when their is not significant concern about you job   194
security.   196

LEVEL TWO
Formatting/typing basic communications

Let's be elemental. A keyboard is made up of several rows of buttons, or keys, which, when struck, operate your machine. This activity of striking is called keyboarding.

Keyboarding certainly seems commonplace enough. It takes on added meaning when you consider that your keyboard is identical to those used to operate an increasingly large number and variety of technical machines, such as computers, microcomputers, word processors, and electronic typewriters. As part of such equipment, the keyboard becomes the instrument through which are transmitted thoughts and ideas, facts and figures, and all sorts of business, academic, social, and scientific data.

How efficiently any machine functions, of course, depends directly upon how skillfully the operator uses it. Its utility increases in ratio to a user's knowledge about it and ability to operate it rapidly and accurately.

By successfully completing Level 1 work, you have gained ability to keyboard by touch and to enter data attractively on a page. Now you are ready to begin a new level of learning, one in which you will learn to put these important skills to professional use.

You will learn, for example, to format and input personal and business correspondence, tables, data sheets, and reports; and you will gain more experience using printed, rough-draft, and handwritten input materials.

In addition, as you enter the practice and problem data, your keyboarding speed should increase; and, with concentrated effort, your accuracy should also improve.

Learning to keyboard and format with skill is a significant accomplishment. From now on, you should realize that future output from equipment you use depends on the input abilities you develop now.

Build statistical-copy skill

1 One 1' writing for speed on each ¶.
2 Two 3' writings for speed on both ¶s combined. Record *gwam* on (LM p. 3).

all letters/figures used | HA | 1.7 si | 6.0 awl | 75% hfw

	gwam 1'	3'
On October 26, 1985, Americana Consolidated, Inc., requisitioned from	14	5	57
us 30 metric tons of Idaho potatoes. However, the invoice stated 30 tons	29	10	62
at $74 per ton, but the $74 rate is for a regular ton--2,000#; the rate	43	14	67
for a metric ton (2,200#) is $82. Therefore, will you please have the	57	19	71
invoice department make the required changes and issue a new invoice for	72	24	76
the correct amount.	76	25	78
Also, the Jamison Cozy invoice needs to be changed because of an	13	30	82
error in the amount shipped. The purchase order dated October 2, 1985,	27	34	87
requested 760# of cornmeal; the shipping documents examined on October 13	42	39	92
specify that the 760# were shipped by Zippo Express, but the invoice	56	44	96
indicates that only 460# were billed. Please make the necessary changes	71	49	101
and forward Jamison Cozy a copy of the new invoice.	81	52	105

gwam 1' | 1 | 2 | 3 | 4 | 5 | 6 | 7 | 8 | 9 | 10 | 11 | 12 | 13 | 14 |
3' | 1 | 2 | 3 | 4 | 5 |

Build script-copy skill

1 One 1' writing for speed on each ¶.
2 Two 3' writings for speed on both ¶s combined. Record *gwam* on (LM p. 3).

all letters used | A | 1.5 si | 5.7 awl | 80% hfw

	gwam 1'	3'
If a survey were conducted of one hundred individuals	11	4	63
and they were asked whether they had enough time to	21	7	67
perform all the duties on their schedules, the answer from	33	11	71
the vast majority of people would probably be a resounding	45	15	75
no. This situation becomes critical when we realize that	56	19	78
few people have adequate time; yet everyone has all the	68	23	82
time that is available. Because all people have an	78	26	86
equal amount of time, the problem becomes not how much	89	30	89
time they have but how effectively they use time.	99	33	93
At some point, most people come to realize that time is	11	37	96
a valuable resource. It cannot be accumulated like	22	40	100
money or stockpiled like raw materials. People are forced	33	44	104
to spend time at a definite rate of sixty seconds every	45	48	107
minute. Time cannot be turned on and off like a	54	51	111
machine or used like a thing. Time is irretrievable.	65	55	114
The only control people can exercise over it is to	75	58	118
allocate it carefully.	80	60	119

30

Learning goals

1 To prepare personal letters in block style.
2 To correct keyboarding errors.
3 To improve ability to keyboard unedited copy.
4 To address envelopes.
5 To align and type over words.

Machine adjustments

1 Position desk and chair at comfortable heights.
2 Elevate book.
3 Set ribbon control to type on upper half of ribbon.
4 Use 60–space line for drills; 50–space line for letters.
5 SS drills; DS paragraphs.
Materials: Monarch–size sheets and envelopes; plain sheets; supplies for correcting errors.

30a ▶ 7
Preparatory practice

each line 3 times SS (slowly, faster, slower); DS between 3-line groups; repeat if time permits

alphabet 1 Jayne Coxx puzzled over the workbooks required for geometry.

a/s 2 This essay says it is easy to save us from disaster in Asia.

figures 3 The box is 6 5/8 by 9 1/2 feet and weighs 375 to 400 pounds.

easy 4 The city auditor paid the proficient man for the fine signs.

| 1 | 2 | 3 | 4 | 5 | 6 | 7 | 8 | 9 | 10 | 11 | 12 |

30b ▶ 43
Prepare personal letters in block style

7¼″ × 10½″ personal stationery [Laboratory Materials pp. 17-19]; 50-space line; 2″ top margin; proofread/circle errors

If personal–size stationery or plain paper cut to size is not available, use full sheets (8½″ × 11″); 50–space line; 2½″ top margin.

1 Study the explanatory paragraphs at the right. Refer to the style letter on page 59 for further illustration.
2 Prepare the letter illustrating the block style shown on page 59. Follow spacing directions given on the letter.
3 On a plain full sheet, do two 1′ writings on the opening lines (return address through salutation) and two 2′ writings on the closing lines (last 3 ¶s through complimentary close).
4 Retype the letter; omit ¶3.

Letter placement information

Many personal letters are prepared on personal-size stationery (Monarch); and Style Letter 1, page 59, is shown with pica (10-pitch) type on that size stationery.

Good letter placement results from the ability to make judgments based on the length of letter, style of stationery, and size of type. Therefore, while it is suggested that letters in Section 7 be started on Line 13 when personal stationery is used (which allows approximately a 2″ top margin) or on Line 16 if full sheets are used (approximately a 2½″ top margin), the starting point can be raised for a longer letter or lowered for a shorter one if you believe it is wise to do so.

Every letter must have a return address. On business stationery, the return address is part of the letterhead. When personal stationery is used, a return address must be typed as part of the letter. The most appro-

priate place for this address, according to common usage, is on the two lines immediately above and aligned with the date.

It is standard procedure to operate the return 4 times, leaving 3 blank line spaces between the date and the letter recipient's address. This procedure is repeated after the complimentary close, leaving 3 blank line spaces for the signature to be written between the complimentary close and the writer's typed name. (For a personal letter, a typed name is not necessary.) These placement procedures should be followed with all letters in Section 7.

For smaller personal stationery, side margins should be no less than 1″ and no more than 1½″. A 50-space line, pica or elite, fits within this standard. It is recommended, therefore, that a 50-space line be used with Section 7 letters regardless of type size.

Supplemental skill-building practice

Build rough-draft copy skill

1 One 1' writing for accuracy.

2 Two 3' writings for accuracy; record *gwam* and number of errors for more accurate writing (LM p. 3).

Difficulty index

	A	1.5 si	5.7 awl	80% hfw
all letters used				

	gwam 1'	3'	

On display at several of the offices ^in our city is a small sign that — 14 | 5 | 54

displays a very important ~~message~~ *word*. The sign says ~~appropriately~~ *quite simply* — 26 | 9 | 58

"think." Busy workers quickly look at the sign, and it is inter- — 40 | 13 | 63

esting to ~~wander if~~ *conjecture that maybe* the sign^s says something a little bit differ- — 55 | 18 | 68

ent to every (one). *who reads it* to some, for example, it might ~~say~~ *portend that* they should — 73 | 24 | 74

exercise greater caution in their work; to others, it offer^s *could* the — 87 | 29 | 79

encouragement to attack ^*a pressing* problem^s that need^s solving; ~~another~~ group *while a third* — 103 | 34 | 84

might ~~think~~ *interpret* it to be a note of stimulation^ *to expand creativity*. That a five-letter — 121 | 40 | 90

wor^d printed on a sign could, like a tiny, mystical beacon, flash — 134 | 45 | 94

^*an individualized* a message to all who read it, is itself thought provoking. — 149 | 50 | 99

Build straight-copy skill

1 One 1' writing for accuracy on each ¶.

2 Two 5' writings for accuracy on both ¶s combined. Record *gwam* and number of errors for more accurate writing (LM p. 3).

Difficulty index

	A	1.5 si	5.7 awl	80% hfw
all letters used				

	gwam 1'	5'	

In the years ahead, the office must be planned for flexibility of — 13 | 3 | 55

space, furniture, and equipment. The time has passed when the needs and — 28 | 6 | 57

demands of the office setting could be predicted for a decade. The of- — 42 | 8 | 61

fice must be designed to enable it to be adjusted quickly and efficiently — 57 | 11 | 64

to any change that might come, whether that change be some progress in — 71 | 14 | 67

high technology or some new technique. Most of the changes that come — 85 | 17 | 70

may impact on space needs, on related needs for furniture and equipment, — 100 | 20 | 72

or on both. Perhaps one of the better approaches to office layout is — 114 | 23 | 75

the new open architectural concept; this is an approach that uses por- — 128 | 26 | 78

table walls to separate the office into its designated areas. — 140 | 28 | 81

Also, the office of the future must provide for modular office fur- — 13 | 31 | 83

niture. Whenever the office layout needs to be changed, there is a cor- — 28 | 34 | 86

responding need to be sure that the office furniture will continue to be — 42 | 37 | 89

functional in the new space arrangement. The office furniture that will — 57 | 39 | 92

most surely continue to be useful for decades to come will be those items — 72 | 42 | 95

that can be made to fit the size of any new office layout that is re- — 86 | 45 | 98

quired. The trend also may be to increase the number of leases for high — 100 | 48 | 101

technology equipment; to lease equipment is one method of hedging against — 115 | 51 | 103

the high probability of obsolescence. — 122 | 53 | 105

gwam 1'	1	2	3	4	5	6	7	8	9	10	11	12	13	14
5'		1				2				3				

Shown in pica type
50–space line

Return
address
Dateline

101 Kensington Place   Line 13
Brockton, MA 02401-5372
August 3, 19-- 2 spaces

Operate return
4 times

Letter
address

Ms. Viola Bargas
6776 Heidelberg Street
Durham, NC 27704-4329
                    DS

Salutation

Dear Viola
        DS

Body
of
letter

It will be great to have you living in Brockton
again. Your promotion to vice-president of the
marketing division is certainly well deserved.

You will find that our town has changed considerably since your last visit three years ago. It is
still a small, close-knit community; but the newly
established Arts Commission has begun to promote
the efforts of many local artists. As a result,
our little village has taken on a bohemian air.

Let me show you one way that Brockton has changed.
I should like you to be my guest on August 23 when
the local theater group presents SCHOOL FOR SCANDAL
at the Whitmore Playhouse. Two of our sorority
members are directing the production.

As you requested, I shall meet you at the airport
(Gate 11) on August 23 at 8:25 a.m. You can spend
the afternoon apartment hunting, and you can relax
in the evening during dinner and the play.

I am very eager to see you, Viola!
                              DS

Complimentary
close
Signature

Cordially

Amanda

This letter is typed with
"open" punctuation; that is,
no punctuation follows the
salutation or complimentary
close.

Style letter 1: personal letter in block style

gwam 1' (total words)	gwam 2'
4	
9	
12	
15	
20	
25	
27	
36	
46	
55	
65	
75	
86	
95	
105	
115	
125	5
135	10
146	15
155	20
163	24
173	29
183	34
193	39
202	44
209	47
211	48

Mr. Riech's assistant has prepared a rough draft of the Chula
Vista balance sheet. Mr. Murtha
gives you this draft and asks you
to prepare the final copy for the
audit report.

First column indentions are
the same as for the other statements you have prepared. Place
8 spaces between Columns 1
and 2, and 2 spaces between
Columns 2 and 3.

CHULA VISTA MANUFACTURING, INC.

Balance Sheet

December 31, 19--

add remaining leaders

Assets

Current assets:		$ 27,150
Cash		
Accounts receivable	$ 57,056	
Less allowance for bad debts	9,346	47,710
Inventories		
Raw materials	$ 16,822	
Work in process	7,477	
Finished goods	39,299	63,598
Prepaid expenses		
Factory supplies on hand	$ 3,738	
Office supplies on hand	1,869	
Prepaid insurance	935	6,542
Total current assets		$ 145,000
Long-term assets:		
Machinery and equipment	$ 105,240	
Less accumulated depreciation	24,299	80,941
Total assets		$ 225,941

Liabilities and Stockholders' Equity

Current liabilities:		
Accounts payable		$ 6,542
Wages payable		9,346
Interest payable		935
Income taxes payable		15,888
Total current liabilities		$ 32,711
Long-term notes payable		
(9%, due 5 years hence)		37,383
Total liabilities		$ 70,094
Stockholders' equity:		
Common stock, $10 par value,		
authorized and issued:		
10,000 shares	$ 100,000	
Retained earnings	55,847	155,847
Total liabilities and		
stockholders' equity		$ 225,941

31a ▶ 7
Preparatory practice

each line 3 times SS (slowly, faster, slower); DS between 2-line groups; then as many 30″ writings on Line 4 as time permits

Goal: Finish Line 4 in 30″.

alphabet	1	Max Jurez worked to improve the quality of his basic typing.
adjacent reaches	2	Bert quickly pointed to where onions grew in the sandy soil.
fig/sym	3	Veronica bought 16 7/8 yards of #240 cotton at $3.59 a yard.
easy	4	The formal gowns worn by the girls hang in the civic chapel.

| 1 | 2 | 3 | 4 | 5 | 6 | 7 | 8 | 9 | 10 | 11 | 12 |

31b ▶ 15
Correct errors

1 Read the information at the right.

2 Keyboard the lines below the information exactly as they appear DS; correct the errors *after* you have typed each line.

Truly finished work contains no errors. Most individuals rely upon an "inner sense" to tell them when they have made an error, and they stop keyboarding at once and correct it. This "inner sense," however, is fallible; and even an expert typist should carefully proofread completed work for undetected mistakes while the paper is still in the machine. Correcting errors before the paper is removed is easier than reinserting paper and trying to realign lines of copy.

There are several acceptable methods that can be used to correct errors, and they are explained below. Whichever one of them is used, one should keep in mind that an error must be repaired skillfully enough so that neither the error nor evidence of the correction can be observed.

Automatic correction

If your machine is equipped with an automatic correcting ribbon, consult with your instructor or the manufacturer's manual for operating instructions.

Correction paper ("white carbon")

1 Backspace to the error.

2 Place the correction paper in front of the error, coated side toward the paper.

3 Retype the error. The substance on the correction paper will cover the error.

4 Remove the correction paper; backspace; type the correction.

Correction fluid ("liquid paper")

1 Be sure the color of the fluid matches the color of the paper.

2 Turn the paper forward or backward to ease the correction process.

3 Brush the fluid on sparingly; cover only the error, and it lightly.

4 The fluid dries quickly. Return to correction point and make the correction.

Rubber eraser

1 Use a plastic shield (to protect surrounding type) and a typewriter (hard) eraser.

2 Turn the paper forward or backward in the typewriter to position the error for easier correction.

3 To keep bits of rubber out of the mechanism, move the carrier away from the error (or move carriage to the extreme left or right).

4 With a sharp edge of the eraser, erase ink from the paper. Move the eraser in one direction only to avoid cutting the paper.

1 Concentrate when you type; fongers can "telegraph" an error.

2 Just as soon as a mistade is made, it ought to be corrected.

3 It pays to be sure that you find evrey error and correct it.

4 Proofread carefully; then remove your work from the nachine.

Job 6
Payroll report with braced heading (full sheet)

Mr. Murtha has finished the weekly payroll for the week of January 11–15. He has made a draft of the payroll report that he must submit to Ms. Skopec each Friday before the checks are signed by her. He asks that you prepare the final copy of this payroll report. If you have any questions about how to do a braced heading, refer to the Office Procedures Manual (see the excerpt on page 245).

As a temporary office worker, you are paid directly by OSTI; therefore, you are not included on the regular payroll report.

Center the table in reading position; allow 4 spaces between columns and an extra ½″ in the left margin for binding purposes.

DENISE SKOPEC, CPA
Payroll Report
Week of January 11–15, 19--

| Name | Gross Pay | Deductions | | Net Pay |
		F.I.T.	F.I.C.A.	
Stanley Riech	480.75	65.00	33.65	382.10
Rosetta Lopez	423.00	78.00	29.61	315.39
Jose Murtha	288.00	28.00	20.16	239.84
Stella Dernovich	250.00	32.00	17.50	200.50
Jimmy Woo	180.00	18.00	12.60	149.40
Totals	1,621.75	221.00	113.52	1,287.23

Job 7
Auditor's opinion statement (full sheet)

Mr. Riech has just completed his audit of Chula Vista Manufacturing, Inc. He has submitted the entire audit report in draft form to Mr. Murtha to be processed. Mr. Murtha hands you a copy of the standard unqualified opinion statement that is used for all audits that do not have to be qualified in any way.

Prepare this statement in the form of a letter; use **December 31** as the examination date in the body of the letter. Date the letter **January 14, 19—**, and address it to:

Mr. Walter P. Lewis, Chairperson
Chula Vista Manufacturing, Inc.
1035 Del Mar Avenue
Chula Vista, CA 92011-3115

This letter will be bound in the client's audit report; therefore, leave an additional ½″ in the left margin for binding.

UNQUALIFIED OPINION STATEMENT

We have examined the balance sheet of the _____ _____ (a California corporation) as of _____, 19___, and the related statements of earnings and retained earnings and changes in financial position for the year then ended. Our examination was made in accordance with generally accepted auditing standards and, accordingly, included such tests of the accounting records and such other auditing procedures as we considered necessary in the circumstances.

In our opinion, the accompanying financial statements referred to above present fairly the financial position of the _____ as of _____, 19___, and the results of their operations and changes in their financial position for the year then ended, in conformity with generally accepted accounting principles applied during the period.

31c ▶ 28
Personal letters in block style

3 personal-size sheets [LM pp. 21-25] or plain paper; see pages 58 and 59 for guides to letter placement; proofread/correct errors

Postal authorities recommend using 2–letter state abbreviations (always with ZIP Code). For a complete list of such abbreviations, see the Reference Guide, p. iv at the back of this book.

Personal titles

As a courtesy to the person to whom a letter is addressed, a letter writer may use a personal or professional title—Miss, Mr., Dr., etc.—with the name in the letter address and on the envelope.

A letter writer, if male, does not ordinarily give himself a title in the signature lines. A female writer, however, may properly use a title before her typed name or, when she writes it, in parentheses before her signature to indicate her preference.

Problem 1

words

900 Beecher Street | Montgomery, AL 36108-4473 | May 18, 19-- | 12
(Operate return 4 times) | Mr. Lymon S. Bohn | 890 Crestview   18
Drive | Rockford, IL 61107-2317 | DS | Dear Lymon | DS   26

(¶) This morning I talked with Debra Tredsaw, a member of the   38
school reunion committee; and I heard a bit of great news--that   51
you plan to attend our class reunion next month.   61

(¶) More great news! Herb Dobynski will also be here, and he   72
and I want to play a little golf that afternoon. Can you arrange   85
to be in town early enough to join us? Maybe I can persuade   98
Jimmy Geddes or Ted Oxward to make it a foursome.   108

(¶) Let me know when you are arriving, Lymon. I'll be glad to   120
pick you up at the airport or to make any other arrangements for   133
you.   133

Cordially | (Operate return 4 times) | Mike Stavros   138

Problem 2

890 Crestview Drive | Rockford, IL 61107-2317 | May 25, 19-- | Mr.   12
Michael Stavros | 900 Beecher Street | Montgomery, AL 36108-   24
4473 | Dear Mike   26

(¶) I do indeed plan to attend the Monroe High reunion of the   38
Class of '78. I wouldn't miss it--nor would I pass up a chance to   51
give you and Herb a drubbing on the golf course.   61

(¶) The trip to Montgomery will also involve taking care of some   74
business. I shall drive down, arriving there during the late   86
afternoon or early evening of the 16th. I have made reserva-   98
tions at the Graymoor for three days. I'll call you when I get in.   112

(¶) I'm really looking forward to this trip, Mike, and to the oppor-   125
tunity to visit many old friends.   131

Cordially | Lymon Bohn   135

Problem 3

900 Beecher Street | Montgomery, AL 36108-4473 | May 27, 19-- | 11
Mr. Herbert Dobynski | 8098 Fairwater Drive | Norfolk, VA   23
23508-6172 | Dear Herb   27

(¶) I have tried to reach you several times by phone, but I have   39
not been successful; hence, this brief note.   48

(¶) Lymon Bohn has confirmed that he'll be in town for the re-   60
union on June 17, and he has agreed to join us for golf that after-   73
noon. Ted Oxward will also join us.   81

(¶) Because I expect things might be hectic at my club that day,   93
I called the pro, Jill Nyles, today and asked her to save us a   105
tee-off time of 1 p.m. If for any reason this time is not good   118
for you, let me know.   123

Cordially | Mike Stavros   127

Job 4
Income statement (full sheet)

Mr. Murtha assigns you to con-tinue finalizing the financial statements for Nick's TV Service. You are handed the income statement form to process, which will be part of the final bound audit report. Follow the specific markings on the form. Indentions in the first column are the same as the indentions used for the balance sheet in Job 3. Place 8 spaces between Col-umns 1 and 2, and 2 spaces be-tween Columns 2 and 3. Place the two depreciation expense items on 2 lines each (be sure to indent the second line an additional 3 spaces). Remember to allow an extra ½-inch in the left margin for binding purposes.

NICK'S TV SERVICE

Income Statement

For the Year Ended December 31, 19--
TS

Income:

Service fees $61,205
TS

Operating expenses:

Rent expense $ 4,800

Wages expense   10,964

SS   Advertising expense   602

Depreciation expense-- delivery truck   1,205

Depreciation expense-- testing equipment 598

Utilities expense   964
Delivery expense   2,048
Supplies and parts expense   4,578

DS   Total operating expenses   25,759

DS   Net income for the year $35,446

Job 5
Statement of owner's equity
(full sheet)

Mr. Murtha still has one of Nick's TV Service statements yet to be processed. He asks you to process it following the same basic procedures as in the previ-ous two statements. In this statement, place 10 spaces be-tween the 2 columns.

NICK'S TV SERVICE

Statement of Owner's Equity   <DS
For the Year Ended December 31, 19--   <TS

Nicholas Dominic, capital
    January 1, 19-- $25,000

Add: <DS
    Capital contributed this year
    Net income for year   DS >   35,446
                                         $60,446

                                           <DS
Less:
    Capital withdrawn during year   26,400
                                           <DS
Nicholas Dominic, capital
    December 31, 19-- $34,046

32a ▶ 7
Preparatory practice

each line 3 times SS
(slowly, faster, still faster);
DS between 3-line groups;
repeat if time permits

alphabet 1 Perry might know I feel jinxed because I have missed a quiz.

figures 2 Buy 147 fish, 25 geese, 10 ponies, 39 lambs, and 68 kittens.

hyphen 3 He won the first-class ribbon; it was a now-or-never effort.

easy 4 The neighbor owns a fox, six foals, six ducks, and six hens.

| 1 | 2 | 3 | 4 | 5 | 6 | 7 | 8 | 9 | 10 | 11 | 12 |

32b ▶ 10
Align and type

It is sometimes necessary to rein-sert the paper to correct an error. The following steps will help you learn to do so correctly.

1 Type this sentence, but do not make the return:

I can align this copy.

2 Locate aligning scale (16), variable line spacer (2), and paper release lever (13) on your machine.

3 Move the carrier (carriage) so that a word containing an i (such as align) is above the align-

ing scale. Note that a vertical line points to the center of i.

4 Study the relation between top of aligning scale and bottoms of letters with downstems (g,p,y).

Get an exact eye picture of the relation of typed line to top of scale so you will be able to adjust the paper correctly to type over a character with exactness.

5 Remove paper; reinsert it. Gauge the line so bottoms of let-ters are in correct relation to top of aligning scale. Operate the vari-able line spacer, if necessary, to move paper up or down. Operate paper release lever to move paper left or right, if necessary, when centering the letter i over one of the lines on the aligning scale.

6 Check accuracy of alignment by setting the ribbon control (28) in stencil position and by typing over one of the letters. If necessary, make further alignment adjust-ments.

7 Return ribbon control to normal position (to type on upper half of ribbon).

8 Type over the characters in the sentence, moving paper up or down, to left or right, as necessary to correct alignment.

32c ▶ 13
Personal letter in block style

1 personal-size sheet [LM p. 27] or plain paper; SS ¶s; DS between ¶s; proofread/correct errors

1 Format the letter at the right, making corrections as marked.

2 For special parts, use:

Return address and date

334 Pittman Street
Olathe, KS 66061-1678
March 22, 19--
Letter address

Miss Evelyn Guione
1352 Pilgrim Place
Pasadena, CA 91108-3307

Salutation **Dear Evelyn**

Closing lines

Sincerely
(Return 4 times)
Trevor Hunter

	words
opening lines	26

As I told you I might, I have changed my plans. I shall be 38

taking three morning classes there at the University during 52

July and august. 55

My expenses would be eased considerably if I could find a 67

part-time job where I might work afternoons or evenings. 78

So would you be kind enough to let me know if you would 89

learn of such a position? May I use your name if I make the 104

application? 106

I value you friendship Evelyn; and I shall be very gratful 119

for any assistnce that you may provide. 127

| closing lines | 129 |

Ms. Lopez has just completed the year–end closing and financial statements for Nick's TV Service, an accounting service client. Whenever possible, financial statement forms have been prepared to make the accountant's job a little easier. Ms. Lopez has filled in the financial statement forms and submitted them to Mr. Murtha for final processing. You have been assigned to prepare the balance sheet and put it in final form. Ms. Lopez has indicated on the form for you to use leaders.

Mr. Murtha reminds you that all financial statements are bound in a report for the client. Therefore, all financial statements have an extra ½–inch in the left margin for binding purposes. Use a 1″ top margin for all statements that are to be bound in a report; use center point for a leftbound report. Indent items at intervals of 3 spaces. SS the body of the document, unless otherwise indicated. Leave 4 spaces between Columns 1 and 2 and 2 spaces between Columns 2 and 3. Correct any undetected errors you may find.

DS {

NICK'S TV SERVICE

Balance Sheet

For the Year Ended December 31, 19--

TS

Add remaining leaders

Assets
DS

Cash		$15,227
Accounts receivable		2,915
Supplies and parts on hand		1,235
Testing equipment	$5,250	
Less accumulated deprecation	1,794	3,456
Delivery truck	17,500	
Less accumulated depreciation	3,012	14,488
DS> Total assets		$37,321

TS
Liabilities

Accounts payable	$2,230	
Utilities	85	
Wages payable	225	
Service fees unearned	735	
DS> Total liabilities		$3,275

Owner's Equity

Nicholas Dominic, capital		34,046
DS> Total liabilities and owner's equity		$37,321

32d ▶ 12
Address envelopes

1 Addressing envelopes is entirely a matter of visual placement. Read the following guides and study the illustrations to help you with the placement of addresses.

2 Type in United States Postal Service (U.S.P.S.) style a Monarch envelope (No. 9) and in standard style a small envelope (No. 6¾) for each address [LM pp. 29–33]. Use your own return address; proof-read/circle errors.

Letter address

Vertically: Visualize a line drawn from side to side across the verti-cal center of the envelope. Begin the first line of the address just below such an imaginary line.

Horizontally: Visualize a line drawn from top to bottom across the horizontal center of the en-velope. Align an address from 5 (for larger envelopes) to 10 (for smaller envelopes) spaces to the left of such an imaginary line.

Return address

Type the writer's name and ad-dress SS in block style in the upper left corner. Start about 3 spaces from the left edge on Line 2.

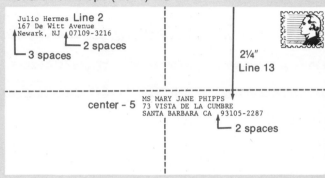

Monarch envelope (No. 9) 7½" × 4"

Small envelope (No. 6¾) 6½" × 3⅝"

The envelope above is typed in ALL CAPS with no punctuation, the form recommended by the U.S. Postal Service.

Mrs. Arthur T. Werther
1321 Fairbanks Road
Concord, NH 03301-1789

Miss Grace Carveck
35 Fox Mill Lane
Springfield, IL 62707-7133

Mr. Brett Reymer
94 Mercer Street
Paterson, NJ 07524-5447

32e ▶ 8
Fold and insert letters

Study the illustrations below. Practice folding 8½" × 11" paper for small envelopes and 7¼" × 10½" paper for Monarch en-velopes.

The folding procedure for Monarch envelopes is also used for large (No. 10) business en-velopes.

Folding and inserting letters into small envelopes

Step 1
With letter face up, fold bottom up to ½ inch from top.

Step 2
Fold right third to left.

Step 3
Fold left third to ½ inch from last crease.

Step 4
Insert last creased edge first.

Folding and inserting letters into Monarch envelopes

Step 1
With letter face up, fold slightly less than ⅓ of sheet up toward top.

Step 2
Fold down top of sheet to within ½ inch of bottom fold.

Step 3
Insert letter into envelope with last crease toward bottom of envelope.

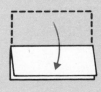
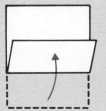

Office job simulation
(LM p. 63)

Job 1
Confirmation of audit visit
(LM p. 63)

For your first keyboarding job, Ms. Skopec hands you a hand-written draft of a letter she has written in order to confirm an audit visit to Office Interiors, Inc.

Date the letter **January 11** and address it to
Ms. Constance Pettiford, President
Office Interiors, Inc.
2385 Broadway
San Diego, CA 92102-3306

Ms. Skopec requests that you prepare a photocopy (pc) for Mr. Stanley Riech. She also wants her name and title typed as follows on all letters:
MS. DENISE SKOPEC, CPA

CONFIRMATION OF AUDIT VISIT

Mr. Stanley Riech, our Senior Auditor, and I will begin the annual audit of your financial records at 9:00 a.m. on Monday, January 21. Our schedule is to spend five working days at your office.

To assist us in being as efficient as possible, will you please do the following prior to our arrival:
1. Arrange for us to have a private office with two desks and a telephone.
2. Notify all officers and employees who need to know of our visit.
3. Complete all year-end financial statements.

If there are any problems with the planned audit dates or in completing needed financial statements, please notify our office as soon as possible.

Job 2
Simplified Memo (plain full sheet)

Ms. Skopec has assigned you to be supervised by Office Manager Jose Murtha. In order to clarify workload assignments, Ms. Skopec has drafted a memo to be sent to Stanley Riech, Senior Auditor, and Rosetta Lopez, Senior Accountant. You have been asked to prepare the simplified memo in final form. Date the memo **January 11, 19—**. Use the subject line: **TEMPORARY OFFICE WORKER EMPLOYED.** Correct any undetected errors that Ms. Skopec may have missed.

I have contracted with office Service Temporaries, Inc., to provide ʌ*us with* a temporary ofice worker for ʌ *the next* six days. This new employee ʌ *is* (insert your name). (She/He) has ʌ *excellent* keyboarding and formating skills and should be of great *assistance* ʌ help to us during our peak ʌ *workload* period.

I have asked our Office Manager, Jose Murtha, to supervise the workload of this ʌ *temporary office* worker. Please continue to submit all keyboarding work ʌ *directly* to Jose for processing.

Improve keystroking technique

60-space line; type 2 times SS; DS between 3-line groups

Technique hint:

Concentrate on each word as you type it.

direct reaches
1 ice cede gun herb deck mute nut shy grunt hunt hymn jump sun
2 Cecelia Haynes and John Lunce hunt in Greece every December.
3 A group of shy, hungry gnus munched on green jungle grasses.

adjacent reaches
4 folk three lion port trite quit pods ankle oil yule were art
5 Opal is prepared to buy gas and oil for her sporty roadster.
6 Tio has a new poncho for sale; it has beading and silk trim.

double letters
7 door veer err skiing lass committee odd off all success inns
8 Ella successfully crossed the creek at the foot of the hill.
9 Deer need access to green grass, weeds, and trees in summer.

Reach for new goals

1 Take a 1' writing on ¶1. Note your *gwam* base rate.

2 Add 4 words to base rate to set a new goal. Note your ¼' subgoals below.

3 Take a ½' writing on ¶1, guided by ¼' guide call. Try to reach your ¼' goal as each guide is called.

4 Take a 1' writing on ¶1, guided by ¼' guide call. Try to reach your ¼' goal as each guide is called.

5 Take two more ½' and two more 1' writings as directed above. If you reach your 1' goal, set a new one.

6 Type ¶2 as directed in 1–5.

7 Take a 3' writing on both ¶s without the call of the guide.

gwam	¼'	½'	¾'	Time
16	4	8	12	16
20	5	10	15	20
24	6	12	18	24
28	7	14	21	28
32	8	16	24	32
36	9	18	27	36
40	10	20	30	40
44	11	22	33	44
48	12	24	36	48

Difficulty index

all letters used	LA	1.4 si	5.4 awl	85% hfw

gwam 3'

Who is happier, a person with much education or one with little? 4

Which of the two is better adjusted, more satisfied, and better able to 9

realize goals? These are not easy questions. Education is no magic 14

elixir. It is only a tool that can help us to use knowledge to win out 19

over problems. The answer lies in how we use that tool. 22

Education will not bring about happiness any more than a hammer will 27

bring about a house. Yet we can use what we learn, through experience as 32

well as through school, to build the kind of lifestyle that will enable 37

us to recognize those values that have great significance for us. We can 41

use them in our best judgment to find the satisfaction we all seek. 46

gwam 3' | 1 | 2 | 3 | 4 | 5 |

Learning goals

1 To develop knowledge about and skills in preparing accounting documents.

2 To become familiar with the various tasks performed in an accounting office.

3 To plan your work efficiently and to complete it correctly.

Machine adjustments

1 Paper guide at *0*.

2 Ribbon control set to use upper half of ribbon.

3 Margins: 70–space line for drills; as appropriate for letters, memorandums, reports, and tables.

4 Space job tasks as directed (or appropriate).

Office Job Simulation

Before you begin the jobs of Section 39, read carefully the material at the right.

Make appropriate notes of any procedures that will save you time as you complete the job activities of this accounting office simulation.

Daily practice plan:

Preparatory practice .... 5'
Work on simulation .... 45'

Work Assignment

You have been assigned by Office Service Temporaries, Inc., to work for Ms. Denise Skopec, a certified public accountant who heads an accounting firm in Chula Vista. Her address is 633 Alpine Avenue, Chula Vista, CA 92010-3040.

Ms. Skopec's office procedures manual specifies that all letters are to be prepared using the AMS simplified letter style. All financial statements are to be bound, unless otherwise indicated. Therefore, leave an extra ½" in the left margin for these financial statements. All documents are to be photocopied; thus, no carbon copies are required to be made of any work done in the office. All work must be proofread carefully and all errors corrected before removing the document from the machine.

Ms. Skopec has based her office procedures manual on COLLEGE KEYBOARDING/TYPEWRITING, so use the Reference Guide and the index of your textbook to look up matters of style and placement when in doubt. When a job requires unusual specifications, she provides them in "Excerpts from the Office Procedures Manual."

When specific job instructions are given, follow them carefully. When specific instructions are not given, make appropriate decisions on the basis of your knowledge and experience. If Ms. Skopec (or your teacher) considers some of your decisions unacceptable, learn from her or his suggestions—just as you would do in any business office.

Excerpts from Office Procedures Manual

Braced Headings. A heading which is centered over 2 or more columns is called a braced heading. This type of heading is found generally in a table that has both horizontal and vertical rulings. However, a braced heading is sometimes used both in a ruled table or in a simple table that has no rulings.

In a table with horizontal rulings, a braced heading will be found within the column heading area—between the double ruling below the main heading and the single ruling below the column headings. Generally, the braced heading is separated from the column headings (or another braced heading) by a horizontal ruling.

As a rule, double-space above and below the double horizontal ruling which follows the main heading. Single-space above and double-space below a single horizontal ruling.

The illustration below shows the placement of a braced heading.

	INVENTORY REPORT				
	DS			DS	
Stock No.	Received*		Shipped*	SS DS	Balance on Hand
	Date	Qty	Date	Qty SS	

*braced heading

118a-121a ▶ 5

Preparatory practice

Type as many times as you can in 5' at the beginning of each class period in this section.

alphabet **1** My exceedingly well-known jazz quintet plays before the lively groups.

fig/sym **2** Sales this year are up 10.6% ($229,872) from $2,168,603 to $2,398,475.

direct reach **3** My brother, the grocer, often hums a tune as he unpacks the groceries.

fluency **4** The quantity of fish at my lake may also be a problem for the visitor.

| 1 | 2 | 3 | 4 | 5 | 6 | 7 | 8 | 9 | 10 | 11 | 12 | 13 | 14 |

Supplemental communication activities

Spelling

70-space line; decide size of paper (full or half sheet), top margin (1″, 1½″, or 2″), and spacing (SS or DS)

1 Clear tab stops; set two new tab stops, one 29 spaces from left margin and one 58 spaces from left margin.

2 Type the first word at left margin as shown; tab and type the word again; then tab and type it a third time, this time without looking at the word in the book or on the paper.

3 Repeat this procedure for each word on the list. Proofread care–fully; correct errors.

4 Use the completed copy as a study list and for future reference.

5 Make comments about your placement decisions on the bot–tom of your typed copy.

SPELLING DEMONS

absence	absence	absence
accumulate		
already		
benefited		
convenience		
develop		
embarrass		
guarantee		
judgment		
likable		
noticeable		
parallel		
receive		
seize		

Capitalization

full sheet; 70-space line; DS; 1½″ top margin; set a tab 5 spaces to right of center point

1 Keyboard the data as shown; tab to type each example.

2 Proofread carefully and correct errors.

3 Study each line and its example from your copy.

Note: Some literary titles may be underlined or shown in all capital letters.

USING CAPITAL LETTERS

		words
		4
	TS	
Capitalize		9
the first word of a complete sentence:	She put the car in the garage.	23
the first word of a direct quotation:	Tio said, "That is my valise."	37
titles that precede personal names:	Introduce me to Senator Reese.	50
main words in literary titles:	I saw Anne of a Thousand Days.	67
adjectives derived from proper nouns:	We always enjoy Italian opera.	81
weekdays, months, and holidays:	Sunday, April 1, isn't Easter.	94
political and military organizations:	The Democrat left by Navy jet.	109
names of specific persons or places:	Jo jogs daily in Central Park.	123
nouns followed by identifying numbers:	They were assigned to Room 14.	137
	TS	
Do not capitalize		144
compass directions not part of a name:	I drive due north to Leesport.	158
a page if followed by a number:	Did he quote Milton on page 9?	171
a title that follows a name:	LeCare is captain of the ship.	183
commonly accepted derivatives:	Put french toast on the china.	196
geographic names made plural:	I sail on Moon and Fish lakes.	209
seasons (unless personified):	Sweet Summer gave way to fall.	221
generic names of products:	Try Magic Mugg instant coffee.	232

Job 10
Prepare an invoice (LM p. 59)

Ms. Fillmore hands you an order taken by one of the sales representatives. She asks you to check the accuracy of extensions and the total and then to prepare an invoice (in duplicate) to be sent to the customer as soon as the confirming purchase order is received and the order has been shipped. She gives you the following additional information:

1. Date: **January 4.**
2. Our Order No.: **B4015627.**
3. Terms: **Net 30 days.**

TauTronics Corp.   (619) 877-4000

1051 Graves Avenue
El Cajon, CA 92021-3001

ORDER FORM

Purchase order No. *PS 705-2841L*

Date *January 2, 19--*

Ship Via *UPS*

Portland Learning Center
2811 NE Holman
Portland, OR 97211-3245

Process order; hold shipment for receipt of purchase order.

Quantity	Cat. No.	Description	Price	Total
15 sets	TO16-3	Lamda MicroType 1 (4-disk)	195.00	2,925.00
15 "	TO17-3	Omicron ElectroType 1	89.95	1,349.25
10 "	TO17-4	Omicron ElectroType 2	115.00	1,150.00
10 "	EO18-3	Lamda MicroEnglish Lab 1 (5-disk)	240.00	2,400.00
1 set	MO19-5	Sigma Math-Pac 1 (Network)	875.00	875.00
				8,699.25

_____   *Leonora Phillips*
Sales Representative   Purchasing Agent

Job 11
Prepare a purchase order
(LM p. 61)

Ms. Fillmore asks you to prepare Purchase Order No. **PO493-2305** to order the items listed in the note at the right. She asks that you figure and enter the extensions in the total column and determine and enter the grand total of the order.

January 4, 19--

Order from Sigma Computer Store, Pacific Design Center, 8687 Melrose Avenue, Los Angeles, CA 90069-3281:

2	No. *8511-1*	Looseleaf diskette binders, 5 1/4" inserts, at *$8.95* each
1	No. *4207*	Sigma printer stand, 30 x 30 x 26 1/2", at *$220*
5 boxes	No. *3481*	Sigma diskettes, 5 1/4", at *$38.95* per box
1	No. *207*	HeatPruf diskette storage cabinet, 19 1/2 x 20 x 22", at *$1,038.95*

Sigma's terms of sale are 2/10, net 30. Have order shipped by Pacific Express.

J. F.

Judith Fillmore

Lessons **113-117** | Section **29** | TauTronics Corp. (production/marketing office)

244

33

Learning goals

1 To prepare business letters in block and modified block styles.
2 To address large envelopes.
3 To develop composing skills.
4 To make carbon copies.

Machine adjustments

1 Check desk/chair adjustments.
2 Set ribbon control to type on upper half of ribbon.
3 Check placement of copy.
4 Set paper guide on 0.
5 Use a 70–space line unless otherwise directed.
6 SS drills; DS paragraphs.

33a ▶ 6
Preparatory practice

each line 3 times
SS (slowly, faster, slower); DS between
3-line groups; repeat if time permits

alphabet 1 One gray antique zinc box was the most favored object kept on display.

figures 2 Please turn to page 350 and answer Questions 2, 4, 6, 7, 8, 9, and 17.

hyphen 3 Pam thinks we have an up-to-the-minute plan for our out-of-town sales.

easy 4 When risk is taken by a giant firm, signs of visible profit may ensue.

| 1 | 2 | 3 | 4 | 5 | 6 | 7 | 8 | 9 | 10 | 11 | 12 | 13 | 14 |

33b ▶ 10
Compose at the keyboard

2 half sheets; 1" top margin;
5-space ¶ indention; DS

1 Keyboard the sentences in ¶ form, inserting the needed information. Do not correct errors.

2 Remove the paper and make pencil corrections. Retype the ¶s. Proofread; correct errors.

(¶ 1) **My name is** (your name). **My home address is** (your complete home address, including ZIP Code). **I am a student at** (name of your school) **in** (city and state), **where I am majoring in** (major area of study). **My school address is** (street address, dormitory name, or other). (¶ 2) **The brand name of the typewriter I use is** (brand name). **I type at approximately** (state the rate in figures) **gwam. My greatest difficulty now seems to be** (name one, as: too many errors, not enough speed, poor techniques, lack of confidence).

33c ▶ 34
Format business letters in block style

plain full sheets

1 Read the special information– tion at the right; then study the style letter on page 78.

2 Prepare a copy of the letter, following directions given on the letter. Correct errors.

3 Take three 2′ writings on opening lines and ¶1. Begin with paper out of the machine. Estimate placement of the date; move quickly from part to part to improve your speed.

Business letter placement information

Letter styles used for business letters are similar to styles used for personal letters, but note the following differences.

When letterhead paper (with a printed return address) is used, the return address is not typed above the date; begin the letter by typing the date.

If the letter is signed by a woman, the personal title she prefers (Ms., Miss, or Mrs.) may be included on the typed signature line. No title, personal or professional, is needed if the writer is male.

The writer's official title may be typed directly beneath the typed signature line.

The initials of the typist may be shown at the left margin a DS below the typed name or title. (In Section 10 letters, reference initials are indicated by xx; you should substitute your own initials.)

If an enclosure notation is used, type it a DS beneath the reference initials.

An attractive appearance is as essential for business letters as for personal letters. Proofreading and correcting must be done well if a letter is to have its desired effect.

The business letters in Section 10 are of average length; such letters fit well on a 60-space line. The date is usually typed on about Line 15, or 2½″ from the top of the page. This placement is recommended for all letters to be typed in Section 10.

Mr. Lambert hands Ms. Fillmore a rough draft of a sales analysis report that he wants prepared in final form for photocopying. Ms. Fillmore asks you to prepare the report in unbound style.

She cautions you to look for unmarked errors and to correct any you find. She asks you to add the side heading

Comments and Projections

between the fourth and fifth paragraphs of the report.

SALES ANALYSIS REPORT
DS   TauTronics Corp.
December 31, 19--
TS

DS

TauTronics Corp. showed an overall ∧*sales* increase this year of 13.1% with total sales of $2,266,380. Percent of gain varied widely among marketing regions and between the home and school market segments. *Sales by Regions* <TS

The Western region lead in total dollar sales with sales of $776,325. The North-Central Region was second with total sales of $500,325. All of the ③ other ∧*younger* regions (Eastern, Mountain-Plains, and Southern) ~~had~~ *posted* sales of over $300,000.

The greatest percentage of total sales increase was enjoyed by the Southern region with a 20.3% gain, followed by the Western Region with 15.6%, the Mountain-Plains Region with 13.8%, the North ∧*-Central* Region with 9.1%, and the Eastern Region with 7.0%.
TS
Sales by Market Segment

The sales leader in both home and school markets in terms of dollar volume was the Western Region. The greatest percentage of sales gain in the school market, however ∧was the Southern Region (38.2%), with the Mountain-Plains Region running a ~~poor~~ *distant* second (18.9%). In the home market, the Western Region lead with a 16.8% sales gain ∧with the North-Central Region ~~showing~~ *posting* an 11.2% increase. School sales over-all increased by 15.3%; *whereas,* home sales ~~jumped~~ *increased by* 11.7%.

Overall, the year just ~~passed~~ *past* was a successful one. Our goal for next year is to increase ∧*total* sales by ∧*at least* 15%, with no region or market segment falling below a 10% gain. ¶Plans already in place should help us attain our goal. Contracts with ∧*new* home suppliers in the Eastern ∧*and Southern* regions should boost sales there dramatically. Pending school adoptions in the Eastern and ∧*North-* Central regions should have a major postive impack on ∧*school* sales in those regions.

The addition of sales ~~reps~~ *representatives* in the Eastern and North-Central Regions, combined with the positive ∧*conditions just mentioned,* ~~above~~ should help ~~us~~ to generate ∧*at least* the projected 15% increase in the coming year.

Communications Design Associates

348 INDIANA AVENUE
WASHINGTON, DC 20001-1438
Tel: 1-800-432-5739

		total words	gwam 2'
Dateline	February 14, 19-- Line 15	4	2
	Operate return 4 times		
Letter address	Mr. Harvey B. Barber	8	4
	Sunstructures, Inc.	12	6
	2214 Brantford Place	16	8
	Buffalo, NY 14222-5147	21	10
	DS		
Salutation	Dear Mr. Barber	24	12
	DS		
Body of letter	This letter is written in what is called "block style." It	36	18
	is the style we recommend for use in your business office for	48	24
	reasons I shall detail for you in the following paragraphs.	61	30
	First, the style is a very efficient one. Because all lines	73	6
	(including the date) begin at the left margin, time is not	85	12
	consumed in positioning special parts of each letter.	96	18
	Second, this style is an easy one to learn. New employees	107	23
	should have little difficulty learning it, and your present	119	29
	staff should adjust to it without unnecessary confusion.	131	35
	Third, the style is sufficiently different from most other	143	41
	styles that it can suggest to clients that your company is a	155	47
	creative one. The style is interesting. It gains attention.	168	54
	I am pleased to enclose our booklet on the subject of letter	180	6
	styles and special features of business letters.	190	11
	DS		
Complimentary close	Sincerely yours	193	13
	Operate return 4 times		
	Kathryn E. Bowers		
Typed name	Ms. Kathryn E. Bowers	197	15
Official title	Senior Consultant	201	17
	DS		
Reference initials	xx	202	17
	DS		
Enclosure notation	Enclosure	203	18

Shown in pica type
60–space line

Style letter 2: business letter in block style, open punctuation

Job 7
Regional sales comparison
(full sheet)

Mr. Jerome Lambert, National Director of Marketing, has put together a comparison of sales by regions. Ms. Fillmore asks you to prepare final copy for photocopying; SS data for each region; DS between regions.

REGIONAL SALES COMPARISON

TauTronics Corp.
December 31, 19--

Region	Last Year	This Year	% Increase
Eastern			
Home Market	$186,750	$198,470	6.3
School Market	132,690	143,285	8.0
Mountain-Plains			
Home Market	162,585	178,605	9.8
School Market	105,990	126,040	18.9
North-Central			
Home Market	271,590	301,920	11.2
School Market	187,045	198,460	6.1
Southern			
Home Market	175,140	189,520	8.2
School Market	118,490	163,755	38.2
Western			
Home Market	398,410	465,200	16.8
School Market	264,715	301,125	13.7
	$2,003,405	$2,266,380	13.1

Job 8
Letter response to new product proposal
(LM p. 57)

After the committee meeting to discuss the Jackson–Williams proposal, Dr. Calo composed a letter to the authors. Ms. Fillmore asks you to prepare the final copy and gives you these direc-tions:

1 Date: **January 3, 19—.**

2 Address:

Dr. Hilda Jackson
Department of Office Systems
Southern California College
1112 E. Artesia Boulevard
Compton, CA 90221-3009

3 Correct any errors in spelling, punctuation, and capitalization you find.

4 Indicate that a photocopy of the letter is being sent to Dr. Mark Williams.

New
Members of our/Products Evaluation Comittee meet yesterday to dis-cuss your Keyboarding Letter-Pac proposal. The reactions were positive and I received approval to work with you in attempting getting the block letter segment ready for field testing.

For field testing we shall need in final tryout form all mate-rials dealing with the modified block style letter; diskette, source document booklet with asignments and directions and all material for the instructor's guide.

Only after the results of field testing is are available will we be able to decide whether to procede in the development of the complete product. We at TauTronics are optomistic that field test results will be positive.

with us
If you and dr. Williams are willling to work/in this way I would like to suggest meet with the two of you soon to discuss some suggestions that we believe will help in the refinement process.

Lessons **113-117** | Section **29** | TauTronics Corp. (production/marketing office)

242

34a ▶ 6
Preparatory practice

each line 3 times SS (slowly, faster, slower); DS between 3-line groups; repeat if time permits

alphabet 1 Ben Jackson will save the money required for your next big cash prize.

fig/sym 2 The 7 1/2% interest of $18.68 on my $249.05 note (dated May 3) is due.

double letters 3 Dell was puzzled by the letter that followed the offer of a free book.

easy 4 In Dubuque, they may work the rich field for the profit paid for corn.

| 1 | 2 | 3 | 4 | 5 | 6 | 7 | 8 | 9 | 10 | 11 | 12 | 13 | 14 |

34b ▶ 9
Compose at the keyboard

2 full sheets; 2″ top margin; DS

1 Center your name horizontally, then TS.

2 Answer the questions at the right in complete sentences.

3 Make pencil corrections on your copy, then retype it. Proofread; correct errors.

1 In what year were you graduated from high school?

2 How long have you been studying at your present school?

3 Have you attended any other postsecondary schools?

4 When do you plan to complete your formal schooling?

34c ▶ 10
Address large envelopes

3 large (No. 10) envelopes [LM pp. 35–37]

1 Read carefully the special placement information.

2 Address a large envelope to each addressee listed below; proofread; circle errors.

3 Fold a sheet of blank 8½″ × 11″ paper for insertion into a large envelope. Use the fold-ing procedure shown for the Monarch envelope on page 63.

Placement information

Some businesses use small envelopes for 1-page letters and large envelopes for letters of 2 or more pages or letters with enclosures. Many firms, however, use large envelopes for all correspondence.

Study the placement of the letter address on the large envelope illustrated below. Set a tab stop about 5 spaces to the left of center or about 4″ from the left edge of the envelope. Space down about 14 lines from the top edge of the envelope and begin typing at the tab stop, thus positioning the address in approximately vertical center and slightly below the horizontal center. Learn to visualize this position so that you can type envelope addresses without special settings or measurements.

Type special messages for the addressee (*Please forward, Hold for arrival, Personal,* etc.) a TS below the return address and 3 spaces from the left edge of the envelope. Underline or type in ALL CAPS.

Type special mailing notations (such as REGISTERED, SPECIAL DELIVERY, etc.) in ALL CAPS below the stamp position.

MR MILO K DECKER PRESIDENT
POPULAR TOOL COMPANY
528 ESSEX LANE
DAVENPORT IA 52803-4163

BERA WALLPAPERS INC
7747 MC ARTHUR CIRCLE
EVANSVILLE IN 47714-3821

Miss Barbara B. Treece
Breummer & Joyner
6234 Reynolds Avenue
Columbus, OH 43201-6822

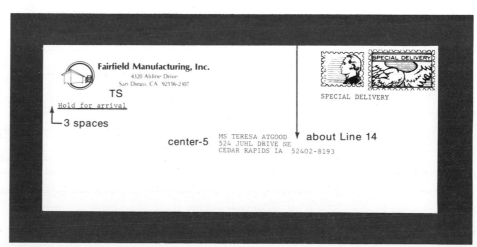

Job 3
Memorandum (LM p. 53)

Dr. Calo has drafted a memo requesting cost estimates from Miss Arlene Simms. Ms. Fillmore asks you to format and type the memo on a memo form. Correct any undetected errors you may find.

Jobs 4 and 5
Adapt a memorandum (LM pp. 53–55)

Dr. Calo has asked Ms. Fillmore to have the rough–draft memo modified to request that Kevin Marx estimate the sales potential of Letter–Pac in the school market and that he send his report to Jerome Lambert by the end of the week. Be sure to inform him of the upcoming meeting on Letter–Pac and its purpose.

He also wants the memo modified and sent to Ms. Sheila Prentiss for an estimate of the sales potential of the new product in the home market. She will need to be informed of the upcoming meeting, and her report should be sent to Jerome Lambert also.

Ms. Fillmore asks you to prepare both memos.

Job 6
Tentative agenda (full sheet)

Dr. Calo has roughed out a tentative agenda for the meeting of the New Products Evaluation Committee. Ms. Fillmore asks you to format and type it in the final form for photocopying.

TO: Arlene Simms

FROM: Dru Calo

DATE: December 23, 19--

SUBJECT: PRODUCTION COST ESTIMATES FOR JACKSON-WILLIAMS PROJECT

A meeting of the New Products Evaluation Committee is scheduled for 2 p.m. 30 December 29, 19-- to discuss the development and marketing of Jackson and Williams' Letter-Pac proposal. Before that meeting you will need to provide production cost information to Jerome Lambert, who sets product prices. I am enclosing a copy of the proposal and protype materials as a basis for your cost estimate. Mr. Lambert wants your cost estimate by the end of this week.

TENTATIVE AGENDA
New Products Evaluation Committee Meeting
2 p.m., December 30, 19--

1. Introductory Comments . . . . Jerome Lambert
2. Presentation of Letter-Pac Proposal . . . Dru Calo
3. Special Reports
    Production Costs . . . . Arlene Simms
    Estimate of School Sales Potential . . Kevin Marx
    Estimate of Home Sales Potential . . Sheila Prentiss
4. Discussion of Proposal . . . . Committee Members
5. Summary of Discussion: Pros and Cons . . Jerome Lambert
6. Call for Vote . . . . Dru Calo
7. Adjournment

Format business letters in block style

2 plain full sheets; 1 large envelope (LM p. 37); 60-space line; begin on Line 15

Problem 1

Prepare the letter; proofread and correct your copy before removing it from the machine.

	words
(Current date)	Mr. Herbert B. Wymore, Jr.	Millikin & Descartes, Inc.	800	15
Hazel Court	Denver, CO 80204-1192	Dear Mr. Wymore		25

(¶) In answer to his request, I am very happy to write a letter of recommendation for Mehti K. Boromand, who worked with our company for about fourteen months. — 40 / 55 / 56

(¶) Mr. Boromand's responsibilities, while he was employed here with us, involved carrying important documents and packages from building to building. He was responsible, prompt, and virtually tireless; cheerful, polite, and very friendly; and above all, discreet and reliable. He was absolutely trustworthy. — 71 / 86 / 102 / 118

(¶) He left our employ at the end of last summer to begin college studies, but he will be welcomed back to our staff at any time that we have an opening in which he might be interested and for which he might be qualified. — 134 / 150 / 161

Sincerely | Miss Kim L. Schuyler | Assistant Vice President | xx — 173

Problem 2

Make a corrected copy of the letter at the right. Insert the longer changes as numbered. Address an envelope.

Note: The total word count is shown as 173/186; the first figure is the letter count; the second is the letter plus the envelope.

June 16, 19-- — 3

Mr. Olin N. Werger — 7
1640 Barnes Land ~e — 10
White Plains, NY 10604-3719 — 16
&i
Dear Mr. Werger — 19

pleasure   *inform* ①
It is my ~~happy opportunity~~ to ~~tell~~ you / that the suggestion you recently submitted ~~has been studied~~ by — 28 / 38
our Management Board. The Management Board has recommended to me its / immediate, implementation. — 52 / 64

② *your* ③
I (too) have studied ~~the~~ suggestion, and I must tell — 73
you that I am extremely enthusiastic about it. Your — 84
explanations makes it quite obvious that by making — 94
the changes in office layout you recommend, our company should be able to save a substantial ~~expense~~. ④ — 104 / 116

Will you attend a brief ceremony to be held in my — 126
office next Friday morning at 9:30? At that time it — 136
will be my pleasure to award to you a check in the — 147
amount of $4,500 in appreciation of your excellent — 157
money-saving recommendation. — 162

Sincerely yours — 166

① *for consideration*
② *has been accepted*
③ *adoption and*
Mrs. Cecelia P. Barbette ④ *amount of money* — 171
President — 173

xx — 173/186

Office job simulation

(LM pp. 67–81)

Job 1

New product proposal (full sheets)

Ms. Fillmore gives you a new product proposal prepared by Dr. Dru Calo, Director of New Products. Dr. Calo wants the material formatted and typed in unbound manuscript style DS. It will later be duplicated for distribution to members of the New Products Evaluation Committee.

Ms. Fillmore asks you to identify and correct any unmarked errors you find in addition to those that have been marked by Dr. Calo.

Job 2

Compose a simplified memo (plain full sheet)

Dr. Calo has asked Ms. Fillmore to have a cover memo composed to accompany the new product proposal. She assigns you the job with these instructions:

1 Use simplified memo style.

2 Date the memo December 23.

3 Address the memo to: Jerome Lambert, Jena Fox, and Ronald Simons.

4 Use the product proposal title as the subject line.

5 Indicate that a copy of the new product proposal, sample storyboards, and diskette are attached.

6 Request a meeting a week from December 23 to discuss the proposal.

7 Use Dr. Calo's name as the originator of the memo.

PROPOSAL FOR NEW PRODUCT:
KEYBOARDING LETTER-PAC

The feedback *reports* to our school products division ~~have~~ *is* ~~show~~ *shows* *clearly* that teachers want computer-aided instructional matrials that go beyond our basic keyboard learning packages. We have been exploring the *possibility* ~~idea~~ of extending computer-aided instruction to the formating and productoin of documents frequently processed in business offices.

Dr. Hilda Jackson *and Mark Williams have* ~~has~~ been working on a microcomputer program to teach students how to fromat and produce letters, using the microcomputer *first* as a tutor to teach format *and procedure* and ~~also~~ *then* as the tool *or medium* for processing letter communications. They have submitted for our consideration some sample storyboards *and a correlated diskette*. They propose the development of a package of materials that consists of:

1. To diskettes
2. A source document printware item of perhaps 64 pages
3. An instructional leader's guide of about 16 pages *plus solutions*

The program is menu driven, giving the operator options in terms of the letter style to be used, preprogrammed formats, and operator-controlled formats. The operator works first from model copy, than from semiarranged and unarranged copy. The operator is first led step by step through the process and is given adequate guidance and frequent prompts. In the learning process, the computer provides evaluation feedback. Later in the production process where the operator does the formatting, the operator (or an instructional leader) evaluates the finsihed products for acceptability. Evaluation of format features is made by comparison with a model in the printware item.

Production costs *data* are being put together by Arlene Simms. An estimate of sales potential for the school market is being prepared by Kevin Marx; for the home market, by Sheila Prentiss. All three reports will be submitted to Jerome Lambert, who will determine a viable cost/price structure.

Among the proposals we have *received* ~~seen~~, this one by Jackson and Williams appears to have the greatest potential for acceptance. Although their original work is on the Sigma Personal Computer, they plan to convert it to other propular microcomputers as soon as the Sigma package is compteted. It is my recomendation that we give the proposal serious consideration, provided the cost/price information is compatable with that of our other comparable products.

35a ▶ 6
Preparatory practice

each line 3 times SS (slower, faster, slower); DS between 3-line groups; repeat if time permits

alphabet 1 The explorer questioned Jack's amazing story about unknown lava flows.

figures 2 I am sending 2,795 of the 4,680 sets now and the remainder on June 13.

capitalization 3 Is the notation on this memorandum Bob's, Edna's, Ralph's, or Myrna's?

easy 4 Work with vigor to shape a theory to make visible and audible signals.

| 1 | 2 | 3 | 4 | 5 | 6 | 7 | 8 | 9 | 10 | 11 | 12 | 13 | 14 |

35b ▶ 12
Use carbon paper

Materials needed:
1 original sheet
2 second sheets
2 carbon paper sheets
1 firm (5"×3") card

70–space line; DS; 2½" top margin; correct errors

1 Study the information and illustrations at the right.

2 Assemble a carbon pack and make an original and 2 carbon copies of the ¶ shown below the illustrations.

Assembling a carbon pack

1 Assemble letterhead, carbon sheets (uncarboned side up), and second sheets as illustrated below. Use one carbon and one second sheet for each copy desired.

2 Grasp the carbon pack at the sides. Turn it so that the letterhead faces away from you, the carbon sides of the carbon paper are toward you, and the top edge of the pack is face down. Tap the sheets gently on the desk to straighten.

3 Hold the sheets firmly to prevent slipping; insert pack into type-writer. Hold pack with one hand; turn platen with the other.

Many companies no longer make carbon copies; of those that do, some do not erase errors on them. If you need to do so, pull the original forward and place a firm card in front of the carbon sheet. Erase the error on the original with a typewriter eraser; erase the carbon copy with a soft pencil eraser. For additional carbon copies, use the card to protect them by placing it between the sheet being erased and the next sheet of carbon paper.

35c ▶ 32
Format business letters in modified block style

3 plain full sheets; copy sheets

Problem 1

1 Study the information at the right and Style Letter 3, p. 71.

2 Type a copy of the letter; proofread; circle errors.

3 Type another copy of letter. Make one carbon copy; correct errors.

Problem 2

Type Problem 2, page 69, in modified block style. Make one carbon copy, no envelope. Proofread; correct errors.

As you study Style Letter 3, page 71, note that the block style has been "modified" by moving the dateline and the closing lines from block position at the left margin. In the modified block style, these lines begin at the center point of the page.

Because stationery with printed letterhead is either used or assumed, the dateline will be the first item typed in these letters. Type the dateline on about Line 15 and use a 60–space line for all letters in Section 8. Spacing between letter parts is the same as was used with the block style. This spacing is standard for all business letters.

Excerpts, continued

Business Forms. Business forms such as purchase requisitions, purchase orders, and invoices can be typed quickly and efficiently if the following procedures are observed by the typist.

1 Set the left margin stop for typing the name and address block.

2 Set a tab stop for aligning the items in the information section to the right of the address block.

3 Set additional tab stops for aligning and typing the columnar entries.

Note: Well-designed business forms permit the left margin stop to be used for positioning both the address and one column of entries beneath the address block (usually the first column). Often, too, the tab stop set for the information section may be used to position the items in one of the columns beneath the information section.

4 Position columnar entries (except Description items) so that they are in the approximate horizontal center of their respective columns. Begin the Description items 2 spaces to the right of the vertical rule.

5 SS the columnar entries when there are 4 or more single-line items. DS the items in the body of the form when there are 3 or fewer single-line items.

6 If an item in the body of the form requires more than 1 line, SS the item and indent the second and succeeding lines 3 spaces.

7 Underline the last figure in the Total column; then DS before typing the total amount.

8 Tabulate and type *across* the form rather than typing all items in the first column.

Properly arranged and typed business forms are illustrated at the right.

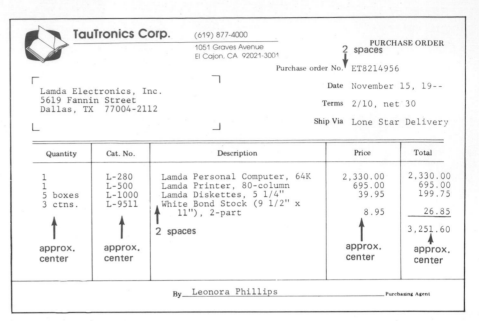

Properly typed purchase order

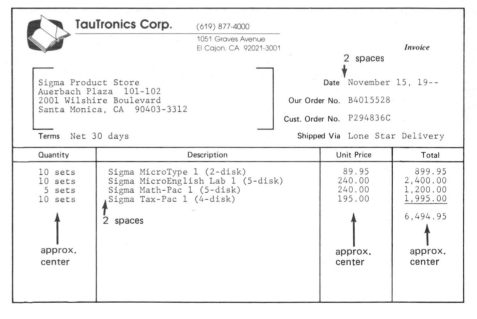

Properly typed invoice

113a-117a ▶ 5

Preparatory practice

Type as many times as you can in 5' at the beginning of each class period in this section.

alphabet	1	Joseph Zbornak meets every degree requirement of six western colleges.
fig/sym	2	On 6/15/85, Kenny & Anderson, Inc., received a 9.4% discount ($2,730).
adjacent key	3	Children on vacation trips like our very popular ice-cream sandwiches.
fluency	4	The box is right for the antique bowl, the panels, or the eighty maps.

| 1 | 2 | 3 | 4 | 5 | 6 | 7 | 8 | 9 | 10 | 11 | 12 | 13 | 14 |

Communications Design Associates

348 INDIANA AVENUE
WASHINGTON, DC 20001-1438
Tel: 1-800-432-5739

Tabulate to center to type
date and closing lines

		total words

Dateline   Line 15   November 28, 19--   4

Operate return 4 times

Letter   Mr. Otto B. Bates, President   9
address   Third Bank and Trust Company   15
9080 Reservoir Avenue   20
New Brunswick, NJ 08901-4476   26
DS

Salutation   Dear Mr. Bates   28
DS

Body of   This letter is written in what is called the "modified block   41
letter   style." It is the style we recommend for use in your office   53
for reasons I shall detail for you in the paragraphs below.   65

First, the style is a fairly efficient one that requires only   77
one tab setting--at center point--for positioning the current   90
date, the complimentary close, and the typed signature lines.   102
All other lines begin at left margin.   110

Second, the style is quite easy to learn. New employees will   123
have little difficulty learning it, and your present staff can   135
adjust to it without unnecessary confusion.   144

Third, the style is a familiar one; it is used by more busi-   156
ness firms than any other. It is conservative, and customers   168
and companies alike feel comfortable with it.   178

I am happy to enclose our booklet on the subject of letter   189
styles and special features of business letters.   199
DS

Sincerely yours   202

Operate return 4 times

Complimentary
close

Kathryn E. Bowers

Typed name   Ms. Kathryn E. Bowers   206
Official title   Senior Consultant   210
DS

Reference   xx   211
initials   DS
Enclosure   Enclosure   213
notation

Shown in pica type
60–space line

Style letter 3: modified block style, block paragraphs, open punctuation

Learning goals

1 To become familiar with the keyboarding/formatting tasks in a firm that produces/markets educational software.

2 To learn selected terms frequently used in word processing.

3 To improve your ability to work from differing copy sources and to detect and correct unidentified errors.

Machine adjustments

1 Paper guide at *0*.

2 Set ribbon control to use upper half of ribbon.

3 Margins: 70–space line for drills and ¶ writings; 1″ standard side margins for reports and correspondence; as appropriate for tables and forms.

4 Space job tasks as directed (or appropriate).

Office Job Simulation

Before you begin the jobs of Section 29, read carefully the information at the right and on page 239.

Make notes of any standard procedures that you think will save you time during the completion of the document production activities.

Daily practice plan:

Preparatory practice .... 5′
Work on simulation .... 45′

Work Assignment

You have been assigned by Office Service Temporaries, Inc., to work in the word processing unit of TauTronics Corp. Tau-Tronics develops, publishes, and markets computer-aided educational products for both school and home markets. The company is located at 1051 Graves Avenue, El Cajon, CA 92021-3001. Your work assignments from various members of the staff will be made by Ms. Judith Fillmore, Supervisor, Word Processing Unit.

TauTronics' word processing manual specifies that all company letters are to be formatted in block style with open punctuation. Closing lines of all letters include the typed name of the person for whom the letters are prepared, followed on the same line by that person's business title. An envelope is addressed for each letter. All documents are prepared for photocopying except business forms which require the preparation of one carbon copy.

When specific job instructions are given, follow them carefully. When specific instructions are not given, make appropriate decisions on the basis of your knowledge and experience. If your supervisor (your instructor) considers some of your decisions unacceptable, learn from her or his suggestions—just as you would do in a business office.

TauTronics Corp. has based its word processing manual and job instructions booklets on *COLLEGE KEYBOARDING/TYPEWRITING*, so use the Reference Guide and the index of your textbook to look up matters of style and placement when in doubt. When a job requires unusual specifications, TauTronics provides special guides in "Excerpts from the Word Processing Procedures Manual."

Excerpts from the Word Processing Procedures Manual

Leaders. Leaders, which are a series of periods (. . .) that are typed between two items in tabular material, are used to make reading easier. They "lead the reader's eye" from one columnar item to another. They are primarily used when the distance between certain items in two columns is so great that matching columnar items is difficult.

Leaders are made by alternating the period (.) and a space. The lines of leaders should be aligned in vertical rows and should end at the same point at the right.

To align leaders, type all periods on either the odd or the even numbers on the line-of-writing scale guided by the position of the first line of leaders. Begin the first line of leaders on the second space after the first item in the column and end the leaders 2 or 3 spaces to the left of the beginning of the next column.

An agenda is one example of a business document that makes use of leaders. Tau-Tronics Corp. uses the *non*justified format for agendas (all items in Column 2 begin at the same horizontal point). Study carefully the agenda shown below.

```
                TAUTRONICS CORP.
       Agenda for Meeting of the Board of Directors
                  February 8, 19--

1.  Call to Order . . . . . . . . . . . . . .  Andrew B. McDaniels

2.  Minutes of Last Board Meeting . . . . . .  Charles L. Black

3.  Special Reports
        Foreign Suppliers  . . . . . . . . .  Kathy Stetson
        Domestic Suppliers  . . . . . . . . . Carl W. Handley
```

Leaders in *non*justified agenda

36a ▶ 6
Preparatory practice

each line 3 times SS (slowly, faster, still faster); DS between 3-line groups; repeat if time permits

alphabet	1	Jim Bond quickly realized that we could fix the pretty girl's vehicle.
fig/sym	2	Serial #815-47 was stamped on the engine; Model #209(36) was below it.
combina-tion	3	Look for the fastest racer to get a big treat at the end of the races.
easy	4	Both of the towns bid for the giant quantity of coal down by the dock.

| 1 | 2 | 3 | 4 | 5 | 6 | 7 | 8 | 9 | 10 | 11 | 12 | 13 | 14 |

36b ▶ 10
Align copy in columns

half sheet, long side up; 50-space line; begin on Line 14; DS

1 Set tab stops according to both the key at the bottom of the table and the guides above the table. Tabs should be set to require the least forward and backward spacing.

2 Format and type the drill; repeat it if time permits.

margin	tab	tab	tab	words
answer	592.79	I	TO:	3
brochure	24.83	I I	FROM:	7
follows	6.02	I I I	DATE:	11
technical	57.42	IV	SUBJECT:	16

key | 9 | 8 | 6 | 8 | 3 | 8 | 8 |

36c ▶ 12
Review modified block letter style

1 letterhead and envelope [LM p. 39]; 60-space line; begin on Line 15

Prepare the letter; proofread and correct your copy before removing it from the machine.

words

(Current date) | Mrs. Lynn Martinez | 431 Poplar Lane | Annapolis, MD 21403-2261   15
| Dear Mrs. Martinez | 19

(¶) Our Credit Department informs me that you recently returned to us for   33
credit a Wilcox Model 24 toaster. It appears from the report that some question   49
was raised about the condition of the toaster when it was returned and that you   65
objected to certain statements made at the credit counter.   77

(¶) I apologize if in any way the routine return of this toaster was questioned. As   93
you know if you are a longtime shopper in our store, we guarantee our mer-   108
chandise to be satisfactory in every way. If you, the customer, are not satisfied,   125
then we, the store, are not satisfied either.   134

(¶) I assure you, Mrs. Martinez, that we have properly adjusted your account to   150
reflect credit for the return. If you have any further questions about this mat-   166
ter, please contact me personally.   173

Sincerely yours | Myles J. Longano, Head | Customer Relations | xx   185/197

Spelling

1 Set margins for a 60–space line.
2 Type each set of words across page, making changes as directed. SS drill lines; TS between sets.

Set 1	Change to plural	analysis soprano premise copy stencil niece century basis calf footnote brother-in-law frogman bypass hero
Set 2	Change to past tense	check circumvent answer mail punish commit leave offend pay send transmit prescribe prove collect
Set 3	Add ing	appraise rattle enclose get put mark dine cross choose run permit chase forget love

Subject/verb agreement

1 Type the paragraph and make the necessary verb agreement corrections. Check the corrected copy with your instructor.
2 Repeat if necessary.

The date and time of the department meeting has not been decided, but the director and her assistant is trying to make a decision. Either of them are capable of making the decision; however, neither she nor her assistant know which date to select. Consequently, I was told that one of us were to be responsible for the final decision--after all, someone has to take responsibility.

Spelling and verb agreement

1 Keyboard and format the paragraph, making any necessary spelling and verb agreement corrections. Check the corrected copy with your instructor.
2 Repeat if necessary.

The Director of Manufacturing, as well as all Production Managers, are well aware of our past procurment problems. They met to intiate procedures to insur that each carton in each shipment arrive in good condition and that a large stock of accesories and materials are always available. The President, in addition to the Baord of Directors, were informed of the new procedures, and everyone knows what needs to be done.

Measure communication skills

plain sheet; 70-space line, 1½" top margin; DS

1 Correct errors in word usage and grammar as you keyboard.
2 Proofread; retype the ¶ if necessary.

Default standards are basic format characteristics that are preprogrammed on a word processing system. Default standards specifies the conditions that apply unless the operator change them. The effect of default standards is to save a operator from having to set margin, tab stops, and other parameter each time a document is prepare. Some firms even adopt there style guides to conform to the default standards of there word processing equipment.

36d ▶ 22
Prepare memorandums

Full-page memorandum
[LM p. 41]

1 Read the information in the memorandum below.

2 Format and type the memo.

3 Address a COMPANY MAIL envelope to:

Mr. Edward Davis, Director
Information Processing
Center

Note: Memorandums are often prepared on printed forms. If a printed form is not available, follow the half–page illustration at the right. Begin the heading on Line 7 for a half–page memo and on Line 10 for a full–page memo. Set 1″ side margins.

		words
TO:	All Information Processors	5
FROM:	Cathy Carapezzi, Director	10
DATE:	December 21, 19--	13
SUBJECT:	Interoffice Correspondence	18

Correspondence within a company is frequently formatted on interoffice forms, either half or full sheets, depending on the length of the message. The following points describe the features of a memorandum prepared on a printed form. — 30 / 44 / 56 / 64

1. Space twice after the colon in the first line of the printed heading and set the left margin. The heading items and the body of the memo will begin at this point. Set the right margin stop an equal distance from the right edge. These margin adjustments will usually give you side margins of 1″. — 79 / 92 / 105 / 117 / 124

2. Full addresses, the salutation, the complimentary close, and the signature are omitted. — 138 / 143

3. Personal titles are usually omitted from the memo heading. They are included on the envelope, however. — 157 / 164

4. TS between the last item in the heading and the body of the message. SS the paragraphs, but DS between them. DS above and below a table or a numbered list when one is included in the message. Space twice after the number in a numbered list; align the whole paragraph under the first line. — 178 / 190 / 203 / 216 / 221

5. Reference initials, enclosure notations, and copy notations are included. — 234 / 236

Special colored envelopes usually are used for memorandums. Type the addressee's name, personal title, and business title or name of department for the address. Type COMPANY MAIL (in ALL CAPS) in the postage location. — 249 / 263 / 276 / 280

xx — 281/**292**

112c ▶ 12
Build rough-draft copy skill

1 Two 1' writings for accuracy.

2 Two 3' writings for accuracy; record *gwam* and number of errors for more accurate writing (LM p. 3).

Difficulty index

| all letters used | A | 1.5 si | 5.7 awl | 80% hfw |

| | gwam 1' | 3' |

When you go to On a job interview, the first few minutes are the most impor- — 15 | 5 | 48

tant. The interviewer's first impressions of you will be more ~~impor-~~ — 27 | 9 | 52

~~tant~~ detailed than what you put on have written your resume. Remember to smile sin- — 42 | 14 | 57

cerely, have a hearty handshake, dress pro perly, and ~~put forth~~ exhibit — 54 | 18 | 61

a pleasant personality. Look confident and be positive about — 66 | 22 | 65

what you , as an employee, have to offer the organization. Be careful that you do — 83 | 28 | 70

not give the impression that you are interested only in hwat — 95 | 32 | 74

you can get from the frim. If you can also articulate your answers — 109 | 36 | 79

to the interview questions, you will have a much better chance to have — 123 | 41 | 84

a job offer , extended to you. — 128 | 43 | 86

112d ▶ 18
Build/measure straight copy skill

1 One 1' writing for accuracy on each ¶.

2 Two 5' writings for accuracy on both ¶s combined. Record *gwam* and number of errors for more accurate writing (LM p. 3).

Difficulty index

| all letters used | A | 1.5 si | 5.7 awl | 80% hfw |

| | gwam 1' | 5' |

Today, most data and text are input into a computer system through a — 14 | 3 | 55
keyboard. Therefore, any individual who will be working with a computer — 28 | 6 | 58
will need to have some basic keyboard skill. The level of keyboarding — 43 | 9 | 61
skill needed is dependent upon the frequency with which a person must — 57 | 11 | 64
work with a computer and the amount of data or text required to be input. — 72 | 14 | 67
For example, a manager who only works on a terminal once in a while and — 86 | 17 | 69
then uses just a few keystrokes does not need to develop the same high — 100 | 20 | 72
skill level that is required of a word processing operator. Obviously, — 115 | 23 | 75
the individual who is required to input large volumes of data or text — 129 | 26 | 78
must develop very good keyboarding skills. — 137 | 27 | 80

The keyboard is divided into two major parts: alphabet and numbers. — 14 | 30 | 82
Many keyboard operators need to develop good skill on both types of key- — 28 | 33 | 85
boards, since they are required to input large volumes of both numeric — 42 | 36 | 88
data and text material into the computer. A person who must input such — 57 | 39 | 91
large quantities of text material will need to spend a great deal of — 71 | 42 | 94
time and effort to learn the alphabet keyboard by the touch method. To — 85 | 44 | 97
learn the number keyboard does not require nearly the time and effort, — 99 | 47 | 99
since there are not as many number keys to learn and since the organiza- — 113 | 50 | 102
tion of the number keys is in a sequential pattern. — 124 | 52 | 104

gwam 1' | 1 | 2 | 3 | 4 | 5 | 6 | 7 | 8 | 9 | 10 | 11 | 12 | 13 | 14 |
5' | 1 | 2 | 3 |

37a ▶ 6
Preparatory practice

each line 3 times SS (slowly, faster, still faster); repeat if time permits

alphabet 1 Gwendolyn Post lives in a quiet area just six blocks from the old zoo.

figures 2 The 1983 edition of this book had 5 parts, 40 chapters, and 672 pages.

hyphen 3 Here is an up-to-date reference for those out-of-this-world questions.

easy 4 The rich man paid half of the endowment, and this firm also paid half.

| 1 | 2 | 3 | 4 | 5 | 6 | 7 | 8 | 9 | 10 | 11 | 12 | 13 | 14 |

37b ▶ 12
Keyboard letter parts

Lines 1-3: Take two 1′ writings on each line. Try to finish each line at least once in the time alloted.

Lines 4-5: Take two 45″ writings on Lines 4-5, arranging them in 3–line address format.

Goal: To complete each address in Lines 4-5 in 45″.

Technique hint:
Type at a controlled, but constant rate. Do not pause before typing figures.

1 123 Brandy Street; 459 Reynolds Drive; 650 River Road; 78 Osage Avenue

2 Erie, PA 16511-4478; Brooklyn, NY 11227-2785; Dayton, OH 45410-3367

3 April 29, 19--; May 18, 19--; June 27, 19--; July 26, 19--; January 17

4 Ms. Deirdre Ann Beebe | 262 Orient Boulevard | Wichita, KS 67213-4976

5 Mrs. Rosetta Hayman | 595 Singingwood Drive | Torrance, CA 90505-3047

| 1 | 2 | 3 | 4 | 5 | 6 | 7 | 8 | 9 | 10 | 11 | 12 | 13 | 14 |

37c ▶ 10
Review memorandums

Half-page memorandum
[LM p. 43]

Format and type the memorandum at the right. Review the format on page 73 if necessary.

1″ side margins; proofread; circle errors.

		words
TO:	All Employees	3
FROM:	Bessie Arthur, Personnel Department	10
DATE:	June 30, 19--	13
SUBJECT:	Booklet on Fringe Benefits	18

Included with your next payroll check will be a booklet developed by 32
our staff that outlines employee benefits. Of particular importance 46
is the section relating to the changes taking place in the Social 59
Security law and how you can make an inquiry to be sure your de- 72
ductions and our contributions are being properly credited to your 85
account. 87

Please call me should you have any questions regarding your fringe 100
benefits or the information contained in the booklet. 111

xx 112

112a ▶ 5
Preparatory practice

each line 3 times SS (slowly, faster, top speed); DS between 3-line groups; repeat selected lines as time permits

alphabet 1 Max Culp knew every answer on today's quiz; he must enjoy being first.

fig/sym 2 The note #65731 (dated 2/09/85 with interest at 14.3%) is due 2/09/89.

shift lock 3 Two typing texts were CENTURY 21 TYPEWRITING and COLLEGE KEYBOARDING.

fluency 4 The title to the land is the endowment held by the panel for the city.

| 1 | 2 | 3 | 4 | 5 | 6 | 7 | 8 | 9 | 10 | 11 | 12 | 13 | 14 |

112b ▶ 15
Build script-copy skill

1 Two 3' writings for accuracy. Record *gwam* and number of errors for more accurate writing (LM p. 3).
2 One 5' writing for accuracy.

Difficulty index

| all letters used | A | 1.5 si | 5.7 awl | 80% hfw |

	gwam 3'	5'

Most large firms are organized into three levels of management. Each of the levels is respon- sible for a specific type of decision-making activity. At the top level, the executive officers make all of the strategic plans and long-range goals of the firm. At the middle level, the managers decide the tactics that are needed to carry out the plans and decisions made by the top-level group. The low-level group is operational and puts into action the tactical decisions of the mid-level group. The paragraph below describes in more detail the func- tions of the three levels.

The executive officers are charged with the basic duty of guiding and directing the firm to a profit- able future. These people who are a part of this top-level group must work with a great deal of uncertainty as they plan. They must not only decide the long-range goals of the firm, but they must also formulate policies and strategies which will cause the goals to be accomplished. In addition to strategic planning, this group must engage in a lot of creative decision-making processes, pri- marily in regard to the introduction of new goods or services.

gwam 3' / 5' values:
3 | 2 | 47
6 | 4 | 49
9 | 6 | 51
13 | 8 | 53
16 | 10 | 55
20 | 12 | 57
23 | 14 | 59
27 | 16 | 61
30 | 18 | 63
33 | 20 | 66
37 | 22 | 68
39 | 23 | 69
42 | 25 | 71
45 | 27 | 73
48 | 29 | 75
52 | 31 | 77
55 | 33 | 79
59 | 35 | 81
62 | 37 | 83
65 | 39 | 85
68 | 41 | 87
72 | 43 | 88
75 | 45 | 90
78 | 46 | 91

37d ▶ 22
Measure skill application: business correspondence

Time schedule:

Assembling materials .... 2'
Timed production .... 15'
Final check; proofread;
   compute *g-pram* .... 5'

Materials needed:

2 letterheads and envelopes, 1 half-page memorandum [LM pp. 43-47], or plain paper
Letters: 60-space line, Line 16.
Memo: 1" side margins, Line 7.

When the signal to begin is given, insert paper and begin typing Problem 1. Keyboard the problems in sequence until the signal to stop is given. Prepare a large envelope for each letter. Proofread all problems; circle errors. Calculate *g-pram*.

$$g\text{-}pram = \frac{\text{total words typed}}{\text{time (15')}}$$

words

	Prob. 1	Prob. 3

Problem 1
block style

(Current date) | Mr. Lonny L. Johnson, Director | The House by the Side of the Road | 679 Truman Street | Abilene, TX 79601-5739 | Dear Mr. Johnson — 15 / 28

(¶) The Executive Board of The House by the Side of the Road has instructed me to express to you how deeply it regrets your resignation as House Director. — 43 / 58 | 28 / 43

(¶) The Board recognizes that you have served as Director for 18 years. Your leadership, loyalty, and perseverance will be missed; and finding your replacement will not be easy. — 73 / 89 / 93 | 58 / 74 / 78

(¶) We shall begin a search for a new Director; but, in the meantime, please let us know of any assistance we can provide. — 108 / 117 | 93 / 102

Sincerely yours | Dale L. Berger | Secretary | xx — 126/**147** | 102

Problem 2
modified block style

(Current date) | Mr. Byung Chung, Manager | Nikki's Paris Shop | 1890 San Luis Street | Las Vegas, NV 89110-7241 | Dear Mr. Chung — 15 / 24

(¶) This letter introduces Gale Senter, our Nevada representative for Cleo Sportswear. Gale will stop at your shop in a day or two to show you samples of our new spring line. — 38 / 54 / 59

(¶) One of the features you should look for in Cleo clothes--and stress to your customers--is the basic, uncluttered look of each style. Our designers fashion clothes that do not have faddish elements that outdate them after one or two seasons. — 74 / 90 / 105 / 107

(¶) Also, examine carefully the fine cloth used to make our Cleo line. All our fabrics are washable and do not need ironing. — 122 / 132

(¶) Gale will be happy to discuss availability and terms of purchase with you. You'll be glad she called. — 147 / 152

Sincerely yours | Miss Celia Murtagh | Sales Manager | xx — 162/**180**

Problem 3

Retype Problem 1 as a memorandum but address it as shown at the right. No envelope.

TO: Lonny Johnson — 3
FROM: Dale Berger — 5
DATE: (Current date) — 8
SUBJECT: Appreciation of Service — 13

(Word count for body of memo is listed in the second column in Problem 1.)

111c ▶ 15

Build rough-draft copy skill

1 Two 1' writings for speed.

2 Three 3' writings for speed; record *gwam* (LM p. 3).

Difficulty index

all letters used	A	1.5 si	5.7 awl	80% hfw

gwam 1' | 3'

Most ~~firms want~~ companies need workers who ~~can type~~ are able to prepare different types ~~fo/~~ of 14 | 5 | 45

tables; ~~they~~ therefore, good typists need to ~~understand~~ know the different 26 | 9 | 49

formats of tables and there ir basic ~~traits~~ characteristics. As a rule, any 39 | 13 | 53

table used in business will be one of three bas_ic types: simple, 53 | 17 | 58

rule d, or boxed. The simple table usually has just a main heading 66 | 22 | 62

and one-line headings above each ~~of the~~ columns of the table. A ruled 80 | 27 | 67

or boxed table is more dif f icult than a simple table to type. 93 | 31 | 71

~~They~~ Both have horizontal rules above and below the column headings and below the 108 | 36 | 76

body. in addition, a boxed table requires vertical ~~ones~~ rulings. 120 | 40 | 80

111d ▶ 15

Build straight-copy skill

1 One 1' writing for speed on each ¶.

2 Two 5' writings for speed on both ¶s combined. Record *gwam* (LM p. 3).

Difficulty index

all letters used	A	1.5 si	5.7 awl	80% hfw

gwam 1' | 5'

Advances in technology have caused many of the changes that have 13 | 3 | 58
taken place in both equipment and procedures in the modern office. Some 28 | 6 | 61
of the changes have had a positive impact on the levels of production 42 | 8 | 63
in the office. One of the first changes came with the arrival of the 56 | 11 | 66
copy machine. If a file copy was desired, the copier ended the need to 70 | 14 | 69
use carbon paper or to retype the job. Now that an electronic photo- 84 | 17 | 72
copier is placed in most organizations and the cost per copy is low, 98 | 20 | 75
there is little need for carbon copies. Another change came with the 112 | 22 | 77
arrival of the electronic calculator which could perform any calculation 126 | 25 | 80
many times faster than a mechanical machine. 135 | 27 | 82

Changes also have been made in the typing area. The use of the 13 | 30 | 85
magnetic-tape typewriter was the beginning of a new period for repeti- 27 | 32 | 87
tive typing jobs. The office staff no longer was required to type the 41 | 35 | 90
same material over and over again; the machine mechanically typed the 55 | 38 | 93
item as many times as was needed. The next change was the word proces- 69 | 41 | 96
sor with its many text-editing functions. The person who uses a word 83 | 44 | 99
processor is able to enter, correct, change, and print data with a mini- 98 | 47 | 102
mum of rekeying. However, for those who do not want a complete word 111 | 49 | 104
processor, there is an electronic typewriter which has only a few of the 126 | 53 | 107
automatic functions and has a limited amount of internal storage space. 140 | 55 | 111

gwam 1' | 1 | 2 | 3 | 4 | 5 | 6 | 7 | 8 | 9 | 10 | 11 | 12 | 13 | 14 |
5' | 1 | 2 | 3 |

Supplemental skill-building practice

Improve keystroking control

each line twice SS; proofread and circle errors before typing the next line; DS between 2-line groups; repeat selected lines as time permits

direct reaches	1 My brother, Mervyn, has my army carbines; Bernice has my breechloader.
adjacent reaches	2 Three guides loped in a column as we stalked over trails after a lion.
double letters	3 Lynn will see that Jill accepts an assignment in the office next week.
long words	4 Governmental departments encourage associations to photocopy booklets.
1st/ fingers	5 Those 456 heavy black jugs have nothing in them. Fill them by June 7.
2d/ fingers	6 Mike Deak, who was 38 in December, likes a piece of ice in cold cider.
3d & 4th/ fingers	7 Zone 12 was impassable; we quickly roped it off. Did you wax Zone 90?
fig/sym	8 General T & T (common stock) had sales of 5,936,067 shares at 142 5/8.

Measure skill growth: straight copy

a 3′ and a 5′ writing; determine gwam; proofread and circle errors

Difficulty index

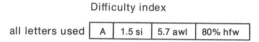
all letters used | A | 1.5 si | 5.7 awl | 80% hfw

gwam 3′ | 5′

Diogenes, quaint little light in hand, journeyed out night after 4 | 3
night looking for an honest man. We don't know exactly how Diogenes 9 | 5
intended to recognize honesty, but he was very serious about his effort. 14 | 8
He really thought he would know such a person when he met one. 18 | 11

Just as a matter of conjecture, do you wonder whether Diogenes, if 22 | 13
he were living today, might look for an educated person? If he were 27 | 16
to undertake such a search, would an educated person be recognizable? 32 | 19
If so, how? What qualities might you expect an educated person to have? 37 | 22

The idea poses interesting questions. Just what is education? Is 41 | 25
it a mental thing? Can it be recognized in the actions or reactions of 46 | 28
a person? Is it backed up by a diploma? Or is it more? Does it perhaps 51 | 30
include such unscholarly elements as experience and observation? 55 | 33

gwam 3′ | 1 | 2 | 3 | 4 | 5
5′ | 1 | 2 | 3

Measure skill growth: statistical copy

1 Keyboard the ¶ once for orientation. Be especially aware of number usage as you prepare the copy.
2 Take two 3′ writings; determine *gwam*.

Goal: at least 19 *gwam*.

Difficulty index

all letters/figures used | LA | 1.4 si | 5.4 awl | 85% hfw

gwam 3′

We started to manufacture Dixie Real Tractors in the back of a small 5
plant at 3720 First Avenue in Quantico, Virginia; and in that first year 9
of 1968, we actually completed only five or six of these small-size 9 hp. 14
machines. Today, in our big, modern factory at One 45th Avenue, we find 19
it hard to realize that we turn out about seventy of our machines in just 24
one day and that our profit for last year was over $1 million. 28

gwam 3′ | 1 | 2 | 3 | 4 | 5

Learning goals

1 To increase basic skill on straight, script, statistical, and rough–draft copy.

2 To improve communication skills.

3 To refine keyboarding tech–nique.

Record results where indicated and compare them to the results recorded in Section 24.

Machine adjustments

1 Set paper guide at *0*.

2 Set ribbon control to type on upper half of ribbon.

3 Margins: 70–space line for drills and ¶ writings; as directed (or ap–propriate) for problems.

4 SS drill lines; DS ¶s; space prob–lems as directed (or appropriate).

111a ▶ 5
Preparatory practice

each line 3 times SS (slowly, faster, slowly); DS between 3-line groups; repeat selected lines as time permits

alphabet	1	If we arrive too quickly tonight, our expectations may be jeopardized.
fig/sym	2	Do you know how to calculate this: 5230 × (14 − 6) / 8 × (397 − 392)?
bottom row	3	Recent bank embezzlements now exceed the maximum government estimates.
fluency	4	The ivory box with an ancient owl emblem is also an authentic antique.

| 1 | 2 | 3 | 4 | 5 | 6 | 7 | 8 | 9 | 10 | 11 | 12 | 13 | 14 |

111b ▶ 15
Build statistical-copy skill

1 Two 1' writings for speed on each ¶.

2 Two 3' writings for speed on both ¶s com-bined. Record *gwam* (LM p. 3).

Difficulty index

all letters used	A	1.5 si	5.7 awl	80% hfw

gwam 1' | 3'

During 1985, the Jacques Renee Company had net profits after federal — 14 | 5 | 75

income taxes of $2,476,302. The Board of Directors has declared a divi- — 28 | 10 | 80

dend of $14.00 per share of common stock for the stockholders of record — 43 | 14 | 85

as of 7/01/85. The total amount of dividends to be paid is $1,500,000; — 57 | 19 | 90

this represents an annual return on investment of about 12.5%, which is — 72 | 24 | 94

3.75% more than the previous year. With the Board's recent decision to — 86 | 29 | 99

invest $1,000,000 of the net profits in new equipment, the outlook for — 100 | 33 | 104

the future is very good. — 105 | 35 | 106

The Board of Directors' 1985 capital investment in export markets — 13 | 39 | 110

will begin to show a sizable increase in gross profits as early as 1987. — 28 | 44 | 115

The Jacques Renee Company's forecast is for gross sales of exports to — 42 | 49 | 120

increase by 3% by the end of 1986; then in 1987, export gross sales — 56 | 53 | 124

should increase by over 12.5%. Of course, the operating costs will — 69 | 58 | 129

also increase during this period, but at a much lower percentage. The — 83 | 63 | 133

1987 net profit after federal income taxes is expected to be at least — 97 | 67 | 138

$2,826,200, which is a 14.1% increase over 1985. — 107 | 71 | 142

gwam 1' | 1 | 2 | 3 | 4 | 5 | 6 | 7 | 8 | 9 | 10 | 11 | 12 | 13 | 14 |
3' | 1 | 2 | 3 | 4 | 5 |

Number usage

half sheet; 74-space line; 1″ top margin; SS sentences; DS between groups

1 Cover the answer key at the bottom of the column. When you have finished keyboarding, check your answers.

2 Study guides for number usage.

3 Keyboard guide number 1a. (with period), space twice, and keyboard review sentence(s), noting guide applications.

4 Keyboard apply sen–tence(s), correcting errors in number usage as you prepare the copy.

Key: 1b. Eight 2c. three, seven 2d. 7 3b. four, 20, two, four 4b. forty, two thirds 5b. Eighty–five 5c. thirty–one

> **Express as words**
>
> **1.** A number which begins a sentence even if figures are used later in the sentence.
> **2.** Numbers ten and lower unless they are used in close proximity to numbers higher than ten, which are expressed as figures.
> **3.** One of two adjacent numbers. Preferably the smaller number should be spelled for efficiency.
> **4.** Isolated fractions and indefinite numbers.
> **5.** Use a hyphen to separate compound numbers between twenty-one and ninety-nine that are spelled out, whether they stand alone or as a part of a number over one hundred.

review 1a. Six players were cut from the 37-member team.
apply   b. 8 altos and 21 sopranos filled the front row of the stage.

review 2a. We saw five or six wild ducks swim away; three were mallards.
review   b. All but 5 of the 15 lamps were turned on.
apply   c. Andrew took 3 sweaters and 7 shirts to the cleaning service.
apply   d. The librarian repaired the loose bindings on seven of the 25 books.

review 3a. The six 200-gallon drums are in the truck.
apply   b. Cora bought 4 twenty-cent stamps; she used only 2 of the 4 stamps.

review 4a. About fifty women registered, but only one half stayed for the meal.
apply   b. Close to 40 attended the meeting; 2/3 offered to help.

review 5a. Seventy-two of the four hundred fifty-eight pages were about Brahms.
apply   b. Eighty five of the one hundred forty-six entry forms were submitted.
apply   c. Out of the one hundred thirty one varieties, sixty-two were hybrids.

Number usage

Follow directions given above.

Key: 1b. Forty percent, 86 percent 1c. 37 percent, 5 per–cent 2c. 75 cents

> **Express as figures**
>
> **1.** Percentages; spell out the word *per-cent*. Use the % symbol in tables, technical writing, and some statistical copy.
> **2.** Large round numbers in the millions or higher with their word modifiers, such as 25 *million* or 63 *billion*; use with or without a dollar sign. Use the word *cents* after figure amounts of less than one dollar.
>
> **Note**
>
> To avoid confusion or error, businesses commonly use figures for all numbers except those which begin a sentence.

review 1a. Attendance was 97 percent; however, 10 percent of the men left early.
apply   b. 40% of the 86% increase came from annual donations.
apply   c. The firm reinvested 37% of last year's five percent profit.

review 2a. They budgeted $12 million for highways and $10 million for parks.
review   b. She took $25 from her savings account; now she has only 14 cents.
apply   c. The group collected $1 million; some donations were only 75¢.

Job 7
Itinerary (full sheet)

Mrs. Wiseman has checked and approved the handwritten draft itinerary you have prepared for her. All of the flights have been confirmed for her business trips for the month of January. Prepare her itinerary in final form in reading position. Place 2 spaces between columns. Be sure to include the horizontal ruling between each horizontal line of copy.

ITINERARY
Regina B. Wiseman
January 2 to January 26, 19 - -

Date	Depart City	Depart Time	Flight No.	Arrive City	Arrive Time
Jan. 2	San Diego	8:04 a.m.	WA 632	Los Angeles	8:45 a.m.
Jan. 4	Los Angeles	12:15 p.m.	UA 415	Kansas City	4:40 p.m.
Jan. 7	Kansas City	9:20 a.m.	OZ 592	St. Louis	10:15 a.m.
Jan. 10	St. Louis	3:20 p.m.	EA 192	Atlanta	5:15 p.m.
Jan. 13	Atlanta	10:35 a.m.	DL 481	New York	12:30 p.m.
Jan. 16	New York	8:00 a.m.	TW 702	London	10:40 p.m.
Jan. 25	London	8:30 a.m.	TW 771	Chicago	12:30 p.m.
Jan. 26	Chicago	3:00 p.m.	TW 235	San Diego	6:45 p.m.

Job 8
Compose a memorandum
(LM p. 43)

Mrs. Wiseman asks you to compose a memorandum to all administrative heads from the sketchy notes shown at the right. The required number of copies will be made on the photocopy machine. Date the memo **December 9, 19—**. The subject of the memo is: **Staff Meeting for Administrative Heads.**

The staff meeting for administrative heads will be held December 20 at 1 p.m. in Room 304. Proposed program enclosed (updated program to be distributed on December 16).

Purpose: present and discuss changes in the training program for computer service technicians, which will be implemented over the next six months. Ms. Sylvia Phillips, Personnel Director, to give formal presentation concerning changes. Any administrative head who cannot attend meeting to inform Ms. Phillips by December 17.

Number usage

Follow directions given on page 77.

> **Express as figures**
>
> 1. Numbers which are preceded by nouns.
> 2. House numbers (except house number One) and street names (except ten and under). When both the street name and house number are expressed as figures, place a dash (--) between them.
> 3. Numbers that precede an abbreviation such as *a.m., lbs., in.,* and *tsp.*
> 4. Dates followed with *d* or *th* when the date precedes the month and is sepa-rated from the month by words. When the day follows the month, express the day in cardinal figures (4, 5, etc.) without *th* or *d* after the number. When the month is not given, the day may be written with figures followed by *th* or *d*; or, if it is ten or lower, it may be spelled.
> 5. Sums of money preceded by a dollar sign.
> 6. Fractions in a series.

review 1a. The Treaty of Ghent is covered in Chapter 9 of the history text.
apply   b. Cesar went to Room forty-three and delivered his application.

review 2a. Pick up the parcel at One Elm Way and take it to 4729 Fifth Avenue.
review b. The new address of the Museum of Modern Art is 2647--56th Street.
apply   c. The taxi stopped at 1 Sixth Street and 234--42d Street.

review 3a. At 8 a.m. the chef simmered the 3 lbs. of beef in the kettle.
apply   b. Their carton (14 in. × 14 in. × eighteen in.) was mailed.

review 4a. She will arrive in Boston between the 2d and the 4th of January.
review b. On May 13 we shall attend the opening of the art exhibit in Richmond.
review c. I shall arrive on the 15th. He will leave Mexico on the 12th.
apply   d. Victoria arrived on the 12th of April, and she left on June 9th.
apply   e. The cast had a rehearsal on the twenty-third.

review 5a. Maxine earned $68 last week for her work at the local garden store.
apply   b. This antique vase, which is made of porcelain, is valued at $400.

review 6a. What is the sum of 1/2, 3/4, and 4 2/3?
apply   b. The tailor cut 2 2/3, 1 1/4, one-eighth, and 4 5/8 yards of fabric.

Proofread/revise as you keyboard

half sheet; 74-space line; 1″ top margin; DS

1 Cover the answer key at the bottom of the column. When you have finished keyboarding, check your answers.

2 Keyboard the guide number (with period), space twice, and type the sentence.

3 As you keyboard each line, decide if the sentence is correct according to the guides for number usage. If the sentence is not correct, make the appropriate correction as you keyboard.

1. A recipe containing two lbs. of veal won Al the 20th annual contest.
2. About 7 20-ounce containers of milk were on the counter yesterday.
3. He gave the clerk $5 and waited for the 25¢ change.
4. Yoko stacked 3 books and 8 magazines on the shelf.
5. Nearly two thirds of the $25,000,000 was spent on medical research.
6. Six hundred forty six graduates receive diplomas on the third of June.
7. Julio read Rule nine and then applied the principle to the problem.
8. We sent the gifts to 1 Laurel Avenue and 231 18th Street.
9. The company increased productivity by approximately 20 percent in May.
10. What is the sum of 2 1/8, one fourth, and one half?

Job 6
News release
(plain full sheet)

Mrs. Wiseman asks that you pre–
pare the news release to an–
nounce the opening of the new
office in the Foreign Region. Use
2″ top margin; 1½″ side margins;
DS the body; TS above and below
the main heading; indent ¶s. Correct any undetected errors.

December 11, 19--

FOR IMMEDIATE RELEASE

CENTEK OFICE SYSTEMS, INC.
OPENS FOREIGN OFFICE

¶ Centec Office Systems, Inc., announced today the opening of its new branch office in London, England. The London office will handle sales, service, and installation of it's microcomputer systems throughout the British Isles and Europe. Also, the London office will serve as the main headquarters for European sales if the current plan to open a Berlin or Munich office materialize. ¶ With the main headquarters located in San Diego, this company has had tremendous growth over the past twelve years since its founding. The company now has five service regions and assets in excess of $18 million. With the opening of the London Office, European sales are expected to assure Centeks success as a leader in micro-computer design in the British Isles and Europe. ¶ The new office is to be located at 30 McGuire Square, London, England. The new office should be operative by June 30.

Learning goals

1 To prepare topical outlines.
2 To prepare unbound reports.
3 To prepare a data sheet.
4 To keyboard spread headings.
5 To develop greater awareness of copy content.
6 To improve ability to think and compose at the keyboard.

Machine adjustments

1 Set paper guide at 0; remove all tab stops.
2 Set ribbon control to type on upper half of ribbon.
3 Use a 70–space line unless otherwise directed.

38

38a ▶ 6
Preparatory practice

each line 3 times SS (concentrate on copy); DS between 3-line groups; repeat selected lines if time permits

alphabet	1	Dixie Vaughn acquired the prize job with a large firm just like yours.
figures	2	The ad said to call 964-5781 before 3 p.m. to order 20 sheets on sale.
shift	3	Rosa and Lazaro spent April in Connecticut and May and June in Hawaii.
easy	4	The eight auto firms may pay for a formal field audit of their profit.

| 1 | 2 | 3 | 4 | 5 | 6 | 7 | 8 | 9 | 10 | 11 | 12 | 13 | 14 |

38b ▶ 14
Align at the right

half sheet; 40-space line; exact vertical center; SS

1 Space forward from left margin 20 spaces; set tab; space forward 20 more spaces; set second tab.

2 Keyboard first column at left margin; use the margin release and backspacer to type "10." Backspace from tab stops to type second and third columns.

			words
1.	I.	one	2
2.	II.	two	4
3.	III.	three	7
4.	IV.	four	9
5.	V.	five	12
6.	VI.	six	14
7.	VII.	seven	17
8.	VIII.	eight	20
9.	IX.	nine	22
10.	X.	ten	24

38c ▶ 14
Preapplication drill: format/type an outline

1 Study the information and the sample outline at the right.

2 Because the lines of the outline are short, set for a 40–space line (center point −20/center point +20); SS; 4–space indentions; 1½″ top margin; full sheet.

3 Use **PREPARING OUTLINES** as a main heading; TS; prepare a copy of the outline.

Preparing outlines

It is important that students and others interested in organizing data be able to use a standard form of outline. As you study and keyboard the example at right, note:

● that 4-space indentions separate divisions and subdivisions of various orders.

● that first-order divisions are typed in all capitals; second-order divisions have main words capitalized; third- and subsequent-order divisions have only the first word capitalized.

● that single spacing is used except above and below first-order divisions.

● that there must be at least two parts to any division.

● that the left margin is set for II. Space forward once for single-digit numerals; use the margin release and backspacer for Roman numerals longer than two digits.

● that the line length used must accommodate the longest line in the outline but not exceed a 70–space line.

I. FIRST-ORDER DIVISION
DS

   A. Second-Order Division
   B. Second-Order Division
      1. Third-order division
      2. Third-order division
   C. Second-Order Division
DS

II. FIRST-ORDER DIVISION

   A. Second-Order Division
      1. Third-order division
      2. Third-order division
         a. Fourth-order division
         b. Fourth-order division
      3. Third-order division
   B. Second-Order Division

Job 5
Letter on executive-size stationery (LM p. 41)

Mrs. Wiseman dictated a letter to you and asked that you type a rough–draft copy so that she could edit it and make changes, if necessary. Now she has edited the letter and asks that you prepare a final copy for her signature on executive–size stationery. Correct any errors she may have missed. Remember that this letter has enclosures. Send a blind photo–copy to Sylvia Phillips.

Mrs. Gosset's address is in the rotary address file on your desk.

Gosset, Carolyn (Mrs.)

Mrs. Carolyn Gosset
1432 Cape Cod Way
Rochester, NY 14623-1433

Send Special Delivery   December 10, 19--

Dear Mrs. Gosset:

Thank you for coming to San diego to ~~meet~~ *visit* with ~~in regards~~ *us about* to the position ~~as~~ *of* Branch manger in London, England. *If you will send us a statement of expenses,* ~~As soon as we receive your expenses~~ we will send you a reimbursement check immediately. Our executive committee has approved my ~~request~~ *recommendation* that we hire you to fill the Branch Manager Position and has ~~told~~ *authorized* me to offer you this position at an annual salary of $50,000. If you wish to accept this offer, you should plan to be in San Diego *by* January 4.

Please complete the enclosed contracts and employment ~~agreements~~ *forms* and return them to our *San Diego* office by December 20. At this time, we can discuss in ~~specific~~ *details* the operations of the London office and make specific arrangments for your move to London.

We ~~are~~ hoping that you ~~can~~ *will* accept this offer and that we may have a long, successful association with you as the Brach manager of our Foreign Reion.

Sincerely,

In addition to the annual salary, our normal fringe benefits package includes a housing and automobile allowance, educational allowances for each child in the family, complete medical and life insurance coverage, and a four-week vacation outside of London.

38d ▶ 16

**Format/type
an outline**

full sheet; 1½″ top mar-
gin; 70-space line;
center heading

words

UNBOUND REPORTS | 3
TS

I. MARGINS | 6

   A. Top Margins | 9
      1. First page: pica, 1 1/2″; elite, 2″ | 17
      2. Other pages: 1″ | 21
   B. Side and Bottom Margins | 27
      1. Left and right margins: 1″ | 33
      2. Bottom margin: 1″ | 38

II. SPACING | 40

   A. Body of Manuscript: Double | 47
   B. Paragraph Indentions: 5 or 10 Spaces Uniformly | 57
   C. Quoted Paragraphs | 62
      1. Four or more lines | 66
         a. Single-spaced | 70
         b. Indented 5 spaces from each margin | 78
         c. Quotation marks not required | 84
      2. Fewer than 4 lines | 89
         a. Quotation marks used | 94
         b. Not separated from text or indented from text margins | 105

III. PAGINATION | 109

   A. Page 1: Usually Not Numbered, but Number May Be Centered 1/2″ | 122
      from Bottom Edge | 125
   B. Other Pages: Number Typed at Right Margin, 1/2″ from Top Edge | 139
      of Paper Followed by a Triple Space | 146

39

39a ▶ 6

**Preparatory
practice**

each line 3 times SS;
(concentrate on
copy); DS between
3-line groups; repeat
selected lines if time
permits

alphabet 1   Our unexpected freezing weather quickly killed Joann's massive shrubs.

figures 2   Invoices 625, 740, and 318 were dated June 5, 1984; and all were paid.

br 3   Brad's brother, Bruce, broke my bronze brooches and brass bric-a-brac.

easy 4   Did the roan foal buck, and did it cut the right elbow of the cowhand?

| 1 | 2 | 3 | 4 | 5 | 6 | 7 | 8 | 9 | 10 | 11 | 12 | 13 | 14 |

39b ▶ 10
Compose at the keyboard

2 full sheets; decide top
margin and spacing

1 Read the questions at the right.

2 Compose an answer for each
question in one or two sentences.
Join the sentences into para–
graphs to make a short essay.
Center the title **MY CAREER** over
the paragraphs.

3 Proofread; mark errors. If time
permits, retype the copy in final
form.

1   What is your career goal as you now see it?

2   What led you to make this career choice?

3   In what part of the world do you think you would like to live
and work?

4   Why do you want to live and work there?

5   Do you see yourself following any other career path in the
years ahead?

Leftbound report (full sheets)

Mrs. Wiseman typed a copy of a report on her typewriter at home, which is to be distributed to the Marketing Department. She asks you to finalize the report by typing it in appropriate report format for a leftbound report.

Job 4
Unbound report (full sheets)

Mrs. Wiseman asks that you retype the report (Job 3) as an unbound report because she will be having it duplicated for distribution by the company's sales representatives.

MEDICAL MICRO-OFFICE SYSTEM

Introduction

The new electronic information processing system designed especially for small medical centers (those staffed by fewer than twelve doctors) was released for promotion and installation on October 30, 19--. This new system is referred to as "Medical Micro-Office System."

Hardware Components

The Medical Micro-Office System is comprised of a 256K microcomputer with a 50-megabyte hard-disk storage system. Up to four terminals and two printers may be connected to the system. The terminals have a standard selectric-type keyboard with a 10-key numerical pad and fifteen special pur-pose control keys. The terminal display is a 12-inch green phosphorous screen. The printers may be either spinwriters (with tractor feed or automatic sheet feeder) or matrix printers.

Each system is supplied with either an 8-inch floppy disk drive or a tape drive to be used as a backup. The floppy disk has a 1.25 megabyte capacity on each side; the tape drive has a 50-megabyte capacity.

Software Package

A comprehensive package of medical software is provided with each Micro-Office System. All accounting, billing, insurance forms, appointments, and patient records are handled efficiently with the software package provided with the Medical Micro-Office System. Most operators can learn to use the system productively with approximately six hours of training.

Pre-Installation Study

A complete study of office operations in each medical center should be completed by our qualified service representative before a prospective cus-tomer places an order. After the office operations of a particular medical center have been analyzed, recommendations for smooth transition to our system should accompany all orders.

Installation and Delivery

Once an order has been authorized, delivery will occur within six weeks from the date of authorization. Installation should take approximately two weeks. The Medical Micro-Office System is guaranteed operational within ten days after installation is completed.

39c ▶ 34
Format/type reports/ spread headings

Problem 1

full sheet; DS; 1″ side margins: 5–space ¶ indention.

1 Read carefully the guides for preparing reports.
2 Follow these guidelines as you keyboard.

Preparing reports

Before you prepare any report, determine whether or not there are specific instructions for its format. In the absence of such instructions, the guides given here are generally accepted for reports that are not to be bound. Follow these guidelines for the reports in Section 9.

• Use a 1½″ top margin (pica) or 2″ (elite) for the first page; otherwise, use 1″ margins for all four sides.

• Use double spacing.
• Do not number the first page.
• Number the second and all subsequent pages in the upper right corner, ½″ (Line 4) from the top of the page.
• Enclose short quotations in quotation marks. Indent longer quotations 5 spaces from each margin; omit quotation marks, and use single spacing.

	words
SIMPLE REPORT FORMAT	4
TS	

It is important that students who prepare term papers, themes, and other — 19
forms of academic writing know the procedures for typing reports. — 32

In the previous sections, your typed work has been set to a stated line — 46
length of 50, 60, or 70 spaces, regardless of whether your machine was equipped — 62
with pica- or elite-size type. Here in Section 9 you will be asked to prepare formal — 79
reports that require placement in accordance to the number of inches in top, — 95
bottom, and side margins rather than to the number of spaces in the writing — 110
line. — 111

Because of the difference in type size, pica and elite solutions will differ — 127
somewhat. When 1-inch side margins are used, a pica line will contain 65 — 141
spaces; an elite line will contain 78 spaces. Both sizes of type, of course, will — 158
accommodate 6 line spaces to a vertical inch. — 167

When side margins of 1 inch are used, 10 pica spaces should be allowed in — 182
each margin; on the other hand, users of elite type should allow 12 spaces. — 197

Problem 2

half sheet; 2″ top margin; center each heading at the far right as a spread heading, as shown in the first heading.

Center spread headings

1 To center a spread heading, backspace from the center point once for each letter, character, and space except for the last letter or character in the heading.
2 From this point, type the heading, spacing once after each letter or character and 3 times between words.

	words
S P R E A D H E A D I N G S	6
SIMPLE REPORT FORMAT	10
SOURCE FOOTNOTES	14
PREPARING AN OUTLINE	18

Problem 3

full sheet

Repeat the report in Problem 1.
Use a spread heading.

Preparatory practice

Type as many times as you can in 5' at the beginning of each practice session during this section.

alphabet	1	A vexing blitz of a very quick opponent was the major cause of defeat.
fig/sym	2	Interest (18.5%) starts today (7/23/85) if bill ($460.79) is not paid.
outside reach	3	Paula and Pasquale always fix pizzas with a lot of sauces and peppers.
fluency	4	The man in the auto and my neighbor on the bicycle both work downtown.

| 1 | 2 | 3 | 4 | 5 | 6 | 7 | 8 | 9 | 10 | 11 | 12 | 13 | 14 |

108b-110b ▶ 45
Office job simulation

(LM pp. 37–43)

Job 1
Memorandum (LM p. 37)

Mrs. Wiseman hands you a sheet of paper on which she has written a memo. She asks you to prepare the memo and send it to Sylvia Phillips, who is the Personnel Director. Today is December 9. The subject of the memo is: **Training Program for Computer Service Technicians.**

Sylvia Phillips, *Personnel Director*

REgina Wiseman, *Executive Vice President*

December 9, 19--

The Executive committee held a meeting *met* yesterday afternoon to discuss and to consider your recommendations concerning the training program of our computer service technicians. They felt that your recommendations will greatly improve the curent program, and they have approved them *with only a few minor changes.*

In particular, They felt that your idea about *suggestion that* a course on computer theory be added to the present curriculum was a fine one. Also, your recommendations that the initial on-the-job training program be extended form one year to 16 months was approved without hesitation and will be implemented soon *within six months.*

Ms. Anna Russo will be visiting you to discuss changes.

 # The Executive Committee wishes to congratulate you for your outstanding work. Over the past two years, the training program has improved substantially as a result of your diligent efforts.

Job 2
Letter (LM p. 39)

Mrs. Wiseman asks you to prepare this letter and send it to a client to confirm installation of one of their microcomputer systems. Send a blind photocopy (bpc) to Victor B. Ruiz. Use executive–size stationery.

December 9, 19-- |Dr. Rudolf Heinz, Director |Dixie Medical Center |325 Main Street |St. George, UT 84770-1245 |Dear Dr. Heinz |INSTALLATION PHASE OF MICRO-OFFICE SYSTEM

(¶) This letter is to confirm our telephone conversation of this morning concerning the installation of your micro-office system. After consulting with the design engineer for your project, we are now able to give you a firm date when the installation of your new system will begin.

(¶) All system components will arrive at your office on or before December 28. Our installation personnel will be in St. George to begin the installation on the morning of January 4. As per our agreement, the system will be installed and operational within ten days from the beginning date of the installation.

(¶) If you have any further concerns, please do not hesitate to phone me at any time.

40a ▶ 6
Preparatory practice

each line 3 times SS (work for fewer than 3 errors per group); DS between 3-line groups

alphabet	1	The objective of the tax quiz was clarified by checking samples of it.
fig/sym	2	Ship the $567 order for 29 1/3 grams of X8-D40 (8% solution) tomorrow.
shift	3	Will Pamela Forsman be quite happy visiting Kansas and Alaska in July?
easy	4	In the land of enchantment, the fox and the lamb sit down by the bush.

| 1 | 2 | 3 | 4 | 5 | 6 | 7 | 8 | 9 | 10 | 11 | 12 | 13 | 14 |

40b ▶ 4
Keystroke the * (asterisk)

The * (asterisk) may be used to refer to a footnote. Find the location of the * on your machine; type the drill line twice.

* ** * I may use * and ** to indicate the first and second footnotes.

40c ▶ 25
Format/type a report with a footnote

full sheet; refer to pages 80 and 81 for format guidelines if necessary

FOOTNOTES

words

4

TS

Formal reports are usually written to put forward some point of view, to 18
convince readers, and/or to convey information in such a way that it will be 34
relied upon, accepted, or believed. To substantiate the contents of a report and 50
to give it greater weight of authority, a writer often cites evidence that other 66
people support his or her conclusions. Sources for such support are then shown 82
as footnotes at appropriate places within the report. 93

Citations for all such opinions or statements of fact spoken or written by 108
someone other than the writer should be documented. This procedure is simply 124
a matter of fair play, of "giving credit where credit is due." Whenever a writer 140
paraphrases or quotes directly from the work of someone else, credit should be 156
given. 158

Footnotes are also frequently used to clarify points, provide additional 172
information, or add other forms of editorial comment that the writer may wish 188
to make. For whatever reason a footnote is included, it must be done with the 204
idea of assisting a reader. 209

Footnotes may be placed at the end of a report, or they may be placed at the 224
foot of the page on which reference to them is made.[*] In either case, the 239
footnotes are typed in sequential order and numbered consecutively throughout 255
the report. Footnotes on a partially filled page may immediately follow the last 271
line of the text, or they may be placed to end one inch from the bottom of the 287
page. 288

SS

1½" underline ———————————— 291

DS

* Footnotes at the foot of the page are usually preferred for academic 305
writing. 307

Learning goals

1 To become familiar with the work in an executive office.

2 To plan and organize your work in an efficient manner.

3 To complete your work neatly and correctly.

4 To integrate your skills and knowledge.

Machine adjustments

1 Set paper guide at *0*.

2 Set ribbon control to type on upper half of ribbon.

3 Margins: 70–space line for drills and ¶ writings; as directed (or ap–propriate) for problems.

4 SS drill lines; DS ¶s; space prob–lems as directed (or appropriate).

Office Job Simulation

Read carefully the material at the right before you begin the work in Section 27. Make notes of any procedures that you think will save you time during the completion of the production activities of this section.

Daily practice plan:

Preparatory practice .... 5′
Work on simulation .... 45′

Work Assignment

You have been assigned by Office Service Temporaries, Inc., to work for Centek Office Systems, Inc., an organization that designs and installs electronic, microcomputer-based office systems. The address where you are to report to work is 300 Lorenz Avenue, San Diego, CA 92114-3002. Your immediate supervisor at Centek will be Mrs. Regina Wiseman, Executive Vice President.

The firm's office manual specifies that all company letters are to be typed in the modified block style with mixed punctuation. The closing lines of all letters should include the typed name of the person for whom the letters are typed followed on the next line by the person's business title. All letters and memorandums require one photocopy (pc) for the file. Some letters require a blind photocopy (bpc) or a blind carbon copy (bcc). Address appropriate envelopes for all letters.

Proofread all work carefully before removing it from your machine; correct all errors. All work that is to leave the company should be "mailable"—technically correct with all errors corrected neatly. All work to be used *within* the company should be "usable"—content correct but with minor "flaws" in format and placement permitted.

When specific job instructions are given, follow them carefully; however, when specific instructions are not given, make appropriate decisions on the basis of your knowledge and experience. If your employer (your teacher) considers some of your decisions unacceptable, learn from her or his suggestions—as you would need to do in any business office.

Centek Office Systems, Inc., has based its office manual on COLLEGE KEYBOARD-ING/TYPEWRITING; therefore, use the Reference Guide and the index of your textbook to check matters of placement and style when you are in doubt. When a job requires unusual specifications, Centek provides them in "Excerpts from the Office Procedures Manual."

Excerpts from the Office Procedures Manual

Executive-size stationery. The size of the paper is 7¼″ by 10½″. When you use stationery that is narrower than the standard 8½″, use 1″ side margins. Begin the dateline on Line 11. The center point is 36, pica; 43, elite.

Blind photocopy notation. If you want to send a photocopy of a letter to someone without disclosing the fact to the addressee of the letter, type a notation on the photo-copy but not on the original. This notation, called *blind photocopy notation* (bpc), is typed at the left margin a double space below the last typed line, for example: bpc Mr. John Howard.

Blind carbon copy notation. The originator of a letter may wish to send a copy of a letter to someone without disclosing this fact to the addressee of the letter. When such a copy is sent, omit the notation from the original copy of the letter. A notation—called *blind carbon copy*—is typed at the left margin a double space below the last typed line on each carbon copy requiring the notation. To type the blind carbon copy notation, insert a heavy piece of paper be-tween the ribbon and the original (first) sheet. Then type the notation, for example: bcc Mr. John Howard. The notation will ap-pear on the inserted paper and the carbon copies but not on the original letter.

If any carbon copy should not have the blind carbon copy notation, insert a piece of paper behind the carbon sheet and in front of the carbon copy lacking the notation; type the notation; it will not appear on the original or any copy for which you inserted a piece of paper.

40d ▶ 15
Preapplication drill: format/type source footnotes

1 Study carefully the guides and models for preparing footnotes.

2 Using the appropriate model (pica or elite) below, type the final lines of a page and its source footnotes. Use 1" side margins. (Note: Since 19 typed and blank lines are needed to complete the 66–line page, begin typing on Line 48.)

3 Compare the appearance and content of your finished product with the model in the textbook.

Format/type source footnotes

Preparing footnotes correctly takes skill, knowledge, and careful planning. The guidelines below will help you to plan and type the footnotes in Section 9.

● Footnotes should be placed at the foot of the page on which reference to them is made.

● Use a superior figure (raised a half line) in the text as reference to the footnote; repeat the superior figure with the footnote.

● Separate footnotes from the body of the report with a single underline 1½" (18 elite or 15 pica spaces); SS before the line and DS after it.

● SS footnotes; DS between them if more than one occurs on a page.

● When one or more footnotes must appear at the foot of a page, allowances must be made for a 1" (6 lines) bottom margin, 3 or 4 lines for each footnote, and 2 lines for the dividing line. As can be seen, it is important to know when to stop keyboarding and when to begin the footnotes.

---

pica   formats as discussed by Guffey and Erickson[1] (business reports)   48

49

and Hashimoto, Kroll, and Schafer[2] (academic reports).   50

SS _____   51

52

DS   [1]Mary Ellen Guffey and Lawrence W. Erickson, _Business Office_   53
Practices Involving the Typewriter with Implications for Business   54
Education Curricula, Monograph 136 (Cincinnati: South-Western   55
Publishing Co., 1981), pp. 17, 27, and 28.   56

DS   [2]Irvin Y. Hashimoto, Barry M. Kroll, and John C. Schafer,   57
58
Strategies of Academic Writing: A Guide for College Students   59
(Ann Arbor: The University of Michigan Press, 1982), p. 1.   60

1" (6 lines)   61
bottom margin   62

63

64

65

66

---

elite   formats as discussed by Guffey and Erickson[1] (business reports) and Hashimoto,   48

49

Kroll, and Schafer[2] (academic reports).   50

SS _____   51

DS   52

[1]Mary Ellen Guffey and Lawrence W. Erickson, _Business Office Practices_   53
Involving the Typewriter with Implications for Business Education Curricula,   54
Monograph 136 (Cincinnati: South-Western Publishing Co., 1981), pp. 17, 27,   55
and 28.   56

DS   57

[2]Irvin Y. Hashimoto, Barry M. Kroll, and John C. Schafer, _Strategies of_   58
Academic Writing: A Guide for College Students (Ann Arbor: The University of   59
Michigan Press, 1982), p. 1.   60

1" (6 lines)   61
bottom margin   62

63

64

65

66

Job 6
Leftbound report with
justified right margin
(full sheet)

Mr. Tullane has asked that you prepare the copy at the right as a leftbound report with justified right margin. The title of the report is **COMPANY PUBLICATIONS,** and the finished report will be added to the Office Procedures Manual as an illustration. You are to have Mr. Tullane check the report before copies are made for the manual.

In the body of the report are two 3–line examples of material to be justified on a 46–space line; be sure to center the 46–space line when typing these two examples. Type them as is, once with the diagonals for extra spaces and once justified.

Note: Many businesses today have word processing equipment that will automatically justify the right margins of reports and other publications. However, Fairfield Manufacturing has not yet purchased such equipment, so the process described in the report and on page 222 for justifying right margins by hand will have to be used.

(¶) All publications of Fairfield Manufacturing, Inc., are prepared and duplicated in our office. Because we want all our publications to have the appearance of a printed page, you should become expert in justifying the right margin.

(¶) A professional-looking effect is achieved by having a right margin that is evenly aligned. Although the procedure for justifying the right margin is time consuming, we feel that it is worth the additional time and expense incurred.

(¶) As you type a line to be justified, come as close to the right margin as possible (without extending beyond the margin). To determine how many extra spaces will be needed in the line, type a diagonal (/) in every space remaining until you reach the right margin. For example, the following material is typed on a 46-space line:

```
All the cards in a card index file should be//
typed in the same form.  Uniformity of style//
facilitates the filing and finding operations.
```

(¶) After you have typed the material the first time, then retype the material and evenly distribute the extra blank spaces throughout the line. For example, the illustration above could be retyped as follows:

```
All the cards in  a card index  file should be
typed  in the same form.   Uniformity of style
facilitates the filing and finding operations.
```

(¶) Please read thoroughly the procedures as outlined in the new Office Procedures Manual.

Mr. Tullane gives you a letter he received from an associate; the body of the letter is shown at the right. He asks you to compose a reply to the letter and instructs you to include a copy of the report you completed above to furnish the information requested. Date the letter **December 6, 19—,** and address it to **Mrs. Sylvia Perry, Office Manager, Ripple, Ripple, and Carey, Attorneys-at-Law, 8505 Black Canyon Highway, Phoenix, AZ 85201-6943.**

Dear Duncan:

We are preparing a new Procedures Manual for our employees at Ripple, Ripple, and Carey. I remember discussing some of our mutual problems last May when we were at the International AMS Conference.

I recall that your company had decided to use the justified right margins for all in-house publications. Could you give me a brief summary of the procedures that a typist should follow when preparing copy with the right margin justified. Perhaps a statement of rationale (at least the major advantage) for using the procedure would be of help to me.

Sincerely,

41a ▶ 6
Preparatory practice

each line 3 times SS (work for fewer than 3 errors per group); DS between 3-line groups; repeat selected lines as time permits

alphabet 1 Jenny Saxon left my squad a week after giving back the disputed prize.

fig/sym 2 I paid $1.95 for 2% milk and $3.87 for 60 rolls at J & D's on June 14.

long words 3 A probability study is particularly helpful for effective forecasting.

easy 4 At a signal, he may sign a name and title at the end of the amendment.

| 1 | 2 | 3 | 4 | 5 | 6 | 7 | 8 | 9 | 10 | 11 | 12 | 13 | 14 |

41b ▶ 44
Format/type reports: second page; two footnotes

Problem 1

full sheet

1 Type copy as the *second* page of a report.

2 Refer to pages 80, 81, and 83 for format directions if necessary.

Problem 2

full sheet

1 Type copy as the *first* page of a report. Use the heading: TECHNOLOGICAL CHANGE

2 Omit the last paragraph before the footnotes.

3 Refer to pages 80, 81, and 83 for format directions if necessary.

words

line 4 2 0

line 7 Today, much of the movement for technological change involves the 14
search for efficiency; that is, shortcutting time and energy, especially as they 30
touch upon the flow of information. Langford says, "Society today is an infor- 45
mation society. Information is what office operations produce."[1] In today's 61
highly competitive business world, accurate information must be readily avail- 76
able; and it is this need, of course, that has given us word processing. 91

Sociologists say that society does not adopt new technology until con- 105
ditions, always changing, make it ready to do so; then it assimilates change very 121
rapidly. The automobile, for example, was invented years before its acceptance 137
as a popular method of transportation. It seems, therefore, that as technology 153
becomes available, society needs pioneers with foresight who will work for its 169
acceptance. Speaking of word processing, Will and Dake say, 181

In order to keep up with technological change and at the same 194
time address human factors, those involved in setting up and run- 206
ning word processing systems must be change agents. Change 218
agents know where to find information on the constant changes in 231
the industry and how to utilize it advantageously.[2] 242

Other "agents of change" must function to prepare a consuming society 256
to trust change; to support it financially; and, above all, to use it. Perhaps the 273
greatest challenge involving technology is not to create change, but to learn to 289
live with it. 292

296

[1] Floyd Langford, "Systems Concept," The Changing Office Environ- 314
ment (Reston: National Business Education Association, Yearbook No. 18, 329
1980), p. 31. 332

[2] Mimi Will and Donette Dake, Concepts in Word Processing: The Chal- 353
lenge of Change (Boston: Allyn and Bacon, Inc., 1981), p. v. 368

Cost sheet (full sheet)

Mr. Tullane asks that you prepare a cost sheet for duplication. Make a first copy for his approval. Have him check it; if he suggests any changes, retype the cost sheet.

Center the cost sheet on a full sheet; leave 4 spaces between columns; make the rules under the column headings and in the total columns 8 spaces wide.

FAIRFIELD MANUFACTURING, INC.

Cost Sheet

Product:
Product Code No.:

Material costs:

Operation	Code	Quantity	Cost	Total
1				
2				
3				
4				
Total				$_____

Variable costs:

Operation	Hours	Cost	Total
1			
2			
3			
4			
Total			_____

Fixed costs:

Operation	Hours	Cost	Total
1			
2			
3			
4			
Total			_____

Total standard cost per unit $_____

42a ▶ 6
Preparatory practice

each line 3 times SS (work for fewer than 3 errors per group); DS between 3-line groups; repeat selected lines if time permits

alphabet	1	We have printed just sixty dozen meal tickets for the banquet meeting.
fig/sym	2	Room #476 is $39 a day, but call 615-2890 (before 2 p.m.) for 7% less.
hyphen/dash	3	Hyphenate a multiword modifier preceding a noun--a hard-and-fast rule.
easy	4	The town may wish to blame us for the auditory problems in the chapel.

| 1 | 2 | 3 | 4 | 5 | 6 | 7 | 8 | 9 | 10 | 11 | 12 | 13 | 14 |

42b ▶ 9
Improve concentration

1 Keyboard a copy of the ¶ DS. Where a blank space occurs, insert either the word **they** or **that**.

2 Using your corrected copy, take as many 1' writings as time permits.

Difficulty index

| all letters used | A | 1.5 si | 5.7 awl | 80% hfw |

gwam 1'

Typically, women and men who are successful give the best _____ can   13

give. _____ do not do this just because _____ have the personality makeup   28

_____ demands it; _____ do so because _____ are seemingly oriented to be   42

achievers. Quite simply, _____ expect to succeed; and _____ refuse to   56

recognize any effort, including theirs, _____ is not top rated.   68

gwam 1' | 1 | 2 | 3 | 4 | 5 | 6 | 7 | 8 | 9 | 10 | 11 | 12 | 13 | 14 |

42c ▶ 35
Format/type a two-page report with footnotes

2 full sheets; standard unbound report format; SS and indent enumerated items 5 spaces from each margin; number second page in upper right corner

1 Review unbound report format on page 80 and the illustrations at the right. Do not type from the illustrations.

2 Format and type the report on pages 86 and 87 as an unbound report.

3 Proofread; correct errors.

1½" pica (Line 10)

Main heading

PREPARING REPORTS: THE PROFESSIONAL TOUCH
TS
Both the writer and keyboard operator, or compositor, share concern for the preparation and ultimate success of a report, but usually the writer must accept final accountability. The composi- tor's contribution, however, is a vital one; and she or he should proceed cautiously. For example, before starting to prepare a final copy of a report, the compositor should determine:

1. the specified purpose of the report and whether some particular format is required;

2. the number, kind, and grade of copies required;[1] and

3. deadlines for completion.

The keyboard operator should be prepared to work from script, rough-draft, or printed copy and yet give the report a final pre- sentation that is as professional as it is functional.
TS
Side heading "Tricks of the Trade"
DS
Those with experience in preparing reports have found that there are special procedures they can use to simplify their tasks. The following paragraphs contain samples of some procedures that can be especially helpful to a person who has not previously key- boarded reports. (Anyone who plans to prepare more than a few reports, however, should read several good books on the subject.)
DS
¶ heading Right margins. Attractive right margins result when good judgment is exercised. Using the warning bell judiciously ensures right margins that approximate left margins in width.

[1]For further information see The Chicago Manual of Style, 13th ed. (Chicago: The University of Chicago Press, 1982), p. 40.

Pica pitch

2" elite (Line 13)

Main heading

PREPARING REPORTS: THE PROFESSIONAL TOUCH
TS
Both the writer and keyboard operator, or compositor, share concern for the preparation and ultimate success of a report, but usually the writer must accept final accountability. The compositor's contribution, however, is a vital one; and she or he should proceed cautiously. For example, before start- ing to prepare a final copy of a report, the compositor should determine:

1. the specified purpose of the report and whether some particular for- mat is required;

2. the number, kind, and grade of copies required;[1] and

3. deadlines for completion.

The keyboard operator should be prepared to work from script, rough-draft, or printed copy and yet give the report a final presentation that is as pro- fessional as it is functional.
TS
Side heading "Tricks of the Trade"
DS
Those with experience in preparing reports have found that there are spe- cial procedures they can use to simplify their tasks. The following paragraphs contain samples of some procedures that can be especially helpful to a person who has not previously keyboarded reports. (Anyone who plans to prepare more than a few reports, however, should read several good books on the subject.)
DS
¶ heading Right margins. Attractive right margins result when good judgment is exer- cised. Using the warning bell judiciously ensures right margins that approxi- mate left margins in width.

[1]For further information see The Chicago Manual of Style, 13th ed. (Chicago: The University of Chicago Press, 1982), p. 40.

Elite pitch

Job 2
Letter (LM p. 29)

The general office does most of the correspondence for the various departments within the company. Mr. Tullane has asked that you type this letter he has written for Mrs. Jacobsen, a design engineer for Fairfield Manufacturing.

December 4, 19-- | Baton Rouge Petrochemicals, Inc. | Attention Mr. Henry I. Franklin | 7899 Jefferson Highway | Baton Rouge, LA 70809-1403 | Ladies and Gentlemen

(¶) Mrs. Anna Jacobsen, our Desk Design Engineer, has asked that I write to you concerning the estimated delivery date for the new plastic laminate product that you recently announced (Shipment No. #A-386).

(¶) Your announcement indicated that the product should be ready for distribution prior to April 1. Mrs. Jacobsen would like to know if a firm date has been established, since one of her major decisions on whether to use the mar-proof top for a new executive desk is dependent upon the date that this new product will be available to us. Would you please let us know within ten days if your delivery schedule will permit a March 1 shipment to us.

(¶) We appreciate your recent performance of providing us with top-quality products for our office furniture and equipment.

Sincerely | Duncan G. Tullane | xx

Job 3
Compose a letter (LM p. 31)

As Mr. Tullane was leaving the office, he stopped by your desk and asked you to take a few notes and compose a letter. Use subject line: OUR PURCHASE ORDER #C-3629. He quickly gave you the following facts:

Data shown on file card:

Roth Office Products Company
535 South Broadway
Wichita, KS 67202-2212

Office
Manager: Miss Thelma Round

December 4, 19-- Write letter to Roth--Attn. Office Manager; Inquire about P.O. #C-3629 sent 2 weeks ago. No confirmation received. We are low on paper. Must have order in 2 weeks (or partial order) or we must cancel. Send duplicate copy of order. Ask for acknowledgment by return mail.

Job 4
Preparing index cards (LM p. 33)

Mr. Tullane maintains a current file of all approved suppliers. The name of each supplier is typed on a 5″ × 3″ index card. You will notice on the sample card that the first line contains the transposed name of the individual. If the supplier is a company, type the company name in place of the transposed name of the person.

Mr. Tullane has given you the names of 4 new suppliers to be added to the file. (See the list below.) You are to prepare an index card for each supplier and arrange the cards in alphabetical order.

```
                            TS
   Frankhauser, Paul L. (Mr.)
                            TS
   Mr. Paul L. Frankhauser
   954 Cabrillo Drive
   Hayward, CA  94545-8091
```

1. Ms. Carlotta Ciminero
   18632 Vale Street
   Santa Ana, CA 92705-1704

2. Miss Sandra Bolivar
   208 International Way, W
   Seattle, WA 99201-7012

3. Tucson Fabrication Company
   809 North Arcadia Avenue
   Tucson, AZ 85711-4023

4. Mr. Faramarz Samadi
   5724 Wandering Way
   Austin, TX 78754-3067

words

preparing REPORTS: THE PROFESSIONAL TOUCH   9
< TS

Both the writer and keyboard operator, or compositor, share   21
a mutual concern for the preparation and for the ultimate suc- 30
cess of a report, but usually the writer must accept final   42
accountability. The compositors contribution, however, is an   54
extremely vital one; and she or he should proceed with great   62
caution. For example, even before they starting to prepare a   73
final copy of a report, the compositor should proceed with   82
determine   84

1. the specified purpose of the report and whether some par- 96
ticular format is required;   102

2. the number, kind, and grade of copies required; and   113

3. deadlines for completion.   119

Thekeyboard operator should be prepared to work from the   130
script, rough-draft, or printed copy and yet give the report a 143
final presentation that is as professional as it is functional. 156

< TS before a side heading
"Tricks of the Trade"   164

Those with experience in preparing reports have found that   176
thereare special procedures they can use to simplify their   188
tasks. The following paragraphs contain samples of some pro- 200
cedures that can be especially helpful to a person who had not 212
previously keyboarded reports. (Anyone who plans to prepare   224
more that a few reports, however, should read several good books on the subject.) 241

Right margins. Attractive right margins result result when   254
good judgment is exercised used. Using the warning bell judiciously 267
ensures right margins that approximate left margins in width. 279

SS { _____   283

[1]For further information see The Chicago Manual of Style,   300
13th ed. (Chicago: The University of chicago Press, 1982),   312
p. 40.   314

(continued on page 87)

Memo Headings on Plain Paper. If a printed memo form is not available or if a memo is to be prepared for duplication, the memo headings TO:, FROM:, DATE:, and SUBJECT: must be typed as a part of the memo. Note the placement of the headings in the illustrations below.

```
        1½" on full sheet
        1" on half sheet

    TO:      All Office Secretaries
                                  DS
    FROM:    Duncan Tullane, Office Manager
1"  DATE:    December 5, 19--                    1"
    SUBJECT: Typing Memo Headings
                                  TS
    Occasionally it is necessary to type an interoffice memorandum on
    a spirit master, a stencil, or a plain sheet of paper.  In such
    cases, the headings which are preprinted on our memo form must be
```

or

```
        1½" on full sheet
        1" on half sheet

       TO:      All Office Secretaries
                                     DS
       FROM:    Duncan Tullane, Office Manager
1"     DATE:    December 5, 19--                  1"
       SUBJECT: Typing Memo Headings
                                     TS
    Occasionally it is necessary to type an interoffice memorandum on
    a spirit master, a stencil, or a plain sheet of paper.  In such
    cases, the headings which are preprinted on our memo form must be
```

105a-107a ▶ 5

Preparatory practice

Type as many times as you can in 5' at the beginning of each class period in this section.

alphabet	1	Major Pluvicky quizzed six officers about their losses during the war.
fig/sym	2	The total is $1,841.71 (sales, $1,762.40; and 4.5% sales tax, $79.31).
shift key	3	Is this Agnes', Emi's, or Jane's new computer? No, it is Carma Lou's.
fluency	4	The chair of the island city panel is to handle the amendment problem.

| 1 | 2 | 3 | 4 | 5 | 6 | 7 | 8 | 9 | 10 | 11 | 12 | 13 | 14 |

105b-107b ▶ 45

Office job simulation
(LM pp. 27–35)

Job 1
Memorandum (LM p. 27)

Mr. Tullane has asked you to prepare this memorandum. It will be photocopied and sent to all office employees. Proofread and correct errors before you remove the memo from the machine.

All Office Staff| Duncan G. Tullane, Office Manager| December 3, 19--| Integration of Information Processing Equipment

(¶) Many of you are already aware that the company has made the decision to implement the recommendation of the consultants to install a new information processing system. This new system will merge many of the present data processing systems and word processing functions. Also affected will be our records management department and our company's resource center.

(¶) The planned implementation schedule shows a conversion to the new system over the next six months. The first phase will be to convert the present company records to a computer compatible medium; in our case, that media will have two large capacity storage disks. The second phase will be the orientation and training of all office personnel on the new information processing equipment. Over the period of three months, we will have present word processing equipment replaced by a more sophisticated system. The third and final phase will be an evaluation of the system. Although this phase is scheduled for a two-month period, the evaluation will be an ongoing one for many months.

(¶) If any of you would like to discuss the implementation schedule of our new information processing system, please come and visit me. xx

words

2   314

     <u>Reference characters</u>. To keystroke a superior figure,   329
turn the platen back half a 1line and type the figure. Aster-   341
isks and other refrence symbols requires no such adjustment.   353
Keyboards equipped with special symbol keys for report writing are also   367
available for regular use.   369

<u>Page endings</u>. A few very simple guides become important when-   383
ever a report has more than one page. For example, never end a   396
page with a hyphenated word. Farther, do not leave a single   408
line a of paragraph at the bottom of a page or at the top of a   420
page (unless the paragraph has only one line, of course.)   432

     <u>Footnote content</u>. Underline titles of <u>complete</u> publica-   446
tions; use quotation marks with <u>parts of publications</u>. Thus,   460
the name of a magazine will be <u>underlined</u>, but the title of an   472
article within the magazine will be placed in quotation marks.   485
Months and location words, such as <u>volume</u> and <u>number</u>, may be   500
abbreviated.   503

     <u>Penciled guides</u>. A light pencil mark can be helpful to   517
mark approximate page endings, planned placement of page numbers,   530
and potential foot note locations. When the report has been   542
finished, of course, erase any visable pencil marks.   553

<u>Conclusion</u>   557

     With patience and skill, the keyboard operator can give a   569
well written report the porfessional appearance it deserves. Says   582
Lesikar, 12   584

     Even with the best typewriter available, the fin-   594
ished work is no better than the efforts of the typist.   605
But this statement does not imply that only the most   616
skilled typist can turn out good work. Even the the   626
inexperienced typist can produce acceptable manuscripts   637
simply by exercising care.   642

   646

—————————————

2 1Raymond V. Lesikar, <u>Basic Business Communcation</u> (Homwood: 657
Richard D. Irwin, Inc., 1979), p. 364.   665

Learning goals

1 To become familiar with the work of a general office.

2 To plan your work and complete it efficiently.

3 To integrate your knowledge and skills in completing office work acceptably.

Machine adjustments

1 Set paper guide at *0*.

2 Margins: 70–space line for drills and ¶ writings; as directed (or appropriate) for problems.

3 Set ribbon control to use the upper half of ribbon.

4 SS drill lines; DS ¶s; space problems as directed (or appropriate).

Office Job Simulation

Read carefully the material at the right and on page 223 before you begin the work of Section 26. Note any standard procedures that you think will save you time during the completion of the production activities.

Daily practice plan:

Preparatory practice .... 5'
Work on simulation .... 45'

Work Assignment

You have been assigned by Office Service Temporaries, Inc., to work for Fairfield Manufacturing, Inc., a firm that manufactures office furniture. The address where you are to report to work is 4320 Aldine Drive, San Diego, CA 92116-2307. Your immediate supervisor will be Mr. Duncan G. Tullane, Office Manager.

The company style manual at Fairfield Manufacturing specifies that all company letters are to be formatted in block style with open punctuation. The closing lines of all letters should include the typed name of the person for whom the letters are prepared followed on the next line by that person's business title. All letters and memorandums require *one* carbon copy for the file. Address appropriate envelopes for all letters.

Proofread all work carefully before removing it from your machine; correct all errors. All work that is to leave the company should be "mailable"—technically correct with all errors corrected neatly. All work to be used *within* the company should be "usable"—content correct but with *minor* "flaws" in format and placement permitted.

When specific job instructions are given, follow them carefully. When specific instructions are not given, make appropriate decisions on the basis of knowledge and experience. If your supervisor (teacher) considers some of your decisions unacceptable, learn from his or her suggestions—just as you would do in a business office.

Fairfield Manufacturing, Inc., has based its office manual and job instruction booklets on COLLEGE KEYBOARDING/TYPEWRITING, so use the Reference Guide and the index of your textbook to look up matters of style and placement when in doubt. When a job requires unusual specifications, Fairfield Manufacturing provides them in "Excerpts from the Office Procedures Manual."

Excerpts from the Office Procedures Manual

Justifying the Right Margin. The process of justifying the right margin gives the finished copy the appearance of a printed page with the right margin evenly aligned. Except for the last line of a paragraph, the words in each line are carefully spaced so that the right margin will be even. When using a standard manual or electric typewriter, all material must be typed twice. The first typing is used to determine how many extra spaces must be added to each line during the final or second typing. The normal procedure is to type as close to the end of the line as possible and then fill the remaining spaces with diagonals.

First typing	A major obstacle to communica-/ ting on a worldwide level lies/ in differences in languages./// People who can't read, write,//
Second typing	A major obstacle to communica- ting on a worldwide level lies in differences in languages. People who can't read, write,

When typing the material in final form, you must use good judgment in distributing the unused spaces throughout the line so they are least noticeable. If you are keyboarding on a computer or electronic typewriter, consult the operator's manual to automatically justify the right margin.

43a ▶ 6
Preparatory practice

each line 3 times SS (work for fewer than 3 errors per group); DS between 3-line groups; repeat selected lines as time permits

alphabet	1	Wilma thinks freezing prices at fixed levels for July is questionable.
fig/sym	2	A grant of $12,367.50 won't fund 10% of the studies; it is $948 short.
direct reaches	3	No doubt my brother Cecil served as an umpire on that bright June day.
easy	4	A fox lay in an island lair; a girl dug a quantity of pale lake worms.

| 1 | 2 | 3 | 4 | 5 | 6 | 7 | 8 | 9 | 10 | 11 | 12 | 13 | 14 |

43b ▶ 14
Format/type a bibliography

full sheet; use standard unbound report format; 1½" top margin recommended

1 Read the guides at the right; study the illustrated bibliography.

2 Keyboard the bibliography; make one carbon copy.

Guidelines for preparing a bibliography

A bibliography is a list of works cited or used in some way in the preparation of a report. Bibliographical entries are distinctive from footnotes, as can be noted in the following items:

• A bibliography is the final part of a report.

• The first surname of an entry is identified first, allowing the list to be arranged in alphabetic order.

• The first line of an entry is placed flush left; all succeeding lines of the entry are indented five spaces.

• Reference characters are not used.

• Items are made more incisive with the elimination of most parentheses and commas.

• Specific page numbers used in a footnote may be omitted.

BIBLIOGRAPHY

Langford, Floyd. "Systems Concept." <u>The Changing Office Environment</u>. Reston: National Business Education Association. Yearbook No. 18, 1980.

pica type

Lesikar, Raymond V. <u>Business Communication: Theory and Application</u>. 4th ed. Homewood: Richard D. Irwin, Inc., 1980.

Will, Mimi, and Donette Dake. <u>Concepts in Word Processing: The Challenge of Change</u>. Boston: Allyn and Bacon, Inc., 1981.

43c ▶ 30
Format/type a personal data sheet

full sheet; 1" top and side margins; set tab stop at center point

1 Read the information about data sheets at the right.

2 Keyboard a copy of the data sheet on page 89.

Developing personal data sheets

A personal data sheet is a summary of pertinent, personal facts, organized for quick reading. Data can be categorized in a number of ways, and the writer should use a form that will best display her or his qualifications. Note the following suggestions:

• The data sheet is accompanied by a well-worded letter of application.

• The appearance of the data sheet is as important as what it says.

• Complete sentences are rarely used.

• The data sheet should stress capabilities, not just aspirations.

• The data sheet should be as brief as possible but as long as necessary. Try not to exceed one page.

Preemployment testing, Part II
(continued)

Problem 2
Unbound, unedited report
(full sheet)

Using correct format, prepare the copy at the right as an un—bound report DS. Correct any errors as you type.

EMPLOYEE BENEFITS 4

OFICE SERVICE TEMPORARIES, INC. 10

Payed Holidays 16

As a OSTI employ you may be eligible to be 25
paid for any of the following holidays: new year's day, 36
memorial day, independence day, labor day, thanks- 46
giving day, and Christmas day. To qualify for each 57
paid Holiday you muts have work 300 hours in the 60 day 69
period imediately preceeding the holiday In addition 80
you must have worked the working day imediately 90
before and the one immediately after the holliday. 100

Vaccation Pay 105

Your eligible for vacation pay when you have 114
werked 1600 ours. Your vacation pay'll be for forty hours 126
at your most resent hourly rate. Once you rech 1600 137
hours and receive vacation pay you begin acumulatin 148
your nest 1600 hours. You must nottify the OSTI ofice 159
manager each time you became eligable. 167

Special Compinsation 175

Your fuly covered by the OTSI workers compen- 185
sation plan if your enjured or killed as a result of 196
an acident that is work related. If you aer injured 207
in a nonwork related accident you maybe eligable 218
for a $1,500 cash benafit. If you are hospitalized as a 229
result of such an accident you may qualify for 239
reimbursement of $25 per day — up to a mapimum 248
of $1,000 in anyone calender year. 255

Problem 3
Employee Record Form
(LM p. 25)

Mrs. DeSoto has in—formed you that you have passed OSTI's pre—employment testing program. She asks you to type the Employee Record Form which will be kept in the files of Office Service Tem—poraries, Inc. Prepare the Employee Record Form, supplying infor—mation about yourself.

Introducing 3

SALLY ANN DUPOIS 6
123 Poinciana Road 10
Memphis, Tennessee 38117-4121 16
(901-365-2275) 19
_{TS}

Present Career Objective 28

Eager to accept part-time position that provides opportunities for 42
additional training and potential for full-time employment. 54
_{TS}

Personal Qualifications 63

Cheerful, outgoing personality; dependable, cooperative worker 76
Very interested in retailing work; find it challenging 87
Excellent health; participate in golf, racquetball, and tennis 100

Experience 104

1985--present   The Toggery, 100 Madison Avenue, Memphis, TN 38103- 117
                 4219; Assistant Manager 122
1984 (summer)   Chobie's, 1700 Poplar Avenue, Memphis, TN 38104- 135
                 2176; Inventory Clerk and Cashier 141
1983 (summer)   Todds, 1450 Union Avenue, Memphis, TN 38104-5417; 154
                 Clerk and Assistant to the Buyer 161
1982 (summer)   Chobie's, 1700 Poplar Avenue, Memphis, TN 38104- 174
                 2176; Salesperson and Utility Helper 181

Education 185

Junior, Marketing, Memphis State University, Memphis, Tennessee 198
AA degree (associate degree/advertising; honors), State Technical 211
Institute, Memphis, Tennessee 217
Graduate (honor student), East High School, Memphis, Tennessee 230

References 233

Mrs. Evelyn J. Quinell   Professor Aldo R. MacKenzie 244
Manager, Chobie's   Department of Marketing Management 255
1700 Poplar Avenue   Memphis State University 263
Memphis, TN 38104-2176   Memphis, TN 38114-3285 273

Ms. Lanya Roover   Mr. Robert E. Tindall, Jr. 282
The Toggery   Attorney-at-Law 287
100 Madison Avenue   1045 Quinn Avenue 294
Memphis, TN 38103-4219   Memphis, TN 38106-4792 304

Preemployment Testing, Part II

After completing Part I of the employment test, Mrs. DeSoto asks you to complete Part II (Problems 1–3). Mrs. DeSoto allots you 45' to take Part II of the test. She suggests that you use 15' of this time to set up problems and to proofread and correct errors.

**Problem 1
Rough-draft letter**
(plain full sheet)

block style, open punctuation; use **December 2, 19—** for the current date

Current date   3

LO Manning Lane   *Use your personal title and name*   6 / 9
San Diego, CA 92154-2221   14

Dear   18

Thank~you for your ~letter concerning~ *recent inquiry about* employment opportunities   31

with Office Service Temporaries, Inc.,   39

OSTI is one~of~ the largest temporary office service *support* sup-   52

pliers in *the* San Diego area. We maintian a working staff of   63

over ~more than~ 600 temporary office ~people~ *workers* who se qualifications   74

fit them for assignment to jobs ranging from general office s *in areas*   88

~work~ to executive offices, from legal offices to medicla cen-   99

ters. We *currently* have people on assignment in more than 350 companies   114

and institutions in San Diego.   120

Because our personel must substitue for regularemployees   who happen to be away for several days at atime, our temporaries   must be able to adjust quickly to different office systems   and working conditions

I would be ~more than~ peleased to have you cometo my office   130

to discuss your qualifications. Thiswill give us the ~chance~ *opportunity*   143

to assess how we might give ~one~ *you* the variety of experience s   155

you want and at the same time provide our clients with the   167

office skills they temporarily need.   175

Sincerely yours   224

Ms. Silvia DeSoto, *Office Manager*   230

xx   231

Enclosed is a brochure which explains in greater detail how   187
OSTI functions and lists the steps in our employment pro-   198
cedure. Please use one of the telephone numbers given on   210
page 8 of the brochure to arrange for an appointment.   220

(Problem 2 is on next page)

Supplemental skill-building practice

Measure straight-copy skill

two 3' writings; proofread; determine *gwam*; circle errors

Difficulty index

all letters used  | A | 1.5 si | 5.7 awl | 80% hfw |

	gwam 1'	3'

Just recently an acquaintance of mine was complaining about how · 13 | 4 | 50

quickly papers accumulated on her desk; she never seemed able to reduce · 27 | 9 | 54

the load down to ground zero. There appeared to be some law working, · 41 | 14 | 59

she explained, that continued to increase the stack each day by exactly · 56 | 19 | 64

the amount she had reduced it the day before. 65 | 22 | 67

My friend ought to be better organized. She should schedule activi- · 14 | 26 | 72

ties so that work is attended to daily. Any paper that requires only a · 28 | 31 | 76

glance, a decision, and swift, final action should get just that. Any · 42 | 36 | 81

paper that must for some reason get closer attention should be subject · 56 | 40 | 86

to a fixed schedule for completion. Self-discipline is the key to order. 71 | 45 | 91

gwam 1' | 1 | 2 | 3 | 4 | 5 | 6 | 7 | 8 | 9 | 10 | 11 | 12 | 13 | 14 |
3' | | 1 | | 2 | | 3 | | 4 | | 5 |

Measure skill growth

Take one 3' and one 5' writing; determine *gwam*; proofread and circle errors.

Difficulty index

all letters used | A | 1.5 si | 5.7 awl | 80% hfw |

	gwam 3'	5'

Usually, writing a report does not seem quite so difficult if the · 4 | 3

writer breaks the task down into smaller jobs. Before even starting to · 9 | 5

write, for example, a writer must know exactly what is to be written, · 13 | 8

for whom, and why; and a request for a report ought to have specific · 18 | 11

directions with it. The next step is to build a working outline that · 23 | 13

summarizes the report. The outline can later be changed to a skeleton · 28 | 17

report with statements of purpose and main headings, subheadings, and · 32 | 19

paragraph headings that will in time grow into a completed report. 37 | 22

Solutions to the problem under study must be found and analyzed; · 41 | 25

and supporting data can be found, among other sources, by observation, · 46 | 28

by experimentation, in books, with a questionnaire, with interviews, · 50 | 30

and by examining all kinds of records. Each bit of data can be jotted · 55 | 33

on a file card, along with a complete citation of its source. As a · 60 | 36

last step, these data are added to the skeleton report; the citations · 65 | 39

are the footnotes. Then all that is needed are the final touches that · 69 | 41

produce a report that is usable, complete, to the point, and readable. 74 | 44

gwam 3' | 1 | 2 | 3 | 4 | 5 |
5' | 1 | | 2 | | 3 |

Office job simulation
(LM pp. 23–25)

Job 1
Letter of inquiry
(plain full sheet)

Your school advisor has given you an example of an inquiry letter which another student has recently sent to a temporary office service agency. Format and type the sample inquiry letter. Use modified block style with mixed punctuation and in-dented paragraphs.

Job 2
Compose a letter of inquiry (plain full sheet)

Study your copy of the in-quiry letter you prepared in Job 1. Compose your own in-quiry letter, using pertinent information about yourself. Use modified block style, indented paragraphs, and mixed punctuation. Date the letter **December 1, 19—;** address it to:

Mrs. Silvia DeSoto
340 Dominican Dr.
San Diego, CA 92128-4411

Job 3
Application form (LM p. 23)

Mrs. DeSoto responds to your letter of inquiry with a return letter and an appli-cation form, which she asks you to fill out, supplying pertinent information about yourself. You are to bring the completed application form with you to OSTI for an initial interview and pre-employment testing.

Preemployment testing, Part I
(full sheet)

Mrs. DeSoto asks you to take the first part of the job application test. Take one 5′ writing on the copy at the right for accuracy; record *gwam* and number of errors on the top of your paper.

words

211 Asbury Court | San Diego, CA 92109-2113 | May 14, 19-- | Mrs. Delores Cuen, 15
Personnel Manager | Temporary Office Personnel Center | 30 Ballinger Avenue | 29
San Diego, CA 92119-2210 | Dear Mrs. Cuen 37

(¶) I will soon complete the course requirements for an associate degree at 52
Coronado College. My major is office systems and administration with a minor 67
in personnel management. I have been on the Dean's List each term, and I need 83
only three more courses to complete my degree. 93

(¶) In addition to taking courses in concepts and principles relating to office 108
systems and administration, I have taken several hands-on courses in the use of 124
office automation equipment. I am also proficient in shorthand, although I have 140
not used the skill in a work setting. 148

(¶) To help me decide the kind of business or office in which I may want to seek 163
long-term employment, I would like to become an office temporary worker for 179
the next several months and to take evening classes to finish my degree. Dr. 194
Fremont Fisher, one of my professors, suggested that I contact you about this 210
kind of employment. 214

(¶) Will you please send me information about your agency and tell me how I can 229
become one of your temporary office personnel staff. 240

Sincerely yours | Roger K. Dastrup 246

Difficulty index

all letters used	A	1.5 si	5.7 awl	80% hfw

gwam 5′

When people in the office work force write in longhand, type on a 3 | 47
standard typewriter, or use an electronic typewriter, they are processing 6 | 50
words. The volume of copy that must be produced in the office of today 8 | 53
continues to grow, and there is more and more a need to simplify and 11 | 56
speed up the handling of words. In order to keep pace with the need to 14 | 59
produce copy more efficiently, office personnel often use more complex 17 | 62
word processing equipment that can record and store the typed material. 20 | 65
Once the material is stored, it may be retrieved and printed rapidly. 23 | 67

Not only does sophisticated word processing equipment allow stored 25 | 70
data to be reprinted quickly, it also provides a very simple way to edit 28 | 73
and correct typewritten material without the need to retype the entire 31 | 76
document on a typewriter. Any size document that needs to be revised 34 | 79
may be retrieved from a file or tape, and only those parts that need to 37 | 81
be corrected are changed. The typist can make the needed changes and 40 | 84
print the new document in just a fraction of the time that it would take 42 | 87
to retype the entire document on a standard typewriter. 45 | 89

5′ | 1 | 2 | 3 |

Period and question mark

1 Make decisions about place–ment of the copy. A full sheet and a 1½" top margin are suggested.

2 Proofread carefully; correct errors.

3 Note your comments about your placement decisions at the bottom of the page.

4 Study the rules and examples from your copy.

THE PERIOD AND THE QUESTION MARK

1. Use a period after a complete sentence; follow the period with two blank spaces.

   Examples: Buy the books. She will use them later.
   I know Don. He is a member of our club.

2. Use a period after an abbreviation. Space once after periods used after abbreviations unless the abbreviation is made up of letters that are combined to represent more than one word; in that case, space only after the final period.

   Examples: Mr. Ogden will be graduated with a Ph.D.
   Mrs. Sipe arrived at 6 a.m. last Monday.

3. Use periods to form an ellipsis. Ellipsis periods, commonly three in number, represent the omission of words from quoted data. Use four periods when an ellipsis ends a sentence. Space once between ellipsis periods.

   Examples: The economy . . . has not yet responded.
   We agree the general won the war . . . .

4. Use a question mark after a direct question--not after an indirect question. Space twice after a question mark that is used to terminate a question.

   Examples: Where is he? I wonder if he had dinner.
   Did she go? I asked if she had tickets.

5. A request that is phrased as a question is usually terminated with a period.

   Examples: Will you please bring me a glass of tea.
   Will you kindly mail that letter for me.

6. Use a question mark after each of a series of short questions that are related to a single thought. Capitalize the first word of each of the questions only if it is a complete sentence. Space once after all but the final question mark.

   Examples: Was it birds? squirrels? rabbits? ducks?
   Who wrote this? Was it Lee? Was it Dale?

Compose at the keyboard

Make all format decisions.

1 Read the ¶ thoughtfully.

2 Compose a second ¶ of five or six lines in which you express your ideas about success. Begin with the word **Personally**.

3 Proofread your ¶.

4 Type a final copy of both ¶s. Center a title over the ¶s.

   Each of us is building a road that is to lead to some ultimate place known as "success." We construct our highway in stages, passing from one objective to another, expecting in time to reach our goal--to be successful. But how shall we recognize success when we reach it? What is success? When is a person successful?

   Personally, (Compose the remainder of the second paragraph.)

Learning goals

1 To prepare a letter of inquiry for job placement.

2 To complete properly a job application form for a temporary office service agency.

3 To complete a job applicant testing program.

4 As time permits, to complete properly an employee record form.

Machine adjustments

1 Set paper guide at *0*.

2 Set ribbon control to type on upper half of ribbon.

3 Use a 70–space line and single spacing for drills; use a 70–space line and double spacing for timed writings; prepare jobs as directed.

Office Job Simulation

Before you begin work in Section 25, read carefully the material at the right.

Daily practice plan:

Preparatory practice .... 5′
Office work simulation ...... 45′

Introduction

You have been searching for just the right job for the past several weeks. You consult with your advisor at school who suggests that you seek employment through a temporary office service agency. According to your advisor, working through such an agency will give you a variety of office experiences, will help you decide the kind of office in which you may wish to work after graduation, and may lead to a permanent position with one of the firms to which you will be assigned.

After making the decision to work as a temporary office worker, you make inquiries about what temporary office help agencies exist in your city. You compile information and send letters of inquiry to the leading agencies in your area. Office Service Temporaries, Inc., (OSTI), sends you a brochure describing the various services it offers and invites you to come in to the office for an interview. You decide to go to OSTI to seek temporary employment.

At the end of the initial interview, the office manager of OSTI, Mrs. Silvia DeSoto, asks you to take an application form home, complete it in typewritten form, and bring it back the next day. Mrs. DeSoto explains that this completed form will help Office Service Temporaries match your qualifications to any of the positions currently available.

Because of your strong qualifications, OSTI decides to have you undergo the final step in its application process. Mrs. DeSoto asks you to undergo OSTI's complete testing process. The test requires you to take a straight-copy timed writing test and to format and prepare a letter and a report. Your ability to proofread and correct errors will also be observed.

After taking the test, OSTI decides that they can use your services. They ask you to type the Employee Record Form for their files so that they can match your qualifications with specific job skills temporarily required by various firms in your community.

103a-104a ▶ 5

Preparatory practice

each line 3 times SS (slowly, faster, top speed); DS between 3-line groups; repeat selected lines as time permits

alphabet	1	Zachary and Jim, both fine young explorers, quickly wanted adventures.
fig/sym	2	Corn is $2.504/bu. (down 13 cents); beans are $6.718/bu. (up 9 cents).
third row	3	Your top priority was to equip your territory people with typewriters.
fluency	4	The auditor may handle the six problems for the firms at half the pay.

| 1 | 2 | 3 | 4 | 5 | 6 | 7 | 8 | 9 | 10 | 11 | 12 | 13 | 14 |

Learning goals

1 To type tables in exact center and in reading position.
2 To type main, secondary, and column headings.
3 To align figures, decimals, and dollar signs in columns.
4 To center announcements horizontally and vertically.

Machine adjustments

1 Set paper guide at 0; remove tab stops.
2 Set ribbon control to type on upper half of ribbon.
3 Use a 70–space line.
4 SS drills; DS paragraphs.

44a ▶ 6
Preparatory practice

each line 3 times SS (work for fewer than 2 errors per group); DS between 3-line groups; repeat selected lines as time permits

alphabet 1 Jack may provide a few extra quiz questions or problems for the group.

figures 2 We can try to add these fractions: 2/3, 3/4, 4/5, 5/6, 7/8, and 9/10.

shift/lock 3 THE LAKES TODAY, published in Dayton, Ohio, is issued in June or July.

easy 4 Enrique may fish for cod by the city docks, but he may risk a penalty.

| 1 | 2 | 3 | 4 | 5 | 6 | 7 | 8 | 9 | 10 | 11 | 12 | 13 | 14 |

44b ▶ 9
Format/type centered announcement

half sheet

Review centering procedures shown at the right.

Use a half sheet (insert long side first). Center the problem verti–cally; center each line horizon–tally; DS.

Vertical centering

1 Count the lines to be centered.
2 Subtract counted lines from total lines available (66 for a full sheet and 33 for a half sheet).
3 Divide the remaining lines by 2 and dis–tribute these lines as top and bottom mar–gins. Ignore fractions.
4 Space down from the top edge of the paper 1 more line than the number of lines figured for the top margin.

Horizontal centering

1 Move margin stops to ends of the scale.
2 Clear all tab stops.
3 From the center point, backspace *once* for each 2 letters, figures, spaces, or punc-tuation marks in the line to be centered. Do not backspace for a leftover stroke at the end of a line.
4 Begin to keyboard where you complete the backspacing. If all lines are of the same length, set a margin stop; if not, repeat Steps 3 and 4 for each subsequent line.

	words
ARS MUSICA	2
under the direction of Serge Chomentikov	10
will present its	14
Annual Spring Concert	18
Friday evening, April 24, at eight o'clock	27
Taer Recital Hall	30

102c ▶ 10
Inventory/build
script-copy skill

1 Two 3' writings for inventory; circle errors. On LM p. 3, record *gwam* and number of errors for the more accurate writings.

2 Two 1' writings to improve speed.

Difficulty index

all letters used	A	1.5 si	5.7 awl	80% hfw

	gwam 1'		3'
A person begins to learn the art of production typing	11	4	36
by first recognizing the basic rules for the placement	22	7	40
and balance of any typing job, whether it is a letter,	33	11	44
manuscript, or table. At first, the typist must have	44	14	47
something concrete upon which to construct a sound	54	18	51
production skill. After a while, improvement is per-	64	21	54
ceived; and the typist is able to format a job without	75	25	58
the exact adherence to rule requirements. Later, the per-	87	29	62
son may not need to refer to the placement rules at all.	98	33	65

102d ▶ 25
Inventory
production skills

Time schedule

Assembling materials .... 2'
Timed production .... 18'
Final check; compute
  n-pram .... 5'

Job 1 (half sheet)
Table with rulings

Center table on half sheet, long side up; insert horizontal rulings as you type; DS body of table; leave 4 spaces between columns.

QUARTERLY SALES REPORT

(January–March, 19--)

Salesperson	January	February	March	Total	
					22
					35
					44
					57
Lois R. Andrus	$ 3,840	$ 3,911	$ 4,870	$12,621	66
Charles A. Cummings	2,130	3,731	2,986	8,847	75
Leslie Q. Owens	4,210	4,560	4,874	13,644	83
Stephanie E. Scott	3,830	3,924	3,870	11,624	92
Jane Y. Zwick	2,870	2,710	3,870	9,450	99
					112
Totals	$16,880	$18,836	$20,470	$56,186	120
					133

(title lines: 5, 9)

Job 2 (full sheet)
Rough-draft table

Center table in reading position; DS body of table; leave 4 spaces between columns; do not use rulings. Use main heading: **EMPLOYEES OF THE SANCHEZ MANUFACTURING COMPANY**; use secondary heading: **(Years of Employment)**.

Note: If time permits, redo Job 1.

words in heading 14

Employees of Less Than 1 Year	Employees of 1 to 5 Years	Employees of 6 to 10 Years	Employees of 11 to 15 Years	
				24
				47
~~Bob~~ Robert Sawyer	~~Pete~~ Peter Dunne	~~Jo~~ Joan Larsen	Sue Patrick / san	57
Patti~~e~~ ricia Jones	Jolynn Kohler	Fran~~k~~ Lopez	Juan Gomez	68
Waku Mori	George McMurd~~o~~ ie	Ded~~~~ ra West	~~Joey~~ Joseph Rozales	78
~~John~~ Jack DeWitt	Mary Hen~~~~drix	Jimmy~~~~ Von Herman	~~R~~ Richard Washington	90
Rich~~~~ ard petersen	~~Maggie~~ Margaret Black	Irma Hardy	Doug~~~~ las Berry	101

44c ▶ 35
Center tables

3 half sheets

Center the tables verti-
cally and horizontally.

Problem 1

Study the information at
the right and the illus-
trations below.

Format and type the illustrated problem on a half
sheet (insert long side
first); SS; exact center;
10–space intercolumn.

Guidelines for centering columns horizontally

1 Take preparatory steps

a Move margin stops to ends
of scale. Clear all tabulator
stops.

b Move carrier (carriage) to
center point.

c If spacing is not given, estimate spacing for intercolumns
(the area between columns)—
preferably an even number
of spaces (4, 6, 8, 10, or 12,
for example).

2 To set left margin stop

Check the longest item in each
column. Then from the center
point, backspace *once* for
each *2* characters and spaces
in the longest items in each
column then for each 2 spaces
to be allowed for the intercolumns. Set the left margin
stop at this point.

If the longest item in one
column has an extra character,
combine the extra character
with the first letter in the
next column. If one stroke
is left over after back-
spacing for all columnar
items, disregard it.

Study the illustration below
used to center two items and a
10-space intercolumn for the
first table.

3 To set tabulator stops

After setting the left margin
stop, space forward once for
each character in the longest
item in the first column, then
for each space to be allowed
for the first intercolumn. Set
tab stop at this point. Follow
this procedure for each subsequent column and inter-
column.

backspace once
for each two
characters ⟶ 1 1 1 1 1 1 1 1 1 1 1 1 1 1 1 1 1 1 1 1 1 1 1

Ca| ro| ly| n| Ly| nn| C| ar| ve| re| Vi| ce| P| re| si| de| nt| 1-2| 3-4| 5-6| 7-8| 9-10|

		words
CALUMINEX BOARD OF DIRECTORS		6
Margin stop	Tab stop TS	
Muriel E. Bouhm	President	11
R. Grady Atgood	Vice President	17
Alonzo J. Cruz, Sr.	Secretary	23
Carolyn Lynn Carvere	Treasurer	29
Myron A. Moilion	Member	34
Sara Harley Beck	Member	39
Key	*Carolyn Lynn Carvere*	*10*	*Vice President*

102a ▶ 5
Preparatory practice

each line 3 times SS (slowly, faster, slowly); DS between 3-line groups; repeat selected lines as time permits

alphabet	1	Max Verbeck set the quartz jewel in antique gold for the lucky person.
fig/sym	2	Please write to us at Box 847, R.R. #1, or phone us at (319) 268-4705.
double letter	3	Access to the accounts will alleviate the need for conferring with me.
fluency	4	The haughty visitor is to pay for the memento and then cycle downtown.

| 1 | 2 | 3 | 4 | 5 | 6 | 7 | 8 | 9 | 10 | 11 | 12 | 13 | 14 |

102b ▶ 10
Inventory/build straight-copy skill

1 One 5' writing for accuracy; on LM p. 3, record *gwam* and number of errors.
2 One 1' writing on each ¶ for speed.

Difficulty index

all letters used | A | 1.5 si | 5.7 awl | 80% hfw

gwam 1' | 5'

The computer age has arrived in the classrooms of many schools in — 13 | 3 | 64
the United States. The advent of the microcomputer, which is small, — 27 | 5 | 67
self-contained, and inexpensive to run, has done much to bring about — 41 | 8 | 70
this change. Microcomputers offer a way for teachers to introduce stu- — 55 | 11 | 73
dents to machines which may do much to shape their careers. Students — 69 | 14 | 76
who learn how to keyboard on these machines will have an advantage over — 83 | 17 | 79
others in a world that is finding more and more uses for the computer. — 97 | 20 | 81

A new type of microcomputer has been increasing in popularity be- — 13 | 22 | 84
cause it can be used by people without the specialized training that — 27 | 25 | 87
made the old-style microcomputers so difficult to use. This new micro- — 41 | 28 | 90
computer is equipped with a "help" key that can aid the user in operating — 56 | 31 | 93
any function on the machine. The user simply pushes the help key and — 70 | 34 | 95
indicates that aid is needed to perform a specific activity. The com- — 84 | 36 | 98
puter responds by giving a series of prompts, at the end of which it — 98 | 40 | 101
offers the answer to the user's problem. — 106 | 41 | 103

Changes in software are also making microcomputers very easy to use. — 14 | 44 | 105
Before the changes, it was often necessary to have large files of floppy — 29 | 46 | 108
disks, each used for a particular job activity. The user had to change — 43 | 49 | 111
the disks as he or she went from one job activity to another. New soft- — 57 | 52 | 114
ware packages are so nearly linked that by simply pressing a key the — 71 | 55 | 117
operator can change from one job activity to another. This ends the — 85 | 58 | 119
need to change software modules between jobs and to deal with new command — 100 | 60 | 122
modes for each business operation. — 107 | 62 | 124

gwam 1' | 1 | 2 | 3 | 4 | 5 | 6 | 7 | 8 | 9 | 10 | 11 | 12 | 13 | 14 |
5' | 1 | 2 | 3 |

44c, continued

Problem 2

Format and type Problem 1 again; use the same directions, but change SS to DS.

Problem 3

Format/type the problem at the right on a half sheet (insert long side first); SS; exact center; 14–space intercolumn.

words

CALUMINEX BRANCH MANAGERS — 5

TS

Gertrude F. Schuyler	Albuquerque	12
Albert C. Chung	Allentown	17
Dale T. O'Hargran	Birmingham	23
F. Janice Montgomery	Denver	28
Rose B. Shikamuru	Honolulu	34
Carla E. Bragg	New Haven	39
Margret G. Bredeweg	St. Louis	45

Key | *Gertrude F. Schuyler* | *14* | *Albuquerque* |

45a ▶ 6

Preparatory practice

each line 3 times SS (work for fewer than 2 errors per group); DS between 3-line groups; repeat selected lines as time permits

alphabet	1	The king and queen brought dozens of expensive jewels from the colony.
fig/sym	2	Check #4690 for $1,375, dated February 28, was sent to O'Neill & Sons.
adjacent reaches	3	As Louise Liu said, few questioned the points asserted by the porters.
easy	4	He may fish for a quantity of smelt; he may wish for aid to land them.

| 1 | 2 | 3 | 4 | 5 | 6 | 7 | 8 | 9 | 10 | 11 | 12 | 13 | 14 |

45b ▶ 16

Preapplication drills: realigning/aligning items

Drill 1

twice as shown DS; 14-space intercolumn

Realigning items at the left

After setting the left margin as usual, adjust it to the right (in this instance 3 spaces) to accommodate the most common line setting. Use the margin release and backspacer for longer lines.

Aligning items at the right

Since spacing forward and backward will be needed to align items at the right, adjust the tab setting for the item length that requires the least forward and backward spacing.

		tab
District 9		
Reset margin → Almont		27
Belden	Backspace once →	150
District 10		
Erie		85
Lamberg	Space forward once →	9
District 11		
Orville		46
Racine		9

Key | *District 10* | *14* | *150* |

Drill 2

half sheet (enter long side first); DS; exact center; 12–space intercolumn

To align a column of words at the right (as in the second column), backspace as usual to set left margin. When spacing forward, set the tab at the end of the second column rather than at the beginning; backspace once for each character in the second column to position for keyboarding.

PROPOSED BANQUET AGENDA

Tab stop ↓

Preliminary remarks	Ellen Prater
Introductions	Grant Dubin
Speaker	Rosalyn Booth
Commentary	Drake Eppingham
Closing remarks	Ellen Prater

Key | *Preliminary remarks* | *12* | *Drake Eppingham* |

101c ▶ 35
Inventory production skills

Time schedule

Assembling materials .... 3'
Timed production .... 25'
Final check; compute
n–pram .... 7'

Job 1
Letter (LM p. 17)

modified block style with in–dented ¶s, mixed punctuation

	words
July 23, 19-- |Ms. Juanita Rosini |7302 East Forest |Detroit, MI 48214-2010 |Dear	16
Ms. Rosini	18

(¶ 1) On July 20, the Board of Directors declared a cash dividend of 30 $2.50 per share of common stock. This dividend will be payable after 44 September 1 to stockholders of record as of July 1, 19--. 56

(¶ 2) The dividend is equal to a 13.9 percent return on the par value 69 investment. The company's profits after taxes for the past fiscal year 83 were $23,987,500, which was a 10.5 percent increase over the previous 97 year. 99

(¶ 3) Your dividend check will be mailed to you on September 1. (92) 110

Sincerely | Ahmad Z. Farouk | President | xx 118

Job 2
Memorandum (LM p. 19)

TO: Robert P. Jones | FROM: Carolyn D. Tew | DATE: November 13, 19-- | 14 SUBJECT: Thanksgiving Holiday Hours 21

(¶ 1) As Personnel Manager, will you please announce to our employees that the 36 office will be closed from noon on Wednesday, November 22, until 8 a.m. on 51 Monday, November 27. 55

(¶ 2) The following policy has been established for any employees who do not 69 have an excusable absence. Office personnel must report for work on Wednes- 84 day morning in order to qualify for the Wednesday afternoon paid holiday. 99 Employees who do not report to work on Wednesday morning will be charged 114 with a full day's vacation for that day. 122

(¶ 3) Please see that the employees are made aware of the policy which has been 137 described above. 140

xx 141

Job 3
Letter with tabulation
(LM p. 21)

block style, open punctuation; SS and center tabular material in two columns; allow 4 spaces between columns

April 6, 19-- | Anderson Lumber Company | Attention Mrs. Pamela Lopez | 3905 14 North Diamond Mill Road | Dayton, OH 45246-3210 | Ladies and Gentlemen 28

(¶ 1) Your order dated April 1 has been filled and shipped with the exception of 43 the following two items: oak paneling, Stock #32-124, and birch paneling, Stock 59 #87-331. We no longer handle these two items; however, we do have the follow- 75 ing two items which are excellent substitutes in stock: 86

Stock #32-X124	Oak Paneling (4' × 8')	93
Stock #87-X331	Birch Paneling (4' × 8')	101

Job 4 (full sheet)
Simplified memo

retype memo in Job 2; simplified style

(¶ 2) Enclosed is a brochure which describes these two items. Please let us know 116 if you would like to substitute these items, and we will ship them to you im- 132 mediately. (106) 134

Sincerely | Miss Loretta V. Conrad | Sales Manager | xx | Enclosure 146

45c ▶ 28
Format/type tables with main and secondary headings

Problem 1

full sheet; DS; reading position; 20–space intercolumn

A TS usually separates a main heading from a table; when a secondary heading is used, DS after the main heading and TS after the secondary heading.

For columns with dollar signs, use the dollar sign only with the top figure and the total (when one is shown). Keystroke $ one space to the left of horizontal beginning point of the longest line in the column. It should be typed again in the same position when a *total line* appears in the table.

		words
CALUMINEX		2
Branch Office Sales for March (DS)		8
(TS)		
Albuquerque	$ 32,791	12
Allentown	47,781	16
Birmingham	60,898	19
Denver	4,558	22
Honolulu	8,432	25
New Haven	104,932	28
St. Louis	13,166	32
San Diego	89,005	35
San Juan	113,364	39
Seattle	21,539	43
	$496,466 (DS)	45

Problem 2

full sheet; DS; reading position; 16–space intercolumn

		words
SOUTH AMERICAN COUNTRIES		5
Approximate Area in Square Miles		12
Argentina	1,072,067	16
Bolivia	424,162	19
Brazil	3,286,470	22
Chile	292,256	25
Colombia	439,512	28
Ecuador	105,685	31
Peru	496,222	34
Uruguay	72,172	37
Venezuela	352,143	40

Problem 3

1 Read the guidelines for deciding intercolumn spacing.

2 Repeat Problem 1. Use a half sheet; exact center; SS. Set a new width for the intercolumn.

Guides for deciding intercolumn spacing
These guidelines will help you decide on the number of spaces to use for intercolumns.

• The body of a table should be wider than its main and secondary headings.

• To center a table, backspace for columns first, intercolumns last.

• Backspace for intercolumns until an appropriate place for setting the left margin has been reached. Set the margin stop; space forward as usual.

Inventory goals

In Section 24, you will take a series of tests to prepare yourself to take an employment test in Section 25. You will determine:

1 Your present straight–copy skill on 5–minute timed writings.

2 Your present production skill performance level. Record the results when indicated.

Machine adjustments

1 Set paper guide at *0*.

2 Set ribbon control to type on upper half of ribbon.

3 Use a 70–space line and single spacing (SS) for drill lines.

4 Use a 70–space line, double spacing (DS), and 5–space ¶ indentions for paragraph copy.

101a ▶ 5
Preparatory practice

each line 3 times SS (slowly, faster, slowly); DS between 3-line groups; repeat selected lines as time permits

alphabet	1	Judge Kerrwick explained very carefully both city zoning requirements.
fig/sym	2	We must pay $2,495 interest (13.8%) on the $18,080 note dated 6/07/85.
adjacent key	3	After we stopped for a look at the poor lions, we pondered about them.
fluency	4	The auditor is to blame for the chaotic problem of the city endowment.

| 1 | 2 | 3 | 4 | 5 | 6 | 7 | 8 | 9 | 10 | 11 | 12 | 13 | 14 |

101b ▶ 10
Inventory/build rough-draft copy skill

1 Two 3' writings for inventory; circle errors. On LM p. 3, record *gwam* and number of errors for the more accurate of the two writings.

2 One 1' writing on each ¶ to improve speed.

Difficulty index

all letters used	A	1.5 si	5.7 awl	80% hfw

	gwam 1'	3'
Today, business firms ~~Many organizations~~ have a great many jobs to ~~give~~ *offer* to	11	4	60
people ~~those~~ who want to accept the unique challenge of ~~trying to~~ *solving*	23	8	64
~~solve~~ some of the ~~greatest~~ *foremost* problems ~~opposing~~ *facing* the business	33	11	67
world. The ~~disciplines~~ *fields* of science, insurance, finance, *sales,* medi-	46	15	71
cine, and law, to name just a few, offers buiness-related jobs.	59	19	76
however, ~~if~~ regardless of the area of business in which you	70	23	79
decide to work certain factors must be considered if you wish	83	27	84
to be a success.	86	29	85
Your Inherent talent and *your* education are two of the primary	13	33	89
factors needed for success. Success rarely ~~happens~~ *comes* to those	25	37	93
with no training or ~~no~~ *little* ability. Also, ~~almost all~~ *most* of the	36	40	97
personnel experts *in the field* will agree that your interest in business	50	45	101
plays a *major* role in *determining* your job success. Success comes more easily	66	51	107
to those who ~~if you~~ are properly equpped and ~~like the~~ *who are zealous about the* work that they do.	83	56	112

46a ▶ 6
Preparatory practice

each line 3 times SS (work for fewer than 2 errors per group); DS between 3-line groups; repeat selected lines as time permits

alphabet	1	Julie began to study the six chapters on vitamins for her weekly quiz.
figures	2	I will send 2,795 of the 4,680 sets now and the remainder on the 13th.
one hand	3	I refereed only a few cases; I regarded waste water as a greater case.
easy	4	May I also fix the shape of the right hand and elbow of the clay form?

| 1 | 2 | 3 | 4 | 5 | 6 | 7 | 8 | 9 | 10 | 11 | 12 | 13 | 14 |

46b ▶ 10
Preapplication drill: center column headings

half sheet; DS; 10 spaces between columns

1 Read the information about centering column headings.

2 Type the drill below; center headings over the columns. Underline the headings.

Guides for centering columnar headings

• A column heading is typed a double space above a column centered over the longest item in the column.

a To determine the center point of the longest item in a column, space forward from the starting point of the column *once* for every *two* strokes or spaces in the longest item. Disregard a leftover stroke.

b The point where the forward spacing stops is the center point of the column. Backspace *once* for each *two* strokes in the heading; disregard a leftover stroke. Starting at the place where backspacing ended, type the heading.

• You may prefer to type column headings after you type the columns. After typing the table headings, space down to the approximate position for the first line of the table, leaving the column heading line vacant. After the columns have been typed, you may enter the column headings.

• If the column heading is longer than its column, use the heading as the longest item in the column for horizontal placement purposes. Then, center the column under the column heading.

Book	Author
Jane Eyre	Bronte
Oliver Twist	Dickens
The Great Gatsby	Fitzgerald
Showboat	Ferber

Key | *The Great Gatsby* | 10 | *Fitzgerald* |

46c ▶ 34
Format/type tables with column headings

Read the information at the right; then format and type the tables on page 97.

Guidelines for formatting a table

To format a table attractively, certain questions must be answered appropriately; as:

• Single or double spacing? Double spacing is more attractive and easier to read, but it may require more space than you have available.

• Full or half sheet? Consider how the table will be used and how much space is available. If more than 20 lines are required, use a full sheet.

• Reading position or exact center? Reading position is recommended for a full sheet, exact center for a half sheet.

• Number of intercolumn spaces? Backspace for columns. Then backspace once for each two spaces to be left between columns (leave an even number of spaces between columns). Be sure the body of the table will be wider than the table heading.

LEVEL FIVE
Processing information
(staff office simulations)

This level of Advanced Keyboarding/Formatting Skill is designed to provide you with ample opportunity to develop your information processing skills in a variety of situations commonly found in sales offices, general offices, accounting offices, and executive offices.

Although the primary emphasis in Level 5 is on the development of your production competence, you should continue to improve your basic speed and accuracy skills. Section 28 and supplemental skill-building practices are devoted almost entirely to speed and accuracy development.

In addition, the final section is a measurement section that tests both your production skills and your speed and accuracy skills. Your two major performance goals are:

- To develop a keen responsibility for high-quality production work.
- To develop the ability to make decisions without direct supervision.

This level provides for about 15 percent of your classroom time to be devoted to basic speed and accuracy development and 85 percent to production activities.

Problem 1

full sheet; reading position; DS;
decide intercolumn spacing

PRINCIPAL WORLD LANGUAGES		words
		5
Language	Millions	12
Arabic	155	14
English	397	17
French	107	19
German	119	21
Hindi	254	23
Japanese	119	26
Mandarin Chinese	726	30
Portuguese	151	33
Russian	274	35
Spanish	258	37

Problem 2

half sheet (insert long side first);
exact center; SS; decide inter–
column spacing

THE SPRINGARN MEDAL		words
		4
Selected Winners		7
Recipient	Year	13
Martin Luther King, Jr.	1956	19
Edward (Duke) Ellington	1958	25
Leontyne Price	1964	29
Sammy Davis, Jr.	1967	33
Henry Aaron	1974	36
Andrew Young	1977	40
Coleman Young	1980	44

Problem 3

Make all decisions about place–
ment of copy.

Notes:

For Column 3, set the tab for the
longest number in the column;
then backspace one space to type
the dollar sign. Align figures at the
decimal.

Many electronic typewriters and
microcomputers have a decimal
tab which automatically aligns
copy at the decimal.

THE ALGONQUIN CLUB			words
			4
Operating Budget, 19--			8
Committee	Chairperson	Budget	19
Business Affairs	C. Villeneuve	$310.50	27
Conservation	D. Treece	95.00	33
Finance	A. Perez	8.50	37
International Relations	F. Heckman	85.00	46
Program	I. Breece	375.00	51

47

47a ▶ 6
Preparatory practice

each line 3 times SS
(work for fewer than
2 errors per group);
DS between 3-line
groups; repeat
selected lines as
time permits

alphabet 1 May the judge quiz the clerks from Iowa about extensive profit-taking?

figures 2 Flight 374 will leave at 10:46 a.m. and arrive in Buffalo at 9:58 p.m.

double letters 3 The school committee will do well to pass on all the Tennessee offers.

easy 4 It is a duty of the civic auditor to aid a city firm to make a profit.

| 1 | 2 | 3 | 4 | 5 | 6 | 7 | 8 | 9 | 10 | 11 | 12 | 13 | 14 |

Problem 2
Leftbound report
DS the report given at the right.

words

RECOMMENDATION FOR IMPROVING EMPLOYEE BENEFITS PLAN 10

Serious consideration should be given to establishing a thrift plan for 25
all employees of your company. A thrift plan is a voluntary supplemental 40
retirement plan that encourages employees to save part of their earnings. 55
Encouragement comes in the form of matching contributions by the employer. 70
Most plans allow limited withdrawals or borrowing to meet emergencies or 84
long-term savings plans for purposes such as the accumulation of equity or the 100
financing of a child's education. 107

A typical thrift plan would allow employees to contribute a maximum of 6 122
percent of salary. Employee contributions would be matched at the rate of 50 138
cents from the employer for each dollar from the employee. The best plans 153
have employer contributions that match those of employees on a dollar-for- 168
dollar basis. 171

Vesting typically occurs faster in thrift plans than in pension plans. A 186
typical plan would have no vesting for five years and would then give 100 200
percent vesting. Vesting refers to the point at which an employee does not 216
forfeit the right to employer contributions in the event of termination of his or 232
her employment. 235

REFERENCES 238

Hess, Mary. "Thrift Plans." Class handout in Business Administration 487, 253
Central University, 1985. 258

Pritchett, Stephen A. "Employee Benefits Plans." Consultant's Report, 273
Columbia, South Carolina, 1985. 279

Problem 3
Second page of
an unbound report
Prepare the material given at the right as the second page of an unbound report.

DS   The value of a evaluation program lies in being continuous 14
and functional. One or more persons involved in the initial 26
evaluation should be given the responsibility of administering 39
the program on a continuing basis. The experience and training 55
given the Job Evaluation Committee qualify uniquely them to 70
administer such a program. ¶ The forms, manuals, and other 80
records contain in the report reflect step-by-step procedures 93
to follow and provide the data needed to administer the program. 107

47b ▶ 12

Compose at the keyboard

Make all decisions about format.

1 Assume that you have agreed to run for president of the student body at your col–lege. Compose a four– or five–line paragraph in which you set forth some of the changes you would attempt to inaugurate.

2 Proofread the ¶; make changes with proofreader's marks.

3 Type a final copy. Center the title **MY PLATFORM**.

47c ▶ 10

Review tables

Make all decisions about format.

			words
CALUMINEX			2
19-- Representatives of the Year			9
Region	Representatives	Sales	20
Eastern	Polly Murger	$357,214	26
Southern	Brent Ortega	542,168	32
Midwestern	Rick Hyatt	497,135	38
Western	Mika Shibasaki	568,900	44

47d ▶ 22

Measure skill application: tables

Time schedule

Assembling materials .... 2'
Timed production .... 15'
Final check; proofread;
   compute *g–pram* .... 5'

Problem 1

half sheet (enter long side first); SS; exact center; decide inter-column spacing

FAMOUS AMERICAN PAINTINGS			words
			5
Painter	Title	Size	12
Mary Cassatt	After the Bath	$26'' \times 39''$	20
Willem de Kooning	Woman I	$76'' \times 58''$	27
Winslow Homer	The Gulf Stream	$28'' \times 49''$	35
Jackson Pollock	Number 27	$11' \times 24'$	42
Robert Rauschenberg	Tracer	$84'' \times 60''$	50
John Singer Sargent	Madame X	$82'' \times 43''$	57
Grant Wood	American Gothic	$30'' \times 25''$	65
Andrew Wyeth	Christina's World	$32'' \times 48''$	73

Problem 2

half sheet; make all decisions for placement of copy

THE UNITED NATIONS			words
			4
Small-Nation Members			8
Country	Admitted	Est. Pop.	18
Belize	1981	146,000	22
Dominica	1978	80,000	26
Grenada	1974	108,000	31
Maldives	1965	150,000	35
St. Lucia	1979	124,000	40
St. Vincent and the Grenadines	1980	120,000	48
Sao Tome and Principe	1975	90,000	55
Seychelles	1976	70,000	60
Vanutu	1981	112,700	64

100a ▶ 5
Preparatory practice

each line 3 times SS (slowly, faster, slowly); DS between 3-line groups; repeat selected lines as time permits

alphabet 1 Wakui analyzed the complex questionnaire just before he gave it to us.

figure 2 The 375 scouts sold 29,648 boxes of good cookies in less than 10 days.

one hand 3 Phillip was in tears at noon; Lynn gave him a red lollipop as a treat.

fluency 4 I am busy, but I may go to the lake and do the usual work on the dock.

| 1 | 2 | 3 | 4 | 5 | 6 | 7 | 8 | 9 | 10 | 11 | 12 | 13 | 14 |

100b ▶ 45
Measure production: reports

full sheets

Time schedule
Assembling materials ... 3'
Timed production ...... 35'
Final check; compute
n–pram .... 7'

1 Arrange supplies for easy handling.

2 When directed to begin, work for 35'. If you complete all three problems in less than 35', start over.

3 Correct errors neatly as you work.

4 Compute n–pram (see p. 125)

Problem 1
Unbound report
Prepare the material given at the right as a short unbound report; DS.

Problems 2 and 3 are on the next page.

words

CATEGORY III JOB EVALUATION 5

A comprehensive study was made of all office positions in Category III. Two major facets of the study were to conduct a complete job evaluation and to establish a salary classification system for all positions in Category III. The objective of the job evaluation was to determine the relative value of individual positions. The objective in developing a new salary classification system was to ensure that all employees are paid equitable and competitive wages. 15 / 27 / 37 / 48 / 59 / 69 / 79 / 88 / 98

Data were gathered from all Category III employees and their supervisors. Data from the questionnaires and the interviews were used to write job descriptions and specifications. The job descriptions and specifications were evaluated by the Job Evaluation Committee. Jobs were ranked on the basis of points ascribed to each of the compensatory factors. Present wages, wages of benchmark positions in competitive industries, and point evaluations were used to determine salary ranges.* 108 / 119 / 129 / 139 / 148 / 158 / 168 / 179 / 189 / 196

199

* A copy of all forms, a summary of the data, and the salary scale are included in the Appendix. 208 / 218

Measurement goals

1 To demonstrate ability to type at acceptable levels average–difficulty writings in straight, rough–draft, and statistical copy for 3' and 5'.

2 To demonstrate ability to type letters, tables, and reports in proper format from semi–arranged copy, according to specific direc–tions.

Machine adjustments

1 Check chair and desk adjust–ment and placement of copy for ease of reading.

2 Set ribbon control to type on upper half of ribbon.

3 Set paper guide at 0.

4 Set 70–space line.

48a ▶ 5
Preparatory practice

each line 3 times SS (slowly, faster, slowly); DS between 3-line groups; repeat selected lines as time permits

alphabet	1	Jack is becoming acquainted with an expert on Venezuelan family names.
fig/sym	2	Our #38065 pens will cost Knox & Brady $12.97 each (less 4% discount).
direct reaches	3	June obtained unusual services from a number of celebrated decorators.
easy	4	It is a problem; she may sue the city for a title to the antique auto.

| 1 | 2 | 3 | 4 | 5 | 6 | 7 | 8 | 9 | 10 | 11 | 12 | 13 | 14 |

48b ▶ 11
Measure skill growth: straight copy

a 3' and a 5' writing; determine *gwam*

Difficulty index

all letters used | A | 1.5 si | 5.7 awl | 80% hfw |

gwam 3' | 5'

Clothes do not "make the person." Agree? Still, clothes form an   4 | 3
integral part of impressions we have of others. Whenever we first meet   9 | 6
people, for example, we quickly look them over (and they us), and we   14 | 8
mentally categorize each other. Inexpert as these conclusions may be,   19 | 11
we all justify them in our own minds on the basis that clothing is the   23 | 14
only evidence of personality we have.   26 | 16

Clothes are, of course, quite practical; we need them for modesty   30 | 18
purposes and to protect us from the hazards of extreme weather. Yet,   35 | 21
clothes are also decorative; they should, beyond just looking nice,   40 | 24
reflect a personality, a mood, and a natural coloring--but not a finan-   44 | 27
cial status. Clothes should be part of a picture--a picture of a per-   49 | 29
son--and the person should be the central part of the picture.   53 | 32

Clothes do serve a purpose. They always make a direct statement   57 | 34
about a person; so they should be suitable, and they should be fresh.   62 | 37
High style (but not quality) is out for usual business occasions, as   68 | 40
are excessive jewelry and tantalizing scents. A good mirror and a bit   71 | 43
of common sense can indicate to a person what clothes are appropriate.   76 | 46

gwam 3' | 1 | 2 | 3 | 4 | 5 |
      5' | 1 | 2 | 3 |

99b, continued

Problem 3
Invoice (LM p. 225)

Prepare on an invoice
form the invoice given at
the right.

			words
	DATE Current		3
SOLD TO The Sports Shop			6
735 Alexandria Drive	OUR ORDER NO. SW86127		10
Macon, GA 31210-3567			16
	CUST. ORDER NO. 3570		17
TERMS 2/10, n/30	SHIPPED VIA Bulldog Express		22

QUANTITY	DESCRIPTION	UNIT PRICE	TOTAL	
24	Champ I racquetball racquet	74.99	1,799.76	30
10	Champ II racquetball	46.75	467.50	38
12	Racquetball bag	21.42	257.04	44
6	Tetherball set	26.49	158.94	49
24	Champ I soccerball	19.25	462.00	55
12	Badminton set	33.90	406.80	60
24	Champ I tennis racquet	94.50	2,268.00	69
			5,820.04	71
	Sales tax		291.00	76
			6,111.04	78

Problem 4
Four-column table

full sheet; DS; exact vertical
center; 6 spaces between
columns

SCHEDULE OF EXPENDITURES FOR 19--   7

(City Manager's Office)   12

Code	Account Classification	Expended	Budgeted	
101	Salaries	$46,680	$51,480	45
210	Printing and Binding	1,597	2,400	52
211	Postage	238	400	55
212	Office Supplies	1,269	2,000	61
214	Memberships and Dues	726	950	67
215	Professional Development	1,584	1,900	74
217	Automobile Expenses	1,111	1,000	80
218	Depreciation Expense	1,508	1,510	87
221	Telephone	738	850	91
226	Maintenance and Contracts	1,843	750	101
	Total	$57,294	$63,240	105

48c ▶ 34
Measure skill application: letters

Time schedule

Assembling materials .... 3′
Timed production .... 25′
Final check; compute
g–pram .... 6′

Materials needed

Letterheads and Monarch sheet [LM pp. 59-63]; copy sheet; carbon paper; large, small, and Monarch envelopes

Format and type as many problems as you can in 25′. Type Problem 1 again if you finish Problem 3 before time has been called. Proofread all problems; circle errors.

Problem 1
Business letter (letterhead)

block style, 1 carbon copy, large envelope; 60–space line; begin on Line 15

Problem 2
Business letter (letterhead)

modified–block style, small envelope; 60–space line; begin on Line 15

Problem 3
Personal letter (Monarch sheet)

modified–block style; Monarch envelope; 50–space line; begin on Line 15

June 9, 19-- | Ms. Debra V. Wynn | 80005 Grand Central Pkwy. | Jamaica, NY 11435-6071 | Dear Ms. Wynn   14 / 19

(¶ 1) Word power! It's important to most people. It's absolutely indispensable to a businessperson like you. Word power commands recognition; it smooths the way to promotion and higher salary; and it brings much personal satisfaction.   34 / 49 / 64 / 65

(¶ 2) Vocabulary is a good place to start, of course; but knowing how to choose words, pronounce and spell them, and fit them together to make meaningful sentences is the added knowledge that makes vocabulary work. This is word power. And it can take a lifetime to achieve it.   80 / 95 / 110 / 120

(¶ 3) SPEAK OUT by Guy Hunter brings you a shortcut to word power. This 175-page book will help you to build your word power and give you confidence to put your thoughts and ideas to work for you. Your copy of SPEAK OUT is on our "save shelf." You can pick it up at your convenience. It's only $17.95.   133 / 148 / 164 / 180

Sincerely | Cesar J. Strongbow | Manager | xx   188/201

October 28, 19-- | Mrs. L. L. Sangtry, President | United Casings, Inc. | 1600 Kirby Street, W. | Shreveport, LA 71103-4923 | Dear Mrs. Sangtry   14 / 27

(¶ 1) Last Tuesday afternoon, a shipment of rubber casings from your company arrived at our receiving dock. It had been rushed to us as requested, and we were grateful.   41 / 57 / 60

(¶ 2) We were not so grateful when we discovered that the shipment was not complete, and I telephoned your sales staff to tell them so. The young lady who answered the telephone listened patiently while I exploded in her ear. Then she went to work.   74 / 90 / 106 / 109

(¶ 3) She asked exactly what was missing and what was happening to our production schedule. She apologized for the mistake and promised to rush the missing casings to us. I bid her a very doubtful goodbye.   123 / 138 / 150

(¶ 4) The parts arrived this morning, just 36 hours after I called.   162

(¶ 5) Mrs. Sangtry, I am impressed with the way your firm handled this very serious problem. To have an error handled promptly and courteously was a pleasant surprise. We shall order from you again.   176 / 191 / 201

Sincerely yours | Miss Phyllis E. Trerrett | Purchasing Director | xx   214/234

---

543 El Caprice Avenue | Hollywood, CA 91605-7168 | August 19, 19-- | Miss Felicia Wymore | 278 Fryman Place | Hollywood, CA 91604-4811 | Dear Felicia   15 / 28

(¶ 1) You asked me to write to you about the interviews and tests I took at the Brewer Publishing Company. I spent most of yesterday morning in the company's personnel office. The tests were intensive--mostly keyboarding, composing, editing, spelling, grammar, and vocabulary.   42 / 57 / 72 / 83

(¶ 2) The interviewer asked about my in-school and out-of-school activities, what magazines I regularly read, and what books I had read recently. We also discussed current events.   97 / 113 / 118

(¶ 3) Frankly, Felicia, I am excited about the prospects of working for Brewer. I'll let you know when I have more news. Thanks for your encouragement.   133 / 148

Yours sincerely | Steve Merrewether   151/176

99a ▶ 5
Preparatory practice

each line 3 times SS (slowly, faster, slowly); DS between 3-line groups; repeat selected lines as time permits

alphabet	1	Joanne Quinn moved four young azalea plants next to the back sidewalk.
figure	2	We ordered 29 lamps, 36 tables, 15 mirrors, 48 rugs, and 705 ashtrays.
adjacent key	3	They were pleased the government responded quickly to help the people.
fluency	4	Did she blend the fuel with dye to make the flame visible at the lake?

| 1 | 2 | 3 | 4 | 5 | 6 | 7 | 8 | 9 | 10 | 11 | 12 | 13 | 14 |

99b ▶ 45
Measure production: tables and invoice

(LM p. 225 and full sheets)

Time schedule

Assembling materials .... 3'
Timed production .... 35'
Final check; compute
n–pram .... 7'

1 Arrange supplies for easy handling.

2 When directed to begin, work for 35'. If you complete all four problems in less than 35', start over on plain paper.

3 Correct your errors neatly as you work.

4 Compute n–pram (see page 125).

Problem 1
Three-column table

full sheet; DS; reading position; 6 spaces between columns

words

BENEFITS COMPARISON FOR CATEGORY III EMPLOYEES			9
Type	Regional Average*	Company Average	23
Term life insurance	$ 3,000	$ 5,000	30
Disability (monthly)	528	550	35
Medical (maximum)	50,000	100,000	41
Dental (yearly maximum)	750	500	47
Retirement (yearly maximum)	4,800	5,000	54
Educational (yearly maximum)	500	500	61
Payment for vacation	500	575	66
Payment for holidays	450	525	71
			75
*Source: Regional Survey by Fred Walters.			83

Problem 2
Four-column table

full sheet; DS; reading position; 4 spaces between columns

PROPOSED SALARY CLASSIFICATION				6
(Category III Employees)				11
Grade	Number of Employees	Present Range	Proposed Range	31
17	6	4.60-6.60	6.00-7.00	36
16	8	4.27-6.50	5.65-6.65	41
15	12	4.52-6.28	5.30-6.30	46
14	34	4.01-5.40	4.95-5.95	51
13	108	3.80-5.09	4.60-5.60	56
12	76	3.45-5.01	4.25-5.25	61
11	69	3.35-4.70	3.90-4.90	66
10	2	3.35-4.25	3.55-4.55	71

Problems 3 and 4 are on the next page.

49a ▶ 5

Preparatory practice

each line 3 times SS (work for smooth, continuous rhythm); DS between 3-line groups; repeat selected lines as time permits

alphabet 1 Max queried Parker about having a jewel box for the many huge zircons.

figures 2 Are those last-minute reports on Bill 3657-84 due on October 19 or 20?

shift/lock 3 Ping-ying Fu typed the notations REGISTERED and CERTIFIED in ALL CAPS.

easy 4 The auditor may laugh, but the penalty for such chaotic work is rigid.

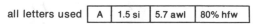

49b ▶ 11

Measure skill growth: statistical copy

a 3' and a 5' writing; determine *gwam*

Difficulty index

all letters used	A	1.5 si	5.7 awl	80% hfw

gwam 3' | 5'

According to a special report of NEWSWEEK (January 17, 1983), the   4 | 3

makeup of the American work force is making some sharp adjustments.   9 | 5

Extracting data from the 1980 census, NEWSWEEK says that the median age   14 | 8

of workers dropped from 39 in 1970 to 34 in 1981. Quite a large number   19 | 11

of women have entered the force--67 percent of women between the ages   23 | 14

of 18 and 34 are working. In fact, a total of 46.8 million women--an   28 | 17

amazing 52 percent of the female population--work.   31 | 19

Fewer men are now working, explains the magazine. Consequently,   36 | 21

their portion of the work force has come down since 1951 from 87.3 per-   40 | 24

cent to just 77 percent, due perhaps to better disability benefits and   45 | 27

early retirement. The departure of males begins at the age of 25 and   50 | 30

speeds up at the age of 45. Of males 65 and older, the portion has de-   55 | 33

clined from 44.6 percent in 1955 to 19.9 percent in 1981.   58 | 35

The magazine also quotes some extraordinary figures about the   62 | 37

situation of males and females who are 75 years old and older and who   67 | 40

have continued to work. A total of 451,000 of them remained active in   72 | 43

the 1981 labor force, and the unemployment rate was just 2.8 percent.   77 | 46

49c ▶ 34

Measure skill application: reports

Time schedule

Assembling materials .... 3'
Timed production .... 25'
Final check; compute
    g-pram .... 6'

Materials needed

2 full sheets

When the signal to begin is given, insert paper and begin typing the problem on page 102, as directed. Type until the signal to stop is given. Begin the problem again if you finish before time is called. Proofread all problems; circle errors. Compute *g-pram*.

98b ▶ 45
Measure production: administrative communications

(LM pp. 221–223 and plain full sheet)

Time schedule

Assembling materials ... 3'
Timed production ...... 35'
Final check; compute
  n–pram .... 7'

1 Arrange supplies for easy handling.

2 When directed to begin, work for 35'. If you complete all three problems in less than 35', start over on plain paper.

3 Correct your errors neatly as you work.

4 Compute *n–pram* (as page 125).

Problem 1
Full-page memo (LM p. 221)

Prepare the memo given at the right.

Problem 2
Full-page memo

(plain full sheet)

Repeat the memo in Problem 1 on a plain full sheet, making the following changes:

1 Add **New Orleans** to enumerated Item No. 1.

2 Delete enumerated item No. 2.

3 Change Item No. 3 to Item No. 2. Total words: 206.

Problem 3
Message/reply memo

(LM p. 223)

Format the memo given at the right on a message/reply form.

	words
TO: Board Members	3
FROM: Elizabeth Hughes, President	9
DATE: Current	12
SUBJECT: Conference Site Selection	17

(¶ 1) The final decision on the site of next year's Youth Club Conference must be made within two weeks. I have reviewed suggestions that were submitted by members of the Youth Club. Our staff has also made suggestions for the site. The following information should be helpful in making our decision: — 32 / 47 / 62 / 77

1. Pittsburgh, Chicago, New York, and San Antonio have been eliminated from consideration because conferences have been held in those cities recently. — 92 / 107

2. New Orleans is still being considered even though we met there three years ago. New Orleans really appeals to the members. — 123 / 133

3. Jacksonville, St. Petersburg, and Newport News were suggested most frequently by the members. Waterfront Inns has an inn in each city and will give us reduced rates. — 149 / 163 / 168

(¶ 2) Please call me and let me know how you rank these cities. You may add other cities to the list if you wish to do so. Messages may be left with my secretary if I am out of the office at the time you call. I will let you know the site of next year's conference when we have made a decision.
xx — 182 / 197 / 214 / 226 / 227

(Message for Problem 3) — words

	words
TO Frank Lopez	Facilities Manager	5 / 6
DATE Current	9
SUBJECT Problems with Electronic Equipment	14 / 16

MESSAGE (¶ 1) We experienced problems with most of our electronic equipment during the electrical storm we had last week. It was my understanding when we purchased superior wiring and placed the wires underground that this type of problem would not occur. — 20 / 27 / 33 / 40 / 46 / 54 / 61 / 65

(¶ 2) Please have one of our best-trained electrical supervisors check the wiring and report to me. — 71 / 78 / 84
SIGNED Alma Thomas, Vice President — 89

(Reply for Problem 3) — words

	words
DATE Tomorrow's date	

REPLY (¶ 1) The problems you experienced during the electrical storm last week are of great concern to us. Bob Bishop and I both checked the wiring today, and we located the cause of the problem. Water seepage caused a short in Transformer #2. — 92 / 96 / 103 / 110 / 118 / 125 / 132 / 138

(¶ 2) We are trying to work out solutions to the problem with the contractor who installed the wiring. As soon as we agree on the best solution, we will schedule the work and see that it is done properly. — 139 / 145 / 153 / 160 / 168 / 175
SIGNED Frank Lopez — 180

Format and type the prob–
lem as a 2–page report.
Center the heading; use a
1½″ (pica) or 2″ (elite) top
margin; 1″ side and bot–
tom margins.

words

BUSINESSPEOPLE WITH A SENSE OF HUMOR?   8

Is there a place in the hurly-burly world of business for humor? Some   22
businesspeople--perhaps even some successful executives--seem to believe not.   38
Business is a very serious undertaking, they say; and there is not much time to   54
be lighthearted about it. Smiles are all right, but only on the way to the bank.   70

On the other hand, Businesspeople With a Sense of Humor--BWSH we   83
can call them--disagree. They say that the best recipe for business success   99
calls for equal parts of dedication and humor.   108

The BWSH know that business does not thrive on a devil-may-care   121
attitude; they know that it does not thrive on melancholy either. For them, a   137
sense of humor creates a "middle" attitude that tells them how to be con-   151
cerned and smile at the same time.   158

The BWSH are champions of the smile. They know that regardless of how   173
critical things become, a smile helps to ease pain and pressure. A millisecond of   189
life is lived only once, they say; and it can be relived only in retrospect. Nothing   206
will change those spent milliseconds, so the BWSH try to be as positive about   222
the disastrous milliseconds as they are about the more fortuitous ones.   236

A sense of humor is what gets BWSH through such calamities as the   250
last-minute Christmas rush, the over-order for 100 mechanized dolls, and the   265
front door that can't be unlocked on the day of the Big Sale. These problems   280
are truly not laughing matters, but how they are viewed determines how they   296
will be handled. With typical good humor, the BWSH keep business moving   310
positively ahead and on the right track.   319

The BWSH know also that a sense of humor helps build their ability   332
to communicate. To paraphrase a daily newspaper item,   343

     If a business executive can speak to people with a little   355
warmth and humor, then those people will be more responsive   367
in listening. If they're paying attention to hear what the speaker   381
says next, he or she will have a better chance to communicate   393
effectively.*   396

Businesspeople With a Sense of Humor? Why not? Why not, indeed?   409
  413

---

 *Detroit Free Press, May 22, 1983, p. 3b.   421

97c ▶ 30
Measure production: business letters

(LM pp. 215–219)

Time schedule

Assembling materials ... 3'
Timed production ...... 20'
Final check; compute
  n–pram .... 7'

1 Arrange supplies for easy handling.
2 When directed to begin, work for 20'. If you complete all three problems in less than 20', start over on plain paper.
3 Correct your errors neatly as you work.
4 Address envelopes.
5 Compute *n–pram* (see page 125).

Problem 1
Block style letter

open punctuation

Problem 2
Modified block style letter

mixed punctuation; indented ¶s

Problem 3
Block style letter

Prepare the letter in Problem 2 a second time in block style, open punctuation. Substitute in the appropriate places the information given at the right.

words

Current date | Mrs. A. W. Marshall | Route 1, Box 258 | Moreauville, LA 71355- 15
5478 | Dear Mrs. Marshall 20

(¶ 1) Thank you for attending the Klienwood Community Council meeting. We 34
were pleased with the participation of so many citizens. 45

(¶ 2) The public hearing was held to assure all of our citizens their right to make 61
their wishes known to the Council. The proposed zoning regulations to upgrade 77
the 200 block of Broad Street from B3 to 04 will affect many people, and we 92
want to consider all of the issues carefully before making a decision. 106

(¶ 3) As you know, the comments ranged from strongly in favor of the regu- 119
lations to strongly against them. We will review all comments to determine 134
what is in the best interest of the community. (122) 143

Sincerely | C. Ralph Walker | Secretary | xx 151

Current date | Mr. Gregg White | 126 Pleasant Street | Claremont, NH 03743-3256 | 15
Dear Mr. White 18

(¶ 1) This letter is to notify you that your automobile, Serial Number 31
3X7R9M4720561, must be taken to one of our authorized dealers for an inspec- 46
tion of the safety system. 51

(¶ 2) We have reason to believe that part of the safety system is not our standard 66
equipment. If standard equipment was not used in the manufacturing process, 81
it is our responsibility to change it. Any repair or replacement of equipment by 99
an authorized dealer will be completed at our expense. 110

(¶ 3) Please accept our apology for this factory error. Our authorized dealer in 125
your area will do the work at your convenience. (114) 134

Sincerely | Ms. Deborah Burge | Customer Care Manager | xx 145

Current date | Miss Sharon Long | Box 257C, Roberts Hill Road | Rye Beach, NH 15
03871-5386 | Dear Miss Long 20

Serial Number 6K85T2B951403   total words 147

98

98a ▶ 5
Preparatory practice

each line 3 times SS (slowly, faster, slowly); DS between 3-line groups; repeat selected lines as time permits

alphabet 1   Zed believes the quarterback was injured long before the complex play.

fig/sym 2   My $762.59 check (No. 304-8) for the June 1 dinner for 25 is enclosed.

direct reach 3   My great uncle and my great aunt brought us both nice and funny gifts.

fluency 4   Did Jane rub the clay to shape it, or did she make the bowl in a form?

| 1 | 2 | 3 | 4 | 5 | 6 | 7 | 8 | 9 | 10 | 11 | 12 | 13 | 14 |

Lessons **97, 98** | Section **23** | Measuring basic/production skills   **207**

50a ▶ 5
Preparatory practice

each line 3 times SS (work for smooth, continuous rhythm); DS between 3-line groups; repeat selected lines as time permits

alphabet	1	Meg was not packed to fly to Zanesville to inquire about her next job.
figures	2	Dial 649-4718 or 469-5709 to obtain your copy of this 32-page booklet.
long words	3	Buyers are ordinarily knowledgeable about performance characteristics.
easy	4	Due to the rigor of the quake, the city may dismantle the old chapels.

| 1 | 2 | 3 | 4 | 5 | 6 | 7 | 8 | 9 | 10 | 11 | 12 | 13 | 14 |

50b ▶ 11
Measure skill growth: rough-draft copy

a 3' and a 5' writing; determine *gwam*

Difficulty index

| all letters used | A | 1.5 si | 5.7 awl | 80% hfw |

	gwam 3'	5'
A lot of people (surprisingly,) measure job potential primarily no	4	3
the basis of the size of the pay check involved. it would be foolish	9	5
to argue that money should plan no essential part in job selection and	14	8
career planning, but money along is not an accurate test to utilize	18	11
when considering a possible career or looking for that first job.	23	14
There is a very subtle difference in philosophy between the person who	27	16
is "hunting for a job" and another who is "beginning a career". These	32	19
position itself, however, is not pivotal to this discussion. Rather,	36	22
the divergence lays in the approach to the job by each applicant. One	41	25
is attracted by what the job bings; the other, by what it take.	45	27
we must acknowledge that everybody, or almost everybody, is required	50	30
to work to purchase the necesities of life; money is used to that	55	33
extent. but when we calculate that we will spend a third of our life-	60	36
times preforming that work, it follows that whatever we do ought to be	64	39
enjoyable, allowing us to make a contribution and help us grow.	68	41

50c ▶ 34
Measure skill application: tables and outlines

Time schedule
Assembling materials .... 3'
Timed production .... 25'
Final check; compute
   g-pram .... 6'

Materials needed
half sheet; 2 full sheets
When the signal to begin is given, insert the paper and begin typing Problem 1 as directed. Type the problems in sequence until the signal to stop is given.

Type Problem 1 again if you finish before time is called. Proofread all problems; circle errors. Compute *g-pram*.

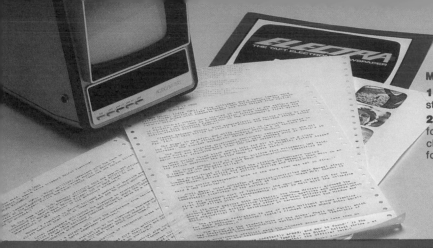

Measurement goals

1 To demonstrate your best straight–copy keyboarding skill.

2 To demonstrate your best skill in formatting communications, including letters, memos, tables, forms, and reports.

Machine adjustments

1 Paper guide at 0.

2 Margins: 70–space line for ¶ writings; as directed for problems.

3 DS ¶ writings; as directed for problems.

4 Indention: 5 spaces for ¶ writings; as appropriate for problems.

97

97a ▶ 5
Preparatory practice

each line 3 times SS (slowly, faster, slowly); DS between 3-line groups; repeat selected lines as time permits

alphabet	1	Can we analyze the next problem quickly and just give a frank opinion?
figure	2	Please request 2,675 copies of Form 8139 and 1,500 copies of Form 462.
outside reach	3	Vasquez was at a park and was puzzled by games he saw Maxwell playing.
fluency	4	Did she pay for the eight enamel emblems or for the six antique bowls?

| 1 | 2 | 3 | 4 | 5 | 6 | 7 | 8 | 9 | 10 | 11 | 12 | 13 | 14 |

97b ▶ 15
Inventory/build straight-copy skill

Two 5' writings for accuracy; circle errors; determine *gwam*.

Difficulty index

all letters used	A	1.5 si	5.7 awl	80% hfw

gwam 1' 5'

Retrieving records is more difficult than filing records. One 13 2 60
reason that records are hard to locate is that they may be requested 27 5 63
under a number of different words or names. Workers who maintain man- 41 8 66
ual record systems often are told to label each file with adequate in- 55 11 69
formation to facilitate easy retrieval of the file. In some cases, 69 14 72
cross-references are placed on the file label. The idea seems to be 83 17 75
that the more data provided, the easier it will be to find the file 97 20 78
that has been ordered. Of course, many other procedures are used to 111 23 81
help locate records in manual record systems. Color codes, indexes, 125 26 84
cross-references, and a wide range of other techniques may be used to 139 29 87
assist the file worker. 144 30 88

Will the same techniques work in computerized records systems? 13 33 91
The idea of labeling the file with as much data as possible will not 27 36 94
work in many electronic filing systems. Most word processing systems 41 39 97
limit the field or amount of space that is available to label a record. 56 42 100
Some systems just assign a number to each record, and an index of all 70 45 103
records is kept. Almost all systems provide space for naming a docu- 84 48 106
ment; but, in many cases, the name can have only a limited number of 98 51 109
characters. In some systems, the number is eight. The procedure used 112 54 112
to shorten the name is called truncating. For example, quarterly may 126 57 115
be written as QTR. 130 58 116

gwam 1' | 1 | 2 | 3 | 4 | 5 | 6 | 7 | 8 | 9 | 10 | 11 | 12 | 13 | 14 |
5' | 1 | 2 | 3 |

words

Problem 1

two-column table

half sheet (enter long side first)

Center and type SS the table in vertical and horizontal center; use a 10–space intercolumn.

LEADING AMERICAN MAGAZINES		5
In 1981		7
Magazine	Circulation	15
Reader's Digest	17,926,542	20
TV Guide	17,670,543	24
National Geographic Magazine	10,861,186	32
Better Homes & Gardens	8,059,717	39
Family Circle	7,427,979	44
Modern Maturity	7,309,035	49
Woman's Day	7,004,367	53
McCall's	6,266,090	59
Ladies' Home Journal	5,527,071	65
Good Housekeeping	5,425,790	71

Problem 2

three-column table

full sheet

Center and type DS the table in reading position; decide inter–column spacing.

EARLY AMERICAN COLLEGES			5
With Dates of Establishment			10
College	State	Year	15
Brown	Rhode Island	1764	20
Columbia	New York	1754	25
Harvard	Massachusetts	1636	30
Moravian	Pennsylvania	1742	36
Pennsylvania	Pennsylvania	1740	42
Princeton	New Jersey	1746	47
Rutgers	New Jersey	1766	52
William and Mary	Virginia	1693	58
Yale	Connecticut	1701	62

Problem 3

outline

full sheet

3″ top margin; 40–space line; add designation numerals and letters for each order; use correct capitalization and spacing

PLANTING LAWN GRASS 4

clear the area 8
 turn over and break up the soil 15
  hand implements 19
  power implements 23
 remove old roots and stems 29
 spread nutrients over area 36
prepare the seedbed 40
 level high and low places 46
  drag 48
  light roller 52
 rake to loosen lumps and clods 59
plant 61
 sow seeds 64
 add protective cover 69
  straw 71
  burlap 73
 wet thoroughly to set seed 79

Measure communication skills: spelling and capitalization

plain sheet; 70-space line, 1½" top margin; DS

1 Find and correct errors in spelling and capitalization as you keyboard.

2 Proofread; retype the copy if necessary.

1 Lay my copy of <u>The King and I</u> on the shelf beside the old china bowls.

2 Dr. Thu gave several analysis of why a person needs some good hobbies.

3 To see huskeys at work in winter, go North to Whaler or Glacier parks.

4 The enemy had already tried to sieze the tower; Kroma would not yield.

5 The partys will meet with their attornies in Room 27 of Yorkton Hall.

6 When it is convient, please vacuum the carpets in the front lobbies.

7 In my judgment, I did not embarass her; her abscence spoke for itself.

8 Demure fall trembled before winter's icy breath. It was now december.

9 He said, "put a few tomatoes in your potatoe salad for these Holidays."

10 If we accumulate enough points, we shall receive three surprise gifts.

Choose the right word

half sheet, long side up; 1" top margin; 74-space line

Keyboard the sentences at the right, selecting the correct word from the words in parentheses. Include the sentence numbers in the 74–space line.

1. Who must (accept/except) the responsibility for (advicing/advising) the (principal/principle) stockholders of the loss?

2. (Its/It's) in the minutes of (passed/past) meetings that the president will (advice/advise) stockholders and company (personal/personnel) of any changes that (affect/effect) our financial position.

3. The (personal/personnel) director was (cited/sited/sighted) for (personal/ personnel) integrity and high (principals/principles).

4. The (cite/site/sight) is excellent (accept/except) for the cost.

5. After (farther/further) consideration, the motion to move (farther/further) from the airport was (passed/past).

Capitalization and punctuation

1 Read the ¶ at the right. Type it line for line with correct capitalization and punctuation.

2 Check your corrected ¶ with your instructor. Use your corrected copy to type two 1' writings.

gwam 1'

eleven people participated in the recent trip to the eiffel tower   13

in paris france the following number were from the united states   27

one was from boise three were from chicago of the remaining seven,   41

one was from quayaquil two were from rio de janeiro three were from   55

vienna and one insisted that she was from reykjavik.   66

| 1 | 2 | 3 | 4 | 5 | 6 | 7 | 8 | 9 | 10 | 11 | 12 | 13 | 14 |

LEVEL THREE
Formatting/typing business correspondence

Now that you have reached a basic competency in keyboarding and achieved a basic understanding of the formatting of business forms, you are now ready to build on this foundation.

In addition to the continued emphasis on speed and accuracy, the 24 lessons that comprise Level 3 are devoted to developing your expertise in solving a wide variety of communication activities. Communication aids that influence the "sound" of communications are combined with the technical aspect of letter formats, special features, and writing styles that influence the "appearance" of the finished product. This careful melding of skill, knowledge, and practical application is a vital link in making your typing ability an integral part of your total education.

Directions and sample solutions are provided throughout Level 3 to give you a feel for acceptable business correspondence and communication. However, the directions leave you flexibility for making decisions in designing, implementing, and producing acceptable business communications. When performed in a dedicated and timely manner, your work on tables, letters, memos, reports, and resumes will result in more efficient production at the keyboard.

Improve concentration

1 Prepare a copy of the ¶ DS. Unscramble the underlined words as you keyboard. Check your answers below.

2 Using your corrected copy, take 1' writings as time permits.

Key: make, been, good, very, read, with, more

gwam 1'

Many people <u>mkae</u> fast work of their letter writing. They com- 12
pose letters on their typewriters. Such a letter has not always <u>bene</u> 26
considered <u>doog</u> form; but now even etiquette experts, whose judgments 40
are accepted by some, recognize and accept typed letters--and for <u>ervy</u> 55
good reasons. A typed letter is easier to <u>rade</u> than a handwritten one; 69
and, as a typist can more easily keep pace <u>hitw</u> his or her thoughts, a 83
typed letter seems to be <u>erom</u> coherent, interesting, and conversational. 98

gwam 1' | 1 | 2 | 3 | 4 | 5 | 6 | 7 | 8 | 9 | 10 | 11 | 12 | 13 | 14 |

Build/measure straight-copy skill

1 Take one 1' writing on each ¶; circle errors and determine *gwam*.

2 Take one 5' writing on all ¶s combined; circle errors and determine *gwam*; compare results with 1' writings.

Difficulty index

| all letters used | A | 1.5 si | 5.7 awl | 80% hfw |

gwam 1' | 5'

Choosing a career is one of the most important decisions affecting | 13 | 3 | 68
your future. One factor that should affect your career choice is the | 27 | 5 | 70
number of available jobs. Unfortunately, this is an ever-changing factor | 42 | 8 | 73
that is difficult to assess, but many regional planning studies are | 56 | 11 | 76
available to help you. You owe it to yourself to learn what types of | 70 | 14 | 79
jobs are likely to be available when you enter the work force. It is | 84 | 17 | 82
quite reasonable to assume that many new career choices will be open in | 98 | 20 | 84
the next several years in both business and government. | 109 | 22 | 87

The chance to enter interesting and varied careers in business is | 13 | 25 | 89
very bright for the near future. Both the natural growth of current | 27 | 27 | 92
jobs and the creation of jobs in new fields will provide such a chance. | 42 | 30 | 95
In the last fifteen years of this century, entirely new industries are | 57 | 33 | 98
likely to develop; and they will provide many career opportunities. | 69 | 36 | 101
Entirely new industries will be created because of new advances in the | 84 | 39 | 103
way we do things and changes in human values that will redirect the ef- | 98 | 41 | 106
forts of our culture. | 102 | 42 | 107

Preparing for future jobs can best be done with the use of a system- | 14 | 45 | 110
atic career plan. However, even with a career plan, you are very likely | 28 | 48 | 113
to change jobs or organizations more than once during your life because | 43 | 51 | 116
you alter your personal goals. Even the best of plans must be altered | 57 | 54 | 119
if the facts warrant. The basic reasons people modify their career | 70 | 56 | 121
plans are because they establish new goals, develop new skills, and | 84 | 59 | 124
acquire new values. Each of us goes through stages of growth and un- | 98 | 62 | 127
certainty in a career. The process of change goes on throughout life. | 112 | 65 | 130

gwam 1' | 1 | 2 | 3 | 4 | 5 | 6 | 7 | 8 | 9 | 10 | 11 | 12 | 13 | 14 |
5' | 1 | 2 | 3 |

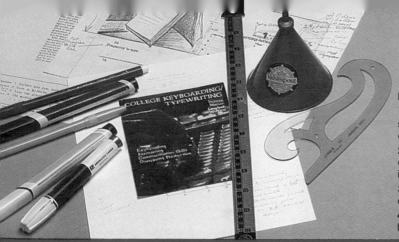

Learning goals

1 To improve basic skill on straight, statistical, and rough-draft copy.

2 To format two- and three-column tables in exact center and in reading position.

3 To format unbound reports (including footnotes).

4 To format business letters in block and modified block styles.

Machine adjustments

1 Paper guide at *0*.

2 Margins: 70–space line for drills and ¶ writings; as directed for problems.

3 Spacing: SS drills; DS ¶ writings; as directed for problems.

4 Indention: 5 spaces for ¶ writings; as appropriate for problems.

51a ▶ 5
Preparatory practice

each line 3 times SS (slowly, faster, slowly); DS between 3-line groups; repeat selected lines as time permits

alphabet	1	Jack asked seven pertinent questions before he analyzed my wage taxes.
figures	2	Between 1985 and 1992, we may open 43 offices and hire 16,078 workers.
fig/sym	3	The deposits of $958 and $1,476 ($2,434 total) were made at 11:30 a.m.
fluency	4	Sue and Henry may wish to fish by the dock when they visit the island.

| 1 | 2 | 3 | 4 | 5 | 6 | 7 | 8 | 9 | 10 | 11 | 12 | 13 | 14 |

51b ▶ 15
Inventory/build straight-copy skill

1 One 5' writing; proofread and circle errors; determine *gwam*.

2 Two 1' writings on each ¶ to improve speed.

Difficulty index

all letters used	A	1.5 si	5.7 awl	80% hfw

gwam 1' | 5'

Traffic jams, deadlines, problems at work, and squabbles at home are some ways in which tension is created. When our tension is about to reach the boiling point, what do people usually tell us? In most cases, they urge us to relax. But relaxation is not always easy to accomplish. We frequently think we cannot find the time for this important part of our daily activity.

13 | 3 | 55
27 | 6 | 58
41 | 9 | 61
55 | 12 | 64
69 | 15 | 67
75 | 16 | 68

To understand how relaxation works for us, we must realize how the stress of contemporary existence works against us. Developed for survival in a challenging world, the human body reacts to a crisis by getting ready for action. Whether we are preparing for a timed writing or for an encounter on a dark street, our muscles tighten and our blood pressure goes up. After years of this type of response, we often find it difficult to relax when we want to.

13 | 19 | 72
27 | 22 | 75
41 | 25 | 78
55 | 28 | 81
69 | 31 | 84
83 | 34 | 87
91 | 35 | 88

Now think about the feeling which is the opposite of this turmoil. The pulse slows down, the breath comes slowly and calmly, and the tension leaves the body. This is total relaxation. And if it sounds good, consider how good it must actually feel. Our bodies are already prepared to relax; it is an ability all individuals have within themselves. What we have to practice is how to use this response.

14 | 38 | 91
28 | 41 | 94
43 | 44 | 97
57 | 47 | 100
72 | 50 | 103
83 | 52 | 105

gwam 1' | 1 | 2 | 3 | 4 | 5 | 6 | 7 | 8 | 9 | 10 | 11 | 12 | 13 | 14 |
5' | 1 | 2 | 3 |

Build/measure statistical-copy skill

1 Two 3' writings; proofread and circle errors; determine *gwam*.
2 Two 1' writings on each ¶ to improve speed.

Difficulty index

all letters/figures used | A | 1.5 si | 5.7 awl | 80% hfw

	gwam 1'	3'
The number of women in the labor force of our nation has been ris-	13	4
ing steadily from 18.2 percent in 1890 to around 51 percent by 1980.	27	9
This indicates that in 1980, 51 percent of all women over the age of	41	14
16 held jobs. In addition, the number of fields which women pursue	55	18
has slowly risen. New technology has brought about new career areas,	69	23
and women are performing jobs today that had never been open to them	83	28
previously. These new opportunities offer pursuits to women of all	97	32
skills and job backgrounds.	102	34
Women are now gaining experience to help them in developing careers.	14	39
In 1974, just 1,000 of the 200,000 coal miners in our land were women.	28	44
Nowadays, over 6,000 female miners are employed. Even as recently as 10	43	49
years ago, relatively few women operated heavy equipment. Now roughly	57	54
1/5 of 1 percent of the women in the work force use apparatus of this	71	59
size. In 1975, just 26 percent of bank managers were women. By the	85	63
early 1980's, that figure had grown to 33 percent.	95	66

gwam 1' | 1 | 2 | 3 | 4 | 5 | 6 | 7 | 8 | 9 | 10 | 11 | 12 | 13 | 14 |
3' | 1 | 2 | 3 | 4 | 5 |

Build/compare straight-copy skill

1 One 2' writing on the first ¶ to set base rate.
2 Two 2' writings on the second ¶. Try to maintain the rate you achieved on the first ¶.
3 Two additional writings on the ¶ on which you had the lower rate. Your goal is to meet or exceed your rate on the faster ¶.

Difficulty index   Difficulty index

all letters used ¶1 | A | 1.5 si | 5.7 awl | 80% hfw | ¶2 | HA | 1.7 si | 6.0 awl | 75% hfw

	gwam 1'		2'
The tools with which office workers do their jobs are undergoing	13	7	49
vast changes right now. Many more changes will take place in the near	27	14	56
future. New tools will save both time and money. One area in which	41	21	63
these new devices will have an effect is in the realm of communica-	54	27	70
tions, especially in documents created and produced in offices. Those	69	34	77
who wish to maximize their chances in this area will learn this new	82	41	84
technology.	84	42	85
Today, most office workers realize that management is very eager	13	7	50
to cut costs. Jobs must be done less expensively, more quickly, and	27	13	57
with high quality. As data flows more rapidly, delays will be very	40	20	63
costly. Millions of new pieces of information will reach offices every	55	27	71
day via computers. This new material will have to be sorted, edited,	69	34	78
stored, retrieved, and disseminated. Efficient means must be found to	83	42	85
do these tasks.	86	43	86

gwam 1' | 1 | 2 | 3 | 4 | 5 | 6 | 7 | 8 | 9 | 10 | 11 | 12 | 13 | 14 |
2' | 1 | 2 | 3 | 4 | 5 | 6 | 7 |

51c ▶ 30
Inventory report skills

2 full sheets

Problem 1

Format the copy at the right in unbound manuscript style: top margin 1 ½″ for pica, 2″ for elite; side margins 1″; DS the first ¶; then reset margins so that the numbered ¶s are indented 5 spaces from both right and left margins; SS the body of each numbered ¶ and DS between the numbered ¶s; center the title **DIVIDING WORDS** above the report.

Problem 2

Reformat the copy at the right as the second page of an unbound report; place the page number in the appropriate place; omit the main heading.

divided

A word may be ~~broken~~ at the end of a line in order to   14
keep right margin as even and attractive as possible. When   26
in dou*b*t about the proper division of a wor*d*k, consult a dic-   38
tion*a*ery or a word-division guide. The following rules will   50
be helpful: 52

1. If you decide that you must divide a word, ~~then,~~   61
    divide it between syllables, as your-self, con-   73
    flict, dif-fer-ent. Even though they may have   86
    two or more syllables, never divide words of   95
    f*iv*le or fewer letters, as offer, onto.   104

2. Divide words between two vowels if each is a   114
    separate syllable, as situ-ations, evalu-ation.   128
    Hyphenated compounds should be divided only at   137
    the point of the hyphen, as know-how, cross-   148
    file, son-in-law.   155

3. When the single-letter syllable a, i, or u is   166
    followed by the ending syllable ble, bly, cle,   177
    or cal, the two ending syllables should be   186
    joined when carried over to the next line, as   195
    cur-able, favor-ably, mir-acle, or cler-ical.   211

4. Regardless of the length of the word, do not   221
    divide a one-letter syllable at the beginning   230
    of it, as e-nough, or a one- or two-letter   240
    syllable at the end of a word, as read-y or   250
    ghast-ly. Words of one syllable cannot be   260
    divided, as thought, trained, or straight.   273

5. Divide words after a prefix or before a suffix   283
    if possible, as pre-scribe. Words should be   294
    divided between double consonants unless the   303
    root word ends in a double letter, as strip-   313
    ping or process-ing.   320

52a ▶ 5
Preparatory practice

each line 3 times SS (slowly, faster, slowly); DS between 3-line groups; repeat selected lines as time permits

alphabet 1 Jack quickly thawed five big boxes of frozen shrimp to make the salad.

figures 2 Holes 9, 10, and 11 had yardages of 378, 526, and 450 for a par of 13.

fig/sym 3 One calculator (used) at $16.84 and a chair at $59.36* came to $76.20.

fluency 4 The ivory tusk, if authentic, is the key to the ancient island ritual.

| 1 | 2 | 3 | 4 | 5 | 6 | 7 | 8 | 9 | 10 | 11 | 12 | 13 | 14 |

Build/measure rough-draft skill

1 Two 1' writings on each ¶ for speed; circle errors; determine *gwam*.

2 One 5' writing for control on all ¶s combined; circle errors; determine *gwam*.

Difficulty index

A	1.5 si	5.7 awl	80% hfw

gwam 1' | 5'

Do you think of yourself as a negotiator? Most people do not. Most | 14 | 3 | 48

people think of negotiation as a process that is used | 25 | 5 | 50

only to resolve major conflicts such as labor problems, polit- | 37 | 7 | 52

ical issues, and salary matters. The truth is that each per- | 49 | 9 | 54

son negotiates dozens of situations every day of the year. Each | 62 | 11 | 56

time you try to gain some thing that you want from somebody else, | 76 | 13 | 58

involved in negotiation negotiate. | 78 | 14 | 59

You cannot negotiate with an other person unless you and the | 12 | 16 | 61

other person both have something to gain and some thing to | 24 | 18 | 63

loose. Why bother to negotiate if you can not gain something you | 37 | 20 | 65

want? Why modify your position if it satisfies you and you have | 50 | 22 | 67

nothing to lose by maintaining it? What each individual wants is to | 64 | 25 | 70

satisfy his or her own needs. The key question is whether both individ- | 78 | 28 | 73

uals can meet their needs. Most, but not all people enter | 82 | 29 | 74

a negotiation expecting to win. You are | 15 | 32 | 77

more likely to win if the other person also wins. just be- | 27 | 34 | 79

cause one individual wins does not mean the other individual looses. | 41 | 37 | 82

The important thing is to discover what the other person | 52 | 39 | 84

really wants and assist that individual to get it so that at the | 65 | 41 | 86

same time you can get what you really desire. This is called | 82 | 44 | 89

"win-win" approach to negotiating strategy. | 86 | 45 | 90

Improve keyboarding technique

each pair of lines 3 times SS at a controlled rate; DS between 6-line groups

hyphen usage
1 Their 10-year-growth plans were run-of-the-mill presentations at best.
2 That 86-year-old woman gave a first-class talk to the 25-member board.

double letters
3 I will call three staff issues to his attention at the weekly meeting.
4 One possibility is to supply small colleges in the Mississippi Valley.

long numbers
5 35,782; 901,562; #97256; 200-30-5754; (617) 448-6799; #10901; 532-2317
6 67-091; 896,358; #52800; 120-55-7633; (412) 593-8082; #05783; 425-7981

long words
7 The representative gave membership information about the organization.
8 Eleven outstanding members completed requirements for the association.

| 1 | 2 | 3 | 4 | 5 | 6 | 7 | 8 | 9 | 10 | 11 | 12 | 13 | 14 |

52b ▶ 10

Review
proofreader's marks

Sometimes typed or printed copy may be corrected with proofreader's marks. The keyboard operator must be able to interpret these marks correctly in reformatting the corrected copy, or *rough draft*, as it may be called. The most commonly used proofreader's marks are shown at the right.

Read the ¶s of 52c below and compare the use of the symbols shown there to the illustrations at the right.

Proofreader's Marks

Capitalize — ≡ or *Cap*

Close up — ⌒

Delete — ℘

Insert — ∧

Insert comma — ∧

Insert period — ⊙

Insert space — # or /#

Insert apostrophe — ∨

Insert quotation marks — ∨ ∨

Move right —

Move left —

Move down; lower —

Move up; raise —

Set in lowercase — *lc* or /

Paragraph — #

Spell out — ○ *sp*

Let it stand; ignore correction — *stet*

Transpose — ∨ or *tr*

Underline or italics —

52c ▶ 12

Inventory/build
rough-draft skill

1 One 5' writing; proofread and circle er–rors; determine *gwam*.

2 Two 1' writings on each ¶ to improve speed.

Difficulty index

all letters used	A	1.5 si	5.7 awl	80% hfw

	gwam 1'	5'

Believe it or not, stress maybe good for ~~you.~~ us. Without | 11 | 2 | 43

stress, we would be a less productive society. we would have | 23 | 4 | 45

~~less~~ fewer ulcers, headaches, and heart seazures, ~~and~~ but we would find | 36 | 6 | 47

it difficult to work. Why the paradox? Actually, stress itself | 49 | 9 | 50

isn't good or bad, but our ~~feelings~~ reactions to pressure situations can | 62 | 12 | 53

be positive or negative. | 67 | 13 | 54

On the positive side, stressful ~~things~~ situations force us to ~~do~~ complete | 13 | 16 | 57

our tasks. if we didnot have dead lines and schedules, | 24 | 18 | 59

~~most~~ many of us would put of untill latter what could be | 34 | 20 | 61

handled ~~quickly~~ immediately. Deadlines give us certain times for | 46 | 22 | 63

completeting our activities. We all require just enough | 57 | 24 | 65

stress to ~~push~~ stimulate us to reach our goals. Thus, stress ~~will~~ can | 69 | 26 | 67

be a positive force in our ~~life~~ lives. | 76 | 27 | 68

But stress can also have a negative aspect. Dead lines | 11 | 29 | 70

are not ~~really~~ necessarily realistic. sometimes we have too many goals to | 25 | 32 | 73

achieve at once, too many requirements to ~~do~~ complete. At these times, | 39 | 35 | 76

we often feel ~~nervous~~ uncomfortable because we are under too much pressure. | 53 | 38 | 79

All of us must learn how much stress we ~~can take~~ need in daly ~~life~~ our lives. | 66 | 41 | 82

Improve keyboarding technique

each pair of lines 3 times SS; DS between 6-line groups; work at a controlled rate

adjacent keys
1 He said new government funds were required for the proposed buildings.
2 A few people support the view that government needs more taxing power.

double letters
3 Their committee may soon recommend that all new agreements be written.
4 My immediate need appears to be getting agreement on all staff issues.

direct reach
5 My annual service contract was brought to the central council offices.
6 My company must urge larger payments to serve these doubtful accounts.

shift lock
7 A contract will be awarded to WJAR-TV in Chicago or WWRN-TV in Boston.
8 Bill Smythe will enter ROTC at SMU, USC, VMI, or UCLA later this year.

| 1 | 2 | 3 | 4 | 5 | 6 | 7 | 8 | 9 | 10 | 11 | 12 | 13 | 14 |

Build/measure script-copy skill

1 Two 1' writings on each ¶ for speed; circle errors; determine gwam.
2 One 5' control writing on all ¶s combined; circle errors; determine gwam.

Difficulty index

| all letters used | A | 1.5 si | 5.7 awl | 80% hfw |

	gwam 1'	5'

¶ Most men and women in executive positions accept travel as a part of corporate life. At the same time, executives try to keep time spent on the road to a minimum. Top management usually supports the efforts to reduce travel time as long as effectiveness is not jeopardized. One of the reasons for this support is that it is quite expensive for executives to travel. Other reasons are that traveling can be tiring and frequently causes stress.

	gwam 1'	5'
	12	2	43
	26	5	46
	38	7	48
	51	9	50
	64	11	52
	76	13	54
	87	15	56
	90	16	57

¶ One suggestion to reduce travel is to find alternatives that will accomplish the objectives of the outing so that no one has to leave the office. In some instances, a letter or telephone call may be appropriate; but a letter or telephone message may not be effectual in many situations. It is much easier to communicate when you can see the person with whom you are talking.

	12	18	59
	24	20	61
	37	23	64
	50	25	66
	62	27	68
	74	29	70
	76	30	71

¶ The technology that is on the market today makes it feasible for executives to hold meetings with people in other sections of the state or country without leaving the office. Teleconferencing with two-way video enables members of a group to see and hear each other even though they may be great distances apart.

	10	32	73
	21	34	75
	33	36	77
	44	38	79
	55	40	81
	62	41	82

**Inventory
report skills**

**Unbound report
with footnote**

full sheet; top margin 2″ elite,
1½″ pica; sides 1″; bottom ap–
proximately 1″; DS; footnote at
bottom of page

words

CORPORATIONS | 2

Most of us take for granted the "Inc." that normally appears after the | 16
legal name of many business firms. Yet not all business enterprises are corpo- | 30
rations. Law firms and many other professional-service businesses custom- | 45
arily work as partnerships. Some businesses that are set up in one individual's | 61
name may operate as a sole proprietorship. However, the fact remains that | 76
corporations are the dominant force in American business. In fact, although | 91
corporations account for only 15 percent of all business enterprises, they col- | 107
lect 77 percent of all business earnings.[1] | 115

The law governing incorporation is complex and varies from state to | 129
state. But any corporation has three fundamental features: limited liability, | 145
eternal life, and greater capital. | 152

Basically, limited liability means that a corporation is liable for only as | 167
much money as it has "capitalized." The corporation may go bankrupt, but the | 183
individuals who started it can lose no more than they have invested. Eternal life | 200
means the corporation lives on and on, and the corporation's life doesn't | 215
depend--as with a partnership or proprietorship--on the life or death of any | 230
person or group of people. Third, a corporation can raise capital by selling | 246
stock. Through the sale of corporate stock, firms are able to raise large | 261
amounts of capital funds. | 266
| 270

[1] William H. Cunningham, Ramon J. Aldag, and Christopher M. Swift, | 283
Introduction to Business (Cincinnati: South-Western Publishing Co., 1984), | 304
p. 63. | 305

**Preparatory
practice**

each line 3 times SS
(slowly, faster,
slowly); DS between
3-line groups; repeat
selected lines as time
permits

alphabet 1 Luckily, we packed just the required number of frozen vegetable boxes.

figures 2 The following 4 classrooms are still unusable: 69, 150, 354, and 728.

fig/sym 3 Helen's 13% note (matures May 25, 1987) will yield a return of $4,690.

fluency 4 The spry buck and the big doe may be visible in the field by the lake.

| 1 | 2 | 3 | 4 | 5 | 6 | 7 | 8 | 9 | 10 | 11 | 12 | 13 | 14 |

96c, continued

Problem 3
Employee record
(LM p. 211)

Prepare the employee record given at the right.

Note: The information contained in this record can be requested after an employee has been hired but cannot be asked for on an application form.

The extra lines for the address and telephone number provide space for updating when an employee moves.

The position history section contains the employee's record with this company only. Information is added to the form as the employee moves to different positions within the company.

The termination record is completed when the employee leaves the company.

words

E M P L O Y E E   R E C O R D

EMPLOYEE _Michi Nitobe_   SOCIAL SECURITY NUMBER _398-84-9085_

STREET _2213 R Street_   CITY _Ft. Smith_   5

STATE _Arkansas_   ZIP _72904_ TELEPHONE _(501) 555-6453_   9

STREET_____ CITY_____   14

STATE_____ ZIP_____ TELEPHONE_____

DATE OF BIRTH _September 6, 1962_ SEX _Female_ U.S.A. CITIZEN _X_ OTHER (NAME)_____

MARITAL STATUS _Married_ SPOUSE _Robert Sumida_   NUMBER OF DEPENDENTS _0_   19

IN EMERGENCY NOTIFY _Robert Sumida_ RELATIONSHIP _spouse_   24

ADDRESS _same_ TELEPHONE_____   28

EDUCATION: HIGH SCHOOL _Sterling Academy_ COLLEGE _Eastern Shores Community College_   29

DEGREE _Associate of arts_ MAJOR _Office systems management_   39

SPECIAL SKILLS _Fluent in Japanese and Chinese_   48

_____   54

COMPANY TRAINING _Orientation and supervisory development_

_____   62

_____

SECURITY CLEARANCE_____

P O S I T I O N   H I S T O R Y

DATE _March 5, 19--_ POSITION _Word Processing Coordinator_

DEPARTMENT _Administrative Services_ SALARY _$16,850_   70

DATE_____ POSITION_____   76

DEPARTMENT_____ SALARY_____

DATE_____ POSITION_____

DEPARTMENT_____ SALARY_____

DATE TERMINATED_____ WOULD WE REHIRE_____

REASON FOR TERMINATION_____

_____

Inventory/build script-copy skill

1 One 1' writing on each ¶; circle errors; determine *gwam*.
2 One 5' writing on all ¶s combined; circle errors; determine *gwam*; compare results with 1' writings.

Difficulty index

| all letters used | A | 1.5 si | 5.7 awl | 80% hfw | | gwam 1' | | 5' |

Forecasting is a means of generating data about such matters | 12 | 2 | 42
as the number, type, or quality of personnel, sales, or raw materials | 26 | 5 | 45
that will be available to or will be needed by a firm. Forecasts | 39 | 8 | 48
do not state ultimate facts or truths about the future. An | 51 | 10 | 50
element of uncertainty, which managers must learn to deal | 63 | 12 | 52
with and to minimize, exists in all forecasts. | 72 | 14 | 54

A high level of uncertainty wastes a great deal of both time | 12 | 16 | 56
and money. In general, the ability to control the course of | 24 | 18 | 58
events and to get reliable data on a regular basis results in | 36 | 20 | 60
a more secure feeling. Unforeseen events and inaccurate data | 48 | 22 | 70
increase uncertainty. A good rule of thumb is the longer the | 60 | 24 | 72
time period for which plans are made, the more tentative | 71 | 26 | 74
the forecast. | 74 | 27 | 75

If ways can be found to make more informed judgments | 11 | 29 | 77
about events, we can improve the value of our forecasts. | 23 | 31 | 79
Today computers can help us to make these decisions. The | 35 | 33 | 81
ability of these machines to store and use data will be a | 47 | 35 | 83
great asset for predicting the results of our decisions. Forecasts | 61 | 38 | 86
for business activity in future decades will be more certain. | 73 | 40 | 88

Inventory proofreading/correcting skills

full sheet; DS; 2" top margin; 1" side margins; format the copy shown at the right, making the corrections indicated; BE ALERT—there are at least 4 additional corrections that have *not* been indicated

words

The ~~Nature of~~ Computers *SOCIETY* | 4

Without a doubt the computer has become a major force in | 16
our society. Schools, corporations, govermnent agencies, an | 28
small business firms rely on computers on a daily basis. Com- | 40
puter have even entered our personal lives with home computers | 53
and electronic games--and that is just the begining. As the | 65
costs or of computar equipment continues to go down, computers | 77
will became an even more integral part of our daily lives. | 89

96a ▶ 5

Preparatory practice

each line 3 times SS (slowly, faster, slowly); DS between 3-line groups; repeat selected lines as time permits

alphabet 1 Vasquez bought expensive jewelry for his mother when he visited Clark.

fig/sym 2 We were given a 45% discount ($381.92) on Invoice #607-25A1 yesterday.

double letter 3 Lee and Ann will see us before the committee meeting tomorrow at noon.

fluency 4 The auditor got the panel to focus on the dual problems in the manual.

| 1 | 2 | 3 | 4 | 5 | 6 | 7 | 8 | 9 | 10 | 11 | 12 | 13 | 14 |

96b ▶ 10

Improve concentration

1 Make a copy of the ¶ DS.
2 Where a blank space occurs, insert a common 4-letter word that fits the context.
3 Using your corrected copy, take 1' writings as time permits.

Key: that, more, must, from, know

Difficulty index

| all letters used | A | 1.5 si | 5.7 awl | 80% hfw |

gwam 1'

Men and women who succeed seem to realize ——— genuine success is   13

much ——— than just turning in one star performance after another. To   27

acquire actual success, they tell us, we ——— measure our achievements   42

by our own standards of excellence. Success truly stems ——— a belief   56

in ourselves and a determination to do well what we ——— we can do.   69

gwam 1' | 1 | 2 | 3 | 4 | 5 | 6 | 7 | 8 | 9 | 10 | 11 | 12 | 13 | 14 |

96c ▶ 35

Prepare follow-up letters and an employee record

Problem 1
Follow-up letter

full sheet

Prepare the letter given at the right in an appropriate letter style.

words

1802 Madison Avenue |New York, NY 10028-5743 |February 19, 19-- |Mrs. Selma   15
Parker |Ozark Insurance Company |P.O. Box 8910 |Ft. Smith, AR 72906-6431 | 29
Dear Mrs. Parker   32

(¶ 1) Thank you for giving me the opportunity to talk with you about the position   47
of word processing coordinator of Ozark Insurance Company.   59

(¶ 2) The tour of your facilities was quite impressive, and I was especially   74
pleased with the satellite-center approach to word processing that you are   89
planning at Ozark. You will be able to take advantage of the productivity of   104
dedicated word processing operators; and, at the same time, you will minimize   120
the control and logistical problems inherent in large, centralized word process-   136
ing centers.   139

(¶ 3) Mrs. Parker, I look forward to hearing from you; and I hope you will give   153
me the opportunity to utilize my word processing supervisory skills as coor-   169
dinator of your satellite word processing centers. (146)   179

Sincerely |Ms. Michi Nitobe   184

Problem 2
Follow-up letter

full sheet

Using the information given at the right, compose and type a follow-up letter.

In Lesson 95b, Problem 3, on page 198, you wrote a letter of application for a position for which you feel qualified. Today, you had an interview for that position. You spoke with the same person to whom you had addressed the letter of application. Now prepare a follow-up letter. You were given a tour of the facilities as part of the interview. You were impressed with the company, the position, and the facilities. Confirm your interest in the position. Your letter should be short, friendly, and sincere.

Inventory problem skills: tables

Problem 1
Table with main heading

half sheet, long side up; DS; exact center; 10 spaces between columns

	words
ROSTER OF NEW EMPLOYEES	5

		words
Administrative Assistant	Maria Georgiopoulos	14
Assistant Registrar	Robert Parks	20
Controller	Cleopatra Sophios	25
Dean of Students	Mary Cadigan-Jones	32
Director of Health Services	Arline Keefe	40
Personnel Administrator	Wally Wong	47

Problem 2
Table with main, secondary, and column headings

full sheet; DS; reading position; 12 spaces between columns

Note: In Column 2, align the numbers at the right and include the letters after the numbers as part of the column.

			words
EVENING DIVISION CLASSROOM SCHEDULE			7
Thursday Evening Classes			12
Class	Room	Instructor	20
General Chemistry I	355R	Tourangeau	27
Typewriting I	31	Parks	31
Management	41	Sandberg	36
Literature	353F	Diepstra	39
Accounting	362R	Zabocki	44
English Composition	23	Costello	50
Marketing	356F	Foster	54
Psychology	310R	da Costa	58

Problem 3
Outline

full sheet; 2″ top margin; 1″ side margins; center heading **MANAGEMENT WORKSHOP OUTLINE**

	words
	in heading 5
I. GETTING THE DESIRED RESULTS	11
A. Characteristics of a Productive Manager	20
B. Problem Analysis	24
1. Identifying the real problem	30
2. Sorting symptoms from causes	36
C. Assigning Work Effectively	42
1. When and how to delegate	48
2. How to maintain control	53
II. IMPROVING COMMUNICATION SKILLS	60
A. How to Deal with Employees in Face-to-Face Situations	71
B. Developing a Rapport with Subordinates	79
C. Recognizing and Overcoming Communication Barriers	90
D. Giving Negative Feedback Effectively	98

95a ▶ 5
Preparatory practice

each line 3 times SS (slowly, faster, slowly); DS between 3-line groups; repeat selected lines as time permits

alphabet	1	Jacob suggested a good way to formalize the complex plan very quickly.
figure	2	The salaries range from $9,705 to $36,841; but the average is $14,264.
direct reach	3	The injection my nurse gave me hurt and left a large bruise on my arm.
fluency	4	She may go to the island with a neighbor to fish and to dig for clams.

| 1 | 2 | 3 | 4 | 5 | 6 | 7 | 8 | 9 | 10 | 11 | 12 | 13 | 14 |

95b ▶ 45
Apply for employment

Problem 1
Letter of application

full sheet

Read the advertisement given at the right; then prepare in an appropriate letter style the letter that follows it.

Problem 2
Help-wanted ad

half sheet, long side up

Compose and type a help–wanted ad for a full–time position for which you feel qualified. Place the ad attractively on the half sheet.

Problem 3
Letter of application

full sheet

Compose and type, in an appropriate style, a letter of application in response to the help–wanted ad you have just written.

EMPLOYMENT OPPORTUNITY—FULL-TIME

Need experienced word processing supervisor to establish and to coordinate three satellite word processing centers. Must be familiar with the insurance industry. Send data sheet to Mrs. Selma Parker, President; Ozark Insurance Company; P.O. Box 8910; Ft. Smith, AR 72906-6431

---

words

1082 Madison Avenue | New York, NY 10028-5743 | February 8, 19-- | Mrs. Selma 15
Parker | Ozark Insurance Company | P.O. Box 8910 | Ft. Smith, AR 72906-6431 | 29
Dear Mrs. Parker 32

(¶ 1) Your ad in today's Ft. Smith News described a position for an experi- 49
enced word processing supervisor who is familiar with the insurance industry. I 65
feel that my background in business administration and my experience super- 80
vising a word processing center in an insurance company make me an ideal 95
candidate for the position. 101

(¶ 2) As a word processing technician, I operated three different brands of word 116
processors and both impact and nonimpact printers. After two years as an 130
operator, I was promoted to supervisor of the center. Recently, I was respon- 146
sible for the evaluation and selection of new software for our information pro- 162
cessors. This experience and my other experiences summarized on the 177
enclosed data sheet will be extremely valuable in setting up new centers. 191

(¶ 3) Our family is scheduled to move to Ft. Smith on March 1; however, I could 205
come for an interview prior to that time. Please give me the opportunity to 221
demonstrate to you that my qualifications are a perfect match for the position 237
you advertised. You may call me at (212) 555-6034 to suggest a convenient time 253
for an interview. (219) 256

Sincerely | Ms. Michi Nitobe | Enclosure 263

54a ▶ 5
Preparatory practice

each line 3 times SS (slowly, faster, slowly); DS between 3-line groups; repeat selected lines as time permits

alphabet 1 My dazed quarterback was very jumpy and frightened from a taxing blow.

fig/sym 2 Their newest model (XL-264) is selling at $1,853.79 less 10% for cash.

adjacent keys 3 In Luis' opinion, a few assets were reported in excess of their value.

fluency 4 She may go with them to the downtown firm to sign the authentic title.

| 1 | 2 | 3 | 4 | 5 | 6 | 7 | 8 | 9 | 10 | 11 | 12 | 13 | 14 |

54b ▶ 15
Inventory/build statistical-copy skill

1 Two 1' writings on each ¶ (1 for speed, 1 for control).

2 One 5' writing; proofread and circle errors; determine *gwam*.

Difficulty index

all letters/figures used | A | 1.5 si | 5.7 awl | 80% hfw

	gwam 1'	5'

Women in the United States continue to gain power in the day-to-day activities of business and government. Part of this power shift is attributable to the changing numerical balance between men and women. In 1950, for the first time in history, there were more women than men in this country. Presently, our nation has nearly 6 million more females than males; and a Census Bureau projection reveals that the gap could widen to 7.2 million by the year 2000.

13 3 64
27 5 67
41 8 70
56 11 72
69 14 75
83 17 78
93 19 80

To examine the numbers in another manner, we can state that in 1910 there were 106 males for every 100 females, but that in the year 2000 there will be only 95 males for every 100 females. Throughout history, more boys than girls have come into the world--the ratio has been approximately 105 baby boys per 100 baby girls. However, the mortality rate of infant boys is always higher than that of infant girls. This discrepancy in the survival rate more than makes up for the greater number of boys born.

13 21 82
27 24 85
40 27 88
54 29 91
68 32 94
83 35 96
97 38 99
102 39 100

Women have consistently had lower mortality rates than men at all stages of life. Girls born in 1900 could expect to outlive boys by less than 3 years. For people born in 1977, women are anticipated to outlive men by about 8 years. During the same 77-year period, life expectancies at birth grew 29 years for women (from 48 in 1900 to 77 in 1977) while increasing just 23 years for men (rising from 46 to 69 years). The greater number of women and their lengthier life spans will be significant in all aspects of commerce and government in future decades.

13 42 103
27 44 104
41 47 108
54 50 111
68 53 114
82 55 117
96 58 119
109 60 122
112 61 123

| gwam 1' | 1 | 2 | 3 | 4 | 5 | 6 | 7 | 8 | 9 | 10 | 11 | 12 | 13 | 14 |
| 5' | | | 1 | | | 2 | | | 3 | | |

Learning goals

1 To develop skill in preparing a personal data sheet and other employment communications.

2 To improve ability to compose communications used in the employment process.

Machine adjustments

1 Paper guide at 0.

2 Margins: 70–space line for drills; as directed for problems.

3 Spacing: SS drills; follow directions outlined for each problem.

94a ▶ 5

Preparatory practice

each line 3 times SS (slowly, faster, slowly); DS between 3-line groups; repeat selected lines as time permits

alphabet 1 James Waverly placed the bronze plaques next to the drinking fountain.

figure 2 We mailed 96,372 brochures; 410 personal letters; and 685 invitations.

adjacent key 3 We were walking quickly to avoid the people trying to view a big fire.

fluency 4 Their enchantment with the robot is a sign they may make a bid for it.

| 1 | 2 | 3 | 4 | 5 | 6 | 7 | 8 | 9 | 10 | 11 | 12 | 13 | 14 |

94b ▶ 45

Prepare personal data sheets

plain sheets

Problem 1
Personal data sheet

The data sheet given at the right illustrates one accept–able style for formatting a data sheet. Prepare the data sheet in the style illustrated, using a 2″ top margin and 1″ side margins. Indent ¶s 5 spaces from left margin.

Problem 2
Personal data sheet

Use your own data and the format you used for a data sheet in Problem 1 to prepare a personal data sheet.

words

MICHI NITOBE   3
1082 Madison Avenue   7
New York, NY   10028-5743   12
(212) 555-6034   15

CAREER OBJECTIVE   18

     Career in administrative office management in the insurance   30
industry.   32

MAJOR QUALIFICATIONS   36

     Knowledge of office management and related areas of business   49
administration. Experience in the insurance industry.   60

EDUCATION   62

     Associate in arts degree, Eastern Shores Community College,   74
June, 1985. Majored in office systems management. Courses   86
in office management, accounting, word/data processing, record   98
management, and management of the automated office.   109

     High school diploma, Sterling Academy, June, 1983. Majored   121
in business and mathematics.   127

EXPERIENCE   129

     Supervisor, Word Processing Center, Hobbs Insurance Company,   141
from June, 1985, to present time. Responsible for supervis-   153
ing 12 employees, analyzing and evaluating work, developing   165
procedures manuals, training technicians, and coordinating   177
with users. Productivity of the Center has increased 20 per-   189
cent, and costs have remained constant under my supervision.   202

REFERENCES   204

     References, including present employer and former instructors,   217
will be provided upon request.   223

54c ▶ 30
Inventory/build letter skill

3 plain full sheets

**Problem 1
Business letter**

modified block style; open punctuation; date on Line 16; 60–space line

words

Current date | Ms. Sylvia Perez | 415 East Plaza Drive | Westmont, IL 60559-8736 | 17
Dear Ms. Perez   20

(¶ 1) You will soon be receiving your Redi-Cash Card. Your card will make it   34
possible for you to enjoy our All-Hours Banking Service.   45

(¶ 2) In order to operate the All-Hours machine, you must utilize your personal   60
identification code. This confidential code must be entered into the keyboard   76
before any machine transaction can be completed.   86

(¶ 3) Never carry the code in written form in the same purse or billfold with   100
your card. If your card were lost or stolen, you would not want the code to be   116
available also. Immediately report any lost or stolen card to your bank.   131

(¶ 4) You will receive your Redi-Cash Card within the next few days. Several   146
days later, your personal identification code will come in the mail. We at First   162
National Bank hope that you will use and enjoy our All-Hours Banking Service.   177

Yours very truly | Mrs. Karen Myers | New Accounts Manager | xx   189

**Problem 2
Business letter**

block style; open punctuation; date on Line 19; 60–space line

May 15, 19-- | Mr. George Fox | 200 Old Tappan Road | Old Tappan, NJ 07675-   15
3126 | Dear Mr. Fox   19

(¶ 1) Although you were notified that Vantage Motor Homes, Inc., has placed   33
your account with us for collection, we at Colby Financial Association have   48
received no response from you to our previous request for payment.   61

(¶ 2) In order to avoid taking further steps to collect this account, it is necessary   75
that we receive the full payment of $345.89 by May 28.   86

(¶ 3) Please make your check payable to Colby Financial Association and send it   101
immediately. If you have any questions about this matter, please direct them to   117
Mr. Robert Wilson, Credit Manager at Vantage Motor Homes, Inc.   129

Yours very truly | Joseph Brennan | Collection Manager | xx   140

**Problem 3
Personal letter**

block style; open punctuation; begin on Line 17; 60–space line

132 Parkside Crescent | Rochester, NY 14617-7337 | June 13, 19-- | Mr. Paul   15
Perine | 308 Myrtle Avenue | Syracuse, NY 13204-4876 | Dear Paul   27

(¶ 1) Today I received my renewal form for season football tickets from the   41
Alumni Relations Office. I hope that you have received yours, also. It would be   57
great to get seats all together this year.   65

(¶ 2) I think it would be a good idea to sign up for seats right on the 40-yard line.   81
Mary and I have requested seats 20A and 21A. Maybe you could get seats 22A   96
and 23A.   98

(¶ 3) Mary and I are eager to see you and Carolyn again. Perhaps we can spend a   113
few weekends together this year!   119

Sincerely | William Sutton   124

Problem 2
Leftbound report
with footnotes
Format the report DS.

words

TRANSPARENCIES AFFECT SUCCESS OF MEETING   8

Communication experts believe that audiovisual aids help make a busi-   22
ness meeting more successful. These devices add to what is being said, help   37
listeners understand complex concepts, and maintain interest and attention.[1]   52
Tables and graphs presenting statistical data are among the most commonly   67
used visual aids.   70

Results of the Wharton study indicate that overhead transparencies have   84
a positive impact on business meetings. Presenters who used overhead trans-   99
parencies in presentations were perceived as significantly better prepared,   114
more professional, more persuasive, more credible, and more interesting than   129
presenters who did not use overhead transparencies.[2]   139

Transparencies must be used effectively if they are to make a positive   153
impact on a meeting. Each participant must be able to read easily the informa-   169
tion that is projected. The information presented on each transparency should   185
be limited. A good transparency uses a few well-chosen words to make one   200
point only. A simple, uncluttered transparency is more effective than a com-   215
plex, cluttered one. Projectors must be turned on only when the attention of the   231
audience is being directed to the screen.   239

242

[1]Allan D. Frank, Communicating on the Job. Glenview, Illinois: Scott,   261
Foresman and Co., 1982, p. 300.   267

[2]"How to Present More Effectively--and Win More Favorable Responses   281
From More People in Less Time." A summary of the Wharton Report. Audio   296
Visual Division/3M, 1981.   301

Problem 3
Title page

Prepare a title page for Problem
2. Use the information given at
the right.

TRANSPARENCIES AFFECT SUCCESS OF MEETING   8

Cynthia Jackson, Training Director   15

Human Resources Department   20

February 8, 19--   23

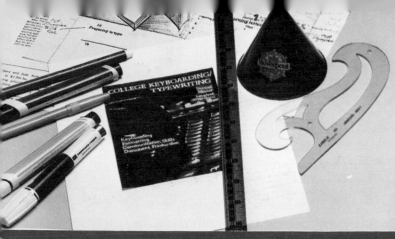

Learning goals

1 To format business letters in the acceptable styles illustrated.
2 To improve basic keyboarding and proofreading skills.
3 To address two sizes of envelopes in an acceptable manner.

Machine adjustments

1 Paper guide at 0.
2 Margins: 70–space line for drills and ¶ writings; as directed for problems.
3 Spacing: SS drills; DS ¶ writings; as directed for problems.
4 Indention: 5 spaces for ¶ writings; as appropriate for problems.

55

55a ▶ 5
Preparatory practice

each line 3 times SS (slowly, faster, slowly); DS between 3-line groups; repeat selected lines if time permits

alphabet 1 Jackie reported sixty-four valuable quartz watches missing on Tuesday.

fig/sym 2 Did their Invoice #9264 for $1,037.88 include a 5% discount of $51.89?

adjacent key 3 Her appointment to the new position pleased many leaders in education.

fluency 4 Do we both wish to work with the panel to enrich the authentic ritual?

| 1 | 2 | 3 | 4 | 5 | 6 | 7 | 8 | 9 | 10 | 11 | 12 | 13 | 14 |

55b ▶ 10
Improve keyboarding technique

each pair of lines 3 times SS; DS between 6-line groups; work at a controlled rate

direct reach 1 They agreed a maximum number of payments for service must be received.
2 We doubt a great many officers must renounce their service agreements.

adjacent keys 3 What equipment do we need to record her weekly news talks on the radio?
4 We outlined for you the six important points in the government report.

double letters 5 A traffic officer suggested we needed three additional gallons of gas.
6 Book orders for all college classes this summer must be submitted now.

shift keys 7 Donna's itinerary included New York, Boston, Los Angeles, and Chicago.
8 Mary Ann attended River College after graduation from Lee High School.

| 1 | 2 | 3 | 4 | 5 | 6 | 7 | 8 | 9 | 10 | 11 | 12 | 13 | 14 |

55c ▶ 7
Learn letter format

plain sheets; 60-space line; begin on Line 14

1 Using Style letter 4, page 115, format and type the opening lines and the first line of the body. Leave proper spacing between parts.

2 Space down to Line 48. Format and type the last 3 lines of ¶4 and the closing lines, leaving proper spacing between them.

3 On another sheet of paper, take a 1' writing on the opening lines and ¶1; a 1' writing on ¶s 2 and 3; and a 1' writing on the last 3 lines of ¶4 and closing lines.

55d ▶ 28
Improve business letter skill

60-space line; begin on Line 13

Note: From this point, LM page references refer to the *Laboratory Materials*, stock number T271.

Problem 1 (plain sheet)
Format and type the letter illus–trated on page 115.
Proofread; use standard proofreader's marks to indicate needed corrections.

Problem 2 (LM p. 71)
Using your corrected copy, pre–pare a final copy of the letter, mak–ing the corrections indicated in your copy.

Problem 3 (plain sheet)
If time permits, take a 5' writing on the entire letter. Determine *gwam* by dividing total words typed by 5.

92d, continued
Problem 2
Bibliography

Prepare the material at the right with the same margins as you need for the leftbound report in Problem 1. Use a full sheet.

Note: Articles or news stories for which no author is given are reported in a bibliography starting with the first words in the title (disregard *a*, *an*, or *the*).

BIBLIOGRAPHY   3

Crawford, T. James, et al. <u>Basic Keyboarding and Typewriting Applications</u>.   28
    Cincinnati: South-Western Publishing Co., 1983.   38

"Electronic Printing Hits Its Stride." <u>Xerox World</u> (Summer 1982), pp. 11-15.   56

Hess, M. Elizabeth. Printing Manager, Effective Office Systems, New Orleans,   72
    Louisiana. Interviewed by Lois Walker, March 20, 1985.   83

Ray, Patrick V. "Electronic Printing Applications." Class handout in BADM   98
    487, Central University, 1985.   104

Toffler, Alvin. <u>The Third Wave</u>. New York: William Morrow and Company,   121
    Inc., 1980.   123

93

93a ▶ 5
Preparatory practice

each line 3 times SS (slowly, faster, slowly); DS between 3-line groups; repeat selected lines as time permits

alphabet 1   Quincy apologized for the lack of objectivity in your complex reviews.

figure 2   Did 387 people pay $695 to attend the training program on April 14-20?

outside reach 3   We saw Wally Maxwell quickly swim past Alex in a show at the zoo pool.

fluency 4   Susie did sign both of the forms, and she did pay half of the penalty.

| 1 | 2 | 3 | 4 | 5 | 6 | 7 | 8 | 9 | 10 | 11 | 12 | 13 | 14 |

93b ▶ 45
Measure production on reports and title page

plain sheets

Time schedule:
Assembling materials ...... 3'
Timed production .... 35'
Final check; compute
   n-pram .... 7'

Problem 1
Unbound report with reference citations

Prepare the report given at the right DS.

                              words

LENDING POLICY FOR COUNTY BANK   6

Limits of Authority   10

    The President of the bank is authorized to make loans up to $100,000 on   24
a secured basis and up to $50,000 on an unsecured basis. Any request for a line   40
of credit in excess of the limit specified for the President must be approved by   56
at least two members of the Loan Committee other than the President. These   71
lending limits are in agreement with recommended standards (Burge, 1985).   86

    The President shall delegate authority to make loans to the senior officers   101
of the bank. Senior officers may approve loans up to $50,000 on a secured basis   117
and up to $25,000 on an unsecured basis. The President may delegate authority   133
to make loans to other officers. Authority delegated to officers other than the   149
senior officers shall not exceed $10,000 and shall be for secured loans only. This 166
policy is based on recommended guides (White, 1985).   176

REFERENCES   178

Burge, S. Michael. "General Lending Policy." <u>South-Western Banking Associa-</u> 189
    <u>tion Report</u>. March 12, 1985, p. 8.   198

White, Deborah B. "Guides for Delegating Lending Authority." Class handout   213
    in Bankers' School, Central University, 1985.   222

Pennsylvania Junior College Association
1500 Academy Street
Harrisburg, PA 15906-4532
(717) 555-1490

| | in parts | total |

Dateline   June 15, 19--   3 | 3

Letter address
Mr. Dana Fox, President   8 | 8
York Community College   12 | 12
West Seventh Avenue   16 | 16
York, PA 17404-5436   20 | 20

Salutation Dear Mr. Fox: 23 | 23

Body of letter   The annual meeting of the Pennsylvania Junior College   34 | 34
Association will take place on Thursday, September 9, at the   46 | 46
Plaza Hotel, Philadelphia, Pennsylvania.   55 | 55

A stimulating program has been developed by the program   11 | 66
committee, chaired by Susan Walker, Dean, Community College   23 | 78
of Philadelphia. This year's speaker will be John Winston,   35 | 90
Assistant Dean of Education, Syracuse University Graduate   47 | 101
School of Education. His address is entitled "Education in   59 | 113
a Time of Change."   63 | 117

Dr. Winston's teaching, research, and administrative   73 | 128
activities focus on lifelong learning, professional develop-   85 | 140
ment, and administration of postsecondary education. He cur-   98 | 152
rently serves as education chairperson of the Institute for   110 | 164
the Development of Lifelong Education.   118 | 172

We are certain that you will find this meeting timely   183
and informative. Please call (717) 281-4339 to register and   195
get any additional information you may desire. The $25 reg-   207
istration fee covers the cost of the meeting, refreshments,   12 | 219
and luncheon. We look forward to seeing you on September 9   24 | 231
at the Plaza Hotel.   28 | 235

Yours very truly,   31 | 239

Complimentary close

Signature   *Pamela Strombom*

Typed name   Pamela Strombom, Ph.D.   36 | 243
Official title   President   38 | 245

Reference initials   xx   39 | 246

In *mixed punctuation*, a colon follows
the salutation and a comma follows
the complimentary close.

Style letter 4: modified block style with indented paragraphs and mixed punctuation

92a ▶ 5
Preparatory practice

each line 3 times SS (slowly, faster, slowly); DS between 3-line groups; repeat selected lines as time permits

alphabet 1 Felix Jiminez hopes to fly back to Quebec to visit with great friends.

figure 2 I ordered 3,750 labels, 1,984 pencils, 625 legal pads, and 95 folders.

double letters 3 Anne will accept the offer and discuss fully the process that applies.

fluency 4 Akeo may go to the big city on the bus to visit with the busy auditor.

| 1 | 2 | 3 | 4 | 5 | 6 | 7 | 8 | 9 | 10 | 11 | 12 | 13 | 14 |

92b ▶ 12
Prepare a title page and a memo

plain sheets

Problem 1

Compose a title page for the unbound report you prepared in 91c. Use your name, your title (Manager of Human Resources), and the current date.

Problem 2

Compose a simplified memo to all supervisors from you. The memo will be sent to each supervisor with a copy of the report you prepared in 91c. Ask each supervisor to read the report and be prepared to discuss it at the staff meeting scheduled one week from today at 2:00 p.m. Use today's date and an appropriate subject line.

92c ▶ 8
Preapplication drill: prepare a bibliography

plain sheet

1 For this drill, use the same margins that you would use for the first page of an unbound report.

2 Start the first line of each entry at the left margin; indent the second and subsequent lines 5 spaces. SS each entry; DS between entries.

BIBLIOGRAPHY

Gates, Calvin. The Micro-Editor. Cincinnati: South-Western Publishing Co., 1983.

Rosen, Arnold, and Rosemary Fielden. Word Processing. 2d ed. Englewood Cliffs: Prentice-Hall, 1982.

Will, Mimi, and Donette Dake. Concepts in Word Processing: The Challenge of Change. Boston: Allyn and Bacon, Inc., 1982.

92d ▶ 25
Prepare a leftbound report and a bibliography

plain sheets

Problem 1
Leftbound report

Prepare the material at the right in leftbound report form on a full sheet. Compose an appropriate title page for the report. Use your name, your title (Manager of Technical Services), and the current date.

ELECTRONIC PRINTING

words

ELECTRONIC PRINTING — 4

We are presently considering using electronic printing in our company. — 28 Products are now available which combine several technologies. These — 42 technologies include digital computers with the capacity of handling informa- — 57 tion at high rates of speed, lasers with the ability to create high-resolution — 73 images, and xerography with the capability of producing high-quality printed — 88 output. The new systems can scan photographs or designs and convert them — 103 into digital images. — 107

Numerous office automation references have been reviewed to determine — 121 the different applications of electronic printing technology in our company. — 137 One application which is being analyzed carefully is forms control. Forms can — 153 now be printed at the same time that they are filled with information. Logos and — 169 signatures can be reproduced. Artwork can be digitized and merged into text. — 184

56a ▶ 5
Preparatory practice

each line 3 times SS (slowly, faster, slowly); DS between 3-line groups; repeat selected lines if time permits

alphabet 1 The six zany jokers might have had backup plans they quickly followed.

fig/sym 2 The bid by Lee & Fox for $28,746 was 9% lower than our bid of $31,590.

direct reach 3 Reserving my doubts should end a great number of technical objections.

fluency 4 The problem is with their firm, so he may sue to enrich the endowment.

| 1 | 2 | 3 | 4 | 5 | 6 | 7 | 8 | 9 | 10 | 11 | 12 | 13 | 14 |

56b ▶ 13
Review envelope format

Postal recommendations

1 Format the address lines in block style (even left margin) in the area on the envelope that the scanner is programmed to read.

2 For a large (No. 10) envelope, begin the address vertically on Line 14 and horizontally about 5 spaces left of the center point.

3 For a small (No. 6¾) envelope, begin the address vertically on Line 12 and horizontally about 10 spaces left of the center point.

4 In the address, capitalize all letters and eliminate all punctuation.

5 Use the standard 2-letter ZIP Code abbreviation for the state. State abbreviations for use with ZIP Codes appear on page iv of the Reference Guide.

6 Place the name of the city, 2-letter state abbreviation, and ZIP Code on the last line of the address. The space below the address must be completely clear.

7 Long city names and street designators may be abbreviated, using the abbreviations found in the *National ZIP Code Directory* or *Customer Service Publication 59* (both available from the U.S. Postal Service).

Recommended placement of additional information

1 When an address contains such notations as *Personal* or *Confidential*, underline them or use all capital letters. Place these notations 3 lines below the return address and aligned with the left edge of the address.

2 Use all capital letters for mailing directions such as SPECIAL DELIVERY or REGISTERED MAIL. Place these directions below the space for the stamp.

3 When an address contains an *attention line*, type it as the second line of the address.

General information

1 If the ZIP Code of an address is not available, use either the state name in full or the traditional abbreviation. You may format this address in either capital and lowercase or all capitals.

2 As a mark of courtesy, always use an appropriate personal title on a letter, envelope, or card addressed to an individual. When a woman's preferred title is unknown, use Ms. as the personal title.

3 Some companies use No. 10 envelopes as a standard practice. Others use No. 10 envelopes for all original copies on 8½" × 11" stationery and No. 6¾ envelopes for half-size stationery or onionskin sheets.

4 Although the U.S. Postal Service recommends the use of ALL CAPS and no punctuation in envelope addresses, many companies continue to use cap and lowercase style with punctuation as illustrated on the No. 6¾ envelope below.

Examples

MISS MELANIE MILLER
BOX 422
WHITTIER CA 90608-4223

MR SUMIO TANAKA
JACKSON ELECTRIC COMPANY
2408 GROVER STREET
OMAHA NE 68105-3542

HANDEL DRY GOODS INC
ATTENTION MRS ANN HANDEL
1300 PACIFIC STREET
PORTLAND OR 97232-5235

Mr. Jonathan Becker
RR 4 Box 120
Woronoco, Mass.

(When ZIP Code is not available)

Large envelope (No. 10) 9½" × 4⅛"

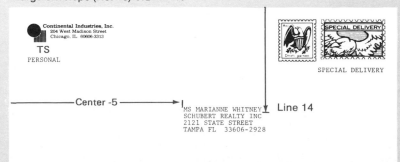

Small envelope (No. 6¾) 6½" × 3⅝"

Style of addressing envelope used above is recommended by U.S. Postal Service to aid mechanical mail sorting.

You see, really and truly, apart from the things any- | 137
one can pick up (the dressing and the proper way of | 147
speaking, and so on), the difference between a lady | 157
and a flower girl is not how she behaves but how | 167
she's treated. I shall always be a flower girl to | 177
Professor Higgins, because he always treats me as a | 187
flower girl, and always will; but I know I can be a | 197
lady to you, because you treat me as a lady, and al- | 207
ways will (Livingston, 1969, 81-84). | 214

Livingston found in his research that some managers tend to | 226
treat subordinates in a manner that improves performance. Other | 239
Managers unintentionally follow Professor Higgins and treat | 251
employees in a way that leads to lowers performance. The way a man- | 264
ager treats handles an employee is often based on the expectations | 276
the that manager has for the employee. High expectations tend to lead to | 290
high productivity. Low expectations tend to cause lower work lead to | 301
productivity. Employees sense can tell how the supervisor superior feels about | 313
their there potential. These workers may then perform in as the role | 325
in which they think they have been cast. Thus, So, a manager's | 337
behavior toward an employee can have a long-range effect on the | 350
employees job performance. | 355

The term "effective cycle" refers to the phenomenon phemonenen that | 366
occurs happens when employees respond to the high expectations of their | 379
managers with high performance (Hersey and Blanchard, 1982). | 391

Managers concerned with worried about developing the talents of all their | 403
employees need to very carefully examine the expectations they | 415
hold for each every employee. Stating Saying what you think an employee can | 427
do is not enough. You have to believe it. | 435

REFERENCES | 437

Hersey, Paul, and Kenneth H. Blanchard. Management of Organiza- | 454
tional Behavior: Utilizing Human Resources. 4th ed. | 474
Englewood Cliffs: Prentice-Hall, Inc., 1982. | 483
Livingston, J. Sterling. "Pygmalion in Management." Harvard | 497
Business Review, July-August 1969, pp. 81-84. | 509
Reber, Ralph W., and Gloria Van Gilder. Behavioral Insights | 525
for Supervision. 2d ed. Englewood Cliffs: Prentice-Hall, | 540
Inc., 1982. | 542

56b, continued

Envelopes

3 No. 10 and 3 No. 6¾ en–velopes (LM pp. 73–77)

Address 3 No. 10 envelopes for the 3 addresses given at the top right and 3 No. 6¾ en–velopes for the 3 addresses given below them (see p. 116 for directions).

Mr. Harold Jackson
4740 Jerald Drive
Monroe, LA 71203-5868

Miss Brenda S. Gara
7800 Carousel Lane
Miles, VA 23114-4692

Dr. Robert Friend
325 Brook Road
Boston, MA 02187-1493
(Confidential)

- -

MRS ROBERTA KING
17027 BIHL AVENUE
TOLEDO OH 43619-8275

MISS JO ANN WHEELER
WESTGAGE PLAZA HOTEL
1641 W 16TH STREET
CHICAGO IL 60608-5993

MR LOU KELLY
SAWYER SCHOOL
917 MAIN STREET
ROCHESTER NY 14605-4458

56c ▶ 7
Learn to use a letter placement table

Study the letter placement table and other information given at the right and below in preparation for completing the following letters.

Letter Classification	5-Stroke Words in Letter Body	Side Margins	Dateline Position	Placement of Second Page Heading
Short	Up to 125	2"	19	Type the first line of second and fol–lowing page headings on 7th line from top edge. TS below head–ing and continue letter.
Average	126–225	1½"	16	
Long	226–325	1"	13	
Two–page	More than 325	1"	13	
Standard 6" line for all letters**	As above for all letters	1¼"	As above for all letters	

*As determined from extensive research conducted on business letters by L. W. Erickson, UCLA.
**Use only when so directed. Some business firms use a standard 6" line for all letters.

Stationery

Business letters are usually typed on 8½" × 11" letterhead paper. For a multipage letter, plain paper of the same size, color, and quality as the letterhead is used after page 1. Onionskin or manifold paper is used for carbon copies.

Margins/vertical placement

Some offices use a set line length for all letters. Others vary the margins according to the letter length.

The placement table given here will help you place letters properly. Use the table as an aid; discon–tinue using it as soon as possible.

For the rest of Division 2, a number in parentheses will appear at the end of the body of each let–ter to indicate the number of 5–stroke words in the body of the letter. This will serve as an aid in determining letter placement. Estimate letter length, and place letters by judgment. Your ability to judge will be vital.

Adjustment guides

As you learn to judge letter placement, consider two factors:

(1) Is your type size pica or elite and (2) does the letter contain extra opening and closing lines, a table, or a list? Allow for these extra lines by raising the dateline from 1 to 3 lines.

If the letterhead prevents typing the date on the designated line, type it on the second line below the last letterhead line.

56d ▶ 25
Format business letters

Problem 1
Block style, open
(LM p. 79)

Determine margins and letter placement from the table above. The number of 5–stroke words in the body of the letter is indicated by the number in parentheses at the end of the body of the letter. Correct errors.

	words
Current date	Mr. Alexander Powers	Sturmer School of Business	2101 South	16
Hamilton Road	Columbus, OH 43227-3757	Dear Mr. Powers	27

(¶ 1) Our company is a distributor of computer equipment and supplies avail- | 41
able from over one hundred manufacturers. We have offices in nine states and | 57
plan offices in two more states in the near future. | 67

(¶ 2) The products we distribute include over twenty mainframe microcomput- | 81
ers, over one hundred input and output devices, software packages from over | 96
two hundred software companies, and any microprocessor books which might | 111
be needed. | 113

(¶ 3) Please add our company to your bid list. We can fill your needs for com- | 128
puters and electronic equipment for use in accounting, computer-assisted in- | 143
struction, student record keeping, text editing, and document preparation. (130) | 158

Sincerely | Soledad Volcy | Sales Manager | xx | 167

91a ▶ 5
Preparatory practice

each line 3 times SS (slowly, faster, slowly); DS between 3-line groups; repeat selected lines as time permits

alphabet 1 Benjamin designed six oversized patchwork quilts for the country fair.

figure 2 We saw 19 dogs, 28 cats, 37 chickens, 46 ducks, 50 cows, and 9 horses.

direct reach 3 Alice doubts that anyone knew my brother wrote the hymn that was sung.

fluency 4 Al did go downtown to turn the signs on an angle to make them visible.

| 1 | 2 | 3 | 4 | 5 | 6 | 7 | 8 | 9 | 10 | 11 | 12 | 13 | 14 |

91b ▶ 10
Preapplication drill: prepare information about citations

plain sheet; DS; use unbound report format

1 Prepare the report given at the right. Use the heading **CITATIONS**.

2 As time permits, study and analyze the content of the report. Discuss the procedures with your teacher.

A citation is a way of referencing quoted material without using traditional footnotes.

A reference citation shows the author's name, the date of publication, and the page number (if a direct quote) placed in parentheses within the text. If the author's name occurs in the sentence, the name is not used in the reference citation. Examples include the following: One study linked job ambiguity and stress (Adams, 1984, 68). OR Adams (1984, 68) linked job ambiguity and stress.

An alphabetical list of references by author names is placed at the end of the report.

91c ▶ 35
Prepare a report with reference citations

2 plain sheets

1 Prepare the material given at the right and on the next page in unbound report form.

2 Make the rough-draft corrections indicated in the copy. Correct errors as you work.

3 Place the references in an alphabetical list 3 spaces below the last line of the report on page 2. Indent the second and succeeding lines of each reference 5 spaces from the left margin.

                                                                    words
                    The Power of Expectations   5

                               to meet the expectations of their
        Students tend to perform at the level their parents and   17
                               Employees also perform to
parents and teachers expect them to. The same is true of   25
meet expectations.
employees. The expectations a supervisor has for an employees   39
        can
affects the way that employee performs. The expectations can   52
                                              Van
be either positive or negative (Reber and Gilder, 1982). The   63
                    have   referred to
effect expectations has on performance is some times labeled   77
         e   c   a
as the self-fulfilling prophesy or the "Pygmalion Effect." The   89
                                                the play on
passage from George Bernard Shaws play Pygmalion (which was   102
which   was based
made into MY FAIR LADY) is used to demonstrate that people may   116

have an influence on others and may not even be aware of it.   127

56d, continued

Problem 2
Modified block style,
mixed

letterhead and envelope (LM p. 81); use the letter placement table on page 117; correct errors

Note: The total word count is shown as 115/**128**: the first fig–ure is the letter count; the sec–ond is the letter plus the en–velope.

	words
Current date	Mr. Walter Anderson	550 Old Country Road	Hicksville, NY	15
11801-8653	Dear Mr. Anderson:	21

(¶ 1) Congratulations on the purchase of your new home. As you know, your   35
home has been schematically prewired for burglar and fire alarms.   48

(¶ 2) When you decide to install your security system, all you have to do is call   63
us. We will be pleased to quote you prices and options to secure your invest-   81
ment.   82

(¶ 3) We will also be happy to send you a list of our services, as well as a few of   98
our many references. (79)   102

Sincerely yours, | Miss Susan K. Patseas | Security Consultant | xx   115/**128**

57a ▶ 5
Preparatory practice

each line 3 times SS (slowly, faster, slowly); DS between 3-line groups; repeat selected lines if time permits

alphabet 1 My chief executives were pleased by the quarterly junkets I organized.

fig/sym 2 Model #TRX-590 has sales of $864,132 or 14% higher than Model #RXL-77.

double letters 3 Employees were happy to support the official committee recommendation.

fluency 4 She may wish to suspend the formal audit if the firm pays the penalty.

| 1 | 2 | 3 | 4 | 5 | 6 | 7 | 8 | 9 | 10 | 11 | 12 | 13 | 14 |

57b ▶ 45
Learn to format multipage letters

1 Study the information at the right and the illustrations below.

2 Format and type the problems that follow (LM p. 83). Make 1 cc and address an envelope for Prob-lem 1.

3 Proofread and circle errors. Check placement of second–page headings.

Second and subsequent pages of a letter: For the second and sub–sequent pages of a multipage let–ter, use plain paper of the same color and quality as the letterhead.

Do not end a page with a divided word. If possible, leave at least 2 lines of a paragraph at the foot of a page and carry at least two lines to the next page.

Place the first line of second–and subsequent–page headings on the 7th line from the top edge. TS after heading and continue typ-

ing. Use the same side margins as for the first page.

If the horizontal style is used for the heading of the second page, center the page number and make sure the dateline ends at the right margin.

Before starting the first page of any long letter, draw a light pencil line 1½" to 2" from the bottom edge of the page as a page–end warning. You can then judge where to end the page if the letter is too long for the page.

Block style heading for second page

Horizontal style heading for second page

Problem 1

Two–page letter in block style, open punctuation, with block second–page heading.

	words
Current date	Mrs. Carmen Quintana	3013 Fountain View Drive	Houston, TX	16
77057-8423	Dear Mrs. Quintana	22

(¶ 1) Thank you for your recent letter requesting clarification of our provisions   37
for the disabled at International Airport. We welcome the opportunity to ac-   52
quaint the public with our provisions for mobility-limited travelers, whether   68
physically handicapped or elderly, and with the many services and facilities   83

(continued on next page)

90c ▶ 37
Prepare title pages and reports
plain sheets

Problem 1
Title page for unbound report

Prepare the title page illustrated at the right for an unbound report; center each line horizontally; use the title **FEASIBILITY OF CENTRALIZED COPY CENTER;** the author is **Thomas Kishpaugh, Operations Manager,** and the date of the report is **August 14, 19--.**

Problem 2
Title page for leftbound report

You are the personnel manager of a corporation. Prepare a title page for your annual progress report on your corporation's affirmative action program. Compose a title; use today's date.

Follow the illustration above right for the title page of a leftbound report; center each line over the line of writing for a leftbound report.

Problem 3
Leftbound report

Prepare the report given at the right.

Problem 4
Title page for leftbound report

Prepare an appropriate title page for the report in Problem 3. The report was written by **Marjorie Sullivan, Vice President of Marketing.** Use today's date.

Title page for unbound report

2½"

FEASIBILITY OF CENTRALIZED COPY CENTER

2½"

Thomas Kishpaugh
Operations Manager

2½"

August 14, 19--

Title page for leftbound report

2½"

FEASIBILITY OF CENTRALIZED COPY CENTER

2½"

Thomas Kishpaugh
Operations Manager

2½"

August 14, 19--

---

words

CUSTOMER SERVICE DEPARTMENT PERFORMANCE   8

¶ The performance of the Customer Service Department for the   20
second quarter was evaluated. Data were compared to the   31
existing company standards and to the departmental per-   42
formance for the past 12 quarters. The individual performance of   55
each customer service representative was also evaluated.   66

¶ Performance met and exceeded every standard except that the   78
complaint ratio increased by 38 percent this quarter. Birsner   91
and Balsley recommend an investigation any time complaint   103
activity increases radically.* An increase of 38 percent   115
is a major increase and merits further study.   124

127

*E. Patricia Birsner and Ronald D. Balsley, _Practical_   140
Guide to Customer Service Management and Operations   160
(New York: AMACOM, 1982), p. 180.   167

words

which are available for their convenience. We also encourage your comments 98
and suggestions regarding these facilities. 107

(¶ 2) Specific policies or requirements with regard to transporting mobility- 121
limited travelers aboard aircraft may differ according to the individual airline. 138
If you have specific questions regarding facilities aboard aircraft or if you 154
desire additional information, call the respective airline you plan to use. 169

(¶ 3) If wheelchair assistance is needed, every major scheduled airline operat- 183
ing at International Airport can provide such assistance. We recommend that 198
you reserve the wheelchair by calling your travel agent or airline in advance of 214
the particular flight arrival or departure. You may find it easier to make all 230
arrangements for special assistance or wheelchair reservations when making 245
your original travel arrangements. 252

(¶ 4) You may also arrange for wheelchair assistance at the airline ticket coun- 267
ters. You can arrange for wheelchair and skycap to meet you within minutes of 283
your arrival at the terminal front curbside or at the airline gate. No charge or 299
deposit is required. Airlines do, however, require a skycap to accompany the 315
wheelchair and passenger to the destination point in the terminal. Gratuity for 331
the skycap's service is at the discretion of the individual. 343

(¶ 5) Airlines Transportation Company, located at the ground level of the termi- 358
nal, operates limousines and vans that can accommodate handicapped travelers 373
proceeding to the downtown area. Van service for groups up to 12 and private 390
lift-van service for wheelchair-bound travelers is available with a minimum 405
one-day advance notice by calling 803-4652. 414

(¶ 6) If you have any additional questions concerning our facilities, please con- 429
tact me. 431

Sincerely | Ms. Betty Nielsen | Director, Department of Aviation | xx 444/**458**

Problem 2
Modified block style

Format the material given at the right as the second page of a two–page letter using horizontal second–page heading.

Dr. Yolanda Ball | 2 | Current date 7

Positions are available both at our plant site near Berwick and at our Allentown 23
headquarters. If your graduates have degrees in mechanical, electrical, civil, 39
or nuclear engineering, we would like to hear from them. 50

Sincerely yours, | Peter A. Stimson | Placement Director | xx 62

58

58a ▶ 5

Preparatory practice

each line 3 times SS (slowly, faster, slowly); DS between 3-line groups; repeat selected lines if time permits

alphabet 1 Roy realized a pair will beat a queen, jack, five, or six in the game.

figures 2 The 89-unit mall built on a 205-acre site can accommodate 37,146 cars.

adjacent key 3 Quickly make three copies of the sales invoice for my equipment parts.

fluency 4 An ancient burial ritual of the island town is the theme of the chant.

| 1 | 2 | 3 | 4 | 5 | 6 | 7 | 8 | 9 | 10 | 11 | 12 | 13 | 14 |

Problem 2
Unbound report
with footnote

Follow the guides given in the outline on page 188 for an unbound report.

words

INTEGRATING MAIL PROCESSING WITH WORD PROCESSING 10

The mailroom is the major bottleneck in the handling of 21
correspondence in your company. The volume of mail currently 33
handled by the mailroom averages 28,000 pieces per day. The bulk 46
of the processing is being done manually. Handling large volumes 59
of mail is a time-consuming and costly operation. 69

Mailing systems are available which streamline office 80
efficiency and enable organizations to concentrate more time on 93
improving communications.* A cost analysis will be made to 105
determine which system is feasible for your company. 115
118

*David Duke, "Mailing Machines Complete Word Processing 129
Cycle," Word Processing & Information Systems (July 1982), p. 35. 149

90a ▶ 5
Preparatory
practice

each line 3 times SS
(slowly, faster,
slowly); DS be-
tween 3-line groups;
repeat selected lines
as time permits

90

alphabet 1 Maxwell brought good quality black pajamas in five sizes for children.

fig/sym 2 My $1,098 raise (22.75%) was excellent; the average was $654 (10.35%).

, (comma)
and figure 3 Should the figure be $13,234,987 rather than the $9,256,087 indicated?

fluency 4 Jane may go to the city to work with the audit panel on the amendment.

| 1 | 2 | 3 | 4 | 5 | 6 | 7 | 8 | 9 | 10 | 11 | 12 | 13 | 14 |

90b ▶ 8
Preapplication drill:
center heading in a
leftbound report

plain sheet; top margin: 1½"
for pica, 2" for elite; left margin: 1½"; other margins same
as for unbound

Read the guides contained in the drill at the right. Then prepare the drill, following the guides pre-sented.

words

GUIDES FOR CENTERING HEADINGS IN LEFTBOUND REPORTS 10

Main headings in leftbound reports are centered over the line of writing. 25
Follow these guides to center the main heading in this report and in other 40
leftbound reports. 44

1. Set the margins for the report. Use a 1½" left margin and a 1" 58
   right margin. 61

2. Determine the horizontal center of the line of writing by adding 75
   the scale number at both margin stops and dividing by 2. 86

3. Backspace from the horizontal center in order to center the 99
   heading. 101

Learn to format letters with mailing notation/attention line

1 Study the information and illustration at the right.

2 Format and type Problems 1–4 below (LM pp. 85–89). Make 1 carbon copy (cc) for each and address an envelope for Problems 1–3.

3 Proofread and circle errors. Check correct placement of special features.

Problem 1
Letter with mailing notation/attention line

block style, open punctuation

Mailing notation in letter: If a special mailing notation (REGISTERED, CERTIFIED, SPECIAL DELIVERY, etc.) is used in a letter, it is shown a double space below the dateline at the left margin of the letter in all capital letters.

Attention line: Place an attention line as the second line of the letter address. (Some companies prefer the attention line placed a double space below the letter address.)

```
Current date

SPECIAL DELIVERY

Nutech Exports Incorporated
Attention Mrs. Wilma Sullivan
2 World Trade Center
New York, NY  10047-4935

Ladies and Gentlemen
```

	words
Current date	SPECIAL DELIVERY	Nutech Exports Incorporated	Attention Mrs.	16
Wilma Sullivan	2 World Trade Center	New York, NY 10047-4935	Ladies and	31
Gentlemen	33

(¶ 1) We at Merchants Bank of New Jersey are happy to see that your company 47
has recently discovered vast new markets overseas. We may be able to help 62
you with your business transactions. 69

(¶ 2) We are one of the nation's leading international banks, with access to an 84
international banking network spanning 40 countries. We can supply any type 99
of international banking service: international letters of credit, trade and term 116
financing, collection, foreign exchange, banker's acceptances, factoring, and 132
others. 134

(¶ 3) Think of us as an important resource for your business and provide us with 149
an opportunity to work with you. (123) 155

Sincerely | John V. Pisani | Marketing Representative | xx 166/190

Problem 2
Letter addressed to job title

modified block style; indented ¶s; mixed punctuation

Note: When a letter is addressed to a job title instead of a particular person, the job title should appear on the line above the company name in the letter address and the salutation *Dear Sir or Madam* should be used.

Current date | Purchasing Manager | Bedford Laboratories | 600 Montgomery 15
Street | San Francisco, CA 94111-6218 | Dear Sir or Madam: 26

(¶ 1) Thank you very much for your request for catalogs and prices. This mate 41
rial will be sent to you today. 47

(¶ 2) You will find that Melrowe Distributors can supply any need you may have 62
for laboratory glassware and related supplies. We appreciate your interest in 78
our products and your giving us the opportunity to serve you. (64) 90

Sincerely, | Kevin Morgan | Sales Representative | xx 100/118

Problem 3
Letter with mailing notation/attention line

modified block style, open punctuation

Problem 4

Using plain paper; retype Problem 2 in block style and open punctuation.

Current date | SPECIAL DELIVERY | United Manufacturing, Inc. | Attention Mr. 16
Jack Farmer | 1724 Chestnut Street | Philadelphia, PA 19103-6423 | Ladies and 31
Gentlemen 33

(¶ 1) In response to your request, we are presently assembling a sample 46
portfolio of various insurance programs Foshee Insurance Agency can offer to 61
your corporation to meet your insurance needs. The portfolio will be sent to you 77
in a few days and will provide all the details of insurance programs relevant to 93
your company. 96

(¶ 2) Once you have had the opportunity to review the material, I will be pleased 111
to meet you at your convenience to discuss how I may be of service. (93) 125

Yours truly | Miss Sandra Goodson | Vice President | xx 135/159

89a ▶ 5
Preparatory practice

each line 3 times SS (slowly, faster, slowly); DS between 3-line groups; repeat selected lines as time permits

alphabet	1	The quarterbacks utilized very good judgment except for a few minutes.
fig/sym	2	The reference manual (Stock No. 2476*) was dated 1983 and cost $10.50.
long number groups	3	437-62-8072; (803) 787-7404; 15,342,679; #21376; 29206-6559; 777-60412
fluency	4	Did she visit the man to sign the form and to pay for the six bushels?

| 1 | 2 | 3 | 4 | 5 | 6 | 7 | 8 | 9 | 10 | 11 | 12 | 13 | 14 |

89b ▶ 15
Preapplication drills: prepare superscript and subscript figures and footnotes

plain sheets

Drill 1

70-space line; DS; do the drill twice

Drill 2

Assume this unbound report ended on Line 20. Place the footnote at the bottom of the page.

> To type a superscript (superior figure), operate the automatic line finder; turn platen backward (toward you); type the figure or symbol; then return the automatic line finder and platen to normal position. Follow the same procedures to type a subscript, except turn platen forward (away from you).
>
> To place footnotes at the bottom of a partially filled page, count the number of lines needed for the footnotes, plus 2 lines for the divider, and 6 lines for the bottom margin. Count from bottom of page to determine the placement of the footnotes.

Drill 1   Statistics quoted were from Xerox,[29] IBM,[30] Apple,[31] and Dictaphone.[32]

Table 2 gives values of critical points: $F_{.90}$, $F_{.95}$, $F_{.975}$, and $F_{.99}$.

Drill 2   _____

[4] Nancy DeMars, "Today's Professional Secretary," The Balance Sheet (September/October 1981), pp. 9-11.

89c ▶ 30
Prepare reports with footnotes

plain sheets

Problem 1
2d page of leftbound report

Prepare the material given at the right as the 2d page of a leftbound report. Follow the guides given in the outline on page 245 for a leftbound report.

	words
The preliminary survey of all _mid-level and top-level_ managers in our company	16
indicates that ~~a fair amount of~~ _some_ resistance _a_ to the installa- _can be expected._	25
tion of desk-top computers ~~is likely,~~ Approximately 40% _percent_ of	40
~~our~~ midlevel managers, and over 60% _percent_ of ~~our~~ top-level managers	52
said they didn't _# need_ ~~want~~ a terminal ~~on their desk;~~ # Management	59
consultants report similar findings in other companies, ~~they~~	73
~~work with.~~ Many ~~businessmen and women,~~ _corporate executives_ are not comfortable	82
with the ~~idea~~ _thought_ of working with a computer. ~~They~~ _Executives_ are often	95
intimidated by the keyboard but _they_ are not honest enough to	108
~~say~~ _admit_ that.[4] _they are afraid of it_	115
	118
_____	
[4]Alexander L. Taylor, III, "Dealing with Terminal Phobia,"	130
Time (July 19, 1982), p. 82.	136

59a ▶ 5
Preparatory practice

each line 3 times SS (slowly, faster, slowly); DS between 3-line groups; repeat selected lines if time permits

alphabet 1 Buck's job experience and high quiz results paved the way for triumph.

fig/sym 2 Their payments totaled $9,642 ($9,305 and $337) but were 18 days late.

direct reach 3 Many large emergency units often were found to be broken or defective.

fluency 4 The city may wish to dismantle the signs; it may make problems for us.

| 1 | 2 | 3 | 4 | 5 | 6 | 7 | 8 | 9 | 10 | 11 | 12 | 13 | 14 |

59b ▶ 10
Improve keyboarding technique

each pair of lines twice SS; DS between 4-line groups; work at a controlled rate

adjacent keys 1 Her proposal was somewhat appropriate, and I'll support her positions.
2 A few union people were aware of new building and safety requirements.

double letters 3 They will soon begin to sell all books for the college summer session.
4 Our total payroll for all employees will exceed three million dollars.

long numbers 5 528; 32.07; 12/28/95; 54,076.94; 536-8853; (717) 844-6799; 189-54-8651
6 868; 45.23; 10/31/86; 23,872.39; 254-4534; (617) 010-9166; 200-30-5753

direct reach 7 I always grant maximum service on any number of my manufactured parts.
8 Branch office space must be enlarged due to increased consumer volume.

| 1 | 2 | 3 | 4 | 5 | 6 | 7 | 8 | 9 | 10 | 11 | 12 | 13 | 14 |

59c ▶ 35
Learn to format letters with subject line/reply reference notation

1 Study the information and the illustrations at the right.

2 Format and type the 3 letters that follow (LM pp. 91–95). Make 1 cc and address an envelope for each letter.

3 Proofread and circle errors. Check correct placement of special features.

Subject line: A subject line in ALL CAPS is placed a DS below salutation at left margin, at paragraph point if paragraphs are indented, or centered. It is not necessary to precede the line with the word SUBJECT.

Reply reference notation: Place the notation as you would a subject line. The word Reference or Re followed by a colon and 2 spaces may be shown before the notation.

```
Ms. Carol Valentino
Hillview Drive
Narragansett, RI  02880-4288

Dear Ms. Valentino

TAX-FREE PROFITS

Recently a Rhode Island municipal bond was
```

```
Mr. Thomas Houston
48 Broadcrest Drive
Philadelphia, PA  15235-3011

Dear Mr. Houston

Reference:  Policy #243067HP

Thank you for choosing your homeowner's insur-
```

words

Problem 1
Letter with subject line

modified block style, blocked ¶s, open punctuation; blocked subject line

Current date | Ms. Carol Valentino | Hillview Drive | Narragansett, RI 02880-4288 | 17
Dear Ms. Valentino | TAX-FREE PROFITS   24

(¶ 1) Recently a Rhode Island municipal bond was issued which returned 11   38
percent interest--COMPLETELY TAX FREE.   46

(¶ 2) Unfortunately, many people did not learn of this offering until it was too   61
late to subscribe. In addition, many people were unaware that interest earned   77
on such securities is free from both federal and state taxes for Rhode Island   93
residents.   95

(¶ 3) If you would like to be notified in advance of such future offerings, please   110
call or drop us a note to get your name on our mailing list. There is, of course,   127
no obligation on your part. (108)   132

Sincerely yours | Mrs. Nancy Watson | Investment Counselor | xx   144/157

88b, continued

Problem 2
Outline

2 full sheets; top mar—gin on first page: 1½″ for pica or 2″ for elite; top margin on second page: 1″; side margins: 1″; bottom margin: approximately 1″; use main heading **GUIDES FOR KEYBOARDING REPORTS OR MANU-SCRIPTS**; TS after main heading

1 Space forward once from left margin to type Roman numeral *I*. Reset left margin 2 spaces to the right of the period following *I*. The margin is now set at the point at which subheading *A* begins.

2 Set 3 tab stops: one 4 spaces, one 8 spaces, and the third 12 spaces from the left margin set for subheading *A*. You will use the mar—gin release and backspace when you come to *II* and *III*.

3 Place the page number for the second page on Line 4, even with the right margin. Begin typing on Line 7.

4 Use a page—end in-dicator or a light pencil mark about 1½″ from the bottom edge of the page to alert you to leave a 1″ bottom margin. If you use a light pencil mark, be sure to erase it. A page—end indicator (page—line gauge) is provided on LM p. 70.

	words
in heading	9
I. MARGINS, SPACING, AND PAGINATION	16
A. Unbound Reports	20
1. Margins	22
a. First page: 1 1/2" pica or 2" elite top margin; 1"	33
side and bottom margins for pica and elite.	42
b. Subsequent pages: 1" top and side margins and at	53
least 1" bottom margin for pica and elite.	61
2. Spacing	63
a. Body: double-space; 5-space paragraph indentions;	74
leave at least 2 lines of a paragraph at top and	84
bottom of page.	87
b. Quoted material: single-space quotes of 4 lines or	98
more; indent 5 spaces from both margins.	106
3. Pagination	109
a. First page: center number 1/2" from bottom or omit	120
number.	121
b. Subsequent pages: number on Line 4 at right margin.	132
B. Topbound and Leftbound Reports	139
1. Margins	141
a. Topbound: 2" pica or 2 1/2" elite top margin for	152
first page; 1 1/2" top margin for subsequent pages;	162
same side and bottom margins as for unbound reports.	172
b. Leftbound: 1 1/2" left margin; other margins same	183
as for unbound.	186
2. Spacing	188
a. Topbound: same spacing as for unbound.	197
b. Leftbound: same spacing as for unbound.	206
3. Pagination	209
a. Leftbound: number pages as for unbound reports.	220
b. Topbound: number first page (or omit) and subse-	230
quent pages 1/2" from bottom; center number.	239
II. HEADINGS AND SUBHEADINGS	245
A. Main and Secondary Headings	251
1. Main: format in ALL CAPS; center over line of writing;	263
leave 1 blank line space between main and secondary	273
headings or 2 blank line spaces between main heading and	284
body if secondary heading is not used.	292
2. Secondary: center over line of writing; capitalize im-	304
portant words; leave 2 blank line spaces between the	315
secondary heading and the body.	321
B. Side Headings (Marginal Headings)	328
1. Triple-space below text to type side heading.	338
2. Place side heading at left margin; use no terminal punc-	350
tuation; capitalize important words; underline.	359
3. Leave 1 blank line space below side headings.	369
C. Paragraph Headings (Run-in Headings)	377
1. Place at paragraph indention point; follow with period;	389
underline.	391
2. Capitalize the first word of each heading.	400
III. DOCUMENTATION	404
A. Footnotes	407
1. Number consecutively; identify by superscript figures in	419
body of report and in footnotes.	425
2. Separate from body of text by a single space and a 1 1/2"	437
divider line; DS below divider line.	444
3. Indent first line of footnotes; single-space footnotes;	456
double-space between footnotes.	462
B. Explanatory Notes	466
1. Reference one note with asterisk or number in order.	477
2. Follow the same spacing guides as used for footnotes.	488

words

Problem 2
Letter with reference notation

modified block style, blocked ¶s, open punctuation; blocked reply reference notation

Current date	Mr. Thomas Houston	48 Broadcrest Drive	Philadelphia, PA	15
15235-3011	Dear Mr. Houston	Reference: Policy #243067HP	27

(¶ 1) Thank you for choosing your homeowner's insurance policy through 40
Foshee Insurance Agency. Your policy has been carefully designed to provide 55
the protection you need. 60

(¶ 2) Your policy will be mailed to you soon in a separate envelope. Please 74
review your coverage carefully. 80

(¶ 3) If you have any questions about your insurance, please let us know. Just 95
contact your agent or drop by our office. We want you to be completely satis- 110
fied with your homeowner's insurance. (92) 117

Sincerely yours | Willard Washington | Customer Service Agent | xx 130/**144**

Problem 3
Letter with subject line

modified block style, indented ¶s, mixed punctuation; centered subject line

Current date | Dr. Jerome Davis, Director | Western College of Optometry | 7008 16
Marin Avenue | Berkeley, CA 94708-8963 | Dear Dr. Davis: | OPTOMETRIC 30
TECHNICIAN PROGRAM 34

(¶ 1) Thank you for taking the time to talk with me last Tuesday. I want to 48
reaffirm the interest of Babcock & Sinclair in organizing a co-op program with 64
your Optometric Technician students. 71

(¶ 2) In a few days, I will call you to set up a meeting time. Best wishes for a 86
successful year. (56) 89

Sincerely yours, | Miss Johanna Dickerson | Director | xx 100/**120**

60

60a ▶ 5
Preparatory practice

each line 3 times SS (slowly, faster, slowly); DS between 3-line groups; repeat selected lines if time permits

alphabet 1 Mary went right for just six blocks and had a quiet view of the plaza.

fig/sym 2 He sold 45 luxury (3-bedroom) suites priced from $189,750 to $296,500.

double letters 3 All necessary issues must be addressed three weeks before the meeting.

fluency 4 Laurie owns a dismal shanty by the lake on the land I may wish to own.

| 1 | 2 | 3 | 4 | 5 | 6 | 7 | 8 | 9 | 10 | 11 | 12 | 13 | 14 |

60b ▶ 45
Learn to format letters with company name in closing/enclosure notation/copy notation/postscript notation

1 Study the information at the right and the Style letter on p. 123.

2 Format and type the 4 problems that follow (plain sheet and LM pp. 97–101).

3 Proofread and circle errors. Check correct placement of special features.

Company name in closing lines: When a company name is used in the closing lines, show it in ALL CAPS a DS below the complimentary close. The writer's name is then placed on the 4th line below the company name.

Problem 1
Learn letter parts

Using plain paper, take a 1' writing on opening lines and ¶ 1 of Style letter 5, p. 123; a 1' writing on ¶s 1 and 2; and a 1' writing on the closing lines. Raise dateline 3 lines because of the special features. Repeat timings.

Enclosure notation: Place an enclosure notation a DS below the reference initials. If there is more than one enclosure, list them on succeeding lines, indented 3 spaces from the left margin:

Enclosures
　Financial Statements
　General Information Survey

Problem 2
Letter with special features

Format and type the letter on page 123. Begin on Line 16. Make 1 cc and address an envelope.

Copy notation: Show a copy notation a DS below the reference initials or enclosure notation. A *cc* is used to indicate a carbon copy; a *pc* is used to indicate a photocopy.

Postscript: Place a postscript a DS below the last item at the bottom of the letter.

88a ▶ 5
Preparatory practice

each line 3 times SS (slowly, faster, slowly); DS between 3-line groups; repeat selected lines as time permits

alphabet 1 Max asked Gwen if the bill would jeopardize the quick market recovery.

figure 2 I need 36 pens, 2,750 labels, 48 legal pads, 9 ribbons, and 1 stapler.

. (period) and figure 3 I paid $4.75 for pens, $8.32 for cards, $6.90 for pads, and $1.09 tax.

fluency 4 It is a risk for me, but I may visit with them to handle the problems.

| 1 | 2 | 3 | 4 | 5 | 6 | 7 | 8 | 9 | 10 | 11 | 12 | 13 | 14 |

88b ▶ 45
Inventory skill on reports and outlines

Problem 1
Unbound report with table

full sheet; DS body and table; 12 spaces between columns; correct errors as indicated in copy

Margins
Top: pica, 1½"
        elite, 2"
sides: 1"

words

PROGRAM ANALYSIS   3

Data on all the programs offered by Effective Office systems   14

during the first quarter of this year have been annalized. The   27

revenue generated income earned during this quarter was 12% higher than the   39

revenue generated income earned during the previous quarter. The ratios of ex-   52

penses to revenue income was considerably higher, however though.   62

One division, sales training, had a significant decrease   73

in revenue this quarter. Three divisions were responsible   85

for the majority of the increase in revenue. They were   96

center table
Secretarial training $128,097   102

Management Training $130,465   108

Communications Training $102,973   114

A complete summary, including the number of programs offered,   126

the revenue generated, the number of participants, the ex-   138

penses incurred, and the net profit, is attached. The projec-   150

tions for next quarter are also attached.   158

Communications Design Associates

348 INDIANA AVENUE
WASHINGTON, DC 20001-1438
Tel: 1-800-432-5739

	words in parts	total

October 15, 19--
DS

<table>
<tr><td>Mailing notation</td><td>SPECIAL DELIVERY</td><td>3</td><td>3</td></tr>
</table>

	in parts	total
October 15, 19--	3	3
SPECIAL DELIVERY	6	6
Search and Recruit International	13	13
Attention Mr. Paul Nugent	18	18
8225 Dunwood Place	22	22
Atlanta, GA 30339-7239	27	27
Ladies and Gentlemen	31	31
SPECIAL FEATURES IN BUSINESS LETTERS	38	38

Mailing notation — SPECIAL DELIVERY
DS

Attention line — Search and Recruit International
Attention Mr. Paul Nugent
8225 Dunwood Place
Atlanta, GA 30339-7239
DS

Ladies and Gentlemen
DS

Subject line or reply reference — SPECIAL FEATURES IN BUSINESS LETTERS
DS

Ms. Darlene Baez asked me to send you a copy of our new
brochure, SPECIAL FEATURES IN BUSINESS LETTERS. This
brochure describes and illustrates many of the special
features that may be used in modern business letters.

	11	49
	22	60
	33	71
	44	82

The special features are presented in this letter in
life-size format. There are variations to the style
presented here; for example, the subject line may be
blocked, indented to match the paragraph indentions, or
centered.

	55	93
	65	103
	76	114
	87	125
	89	127

The likelihood of using all these special features in a
single letter is remote. However, a good typist under-
stands their functions and uses good judgment as to how
and when to apply them. I hope you will find the information in the enclosed brochure interesting and useful.

	100	139
	111	150
	123	161
	134	172
	145	183

DS

Sincerely yours
DS

Company name — COMMUNICATIONS DESIGN ASSOCIATES

| Sincerely yours | 3 | 186 |
| COMMUNICATIONS DESIGN ASSOCIATES | 8 | 191 |

Leona Shamura

Ms. Leona Shamura
Communication Specialist
DS

| Ms. Leona Shamura | 12 | 195 |
| Communication Specialist | 17 | 200 |

xx
DS

| xx | 18 | 201 |

Enclosure notation — Enclosure
DS

| Enclosure | 20 | 203 |

Copy notation — cc Raymond Sink
DS

| cc Raymond Sink | 23 | 206 |

Postscript — Additional free copies of the brochure are available.

| Additional free copies of the brochure are available. | 33 | 216 |
| | | **240** |

Style letter 5: Modified block business letter illustrating special features

---

Forming plurals

full sheet; 70-space line, SS, DS between ¶s, listed items, and examples; 1″ top margin; 5-space ¶ indention; set a tab 10 spaces to left of center point to type examples

1 Prepare the data as shown; tab to type each example.

2 Proofread and correct errors.

3 Study the rules from your typed copy.

Note: The abbreviation e.g. may be used in place of the phrase *for example*.

FORMING PLURALS
TS

To achieve the regular plural form for most nouns, simply add s to the singular form; e.g., hats. Some nouns, such as men and oxen, take an irregular plural form. These nouns have to be memorized. A few nouns, such as deer and sheep, have no plural form at all. To achieve the plural form for still other groups of nouns, certain guidelines, some of which are given below with examples, should be followed. In every instance of doubt, of course, consult a dictionary.
DS

1. To form the plural of a noun ending in y preceded by a consonant sound or a consonant (any letter except a, e, i, o, or u), change the y to i and add es.

husky--huskies
hobby--hobbies
colloquy--colloquies

2. To form the plural of a noun ending in y preceded by a vowel, just add s.

attorney--attorneys
decoy--decoys
holiday--holidays

3. To form the plural of most nouns ending in o, add es.

tomato--tomatoes
hero--heroes
mosquito--mosquitoes

4. To form the plural of nouns ending in o preceded by a vowel, add s to the singular.

cameo--cameos
ratio--ratios
taboo--taboos

5. For singular nouns ending in sis, change the sis to ses to form the plural.

basis--bases
analysis--analyses
crisis--crises

6. To form the plural of most nouns ending in s, ss, ch, sh, or x, add es.

kiss--kisses
box--boxes
lash--lashes
match--matches

60b, continued

Problem 3
Letter with company name in closing lines and enclosure notation

Format and type the letter given at the right in block style, open punctuation. Address an envelope.

Current date | Dr. Susan Yamada, Director | Electronic Education Systems, Inc. | 200 Fifth Avenue | Seattle, WA 98121-0159 | Dear Dr. Yamada — 15 / 27

(¶ 1) Enclosed are five copies of our audited financial statements for Electronic Education Systems, Inc., for the year ended June 30. I have also enclosed three copies of the U.S. Department of Education General Information Survey. — 41 / 56 / 71 / 73

(¶ 2) Forward one copy of the Department of Education General Information Survey to the Department of Education after you have signed it. — 87 / 99

(¶ 3) If you have any question regarding the enclosed items, call me. (85) — 112

Sincerely | BAKER, SEXTON, AND CAVELL | Miss Cindy Sexton, CPA | xx | Enclosures | Financial Statements | General Information Survey | pc Jay Cavell — 126 / 139/159

Problem 4

Format and type in block style, open punctuation, the script letter shown at the right. Block the subject line. Make two carbon copies; make one a blind carbon copy (bcc) for *John Denby*. Address an envelope.

Blind copy notation (bcc): a blind copy notation appears only on the carbon copy of the letter. For a carbon copy, type the notation on a piece of paper held between the typewriter ribbon and the original (top) sheet of paper. Type the notation as:

bcc Miss Linda Wilson

For a photocopy, type the *bpc* (blind photocopy notation) notation on the photocopy after the photocopy has been made.

Current date | Mr. Thomas Fornabio, President | Dunhill Container Corporation | 110 Summit Avenue | Montvale, NJ 07645-2211 | Dear Mr. Fornabio | ITEMS NEEDED FOR SECURITY ANALYSIS — 12 / 22 / 30 / 36

(¶) In order to provide the best security analysis possible for your firm, we will need several items from you. First, we will need a roster of your employees, listing the hours they work and the departments in which they work. We will need an inventory of the number and types of vehicles used for official business, along with the license tag numbers of the vehicles. Also, we will need a map of your plant site and facilities, showing the property boundaries and all points of access to and from the site. — 47 / 59 / 71 / 82 / 92 / 104 / 116 / 127 / 138

(¶) Our security analysis should be completed about two weeks after we receive these items. Mr. Denby will call you to discuss our findings and present our solutions to your security needs. — 148 / 159 / 170 / 175

(¶) You can be assured that Denby Security Systems offers the finest protection systems available today. The enclosed brochure describes just a few of the security systems we can provide your firm. (178) — 184 / 195 / 205 / 213

Sincerely yours | Ms. Carmen Zapata | Security Consultant | xx | Enclosure | bcc John Denby — 222 / 230/251

Choose the right word

half sheet, long side up; 1″ top margin; 74-space line

1 Cover the answer key at the bottom of the column. When you have finished keyboarding, check your answers.

2 Study the definitions of the closely related words at the right. Then type the sentences, selecting the appropriate word from the words in parentheses. Include the sentence numbers in the 74-space line.

Key: 1. accept, advice, further
2. except, farther, advised
3. further, accept, advice

accept — (verb) to receive; to agree	except — (verb) to exclude; (preposition) with the exclusion of
advice — (noun) counsel; suggestion	advise — (verb) to give counsel
farther — (adverb) more remote (distance)	further — (adverb) to a greater degree (thought)

1. Did he (accept/except) her (advise/advice) to study the matter (farther/further)?

2. All of us (accept/except) John traveled (farther/further) than we were (adviced/advised) to travel in one day.

3. Jane said she would question Tom (farther/further), but she did not think she could (accept/except) his (advice/advise).

Choose the right word

half sheet, long side up; 1″ top margin; 74-space line

Keyboard and format as directed above.

Key: 1. It's, site, affect 2. cite, effect, its 3. sight, its, affected 4. It's, effect, site

affect — (verb) to influence; to change	effect — (noun) result; (verb) to produce a result; to cause
cite — (verb) to quote	sight — (noun) view; (verb) to see
site — (noun) place; location	
its — (pronoun) possessive of it	it's — (contraction) it is

1. (Its/It's) certain that the (cite/sight/site) selected will (affect/effect) attendance.

2. Did the manager (cite/sight/site) the (affect/effect) of the hotel's not having (its/it's) own parking lot?

3. The (cite/sight/site) of the canyon with (its/it's) majestic view (affected/effected) all of us.

4. (Its/It's) true that the (affect/effect) of moving to the new (cite/sight/site) will be an increase in rental costs.

Choose the right word

half sheet, long side up; 1″ top margin; 74-space line

Keyboard and format as directed above.

Key: 1. principal, passed, personnel 2. past, personal, principle

passed — (verb) past tense of pass	past — (adjective) ended, gone by (noun) time gone by
personal — (adjective) private, individual	personnel — (noun) employees
principal — (adjective) main (noun) leading person; head of a school	principle — (noun) basic truth, rule

1. The (principal/principle)(passed/past) out the report but referred questions to the director of (personal/personnel).

2. The manager was out for the (passed/past) five days conducting (personal/personnel) business and, as a matter of (principal/principle), would not disclose the nature of the business.

61a ▶ 5
Preparatory practice

each line 3 times SS (slowly, faster, slowly); DS between 3-line groups; repeat selected lines if time permits

alphabet 1 All the fighters worked quietly to jazz music at various boxing camps.

fig/sym 2 This year, 80% of the 4,697 workers received a 13% increase of $1,575.

adjacent key 3 We took fast action to stop the development of wells on this property.

fluency 4 If their giant hayfork is an authentic antique, when may they be paid?

| 1 | 2 | 3 | 4 | 5 | 6 | 7 | 8 | 9 | 10 | 11 | 12 | 13 | 14 |

61b ▶ 12
Build/measure straight-copy skill

1 One 1' writing on each ¶; circle errors; determine *gwam*.

2 One 5' writing on all ¶s combined; circle errors; determine *gwam*; compare results with 1' writings.

Difficulty index

all letters used | A | 1.5 si | 5.7 awl | 80% hfw |

gwam 1' | 5'

Americans have always known the value of wisely managing their own   13 | 2 | 49
finances. The general rise in prosperity during the present century   27 | 5 | 52
has helped many people to build savings. People have begun to want a   41 | 8 | 55
means to gain a greater return on their money than the amount they can   55 | 11 | 58
get with just simple bank interest. One option is the buying of stock   69 | 14 | 61
in multiple firms.   73 | 15 | 62

Two basic attitudes toward the stock market exist nowadays. Some   13 | 17 | 64
people believe that the overall trend of the stock market is upward.   27 | 20 | 67
Individuals who hold this optimistic attitude about the future are   41 | 22 | 69
known as "bulls." These people buy stock with the idea that the value   55 | 25 | 72
of the stock will rise and that they will undoubtedly be able to sell   69 | 28 | 75
at a higher price than they have originally paid.   79 | 30 | 77

"Bears," on the other hand, are individuals who are not so opti-   13 | 32 | 79
mistic about stock market trends. These people feel that a decline in   27 | 35 | 82
the market is always imminent. When bears anticipate a loss on the   41 | 38 | 85
market, they quickly sell their stock in order to get back as much   54 | 40 | 87
money as they can before the drop takes place. But whether people are   68 | 43 | 90
bulls or bears, their hope is to realize a reasonable profit on their   82 | 46 | 93
personal investments.   87 | 47 | 94

gwam 1' | 1 | 2 | 3 | 4 | 5 | 6 | 7 | 8 | 9 | 10 | 11 | 12 | 13 | 14 |
5' | 1 | 2 | 3 |

61c ▶ 33
Measure letter production skill

Time schedule

Assembling materials .... 3'
Timed production .... 25'
Final check; compute
 n-pram .... 5'

1 Follow time schedule shown at the left. Arrange letterheads and envelopes (LM pp. 103–107) and supplies for easy handling. Correct errors neatly as you keyboard. Address envelopes.

2 When directed to begin, format and type for 25' the problems given on page 126. If you complete the problems in less than 25', start over on plain full sheets.

3 Proofread and circle uncorrected errors found in the final check.

4 Compute *n-pram*:

$$\frac{\text{Gross (total words)} - \text{penalty*}}{\text{Length (in minutes) of writing**}}$$

*15 words deducted for each error
**25 minutes in this instance

Improve keyboarding technique

each pair of lines 3 times SS at a controlled rate; DS between 6-line groups

For Line 7, beginning at the left margin, set 6 tab stops 10 spaces apart. For Line 8, set 4 tab stops 15 spaces apart.

adjacent reach	1	Yes, I buy premium goods requiring minimum service on operating parts.
	2	Twenty-three new power saws were opened quickly and serviced properly.
space bar	3	In the big city, with a map, I did go by bus to my own auto to fix it.
	4	I may work to pay for the coal, the big fur rug, and the worn oak box.
direct reach	5	An excessive number of people in my survey agreed the economy is weak.
	6	Why not obtain a large company grant from my bank to make the payment?

tab/ figures	7	$49.07	$2,365	#543-1	79,823	59-286	$39.27	9032-15768
	8	243,879	#612793	$17,985		#793-21		13,928,543

| 1 | 2 | 3 | 4 | 5 | 6 | 7 | 8 | 9 | 10 | 11 | 12 | 13 | 14 |

Build/measure straight copy skill

1 Two 1' writings on each ¶ for speed; circle errors; determine *gwam*.
2 One 5' control writing on all ¶s combined; circle errors; determine *gwam*.

Difficulty index

all letters used	A	1.5 si	5.7 awl	80% hfw

	gwam 1'	5'
People spend far more time listening than they spend communicating	14	3	70
in any other way, but only a very few people have developed good listen-	27	6	73
ing skills. There is a big difference between hearing and listening.	41	9	76
Hearing does not require major effort, but listening is hard work. One	55	12	79
of the problems with listening is that we can listen about three times	68	15	82
faster than most people speak. We are able to hear what the speaker	81	18	85
is saying and still have extra time for our minds to wander to other	94	21	88
things.	95	22	89
An active listener utilizes the difference between the listening	13	25	92
and the speaking rates to make mental summaries of the conversation.	27	28	95
One way to listen actively is to try to anticipate the next point that	41	31	98
the individual will make. It is also important to clarify in your own	55	34	101
mind what is being said. Generally, people try to assume too much. A	69	37	104
good listener will let the person explain in her or his own words ex-	83	40	107
actly what she or he would like to say. Paraphrasing is a good way to	97	43	110
confirm that the message is understood.	115	45	112
A person who has developed good listening skills will not interrupt	14	48	115
the person who is speaking. The problem is that most people prefer to	28	51	118
speak than to listen. Sometimes it takes a considerable amount of	41	54	121
effort to give the person an opportunity to get the message across.	55	57	124
Showing that you are interested in what is being said helps to put the	69	60	127
speaker at ease. It is not enough just to listen; you also have to look	84	63	130
like you are listening. The effective use of body language enhances	98	66	133
listening.	100	67	134

| gwam 1' | 1 | 2 | 3 | 4 | 5 | 6 | 7 | 8 | 9 | 10 | 11 | 12 | 13 | 14 |
| 5' | | 1 | | | 2 | | | 3 | |

61c, continued

Problem 1
Letter with subject line

modified block style, indented ¶s, mixed punctuation; centered subject line

Current date | Mr. John Lundstrom | 415 Lantana Avenue | Englewood, NJ 07631-2192 | Dear Mr. Lundstrom: | ADJUSTABLE RATE MORTGAGE

16
26

(¶ 1) As an apartment dweller, you may be interested in learning more about how an adjustable rate mortgage from Merchants Bank of New Jersey can enable you to afford your own home today.

40
54
62

(¶ 2) Merchants Bank offers a budgeted monthly payment plan with an affordable rate mortgage loan where the rate of interest changes periodically according to a preset index. Rate adjustments to the mortgage are made every six months based on the commercial bank money market certificate rate.

76
92
107
120

(¶ 3) Are you interested in learning more about home financing in the current economic environment? If so, please contact our Mortgage Department at 445-7834. (125)

134
148
150

Sincerely, | Mrs. Alice Rivera | Loan Advisor | xx

159/**172**

Problem 2
Letter with mailing notation, attention line, reference notation, company name in closing lines, and pc notation

block style, open punctuation

May 18, 19-- | REGISTERED | Data Information Corporation | Attention Purchasing Director | 1945 West Parnall Road | Jackson, MI 49201-1638 | Ladies and Gentlemen | Reference: Claim #5489

15
30
37

(¶ 1) Electronics Manufacturing, Inc., has agreed to make payment of $2,500 in full settlement of your claim for defective equipment purchased on January 24.

52
68

(¶ 2) In agreeing to this settlement, they are in no way accepting responsibility for any additional claims or damages as the result of the faulty equipment.

83
98

(¶ 3) Please have a representative of your firm at my office at 9 a.m. on June 1. At that time, I will present a check for $2,500 in exchange for the completion of the waiver forms. (94)

113
129
132

Sincerely yours | DONNELLY, EVERETT, AND SLOANE | Ms. Susan Everett | Attorney | xx | pc Bruce Donnelly

146
152/**175**

Problem 3
Letter with subject line and pc notation

modified block style, blocked ¶s, mixed punctuation; blocked subject line

Current date | Ms. Debbie Peterson | 1078 Lewis Road | Linfield, PA 19468-4353 | Dear Ms. Peterson: | METRO SERVICE

16
23

(¶ 1) Metro Cable TV is pleased to announce that it has been awarded the contract by the Linfield Civic Association for the installation of Metro's cable television system in your subdivision. Our installers should begin hanging cable in your neighborhood within the next month.

37
54
70
78

(¶ 2) The system being installed has a 35-channel capacity with 25 of the channels operational at "turn on." The system is bi-directional, permitting Metro to offer, when completed, an optional security package.

92
108
118

(¶ 3) We at Metro are excited about the opportunity to serve your neighborhood. If you wish further information or have specific questions, please call one of our service representatives at 981-6742. (136)

133
149
157

Cordially, | Robert Hartman | Vice President | xx | pc Linfield Civic Association

172/
184

Supplemental skill-building practices

Improve keystroking control

each line twice SS; proofread and circle errors before typing the next line; DS between 2-line groups

Type at a steady rate; concentrate on the copy.

1st row   1   Uncle Xavier mines zinc, cobalt, and silver on vacant land in Bavaria.

2d row   2   As she dashed to Dad's lake last fall, Sarah had half a glass of soda.

3d row   3   Terrie, try to work quietly if you operate our out-of-date typewriter.

4th row   4   A 4-act play, to be given June 17, 26, and 30, will begin at 8:59 p.m.

fingers 1/2   5   Trudy knew by her voice that Martha had broken the hush of the jungle.

fingers 3/4   6   Polly was puzzled by six quaint wax dolls in an antique dealer's shop.

| 1 | 2 | 3 | 4 | 5 | 6 | 7 | 8 | 9 | 10 | 11 | 12 | 13 | 14 |

Build/compare progressive straight-copy skill

1 Three 1' writings on ¶1. Use the highest rate as the base rate for the next writings.

2 Three 1' writings on ¶2. Try to equal or exceed the base rate established on ¶1.

3 Three 1' writings on ¶3. Try to equal or exceed the base rate established on ¶1.

4 One 5' writing on all ¶s. Try to maintain the ¶1 base rate on all ¶s.

all letters used

¶1 Difficulty index				¶2 Difficulty index				¶3 Difficulty index			
E	1.2 si	5.1 awl	90% hfw	A	1.5 si	5.7 awl	80% hfw	HA	1.7 si	6.0 awl	75% hfw

gwam 1'   5'

Just who is a leader? Could you learn to be a leader if you wanted   14   3 | 60
to be one? A number of people have done studies on the traits of lead-   28   6 | 63
ers and on leadership style. For many years, studies were done to see   42   9 | 66
if traits could be found in people who were leaders that were not found   56   12 | 69
in people who were not leaders. Not a single one has been found that   70   15 | 72
can be used to separate persons who are leaders from persons who are   84   18 | 75
not.   85   19 | 76

Recent studies seem to focus on style of leadership. One way to   13   22 | 79
define leadership is that it is a means of influencing the actions or   27   25 | 82
behavior of others in an effort to reach a goal. A leader, thus, must   41   28 | 85
care about working with others and about getting a job done. Concern   55   31 | 88
about working with others is called relationship behavior. Concern   69   34 | 91
about getting a job done is called task behavior. Both kinds of be-   82   37 | 94
havior are very important.   87   38 | 95

Effective use of leadership style requires a leader to vary the   13   41 | 98
leadership style depending on the situation that exists. Some situ-   26   44 | 101
ations call for a leadership style that is relationship oriented; some   40   47 | 104
call for a leadership style that is task oriented; and others call for   54   50 | 107
a leadership style that is a combination of the two. Varying the style   68   53 | 110
is not easy because each person in an organization tends to feel more   82   56 | 113
comfortable with a given style.   87   57 | 114

gwam 1' | 1 | 2 | 3 | 4 | 5 | 6 | 7 | 8 | 9 | 10 | 11 | 12 | 13 | 14 |
      5' | 1   2   3 |

Supplemental skill-building practice

Build statistical-copy skill

1 One 5' writing to determine base rate; circle errors; determine *gwam*.
2 Two 3' writings to build speed; circle errors; determine *gwam*.

Difficulty index

all letters/figures used | A | 1.5 si | 5.7 awl | 80% hfw

	gwam 3'		5'
Developing fair and equitable expense policies for the 3,796 sales	4	3	29
representatives we employ is very hard to do. Over 85 percent of our	9	5	32
sales force drive more than 48,000 miles a year. The outlay for main-	14	8	35
taining a fleet of 4,215 cars is significant. About 74 percent of our	19	11	38
travel budget is consumed by automobile costs. The most equitable way	23	14	40
of paying automobile expenses for a very mobile sales force is to give	28	17	43
a company automobile to each person who drives at least 18,000 miles	33	20	46
a year for sales work and to pay for the operating costs. Represen-	37	22	49
tatives who drive 17,999 or fewer miles a year are paid 23 cents a mile	42	25	52
for driving their own vehicles.	44	26	53

gwam 3' | 1 | 2 | 3 | 4 | 5
5' | 1 | 2 | 3

Build straight-copy skill

1 Two 1' writings on each ¶ (1 for speed, 1 for control).
2 One 5' writing; proofread and circle errors; determine *gwam*.

Difficulty index

all letters used | A | 1.5 si | 5.7 awl | 80% hfw

	gwam 1'		5'
You have probably noticed that money seldom stays in your pocket	13	3	57
for very long. The fact is, money never stays in any one location for	27	6	60
very long. Cash deposited in a bank is immediately put to work in the	41	9	63
form of loans and investments. When you buy merchandise at a business	55	12	66
establishment, your money travels on to pay employees, wholesalers, and	64	15	69
anyone else to whom the proprietor has an obligation. The role of money	79	18	72
is to circulate through the economy.	86	19	73
Money is required by companies of any size. Working with the fi-	13	22	76
nances of a firm means always thinking about assets and liabilities.	27	25	79
Assets are the items of value that a firm owns. Money held by a company	42	28	82
is one of its assets. Liabilities are debts, the money that the firm	56	31	85
owes to other people or groups. By subtracting the liabilities from the	71	34	88
assets, company officials can judge the financial strength of their firm.	86	37	91
Company financial managers must know how to regulate the movement	13	40	94
of money into and out of the firm. The fiscal operation of an organi-	27	43	97
zation is quite a complex area. A small business venture may have one	41	46	100
person directing its financial matters. But in a large firm, a whole	55	49	103
department is occupied with keeping track of the flow of funds and the	69	52	106
optimum ways to acquire and invest money.	77	54	108

gwam 1' | 1 | 2 | 3 | 4 | 5 | 6 | 7 | 8 | 9 | 10 | 11 | 12 | 13 | 14
5' | 1 | 2 | 3

Improve keystroking technique

70-space line; keyboard each line 3 times SS; DS between each 2-line group

1st/ fingers
1 Those 456 heavy black jugs have nothing in them. Fill them by June 7.
2 A youth of just over 6 or 7 years of age ran through the orange grove.

2d/ fingers
3 Mike Deak, who was 38 in December, likes a piece of ice in cold cider.
4 Eddie decided to crate 38 pieces of cedar decking behind the old dock.

3d & 4th/ fingers
5 Polly made 29 points on that quiz; Wex made 10 points. Did they pass?
6 Zone 12 was impassable; we quickly roped it off. Did you wax Zone 90?

| 1 | 2 | 3 | 4 | 5 | 6 | 7 | 8 | 9 | 10 | 11 | 12 | 13 | 14 |

87d ▶ 12

Build/measure statistical-copy skill

1 One 1' writing on each ¶; circle errors; determine *gwam*.
2 One 5' writing on all ¶s; circle errors; determine *gwam*; compare results with 1' writings.

Difficulty index

all letters/figures used | A | 1.5 si | 5.7 awl | 80% hfw |

gwam 1' | 5'

	1'	5'
Inflation is defined as a continuous rise in prices for an extended	14	3	52
period. It can also be defined as a reduction in the purchasing ability	28	6	55
of your savings and earnings. How much impact will inflation have on	42	8	58
your future? Plenty, if it continues to increase at the present rate!	56	11	61
For example, let us hypothesize that the price of an average house is	70	14	64
$85,000 in 1985 and that the rate of inflation is 10 percent annually for	85	17	67
10 successive years. In 1986, the same house would cost $93,500; in 1991,	100	20	70
it would cost $150,582; and in 1996, it would total a whopping $242,515.	115	23	73
That is just one example of inflation.	123	25	74
When comparing past salaries with present salaries, inflation again	14	27	77
becomes a big consideration. For example, if your take-home pay in 1950	29	30	80
was $10,000, in 1980 you would have needed $35,659 just to equal that	43	33	83
former spending power. Inflation becomes a startling realization when	57	36	86
we see $25,659 eroded from our income. What will the figure be in	71	39	88
about another 30 years, say in the year 2017? No one knows the answer	85	41	91
to that question; however, it is a safe bet that some level of inflation	100	44	94
will exist in the years ahead. Now may be the time to begin thinking	114	47	97
about ways you can improve your protection against inflation.	126	50	99

gwam 1' | 1 | 2 | 3 | 4 | 5 | 6 | 7 | 8 | 9 | 10 | 11 | 12 | 13 | 14 |
    5' | 1 | 2 | 3 |

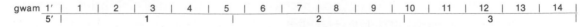

87e ▶ 10

Measure communication skills

plain sheet; 70-space line, 1½" top margin; DS copy

Read the ¶, noting corrections in capitalization and punctuation that must be made. Format and type the ¶; proofread; retype the paragraph if necessary.

president smith said to henry you will receive state of the art equipment good software and ergonomic furniture and you will be given adequate training on the equipment. the vice president of the human resources division is responsible for scheduling and coordinating the training program. although the training program will be conducted by the vendor it will be held in our facilities.

Improve keyboarding technique

each pair of lines 3 times SS at a controlled rate; DS between 6-line groups

double letters
1 Many employees will attend the annual meeting to support their issues.
2 Their accounting staff will need supplies in approximately three days.

adjacent reaches
3 Portia asked that we talk to various teachers about the ruined chairs.
4 A reasonable understanding was quickly developed joining both parties.

direct reaches
5 Many hungry soldiers brought much of the food which they had received.
6 The survey continued to project gradual gains for many technical jobs.

shift-key reaches
7 Janette and Tommy will probably meet Harriet on Sunday in Kansas City.
8 Today, the Boston Red Sox played the Toronto Blue Jays in Fenway Park.

| 1 | 2 | 3 | 4 | 5 | 6 | 7 | 8 | 9 | 10 | 11 | 12 | 13 | 14 |

Build straight-copy skill

1 One 1' writing on each ¶; circle errors; determine *gwam*.

2 One 5' writing on all ¶s; circle errors; determine *gwam*; compare results with 1' writings.

Difficulty index

all letters used | A | 1.5 si | 5.7 awl | 80% hfw

gwam 1' | 5'

Beginning typists, like other people who are first learning a 12 | 2 | 60
skill, often experience times when their progress seems to stagnate 26 | 5 | 63
and they seem to be going nowhere. It takes more than just repetition 40 | 8 | 66
or rote practice to change an amateur into a professional. Profes- 54 | 11 | 68
sionals practice not only to achieve accuracy but also to improve 67 | 13 | 71
their methods so as to overcome any setbacks. Just working on a job 81 | 16 | 74
in the same old way does not mean you will master it. 91 | 18 | 76

When people are learning to keyboard, they spell out words letter 13 | 21 | 79
by letter. This process raises a barrier to speed, and soon a plateau 27 | 24 | 81
is hit. But as the serious learners keep working, they slowly begin 41 | 27 | 84
to see words as combinations, not merely as letters. The words used 55 | 29 | 87
more often become keyboarding units rather than single strokes. It is 69 | 32 | 90
not greater finger speed but larger working units that make it possible 84 | 35 | 93
for new typists to pass each level. 91 | 37 | 94

When a plateau is encountered, it is helpful to analyze the way 13 | 39 | 97
in which a learner is working in order to find out how to improve. 26 | 42 | 99
Keyboard operators, for example, may be held at a certain level by 40 | 44 | 102
faulty techniques. It is possible that they are reading too far ahead 54 | 47 | 105
in their copy. Too many learners decide that they have achieved their 68 | 50 | 108
maximum potential at their initial plateau and quit trying too soon. 82 | 53 | 111
But these students must keep persevering. A block in progress should 96 | 56 | 113
be an opportunity to discover how to push ahead. 106 | 58 | 115

gwam 1' | 1 | 2 | 3 | 4 | 5 | 6 | 7 | 8 | 9 | 10 | 11 | 12 | 13 | 14 |
5' | 1 | 2 | 3 |

87a ▶ 5
Preparatory practice

each line 3 times SS (slowly, faster, slowly); DS between 3-line groups; repeat selected lines as time permits

For Line 3, beginning at the left margin, set 4 tab stops 14 spaces apart.

alphabet	1	Six zany questions provoked even the cool members of the working jury.
fig/sym	2	The billing error of $295.86 (Invoice #2473) was corrected in 10 days.
tab/cap	3	Jane Bill Mary Dick Beth and James
fluency	4	The city may make the firm pay a penalty for their toxic odor problem.

| 1 | 2 | 3 | 4 | 5 | 6 | 7 | 8 | 9 | 10 | 11 | 12 | 13 | 14 |

87b ▶ 15
Build/measure rough-draft skill

1 Two 1' writings on each ¶ for speed; circle errors; determine *gwam*.
2 One 5' writing for control on all ¶s combined; circle errors; determine *gwam*.

Difficulty index

all letters used	A	1.5 si	5.7 awl	80% hfw

gwam 1' | 5'

It is ~~necessary~~ *important* that ~~every~~ *each* employee learns how to make   11 | 2 | 50

wise decisions. an ~~employee~~ *worker* who helps to make a decision   22 | 4 | 52

about her *or his* job is much more likely to support than decision   35 | 7 | 55

than is an employee who is not given the chance to make   46 | 9 | 57

job-related decisions. Decisions made by a group *or*   56 | 11 | 59

~~groups~~ of ~~employees~~ *workers* (will normally) be better than deci-   65 | 13 | 61

sions made by one person. ~~Group~~ *cooperative* decision-making pro-   77 | 15 | 63

duces a synergistic effect. # Synergy ~~is~~ *means* working ~~together,~~   82 | 16 | 64

cooperatively. A synergistic effect produces out comes   15 | 19 | 67

that are far greater than the sum of all the separate   26 | 21 | 69

actions. ~~Every~~ *Each* person who analyzes a problem brings to   37 | 23 | 71

the problem-solving process a ~~different~~ *unique* view of the thing *problem*   48 | 25 | 73

and how to solve it. The idea that one worker may bring   59 | 27 | 75

to discuss with the group may cause others *workers* to think of   71 | 29 | 77

something else that is related.   77 | 30 | 78

Workers cannot be expected to make wise decisions   10 | 32 | 80

unless they are taught how to make decisions, *the process of decision making.* The first   23 | 35 | 83

step is ~~to try,~~ to identify the basic problem. The second   33 | 37 | 85

step is to ~~look for~~ *seek* all of the feasible ways to solve ~~it,~~ *the problem.*   46 | 40 | 88

The third step is to analyze each ~~of the~~ alternatives in   56 | 42 | 90

an objective fashion. # Then the fourth step is to decide   67 | 44 | 92

which of the *various* alternatives would be ~~a good~~ *the best possible* solution to   92 | 47 | 95

the problem.   94 | 48 | 96

Capitalization

full sheet; 1″ top margin;
74-space line

1 Cover the answer key at the bottom of the column.

2 Study carefully each guide under *Capitalize* presented at the right.

3 To assure understand–ing, read and then type each *review* and *apply* sentence, including the guide number, to which the communication guide applies.

4 Check your corrected sentences. Make any additional corrections in pencil or pen.

5 Repeat any *apply* sen–tence containing an error, correcting the error as you type.

Key: 1b. This 2b. Shakespearian, Elizabethan 3b. Jove, Maurice Building 4b. Memorial Day, Monday, May 5b. Street, Company 6b. to the, Lenox Theater 7b. editor 8b. Left Bank 9b. Column 1 10b. ex–President

Capitalize

1 The first word of a sentence or of a complete direct quotation, and the first word after a colon if the word introduces a complete sentence.

2 Proper nouns and their derivatives or names or nicknames that designate a per-ticular person, place, or thing.

3 Names of organizations, clubs, build-ings, and brand names, but usually not the commodity they identify.

4 Words that indicate time, such as days of the week, months, holidays, historical events or periods; seasons of the year only if personified.

5 Street, avenue, company, etc., when used with a proper noun.

6 The first and all other important words in the titles of books, articles, periodicals, headings, plays, movies, songs, and works of art, but not the conjunctions, articles, or prepositions having four or fewer letters.

7 Official titles before personal names but not occupational titles which follow per-sonal names. (Company policy may vary regarding this rule.)

8 Words which identify specific locations or geographic regions but not general di-rections or compass points.

9 Nouns followed by a number or letter except common nouns such as line, page, sentence, etc.

10 Both parts of a hyphenated word if both initial letters are usually capitalized.

review 1a. Amy announced, "They drove south to Peoria to attend a meeting."
apply b. Leo spoke confidently: "this is the only way to Central Plaza."

review 2a. Moving the large painting by Manet required a Herculean effort.
apply b. The shakespearian actor performed in the elizabethan drama.

review 3a. The Chamber of Commerce held a fund raiser in the Endicot Complex.
apply b. The jove electrical outlets were installed in the maurice building.

review 4a. This fall, Thanksgiving Day occurs on Thursday, November 24.
apply b. We celebrated memorial day on monday, may 30.

review 5a. The J. A. Tempe Company, located on Iris Avenue, gave prompt service.
apply b. One Locust street is the new address of the Hammersmith company.

review 6a. The Last of the Mohicans is an early adventure novel by Cooper.
apply b. I saw The Road To The Republic at the lenox theater last Sunday.

review 7a. Marion Kemper, attorney, had dinner at the home of Senator Bristol.
apply b. Marvin Silvers, an Editor, will speak before a group of doctors.

review 8a. The Mason and Dixon Line does not extend west of the Ohio River.
apply b. Both Houses of the French Parliament were situated on the left bank.

review 9a. All the important information is contained in line 21 of Appendix B.
apply b. The merchandise in column 1 is less expensive than in Column 2.

review 10a. The Spanish-American War was a favorite topic of the ex-Green Beret.
apply b. The political science students hosted ex-president Carter.

Proofread/revise as you keyboard

half sheet; 1″ top margin; 70-space line

1 Keyboard the sentences at the right, providing needed capitals.

2 Check your answers below.

Key: 1 Lee, Room, He, Chapter **2** You, New York **3** They, Thursday's **4** Jan, Mo, I, Chicago, Thanksgiv-ing **5** Did, Shaw, Caesar, Cleopatra, I, Memphis

1 lee left his history book in room 27. he must study chapter 15 today.

2 you will reach the new york state line if you drive east for 21 miles.

3 they announced their fall hosiery sale on page 15 of thursday's paper.

4 jan said, "mo and i should arrive in chicago on thanksgiving evening."

5 did shaw write "caesar and cleopatra"? i saw it at a memphis theater.

Improve keyboarding technique

each pair of lines 3 times SS at a controlled rate; DS between 6-line groups

letter response

1 Kinuyo, in my opinion, deserves only a few bad grades on tests in art.
2 We regret Lynn started at only minimum wage in a union garage in July.

word response

3 The amendment to their bid is a civic problem for the towns to handle.
4 The auditor did the work, and the firms paid the city with the profit.

combination response

5 We did imply they may have to limit the work they do on the editorial.
6 Ted plans to visit with the vendor to look at the quality of the loom.

| 1 | 2 | 3 | 4 | 5 | 6 | 7 | 8 | 9 | 10 | 11 | 12 | 13 | 14 |

86d ▶ 15

Build/measure script-copy skill

1 Three 1' writings on each ¶ for speed; circle errors; determine *gwam*.
2 One 5' control writing on both ¶s combined; circle errors; determine *gwam*.

Difficulty index

all letters used	A	1.5 si	5.7 awl	80% hfw

gwam 1' | 5'

We hear a tremendous amount about the negative side   10 | 2 | 45
of stress, but we do not hear very much about the   20 | 4 | 47
positive side. Stress can be very healthful. It can be a   32 | 6 | 49
motivating or an energizing force. It is important to   43 | 8 | 51
learn to control our frustrations and to incorporate   54 | 10 | 53
some satisfying activities into our work. Before we can   65 | 12 | 55
manage our stress, we must identify the cause of   75 | 14 | 57
it. Identifying the cause of a problem is not always   86 | 16 | 59
simple. Frequently, we deal with symptoms rather   96 | 18 | 61
than the actual problem.   101 | 19 | 63

It might be necessary to alter our life-style sig-   10 | 21 | 65
nificantly if we wish to manage stress effectively.   21 | 23 | 67
We cannot separate stress caused by our work from   31 | 25 | 69
that caused by other factors in our lives. The first   42 | 27 | 71
step is to reassess our priorities in life. We should   53 | 29 | 73
question ourselves seriously about those things in   63 | 31 | 75
life that are most precious to us. The second step   73 | 33 | 77
is to examine carefully our job priorities. Then we   84 | 35 | 79
can work to balance the two. Trying to do too   93 | 37 | 81
much causes most of the pressures we experience.   103 | 39 | 83
We need to recognize the things that are most   112 | 41 | 85
important and put our emphasis on those things.   121 | 43 | 87

Punctuation

Use a period	**Use a question mark**
1. At the end of a sentence that makes a direct statement or at the end of a request expressed as a question.	4. At the end of a sentence that is a direct question; however, use a period after an indirect question and a request which does not give the option of refusal.
2. After initials representing names.	**Use an exclamation point**
	5. After emphatic interjections which are stated as single words, phrases, or expressions.
3. After each element of an abbreviation, except for ALL-CAP abbreviations such as CIO and USPS.	6. After sentences which express strong emotions.

review 1a. Won't you please lend your support to this good cause.

apply   b. Can you give your answer to us by the end of the next week?

review 2a. This book is by R. J. Gould with a foreword by D. K. Adler.

apply   b. Alan E Dodd wrote the play; O D Brooks adapted it for the movies.

review 3a. The 10 a.m. class on data entry will be taught by Elvin Jones, Ph.D.

review b. The USPS has already begun implementing the 9-digit ZIP Code.

apply   c. Lou Cole, R N., joined the A.F.L.-C.I.O. meeting at 8:30 pm.

review 4a. Did you see seven or eight people run out of the burning building?

review b. The director has asked when the new microcomputers will be installed.

apply   c. Have you seen the annual report of Hornbacker Corporation.

review 5a. Oh! You surprised me. Look out! That car almost hit you.

apply   b. Fabulous. What a concert.

review 6a. You have exaggerated the facts completely beyond recognition!

apply   b. I can't believe you said that to such a nice person.

Check communication skills

1. A budget of $9,000,000 was voted; $10 million was projected.

2. Will you go to the army and navy game with me, Pete.

3. "Mark that spot," Valerie said, "And measure another five feet."

4. Read Page 8 for homework; outline chapter 2.

5. The works of J D Salinger are admired and sharply criticized.

6. The louisiana territory was purchased from napoleonic france.

7. Ted finished about 1/3 of his project which is due march 5th.

8. Dr Howard volunteered her services to V.I.S.T.A.

9. My order for 12 50-gallon drums and 100 ten-gallon drums is here.

10. Stop that immediately.

11. All thirty-seven entries were sent to 271--Forty-second street.

12. We admired the architecture of Cincinnati union terminal.

13. Did he plan to arrive in London on the twenty-ninth of april.

14. Business must be constantly alert to changes in Consumer demands.

15. Joyce introduced senator Hunt during the republican convention.

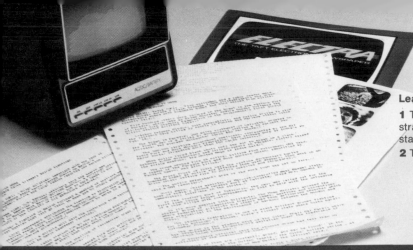

Learning goals

1 To improve basic skill on straight, script, rough–draft, and statistical copy.
2 To improve proofreading skills.

Machine adjustments

1 Paper guide at 0.
2 Margins: 70–space line for drills and ¶ writings.
3 Spacing: SS drills; DS ¶ writings.
4 Indention: 5 spaces for ¶ writings.

86a ▶ 5
Preparatory practice

each line 3 times SS (slowly, faster, slowly); DS between 3-line groups; repeat selected lines as time permits

alphabet	1	Kevin may be required to utilize six large units on the wharf project.
figure	2	Maria said 827 men, 934 women, and 1,056 children attended the picnic.
adjacent key	3	Are you going to shop there because pop art and coins are on sale now?
fluency	4	Eight of the downtown firms paid for the city to do the work for them.

| 1 | 2 | 3 | 4 | 5 | 6 | 7 | 8 | 9 | 10 | 11 | 12 | 13 | 14 |

86b ▶ 15
Build/measure straight-copy skill

1 Two 1' writings on each ¶ for speed; circle errors; determine *gwam*.
2 One 5' control writing on all ¶s combined; circle errors; determine *gwam*.

Difficulty index

all letters used	A	1.5 si	5.7 awl	80% hfw

gwam 1' | 5'

At one time it was thought that managers were the primary employees — 14 | 3 | 62
who needed to be able to cope with occupational stress. Today, however, — 29 | 6 | 65
research has shown that blue-collar workers and office employees are — 43 | 9 | 68
also victims of job pressures and tensions. In fact, these two groups — 57 | 12 | 71
are rated on many scales as having very high-stress jobs. Companies — 71 | 15 | 74
are spending a major amount of time and money to help workers in these — 85 | 18 | 77
jobs learn how to manage job pressure. — 93 | 20 | 79

One factor that seems to have an effect on the amount of stress a — 13 | 23 | 82
person experiences at work is the perception the individual has of how — 27 | 26 | 85
the requirements of the job match her or his ability. A person who — 41 | 29 | 88
perceives a poor fit between his or her ability and the job require- — 55 | 32 | 91
ments seems to experience more stress than a person who believes his or — 69 | 35 | 94
her ability matches the job. A challenging position is not necessarily — 83 | 38 | 97
a stressful position. — 88 | 42 | 101

Another factor that appears to have an effect on the amount of — 13 | 45 | 104
stress a worker experiences on the job is the amount of control that she — 28 | 48 | 107
or he can exert over the work. Those individuals who have the chance — 42 | 51 | 110
to help make decisions that affect their jobs seem to encounter fewer — 56 | 54 | 113
problems than individuals in organizations that do not permit them to — 70 | 57 | 116
take an active part in making job-related decisions. — 80 | 59 | 118

gwam 1' | 1 | 2 | 3 | 4 | 5 | 6 | 7 | 8 | 9 | 10 | 11 | 12 | 13 | 14 |
5' | 1 | 2 | 3 |

Punctuation

full sheet; 1″ top margin;
74-space line

Keyboard and format as
directed on p. 129.

Key: 1c. museum, Chad,
Togo, 2b. said, 3d. man–
ager, Diaz, today, tomor–
row, 4b. building, 5b.
Roanoke, Virginia, 12, 6b.
cunning, experienced, 6d.
huge elm 7b. 1984, 8b.
paints, scrapers, brushes,
etc.,

Use a comma

1. After an introductory word, phrase, or clause, and to separate words in a series.
2. To set off a short direct quotation.
3. To set off appositives, words in direct address, and contrasting phrases and clauses.
4. To set off nonrestrictive clauses (not essential to the meaning of the sentence). Do not set off information with comma(s) which is essential to the designation or identification of that which is modified.
5. To separate the day from the year and the city from the state.
6. To separate coordinate adjectives in a series. Each coordinate adjective modifies the noun independently. Do not use commas to separate closely related adjectives which seem to form a single unit with the noun they modify.
7. To separate adjacent groups of figures which are unrelated and whole numbers into three digit groups. However, policy, page, room, telephone, and most serial numbers are typed without commas.
8. Before and after the abbreviation etc.

review 1a. After separating the socks, he folded each pair.
review   b. Yes, I do like fruits, vegetables, and cheeses.
apply   c. While touring the museum I saw exhibits from Chad Togo and Mali.

review 2a. "I shall be home early this evening," Charlotte told her mother.
apply   b. Ann said "That is the only way."

review 3a. Our mayor, Lucinda Allen, provides the leadership our city needs.
review   b. Is this the letter you wish to send, Mr. Cheng?
review   c. This book, not the one on the desk, is the one I want.
apply   d. Our manager Ms. Diaz will speak with you today not tomorrow Eve.

review 4a. Mr. Arnold Meyer, Jr., a stockbroker, handles my portfolio.
apply   b. My office, a red brick building is only 15 minutes from downtown.

review 5a. Edmund moved to Sandusky, Ohio, on June 8, 1985.
apply   b. My family reunion in Roanoke Virginia was held on April 12 1984.

review 6a. The boat disappeared in the dark, cold, icy water.
apply   b. My opponent was cunning experienced and agile.
review   c. Growing gardenias is easy along this white picket fence.
apply   d. We had a picnic under the huge, elm tree.

review 7a. During 1984, 29 maintenance calls were made to Room 312.
apply   b. In 1985 12 errors were noted and corrected on page 7 of the text.

review 8a. All books, notes, etc., should be removed from the desk.
apply   b. All paints scrapers brushes etc. were reduced for the big sale.

Communication aid: capitalization/punctuation

full sheet; 1″ top margin;
DS; 70-space line

1 Read the ¶ at the right. Type it with correct capitalization and punctuation.

2 Check your corrected ¶ with your teacher. If necessary, repeat the paragraph correcting any errors you made.

3 Take two 1′ writings on your corrected copy.

gwam 1′

she remembered her feelings as precisely as she remembered the   13

sights smells and sounds around her as she sang each solo. the crowd   27

which contained a large number of college students had applauded her   41

enthusiastically she had shown no emotion. yet anxiety and a little   54

nervousness must have been hiding behind the all too cheerful mask   67

of her face.   70

85b, continued

Problem 2
Invoice

SOLD TO	The Cook's Nook	DATE	January 15, 19--	6
	235 Adams Street	OUR ORDER NO.	Rm-160472	11
	New Orleans, LA 70118-5723	CUST. ORDER NO.	C-351908	18
TERMS	2/10, n/30	SHIPPED VIA	Palmetto Express	23

QUANTITY	DESCRIPTION	UNIT PRICE	TOTAL	
6	Espresso maker, #PO16	86.95	521.70	29
24	Bird's nest fryer, large, #9R6	14.39	345.36	37
12	Soda siphon, chrome, #7N29	37.95	455.40	42
6	Silver decanter label sets, #J5	41.75	250.50	48
9	Beverage warmer, #G243	27.89	251.01	55
			1,823.97	57
	Sales tax		72.96	61
			1,896.93	63

Problem 3
Statement of account

DATE	February 28, 19--		3
TO	The Gourmet Shop		6
	214 Burnett Drive		9
	Baytown, TX 77520-4891		14

DATE	ITEMS	DEBITS	CREDITS	BALANCE	
February 1	Balance			694.28	19
7	Invoice L-6174	285.79		980.07	24
11	Invoice L-6923	410.80		1,390.87	30
15	Payment on account		550.00	840.87	36
18	Credit Memo 752		39.98	800.89	42

Problem 4
Inventory of equipment

Problem 5

Retype Problem 4 making these changes:

Manager: **T. J. Brennan**
Telephone: **325-6948**
Employee responsibile for first three items is **J. Rafferty** and for the last two items, **D. Fleming.**

DEPARTMENT	Sales	DATE	December 31, 19--	4
MANAGER	L. A. Matthews	TELEPHONE	555-2918	8

LOCATION	ITEM	SERIAL NUMBER	EMPLOYEE RESPONSIBLE	
122	Telecopier	8942R64	D. Steranka	14
122	Photocopier	628150JT	D. Steranka	19
122	Electronic typewriter	RM62943	D. Steranka	28
122	Shredder	1240635	D. Steranka	34
124	Word processor	X860-29	V. Johnson	41

Learning goals

1 To review half-page and full-page interoffice communications.
2 To learn to format letters in AMS style.
3 To refine keyboarding techniques.

Machine adjustments

1 Paper guide at 0.
2 Margins: 70-space line for drills and ¶ writings; as directed for problems.
3 Spacing: SS drills; DS ¶ writings; as directed for problems.
4 Indention: 5 spaces for ¶ writings; as appropriate for problems.

62a ▶ 5

Preparatory practice

each line 3 times SS (slowly, faster, slowly); DS between 3-line groups; repeat selected lines as time permits

alphabet 1 Sammy quickly explained it to the girl in a fuzzy brown velvet jumper.
fig/sym 2 Hunt & Dwyer's $623.75 check (Check 1489) was delivered on January 10.
double letters 3 Kelly aggressively guaranteed the current fees at the school meetings.
fluency 4 He laid the blame for the penalty on their dismal work on the problem.

| 1 | 2 | 3 | 4 | 5 | 6 | 7 | 8 | 9 | 10 | 11 | 12 | 13 | 14 |

62b ▶ 7

Improve keyboarding technique

each pair of lines 3 times SS at a controlled rate; DS between 6-line groups

letter response 1 As you were aware, you debated in a few cases after we were in a poll.
2 Seven million readers were in great fear after I stated a new opinion.
word response 3 Sign the right forms so the big civic panel may handle their problems.
4 The big problem with their theory is the risk to the eight lake towns.
combination response 5 Such key cases as ours are treated as secrets by a great number of us.
6 It is the duty of the big star and extras to create a loony art craze.

| 1 | 2 | 3 | 4 | 5 | 6 | 7 | 8 | 9 | 10 | 11 | 12 | 13 | 14 |

62c ▶ 38

Format interoffice communications

Problem 1
Memorandum (LM p. 115)

Prepare the memo; correct errors. Address a COMPANY MAIL envelope to:

Janice Fox, Supervisor
Word Processing Center

Note: If a printed form is not available, refer to page vi of the reference section.

words

TO: Janice Fox, Word Processing Supervisor — 8

FROM: Eric Shimmel, Training Supervisor — 15

DATE: June 30, 19-- — 17

SUBJECT: Seminar/Demonstration for Word Processing Staff — 27

Midwest Electronics has agreed to conduct a seminar for all members of our word processing staff. The seminar will be presented twice: once on July 14 at 1:30 p.m.; again on July 21 at 9:30 a.m. — 39 / 51 / 64 / 67

New equipment and new software packages for the processing of information will be demonstrated. In addition, new automated systems will be presented and analyzed in terms of our current and future word processing needs. — 79 / 91 / 104 / 111

You should divide your work force into two groups and assign one group to the July 14 session; the other group, to the July 21 session. In this way, total work stoppage in your unit can be avoided. — 123 / 136 / 149 / 151

xx — 151/160

84c, continued

Problem 3
Statement of account

Prepare the state-ment of account shown at the right; make 1 cc.

Date   April 30, 19--

To

┌   ┐
   Wilder & Sons, Inc.
   3982 Redwood Drive
   Kansas City, KS 66112-4579
└   ┘

Statement of Account

King Manufacturing Co.

625 Allerton Avenue
Milwaukee, WI 53221-4723
(414) 555-7225

Date	Items	Debits	Credits	Balance	
Apr. 1	Balance			684.72	20
4	Invoice J2345	146.35		831.07	25
8	Invoice J7890	371.83		1,202.90	31
10	Credit Memo 864		48.95	1,153.95	37
12	Invoice J9284	269.37		1,423.32	43
15	Payment on account		950.00	473.32	49

85

85a ▶ 5
Preparatory practice

each line 3 times SS;
DS between 3-line groups

For Line 3, leave 3 spaces between number groups.

alphabet 1 Meg quickly asked if the annexation project was criticized very badly.

figure 2 I need $1,536.70 and a 48-hour notice before I can begin Project 2819.

long numbers 3 437-62-8072   803-787-7404   29163   903-41-5862   318-842-528   94545

fluency 4 Jana may go with them to the lake at dusk to sit on the dock and fish.

| 1 | 2 | 3 | 4 | 5 | 6 | 7 | 8 | 9 | 10 | 11 | 12 | 13 | 14 |

85b ▶ 45
Measure production: business forms

Time schedule
Assembling materials . 5'
Timed production ..... 30'
Final check; compute
n-pram .... 10'

1 Arrange forms (LM pp. 195–203) and supplies for rapid handling.

2 When directed to begin, work for 30'. Make 1 cc of each problem.

3 Erase and correct errors; proofread carefully; com-pute n-pram.

Problem 1
Purchase requisition

words

FILLMORE recording specialists. inc.

2335 IOWA AVENUE
OGDEN, UT 84401-5332
(801) 555-3238

PURCHASE REQUISITION

Deliver to: M. C. Luke   Requisition No. 59374   3
Location: Front Showroom   Date April 27, 19--   8
Job No. 57398   Date Required As soon as possible   12

Quantity	Description	
1	Quartz guitar tuner	15
12	Battery, 9 volt	18
6	AC adaptor, 12 volt	21
1	Record cleaner, #J7328	25
1	Stylus care kit, #ST157	29

Requisitioned by: _____

62c, continued

Problem 2
Page 2 of a memorandum
(plain full sheet)

1 Format the copy at the right as page 2 of a memorandum. Begin page 2 heading SS on Line 7; use 1″ side margins; TS between heading and body of memo.

2 Proofread; correct errors.

Second–page headings for memos are the same as second–page headings for let–ters. This memo uses block style heading.

words

Charlene Post, Director Line 7	5
Page 2	6
February 13, 19--	9

TS

participants who responded to our survey, 77 percent stated that they used   24
message/reply forms. The main reasons given for adopting the message/reply   39
form were its ease of handling and its ease of filing.   50

A message/reply form can be used in any situation that is appropriate for a   65
memorandum. The following procedure should be used when preparing our   79
message/reply forms: 83

  1. The sender types a message in the left-hand section of the form,   97
    keeps the second (yellow) copy, and sends the other (white and   110
    pink) copies to the addressee.   116

  2. The addressee replies in the right-hand section of the form, keeps   130
    the third (pink) copy, and returns the original (white) copy to the   144
    sender.   145

  3. Signatures of both persons may be handwritten, or they may be   158
    typed and then initialed.   163

  4. The envelope address depends upon whether the message travels   176
    through the U.S. Postal Service or through COMPANY MAIL. The   188
    message form is creased down the center of the page and inserted   201
    into an envelope.   204

We will begin using message/reply forms on the first of next month. Data will   218
be collected by my office over the next six months to see how well the forms are   234
accepted.   236

xx   237

Problem 3
Message/reply memo

1 On a message/reply form (LM p. 117), prepare the message and reply given at the right, using the format shown in the illustration below.

2 Address an envelope marked COMPANY MAIL.

TO: Jonathan Kappel | Director, Employee Development | 126 Hancock Tower   13
DATE: January 22, 19-- SUBJECT: Conference on Employee Development   23

MESSAGE: The attached brochure was received from the National Center for   36
the Advancement of Business Practices. Since employee development will be a   51
priority for us for some time, these conference topics should be relevant.   66
Please let me know your opinion.   72

SIGNED: Maria Gonzalez, Vice President   78

DATE: January 23, 19--   81

REPLY: The topics listed are timely and relevant to our long-range plans. I   95
suggest that I attend the conference in New York in March and make a formal   110
proposal to the corporate officers by April 1.   119

SIGNED: Jonathan Kappel   122 | 124

84b ▶ 15
Preapplication drill: prepare rules (lines); place copy on printed rules

half sheet, long side up; 1″ top margin

Preparing horizontal rules

Depress the shift lock and use the underline key.

Drawing vertical rules

Operate the automatic line finder. Place the point of a pencil or pen through the cardholder (or on the typebar guide above the ribbon). Roll the paper up until you have a ruling of the desired length. Remove the pen or pencil and reset the line finder.

You can also remove the paper from the typewriter and, using a pen with black ink and a ruler, draw the vertical rules.

Drill

1 Prepare a 5″ horizontal rule; DS; prepare another 5″ horizontal rule. Remove paper; reinsert it; align the first ruled line with the aligning scale. Place your name on the first rule and your address on the second rule. Check to see that you have placed the words close to the rule, but that you have not cut the rule.

2 Prepare three 5″ horizontal rules a double space apart; draw a vertical rule 3″ from the left edge of the rules; draw a second vertical rule 4″ from the left edge of the rules. Place the following items on the rules:

Mike Brittan	215 lbs.	6′10″
Jimmy Foster	204 lbs.	6′10″
Duane Kendall	206 lbs.	6′11″

84c ▶ 30
Prepare inventories of equipment

(LM pp. 189–193)

Problem 1
Inventory of equipment

Prepare the inventory at the right.

words

INVENTORY OF EQUIPMENT

DEPARTMENT *Technical Services* DATE *December 30, 19--* · 7

MANAGER *Margaret Vickery* TELEPHONE NUMBER *555-6072* · 12

LOCATION	ITEM	SERIAL NUMBER	EMPLOYEE RESPONSIBLE	
10A	Electronic typewriter	2P182469	L. Bordelon	21
10A	Electronic typewriter	2P174932	L. Laborde	30
12B	Microcomputer	86284JRL	E. Gentry	37
12B	Disk drive	71490JRL	E. Gentry	43
12B	Printer	78213JRL	E. Gentry	49
14A	Copier	69083247	D. White	54
14A	Word processor	52971638	C. Jeansonne	62
14A	Transcriber	28375642	C. Jeansonne	69

Problem 2
Inventory of equipment

Use the information at the right to prepare the inventory for the Training Department. Follow the style illustrated in Problem 1.

Department: **Training** | Manager: **Dale McKee** | Date: **June 30, 19--** | 6
Telephone: **555-7000** · 8

Location: **A** | Employee Responsible: **M. Snowden** | Item: **Overhead projector,** 14
68429071; Slide projector, 29168415; Movie projector, 91652930; Video 28
recorder, 7829431; TV monitor, 37281450; Camera, 39184560 · 40

Location: **B** | Employee Responsible: **C. Warner** | Item: **Typewriter, 2R197638;** 47
Lettering machine, 4K261375 · 52

63a ▶ 5
Preparatory practice

each line 3 times SS (slowly, faster, slowly); DS between 3-line groups; repeat selected lines as time permits

alphabet 1 A dazzling lake view just beyond the quaint farm was exciting to Paul.

fig/sym 2 A premium of $864.50 is due May 19 on Policy #32-770H, a 15% increase.

direct reach 3 Our group must agree to urge any number of new organizational changes.

fluency 4 Ruth and my neighbor may visit the ancient island city in a dirigible.

| 1 | 2 | 3 | 4 | 5 | 6 | 7 | 8 | 9 | 10 | 11 | 12 | 13 | 14 |

63b ▶ 5
Improve keyboarding technique

each pair of lines 2 times SS at a controlled rate; DS between 4-line groups

adjacent reaches
1 She quickly showed them samples of government bonds to buy or to sell.
2 They assured the developer we would support the three required points.

double letters
3 Abbott suggested all staff personnel make an effort to arrive by noon.
4 All classes will meet in this room to discuss the latest school offer.

direct reaches
5 A great many payments must continue to be processed until you balance.
6 Their library recently obtained my lengthy brochure about the economy.

| 1 | 2 | 3 | 4 | 5 | 6 | 7 | 8 | 9 | 10 | 11 | 12 | 13 | 14 |

63c ▶ 10
Review memo format

half-page memorandum (LM p. 119)

Format the memo given at the right. Proofread and correct errors.

words

TO: Regional Sales Managers FROM: Charles Harbottle, Sales Manager   11
DATE: October 3, 19-- SUBJECT: National Sales Meeting   19

(¶ 1) This memo will confirm that each of you will be participating in our   33
national sales meeting on November 3-6. We have made reservations for you to   49
stay at the Ritz-Carlton, 2100 Massachusetts Avenue, N.W., Washington, D.C.,   64
where the telephone number is (202) 555-2100. The reservations arc for late   79
arrival on November 2 and departure on November 6.   89

(¶ 2) The agenda for this meeting is enclosed.   97

xx | Enclosure   100

63d ▶ 30
Format a letter and a memo

2 plain sheets
1 half-page memorandum (LM p. 119)

Problem 1
Learn letter format

1 Prepare machine for formatting Style letter 6, page 135; plain sheet; 1½" margins; date on line 14.
2 Using the letter on page 135, format and type the opening lines and the first line of the body. Leave proper spacing between letter parts. Space down 22 times. Type the last paragraph and closing lines.

Problem 2
AMS Simplified letter

1 On a plain full sheet, format the letter given on page 135 in the style shown, using the dateline placement and margins given. You will later format other AMS Simplified letters using the placement table given on page 117.
2 Proofread; correct errors.

Problem 3
Half-page memorandum

Compose a memo to all department heads from you informing them that your company is adopting the AMS Simplified letter style. Briefly explain the benefits of this style. Use today's date and an appropriate subject line.

words

BENNETT & BENNETT SPORTING GOODS

230 ASHFORD STREET
RALEIGH, NC 27610-5723 (919) 555-9460

Invoice

Seven Devils Ski Shop
1294 Wildcat Rocks Road
Banner Elk, NC 28604-3789

		words
Date	November 6, 19--	3
		7
Our Order No.	SE87304	13
		18
Cust. Order No.	3207	19
Shipped Via	Mountain Express Lines	28

Terms 2/10, n/30

Quantity	Description	Unit Price	Total	
12 prs.	Beginners' skis, Stock No. 834	55.98	671.76	38
12 prs.	Beginners' skis, Stock No. 884	68.25	819.00	48
8 prs.	Intermediate skis, Stock No. 934	75.50	604.00	58
10 prs.	Intermediate skis, Stock No. 984	84.98	849.80	68
48 prs.	Fiberglass ski poles, Stock No. 329	4.15	199.20	78
24 prs.	Bindings, Stock No. 582	39.99	959.76	86
6 prs.	Bindings, Stock No. 592	46.78	280.68	96
			4,384.20	98
	Sales tax		175.37	103
			4,559.57	105

Problem 3
Half-page memorandum

Compose a memo, using the information at the right.

TO: June Schmidt, Coordinator, Graphics Department
FROM: (your name), **Office Administrator**
DATE: (current)
SUBJECT: **Request for New Invoice Forms**

Request that June Schmidt have new invoice forms designed on 8½″ × 11″ paper for large orders. You will continue to use the 8½″ × 5½″ forms for regular orders. Suggest that 10,000 copies (100 pads of 100 invoice forms) be printed initially.

84a ▶ 5
Preparatory practice

each line 3 times SS (slowly, faster, slowly); DS between 3-line groups; repeat selected lines as time permits

84

alphabet	1	Mercedes was just given the deluxe bronze plaque for her charity work.
figure	2	My telephone number was changed from 392-0174 to 853-6927 on March 18.
shift key	3	Jan, Don, Tom, and May wrote "Bonn on Less than $10 Per Day" for Life.
fluency	4	A neighbor owns key land downtown, and she also owns a dock on a lake.

| 1 | 2 | 3 | 4 | 5 | 6 | 7 | 8 | 9 | 10 | 11 | 12 | 13 | 14 |

Communications Design Associates

348 INDIANA AVENUE
WASHINGTON, DC 20001-1438
Tel: 1-800-432-5739

		words	in parts	total

Begin all major lines at left margin

May 9, 19--   words   2 | 2

Begin address 3 blank line spaces below date

Mr. William S. Rapp, Manager   8 | 8
American Production Systems   13 | 13
98 Clutter Mill Road   17 | 17
Great Neck, NY 11021-4527   22 | 22

Omit salutation

Subject line in all capital letters with a triple space above and below it

AMS SIMPLIFIED STYLE   26 | 26

This letter is typed in a simplified style that is recom-   37 | 37
mended by the Administrative Management Society. It is   48 | 48
designed to save you time. The following points outline   59 | 59
the basic features of a letter typed in the AMS style.   70 | 70

Begin enumerated items at left margin; indent unnumbered items 5 spaces

1. Use block format.   4 | 74

2. Omit the salutation and the complimentary close.   14 | 84

3. Include a subject heading in ALL CAPS a triple space   25 | 95
    below the address; TS from the subject line to the   35 | 105
    first line of the body.   40 | 110

4. Begin enumerated items flush with the left margin;   51 | 121
    indent unnumbered items five spaces.   58 | 128

5. Place the writer's name and title in ALL CAPS on the   69 | 139
    4th line space below the last line of the letter body.   80 | 150

6. Place the reference initials (typist's only) a double   92 | 162
    space below the writer's name.   98 | 168

Correspondents in your company may like the AMS Simpli-   12 | 180
fied letter style not only for the eye appeal it gives   23 | 191
to letters but also for the potential reduction in letter-   35 | 203
writing costs.   36 | 204

Omit complimentary close

Carolyn Jackson

Writer's name and title in ALL CAPS at least 3 blank line spaces below letter body

MRS. CAROLYN JACKSON, PRESIDENT   42 | 210

xx   43 | 211

Style letter 6: AMS Simplified

Problem 2
Purchase order

Prepare the purchase order given at the right; make 1 cc.

Problem 3
Purchase order

Repeat the purchase order given in Problem 2, making these changes:

1 Purchase Order No. **4025-3830.**

2 Date: **January 14, 19--.**

3 Double the quantity of each item; compute the total.

words

Office Services, Inc.
530 Montgomery Street
San Francisco, CA   94111-4225

(414) 555-3520

Custom Forms, Inc.
2438 Bay Shore Boulevard
San Francisco, CA   94134-3733

PURCHASE ORDER

Purchase order No.	3028-1739	2
Date	September 24, 19--	6
Terms	Net	10
		15
		21
Ship Via	Rapid Express	23

Quantity	Cat. No.	Description	Price	Total	
4 boxes	SR-253-25	Stock requisition, 6" x 9 1/2"	23.56	94.24	34
12 pads	QF-309-21	Quotation form	2.85	34.20	42
24 pads	PF-957-72	Proposal form	3.00	72.00	50
8 pads	TS-264-18	Daily professional time sheet	4.12	32.96	61
12 boxes	IS-725-41	Invoice for services	24.75	297.00	71
6 boxes	ER-284-31	Weekly expense report	37.68	226.08	81
20 boxes	TM-399-04	Telephone message pad	5.23	104.60	92
				861.08	93

By_____Purchasing Agent

83

83a ▶ 5
Preparatory practice

each line 3 times SS (slowly, faster, slowly); DS between 3-line groups; repeat selected lines as time permits

alphabet 1 Jacobsen asked why the quiet farmer gave him six pretty azalea bushes.

fig/sym 2 He got 34 rolls of 1/2″ × 360″ tape at $5.79 each, a total of $196.86.

space bar 3 The big oak box by the fur rug is also a bit worn, and she may fix it.

fluency 4 Did she bid for the bicycle, the antique chair, and the enamel emblem?

| 1 | 2 | 3 | 4 | 5 | 6 | 7 | 8 | 9 | 10 | 11 | 12 | 13 | 14 |

83b ▶ 45
Prepare invoices and a memorandum
(LM pp. 185–189)

Problem 1
Invoice

An invoice is a bill prepared by the seller.

Prepare the invoice illustrated on p. 175; make 1 cc.

Problem 2
Invoice

Prepare an invoice, using the information at the right; make 1 cc.

				words
SOLD TO	Appalachian Ski Shop	DATE	November 14, 19--	7
	905 Blowing Rock Road			11
	Boone, NC 28607-5348	OUR ORDER NO.	SE87492	17
		CUST. ORDER NO.	R83023	18
TERMS	2/10, n/30	SHIPPED VIA	Speedy Express	23

(Increase the quantity of each item in Problem 1 by adding 2 to it; use the same description and unit price as in Problem 1; compute the total. Use 4% to compute sales tax.)

Total 101

64a ▶ 5
Preparatory practice

each line 3 times SS (slowly, faster, slowly); DS between 3-line groups; repeat selected lines as time permits

alphabet 1 Major excavation was taking place quietly behind Zone Four on the map.

fig/sym 2 Our Invoice #58* and their Check #902 for $1,437.06 were mailed May 8.

long words 3 Arrangements were announced to honor outstanding accounting graduates.

fluency 4 When may the auditor work with the city panel to cut down on the risk?

| 1 | 2 | 3 | 4 | 5 | 6 | 7 | 8 | 9 | 10 | 11 | 12 | 13 | 14 |

64b ▶ 15
Build/measure straight-copy skill

1 Two 1' writings on each ¶; circle errors; determine *gwam*.
2 One 5' writing on all ¶s combined; circle errors; determine *gwam*; compare results with 1' writings.

Difficulty index

all letters used | A | 1.5 si | 5.7 awl | 80% hfw

gwam 1' | 5'

Many business people have found the new microcomputers to be a 13 | 3 | 55
good management tool. These small computers can now be seen on the 27 | 5 | 58
desktops of a rising number of managers. The typewriter-size tools 40 | 8 | 61
seem well on their way to becoming as important as calculators. Micro- 54 | 11 | 64
computer creation is a rapidly expanding field and will continue to be. 69 | 14 | 67
In fact, sales of these new machines now amount to over a billion dol- 83 | 17 | 69
lars a year. 85 | 17 | 70

These machines have something for just about everyone. Business 13 | 20 | 73
is using them to analyze, store, and locate data for tasks ranging 26 | 22 | 75
from billing work to long-term sales projections. The machines can 40 | 25 | 78
also develop budgets and cash-flow plans as well as follow market trends. 55 | 28 | 81
With the computer, a telephone, and an add-on device called a modem, 69 | 31 | 84
researchers can have contact with other data bases to get a greater 82 | 34 | 87
amount of news or facts right off the wire services. 93 | 36 | 89

The assets of these machines are speed, versatility, and ease of 13 | 38 | 91
use. Tasks that previously required hours to do can be done in seconds 27 | 41 | 94
just by tapping a few keys. In fact, with a feature called "data base 42 | 44 | 97
management," a file can be created which can be instantly called up by 56 | 47 | 100
using various approaches. Thus, once the proper data have been put 69 | 50 | 102
into the data base, managers can easily summon customers' files or 83 | 52 | 105
workers' names. 86 | 53 | 106

gwam 1' | 1 | 2 | 3 | 4 | 5 | 6 | 7 | 8 | 9 | 10 | 11 | 12 | 13 | 14 |
5' | 1 | 2 | 3 |

82a ▶ 5
Preparatory practice

each line 3 times SS (slowly, faster, slowly); DS between 3-line groups; repeat selected lines as time permits.

For Line 3, beginning at the left margin, set 7 tab stops 9 spaces apart.

alphabet	1	Josefina Vazquez will spend about six days working on those documents.
figure	2	The pet shop has 149 dogs, 72 cats, 58 rabbits, 60 birds, and 93 fish.
tab	3	look hear talk read open shut walk advance
fluency	4	The proficient auditors may handle the usual big problems of the city.

| 1 | 2 | 3 | 4 | 5 | 6 | 7 | 8 | 9 | 10 | 11 | 12 | 13 | 14 |

82b ▶ 15
Preapplication drill: tabulate

half sheet, long side up; 1½″ top margin; 1½″ left margin; set tab stops every 10 spaces, beginning at the left margin; align decimal points in decimal columns and colons in colon column; SS; DS between groups

$184.29	a.m.	23″	10 lbs.	3 5/8	25.4 mm	12:30
$178.40	p.m.	6′	8 oz.	6/2/89	2.54 cm	9:15
$350.17	FICA	75%	4 ft.	27 1/2	1.305 m	7:45
$692.53	Ph.D.	#38	7 in.	B4-53	1.61 km	6:29
$159.06	i.e.	(4)	9 ea.	n/30	4.785 l	11:27
$804.31	Inc.	12*	1 doz.	Z-104	0.47 L	6:32
$572.93	COBOL	36#	12 v.	6 1/4	0.45 kg	10:48
$831.82	No.	*90	1 tsp.	2/7/90	28.35 g	8:03

82c ▶ 30
Prepare purchase orders

(LM pp. 179–183)

Problem 1
Purchase order

A purchase order is completed by the purchasing department to order requisitioned supplies or equipment.

Prepare the purchase order given at the right; make 1 cc.

words

King Manufacturing Co.

625 Allerton Avenue
Milwaukee, WI   53221-4723   (414) 555-7225

Benchmark Supply Company
P.O. Box 3927
Madison, WI   53707-3906

PURCHASE ORDER

Tab

		words
Purchase order No.	P-392840	2
Date	April 6, 19--	5
		10
Terms	2/10, n/30	15
		20
Ship Via	UPS	21

Quantity	Cat. No.	Description	Price	Total	words
4	S2-P1046	Printwheel, Courier 10	7.25	29.00	29
4	S2-P1052	Printwheel, Courier 72	7.25	29.00	37
12	S2-R3276	Multi-strike film ribbon	5.12	61.44	46
1	F3-M8210	Anti-static chair mat, brown,			54
		60" x 48" x 1/8"	170.98	170.98	60
30	S5-D7539	Flexible disk, double density	8.30	249.00	70
6	S8-3176	Disk library case	5.80	34.80	77
2	F4-7285	Adjustable turntable	31.98	63.96	86
				638.18	87

(Set tab 2 spaces from rule) — Description
Indent 3 spaces
Approximate center
DS

By _____ Purchasing Agent

64c ▶ 30
Measure production

Time schedule

Assembling materials ...... 3'
Timed production .... 20'
Final check; compute
n–pram .... 7'

Problem 1
Full-page memorandum
(LM p. 121)

Format and type the full–page memorandum given at the right; proofread; correct errors; ad–dress a COMPANY MAIL envelope.

TO: Floyd Vasquez, Supervisor, Data Processing | FROM: Nancy Finch, Director   13
of Employment Programs | DATE: December 15, 19-- | SUBJECT: Educational   24
Programs   26

(¶ 1) Walton, Incorporated, has a full agenda of educational program offerings   41
planned for the coming year. Specialized sessions on estate planning, personal   57
computer systems, tax planning, gourmet cooking, literature, and much more   72
are featured.   75

(¶ 2) Enclosed is the schedule of programs, which explains many of the courses   90
to be offered. Also included are registration forms for the convenience of your   106
staff. Please inform your staff of the schedule of programs and make the regis-   122
tration forms available to them.   128

(¶ 3) Please contact me if you have any questions or if I can provide further   142
information about these course offerings. | xx | Enclosure   153 | **155**

Problem 2
AMS Simplified letter
(LM p. 123)

Format and type the letter given at the right; proofread; correct errors; address an envelope.

March 9, 19-- | Mr. Edward Fisher, President | St. Louis Business Institute | 12115   16
Lackland Road | St. Louis, MO 63141-4587 | SOFTWARE EDUCATIONAL PRO-   29
GRAMS   30

(¶ 1) If your institution is like most institutions, you have been buying com-   44
puters for educational purposes and now are face to face with the "software   59
problem": You need specific programs that will make your computers more   74
effective as educational tools.   80

(¶ 2) We may be able to help! As members of a nonprofit agency, we at Com-   94
munications Design Associates have been working on the software problem for   109
over ten years. We have reviewed and tested more than 1,000 educational pro-   124
grams and compiled a catalog of the small percentage that meet our rigid   139
standards.   149

(¶ 3) Take the time to look through the enclosed publication and consider what   164
Communications Design Association has to offer. Order forms for instruc-   178
tional packages are included in the catalog sections, and you can get on our   193
mailing list by using the request card provided in thc catalog. (168)   206

MRS. MARY G. PETERS, EDITOR | xx | Enclosure   214 | **234**

Problem 3
Message/reply memo
(LM p. 125)

Format and type the mes–sage/reply memo given at the right; proofread; correct errors; address a COMPANY MAIL en–velope.

Problem 4

If you complete the 3 problems in less than 20', start over on plain paper.

TO: Lisa Woo | Director of Operations | 190 Communications Center | DATE: 12
October 10, 19-- | SUBJECT: School Visit   18

MESSAGE: I have received a request from Linda Akers, Chairperson, Business   31
Education Department, Fall River Community College, to visit our Information   46
Processing Center on October 19. Thirty-five students would visit for approxi-   62
mately two hours. They are interested in the equipment we use and the skills   78
we require for our entry-level positions. Can we accommodate these students   93
at the time requested? | SIGNED: Don Long, Director of Information   104

DATE: October 11, 19-- | REPLY: I do not see a problem with the request. Ms.   117
Akers has worked with us in the past in placing her students with us for summer   133
employment. Please let me know if you would like me to contact her to make   148
the final arrangements. | SIGNED: Lisa Woo   155 | **157**

Learning goals

1 To improve facility with figure and symbol reaches.

2 To improve tab control.

3 To develop skill in typing purchase requisitions, purchase orders, inventory forms, invoices, and statements of account.

Machine adjustments

1 Paper guide at 0.

2 Margins: 70–space line for drills; as directed for problems.

3 Spacing: SS drills; as directed for problems.

4 Indention as appropriate for problems.

81a ▶ 5
Preparatory practice

each line 3 times SS (slowly, faster, slowly); DS between 3-line groups; repeat selected lines as time permits

alphabet	1	Maxwell visited the quaint shopping plaza just sixty blocks from here.
figure	2	The waterfront lot was 147 feet wide, 239 feet deep, and cost $38,650.
fig/sym	3	I paid 25% ($3,749) down and 60% ($6,748.21) of the balance last week.
fluency	4	Jane and Sidney may both go to work for the big firm down by the lake.

| 1 | 2 | 3 | 4 | 5 | 6 | 7 | 8 | 9 | 10 | 11 | 12 | 13 | 14 |

81b ▶ 10
Study business forms

Study the illustrations of a purchase requisition (below), a purchase order (page 173), an invoice (page 175), an inventory form (page 176), and a statement of account (page 177).

Read the following tips carefully before preparing the business forms in this section.

1 Set left margin stop for the address and first column; set tab stops for other columnar items.

2 Begin entries in the "description" or "items" column two spaces to the right of the vertical line; center the other columns under the headings.

3 If 3 or fewer entries are to be typed on a form, DS them. SS for 4 or more entries.

4 If an entry will take more than one line, indent the second and succeeding lines 3 spaces.

5 Underline the last item in a column for which a total is to be shown; DS, then type the total.

81c ▶ 35
Prepare purchase requisitions

(LM pp. 175–177)
Problem 1
Purchase requisition

A purchase requisition is completed by a department in a company that needs the supplies or equipment.

Prepare the purchase requisition given at the right; make 1 cc.

Problem 2
Purchase requisition

Reformat Problem 1, making the following changes:

1 Requisition No. **49658**.

2 Date: **February 6, 19—**.

3 Increase order for pad holders and ballpoint pens to 100.

4 Alphabetize the entries in the description column. Rearrange quantities accordingly.

words

Communications Design
Associates

348 INDIANA AVENUE   WASHINGTON, DC 20001-1438

PURCHASE REQUISITION

Tab ↓

Deliver to:	Starr Askew	Requisition No.	49650	5
Location:	Suite 28B	Date	January 12, 19--	10
Job No.	37528	Date Required	As soon as possible	15

Quantity	Set tab 2 spaces from rule / Description	
DS	↓	
6	Perforated pads for easel presentation	23
12	Felt-tip markers with black ink	30
6	Felt-tip markers with blue ink	36
6	Felt-tip markers with red ink	42
24	Walnut pad holders, 8 1/2" x 11"	49
24	Ballpoint pens, fine point, black ink	57
24	Clear transparencies	62
Approximate center ↑		

Requisitioned by: _____

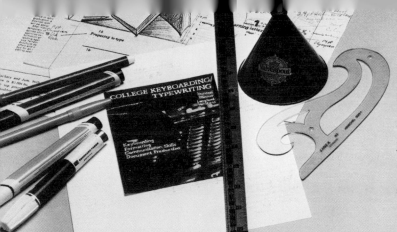

Learning goals

1 To learn to format various kinds of administrative communications.

2 To produce usable copy under time pressure over an extended period.

3 To improve basic proofreading skills.

Machine adjustments

1 Paper guide at 0.

2 Margins: 70–space line for drills and ¶ writings; as directed for problems.

3 Spacing: SS drills; DS ¶ writings; as directed for problems.

4 Indention: 5 spaces for ¶ writings; as appropriate for problems.

65a ▶ 5
Preparatory practice

each line 3 times SS (slowly, faster, slowly); DS between 3-line groups; repeat selected lines as time permits

alphabet	1	Megg sat by the park to relax with a cup of java on a quiet, lazy day.
fig/sym	2	Will Flight #739 leave at 10:48 p.m. and arrive in Miami at 2:56 a.m.?
shift key	3	Bob Pack, Jane Epworth, and Marie Appel will go to New York City soon.
fluency	4	They did laugh at the sight of the neighbor in the rich field of corn.

| 1 | 2 | 3 | 4 | 5 | 6 | 7 | 8 | 9 | 10 | 11 | 12 | 13 | 14 |

65b ▶ 10
Review/apply communication skills: punctuation

full sheet; 1" top margin; 74-space line

Keyboard and format as directed on p. 129.

Key: 1b. reservations; 2c. implemented; con–sequently, 3b. navy; 4b. job; namely,

Use a semicolon

1. Between two independent clauses of a compound sentence when the conjunction is omitted.

2. To separate independent clauses when they are joined by a conjunctive adverb (however, therefore, consequently, etc.).

3. Before a coordinating conjunction (and, but, for, or, nor) between two independent clauses when either or both contain internal punctuation

4. Before an expression which introduces an explanatory statement.

review 1a. The computer course was easy; I received top grades.
apply   b. I shall make the reservations she will provide transportation.

review 2a. The highway was impassable; consequently, traffic was rerouted.
review b. I dialed the right number; however, no one answered the phone.
apply   c. New procedures were implemented consequently efficiency was improved.

review 3a. Yes, we ordered Beef Wellington; and they ordered Crab Imperial.
apply   b. My skirt was brown, tan, and navy and hers was a solid color.

review 4a. Some conditions promote effective study; for example, a quiet place.
apply   b. He is qualified for the job namely he has training and experience.

65c ▶ 35
Format letters on executive-size stationery

Problem 1

Executive–size letter (LM p. 141) or paper cut to size (7¼" × 10½")

Format the letter illustrated on page 139. Use ¾" side margins (spaces: 7 pica, 9 elite) for this letter because it is long; begin date on Line 13.

Proofread; use standard proofreader's marks to indicate needed corrections.

Problem 2

Executive–size letter (LM p. 143) or paper cut to size

Using your corrected copy, pre–pare a final copy of the letter in Problem 1. Correct errors as you type.

GUIDE FOR CORRESPONDENCE ON SPECIAL-SIZE STATIONERY		
Stationery	Margins	Date Placement
Executive–size	¾"–1"	Lines 10–16
Postal card	3 spaces	Line 3

Problem 3
4-column table

full sheet; reading position; DS
body of table; decide spacing
between columns

SCHEDULE OF DIRECT REDUCTION OF LOAN

19--

Month	Interest	Principal	Loan Balance	
				22
January	$157.08	$59.43	$14,440.57	28
February	156.44	60.07	14,380.50	34
March	155.79	60.72	14,319.78	39
April	155.13	61.38	14,258.40	44
May	154.47	62.04	14,196.36	49
June	153.79	62.72	14,133.64	54
July	153.11	63.40	14,070.24	59
August	152.43	64.08	14,006.16	64
September	151.73	64.78	13,941.38	70
October	151.03	65.48	13,875.90	75
November	150.32	66.19	13,809.71	81
December	149.61	66.90	13,742.81	87

(7)
(8)

Problem 4
4-column table

full sheet; reading position; DS
body of table; 8 spaces between
columns

DANIEL MANAGEMENT CENTER
Program Analysis for February

Program	Income	Expenses	Profit	
				22
C 2810	$4,820	$2,975	$1,845	27
C 2824	3,975	2,480	1,495	31
M 3612	7,655	4,375	3,280	35
M 3634	8,534	5,150	3,384	39
M 3639	6,895	4,767	2,128	43
S 4123	9,256	5,348	3,908	47
S 4130	8,850	5,025	3,825	51
S 4138	8,775	4,987	3,788	55
W 5204	5,134	3,266	1,868	59

(5)
(11)

Lammey Printing & Paper Supply Co.
425 South Wabash Avenue
Chicago, IL 60605-3259   (3l2) 555-l503

	words	in parts	total

Line 13   August 25, 19-- | | 5 | 5 |

Mr. Frederick Rozier, President | | 11 | 11 |
Household Products Corporation | | 17 | 17 |
444 W. St. James Place | | 22 | 22 |
Chicago, IL 60614-5739 | | 27 | 27 |

Dear Mr. Rozier | | 30 | 30 |

Thank you for your recent order for the multicolor | | 40 | 40 |
printing of your new catalogs and manuals. We at Lam- | | 51 | 51 |
mey Printing Company are pleased to have the opportu- | | 61 | 61 |
nity to serve you. | | 65 | 65 |

¾″   Sharp eyes and unfaltering attention to detail will   ¾″ | 10 | 75 |
follow your work through every stage--from the first | | 21 | 86 |
planning session through final production. You can | | 31 | 96 |
depend on expert handling, conscientious proofreading, | | 42 | 107 |
and efficient service because our employees have the | | 53 | 118 |
same commitment to quality as you have. | | 61 | 126 |

We know you will be impressed with the superior appear- | | 11 | 137 |
ance of your finished catalogs and manuals. We hope | | 22 | 148 |
that you will continue to think of our printing company | | 33 | 159 |
whenever you need graphics work done to perfection. | | 43 | 169 |

Sincerely yours | | 46 | 172 |

LAMMEY PRINTING & PAPER SUPPLY CO. | | 51 | 177 |

Richard Laramie

Richard Laramie | | 54 | 180 |
Production Manager | | 58 | 184 |

xx | | 59 | 185 |

Style letter 7: Executive-size letter

80a ▶ 5

Preparatory practice

each line 3 times SS (slowly, faster, slowly); DS between 3-line groups; repeat selected lines as time permits

alphabet 1   Hal Jimenez fixed twelve good pancakes quickly for my breakfast today.

figure 2   They had 532 men, 498 women, and 1,067 children volunteer for 36 jobs.

outside reach 3   Polly was at the Dallas Plaza last fall; she sold Max two quilts then.

fluency 4   The key goal of the city panel is to audit the six big downtown firms.

| 1 | 2 | 3 | 4 | 5 | 6 | 7 | 8 | 9 | 10 | 11 | 12 | 13 | 14 |

80b ▶ 45

Measure production: tables

Time schedule

Assembling materials .... 5'
Timed production .... 30'
Final check; compute
  n–pram .... 10'

1 Organize your supplies.

2 When directed to begin, work for 30'.

3 Erase and correct errors; proofread carefully; compute *n–pram*.

Problem 1
2-column table

half sheet, long side up; exact vertical center; SS body of table; 12 spaces between columns

		words
ESTATE DIAMOND SOLITAIRES		5
Emerald (3.71 ct.)	$13,650	10
Pear (5.05 ct.)	23,795	15
Marquise (2.79 ct.)	9,875	20
Oval (3.04 ct.)	16,650	25
Oval (7.91 ct.)	32,495	29
Oval (1.89 ct.)	7,635	34
Heart (6.48 ct.)	27,865	39
		42
Source: Anderson Estate Jewelers.		49

Problem 2
Ruled table

full sheet; reading position; DS body of table; decide spacing between columns

Region	Travel	Entertainment	words
REGIONAL EXPENSE ANALYSIS			5
(First Quarter)			8
			17
			26
			31
			40
Midwest	$ 48,650	$12,375	44
Northeast	41,725	10,675	48
Northwest	54,374	9,350	52
Southeast	43,679	14,795	56
Southern	44,750	13,684	60
Southwest	51,287	10,596	64
			73
Total	$284,465	$71,475	77
			86

Problem 3
Simplified memo
(LM p. 145)

1 Read the information in the simplified memo shown at the right.

2 Format and type the memo, following the directions in the memo.

3 Proofread; circle any errors you have made.

oei

OFFICE EFFICIENCY, INC.
EXPERTS IN OFFICE RESEARCH

35 E. South Water
Chicago, IL   60601-4737

(312) 575-2121

DS

words

January 23, 19--   3

TS

William A. Johnston, Office Manager   10

TS

SIMPLIFIED MEMORANDUM   14

TS

This is an example of the simplified memorandum you and I discussed at the   29
recent AMS meeting. Its features are listed below: 39

DS

1. The memorandum may be prepared on standard letterhead or plain paper.   53

2. It is formatted in block style with 1″ side margins, eliminating those pesky   69
tabulator stops that some memo forms require.   78

3. The date is placed a double space below the last line of the letterhead or 1 1/2   95
inches below the top edge of a plain sheet.   104

4. A triple space separates all major parts (date, name of recipient, subject line,   121
body, name of originator, reference initials, enclosure notation, and copy   136
notation).   138

5. The message is single-spaced with double spacing between paragraphs.   152

6. Enumerated items are single-spaced with either double or single spacing   167
separating individual items.   173

DS

Because of its uncomplicated format, the simplified memorandum can be pro-   188
cessed easily on microcomputers and other word processing equipment that   203
utilizes standard-size continuous-feed stationery or plain paper. It can also be   219
used for short messages on half sheets; but automated offices, including the   234
U.S. Government, seem to be moving rapidly toward standard 8 1/2- by 11-inch   250
stationery and plain paper for word processing operations.   261

DS

If I can be of further assistance, please let me know what I can do to help you.   277

TS

MRS. SUSAN RANDALL, MANAGER OF TECHNICAL SERVICES   287

TS

xx   288

Prepare documents

Problem 1
Boxed table

full sheet; exact vertical center; DS body of table; 10 spaces between columns; insert vertical rules

				words
PHOTOCOPIER RENTAL PLAN				4
Effective January 1, 19-- Through December 31, 19--				14

Model	Monthly Charge	Copy Allowance	Excess Copy Charge	
				26 / 38 / 42 / 47 / 59
3170	$100	3,090	.0121	63
3405	176	5,150	.0135	66
5455	210	7,725	.0093	69
2480	150	10,300	.0051	73
3695	227	10,300	.0051	77
8280	443	41,200	.0083	81
9290	451	51,500	.0051	85
9495	529	61,500	.0043	89
9594	637	81,500	.0041	93
				105

Problem 2
Boxed table

full sheet; reading position; DS body of table; 6 spaces between columns; insert vertical rules

Problem 3
Boxed table

If time permits, repeat Problem 2 with 8 spaces between columns.

				words
SCHEDULED PERSONAL PROPERTY ENDORSEMENT				8
Policy 39-549718				11

Article	Number	Value Per Piece	Insurance	
				23 / 35 / 42 / 54
Teaspoons	18	$ 86	$1,548	58
Dinner knives	12	90	1,080	62
Dinner forks	12	122	1,464	66
Serving spoons	4	277	1,108	71
Salad forks	12	97	1,164	75
Soup spoons	12	115	1,380	79
Meat fork	1	177	177	82
				94
Total			$7,921	96
				108

66a ▶ 5
Preparatory practice

each line 3 times SS (slowly, faster, slowly); DS between 3-line groups; repeat selected lines as time permits

alphabet	1	A few lazy boys parked next to the back hedge and quickly jumped.
figures	2	A new profit of $21,894,650 from a gross of $297,807,319 set a record.
fig/sym	3	Order #3950-8 (dated 6/14) must be shipped to Wells & Wall by June 27.
fluency	4	Their half of the map did make big problems for me and for the ensign.

| 1 | 2 | 3 | 4 | 5 | 6 | 7 | 8 | 9 | 10 | 11 | 12 | 13 | 14 |

66b ▶ 10
Review/apply communication skills: punctuation

full sheet; 1" top margin; 74-space line

Keyboard and format as directed on p. 129.

Key: 1b. thirty–seven 2b. short–term 3b. first–, second–, third–class 4b. time–out 5b. s–e–p–a–r–a–t–e

Use a hyphen
1. To join compound numbers from twenty-one to ninety-nine that are typed as words.
2. To join compound adjectives to the noun which is modified, unless the adjective is in the comparative or superlative form.
3. To join two or more compound words or figures with a common base which they modify as a unit. Use suspended hyphens rather than repeating the base word.
4. To form certain compound nouns.
5. To indicate the spelling of a word or a name.

review 1a. Forty-two applicants responded to the newspaper advertisement.
apply b. About thirty seven executives attended the conference.

review 2a. The worn-out notebook was discarded.
apply b. I obtained a short term loan at a reasonable rate of interest.

review 3a. You respond to the items on page 55 with—one- or two-word answers.
apply b. Harry checked the rates on first, second, and third class mail.

review 4a. The head bolts must be torqued to approximately 75 foot-pounds.
apply b. The officials called time out.

review 5a. The preferred spelling is e-e-r-i-e.
apply b. Many people have difficulty spelling the word separate.

66c ▶ 35
Format special messages

Problem 1
Telegraphic message

plain sheet; 2" top margin; 60-space line; DS message; proofread and correct errors

words

PHONED TELEGRAM | 3
TS

Telegram | 5
DS
July 5, 19--, 3:15 p.m. | 10
DS
Mrs. Clare Payne | 13
Duffy and Larue Real Estate | 19
1500 Main Street | 22
Houston, TX 77002-5519 | 27
Phone: (713) 555-4562 | 31
DS
Harry E. Clifford agrees to sell to Gail D. Lenehan property at 10607 Glenway | 47

Drive, Houston, Texas, with cash down of $85,000 and loan of $140,000. Total | 63

sales price of $225,000. Closing date of September 3, 19--, and other terms as | 79

agreed. | 80
DS
Harry E. Clifford | 83
DS
xx | 84

Problem 2
4-column table
with horizontal rulings

full sheet; reading position; DS body of table; decide spacing between columns

Problem 3
3-column table
with horizontal rulings

If time permits, repeat Problem 1; SS the columnar items; decide spacing between columns.

				words
VAN CONFERENCE CENTER				4
Capacity Based on Seating Arrangement				11
				23
				35
Room	Conference	Schoolroom	Auditorium	42
				54
Birch	24	80	150	56
Cedar	18	60	110	58
Maple	18	60	110	60
Oak	12	40	65	62
Pecan	40	120	225	64
Pine	36	100	185	66
Walnut	20	70	135	69
				81

79

79a ▶ 5

Preparatory practice

each line 3 times SS (slowly, faster, slowly); DS between 3-line groups; repeat selected lines as time permits

alphabet	1	Jaklynne characterized Quemoy as a very exotic paradise with big fish.
figure	2	Our income for 1975 was only $26,870; our income for 1985 was $43,275.
direct reach	3	Johnny brought a great present for Mary--a brown and grey hunting bag.
fluency	4	Eight men pay the city for the right to hang their own signs downtown.

| 1 | 2 | 3 | 4 | 5 | 6 | 7 | 8 | 9 | 10 | 11 | 12 | 13 | 14 |

79b ▶ 10

Preapplication drill: format a boxed table

half sheet, long side up; 1½" top margin; 16 spaces between columns

To insert vertical rulings, remove the page from the typewriter; use a pen with black ink and draw vertical lines at the midpoint between columns.

PURCHASE AGREEMENT--TRANSPARENCIES

(Price Based on Boxes Ordered)

Order Number	50-99	100+
3R20341 CL	$22.85	$19.95
3R87034 RD	24.55	21.50

66c, continued

Problem 2
Night letter

plain sheet; 2″ top margin; 60–space line; DS message; proofread and correct errors

Problem 3
Night letter

Format the same message used in Problem 1 as a night letter, using the current date and **6:10 p.m.** Substitute the words **Night Letter** for **Telegram** in the heading and at the left margin. Address the night letter to:

Mr. Charles Kuo
Kuo and Ryan Properties, Inc.
1802 Vine Street
Houston, TX 77002-4328
Phone: (713) 555-2800

Total words: 85

NIGHT LETTER   2
                                    TS
Night Letter   4
          DS
August 13, 19--, 5:30 p.m.   9
                      DS
Ms. Wendy Peters, Director   14
American Business School   19
362 Robert Street   22
St. Paul, MN 55115-3789   27
                      DS
Our competitors envy our success. We take their profits and give them to you.   43

Many managers of area businesses have already switched to Vendors Ex-   60

change. The reasons are obvious! With the Vendors Exchange program you get   75

the advantages of keeping all your vending profits; fast, dependable local pro-   91

duct and repair service; and new vending equipment with no investment. Call   106

555-8100 for additional information.   113
                              DS
Peter Paulos, President   118
Vendors Exchange   121
                    DS
xx   122

Problem 4
Postal card (LM p. 147)

1 Format the message side of a postal card as illustrated in the first model at the right.

2 Format the return address and the receiver's address as shown in the second model at the right.

Problem 5
Postal card (LM p. 147)

1 Compose a response to the postal card in Problem 4.

2 Format the proper receiver's address and return address.

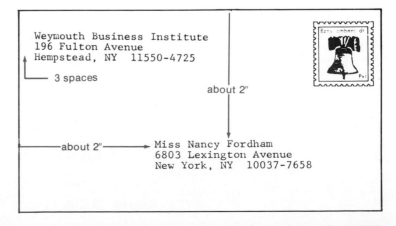

TS
September 23, 19--
└─ 3 spaces   TS
Dear Miss Fordham
                    DS
We are sorry that you were unable to keep your
appointment. We realize that circumstances beyond your control may have prevented your visit.
                                            DS
We would like to extend an invitation to visit
with us at a time convenient to you. Please
visit or call us to arrange a suitable time for
your informal tour.
                              DS
Miss Susan Wong, Admissions Director

Weymouth Business Institute
196 Fulton Avenue
Hempstead, NY 11550-4725
└─ 3 spaces

about 2″

├──── about 2″ ────→ Miss Nancy Fordham
                      6803 Lexington Avenue
                      New York, NY 10037-7658

78a ▶ 5
Preparatory practice

each line 3 times
SS (slowly, faster, slowly); DS between 3-line groups; repeat selected lines as time permits

alphabet	1	Joaquin bought a new executive desk and credenza from Polly last week.
figure	2	Write a $382 check for Invoice 4109 and a $578 check for Invoice 3926.
combination response	3	I may go with Lulu to visit the great estate on the rich reserve land.
fluency	4	Andy may pay for half of the bus, and the city may pay for half of it.

| 1 | 2 | 3 | 4 | 5 | 6 | 7 | 8 | 9 | 10 | 11 | 12 | 13 | 14 |

78b ▶ 10
Preapplication drill: horizontal rulings

Format the drill on a half sheet, long side up, according to the instructions given at the right; leave a 1½″ top margin; 12 spaces between columns; DS column entries.

If time permits, space down 4 lines and repeat the drill with 8 spaces between columns.

Horizontal rulings
Center the heading; DS; determine placement of the columns; set left and right margin stops; type first line of double ruling; operate the variable line spacer and move cylinder slightly forward; (electronic typewriters may have an index key that will space up ¼ line); type the second ruling. Type the body of the table. After the last item in columns has been typed, SS and type a single ruling. DS and type the footnote.

Drill

NEW PRODUCTS*
DS

Model	Release Date
X3836	June 2, 19--
X6837	July 7, 19--

*Low-Volume Division

78c ▶ 35
Prepare documents

Problem 1
3-column table
with horizontal rulings

full sheet; exact vertical center; DS body of table; 10 spaces between columns

SMITH COUNTY

Sales Tax Revenue Bonds, Series A

Principal Amount	Maturity	Interest Rate
$2,235,000	1985	8.25
2,415,000	1986	8.50
2,625,000	1987	8.75
2,850,000	1988	9.00
3,110,000	1989	9.25
3,395,000	1990	9.50
3,720,000	1991	9.75
4,080,000	1992	10.00
4,490,000	1993	10.25
4,950,000	1994	10.50
5,470,000	1995	10.75

Source: Smith County Auditor's Records.

words
2
9
21
33
40
52
56
59
62
65
68
71
74
78
82
86
90
102
110

67a ▶ 5
Preparatory practice

each line 3 times SS (slowly, faster, slowly); DS between 3-line groups; repeat selected lines as time permits.

alphabet 1 Excessive assignments will often jeopardize both joy and zeal quickly.

fig/sym 2 Item #30254 (pens) will cost Mack & Fox $17.89 each, less 6% discount.

shift key 3 Tommy attended Lake College; Marianne, Cooke; and Bobbie, Maine State.

fluency 4 The firms may go to the big city panel with the problem of the profit.

| 1 | 2 | 3 | 4 | 5 | 6 | 7 | 8 | 9 | 10 | 11 | 12 | 13 | 14 |

67b ▶ 10
Improve skill transfer

60-space line; two 1' writings on each line; additional 1' writings on each line for which your *gwam* was less than on Line 1

words

straight copy 1 Executives today frequently confront the question of ethics. 12

script 2 *New firms need capital to get started in the business world.* 12

statistical 3 In 1989, the group will employ 43,627 workers in 105 cities. 12

rough draft 4 successfull businesses set real goals so they can succeed. 12
definite *in order to thrive.*

67c ▶ 35
Format schedules

plain sheets

Problem 1
Agenda of meeting

1 Format and type the agenda, centering it both vertically and horizontally. Leave 4 spaces between columns.

2 Use spaced leaders between columns.

3 Correct errors as you type.

Typing leaders: After the first item in the first column, space once and then alternate a period and a space to a point 2 or 3 spaces short of the next column. Note whether you type the periods on odd or even line–of–writing numbers; align sub–sequent rows by starting them in a like manner.

APEX MANUFACTURING COMPANY	5
Agenda for Meeting of the Board of Directors	14
April 30, 19--	17
1. Call to Order . . . . Wilma Jackson	30
2. Reading and Approval of Minutes . . . . Alice A. William	44
3. Reports of Officers	49
President . . . . Wilma Jackson	61
Vice President, Marketing . . . . Matt L. Lyle	73
Vice President, Research and Development . . . . Lupita Diaz	84
Vice President, Finance . . . . Jane E. Allerton	96
Vice President, Manufacturing . . . . Arthur I. Cooper	108
4. Report of Special Actions	114
Status of the amendment to the Certificate	122
of Incorporation to eliminate preemptive	130
rights . . . . Alice A. William	142
5. Dividend Declaration . . . . Jane E. Allerton	156
6. New Business	159
Review of Long-Range Objectives . . . . Lupita Diaz	170
7. Adjournment . . . . Wilma Jackson	183

DS ... DS ... TS ... DS ... SS

Problem 2
4-column table

full sheet; reading position; DS
body of table; 4 spaces
between columns

words

SALES REVENUE — 3

(Gross Sales for Third Quarter, 19--) — 10

Region	Arcade	Home Video	Microcomputer	
Alaska/Canada	$ 16,123.70	$ 32,819.06	$ 102,835.42	33
Great Lakes	19,483.42	26,804.55	108,384.52	41
Gulf States	17,467.97	30,279.64	112,742.93	4S
Islands	9,876.54	11,310.82	78,315.36	56
Mid-Atlantic	21,739.40	34,619.37	121,327.52	64
Midwest	18,290.41	31,214.83	118,369.02	71
Mountain Plains	10,746.35	14,987.35	90,472.41	79
New England	15,376.31	27,493.20	109,346.74	87
Northeast	22,947.63	32,617.49	120,983.45	94
Northwest	12,593.48	17,439.94	98,765.31	101
Southeast	20,639.27	33,949.31	132,659.52	108
Southwest	14,329.60	17,383.63	96,418.33	122
Totals	$199,614.08	$310,919.19	$1,290,620.53	130

Problem 3
4-column table

full sheet; reading position; DS
body of table; decide spacing
between columns

Problem 4
4-column table

It time permits, repeat Problem 3
with different spacing between
columns.

words

Incentive Compensation Statement — 7

(Salary Suplement for Third Quarter) — 14

center column heading

Sales Rep~~t~~ *resentative*	Budgeted Units	Perf~~ormance~~	Commission	
DS Peter Perkins	[128	[225%	$ [8,575.70	42
Margaret Walters	115	212%	DS 8,080.21	48
Tom Fernandez	130	167%	6,365.07	54
Sharon Kinser	140	156%	5,945.82	60
Doris Dunlop	120	(3)4%	5,107.30	65
Richard ~~Tom~~ Robinson	110	127%	4,840.50	71
(Lynn Ligon	116	63ø%	2,401.19)	87
Timothy Kurtis	90	104%	3,963.~~00~~ 88	77
Yang Shih	117	85%	3,239.71	82
Jeannette Alexander	142	35%	1,334.00	96
DS Total Paid			DS $49,853.38	100

67c, continued

Problem 2
Appointment schedule

1 Format and type the schedule with 2" top margin and 1½" side margins.

2 Center the following heading in this way:

APPOINTMENT SCHEDULE
FOR
WILMA JACKSON
DS
April 29, 19--
TS

SS appointment listings; DS below each listing.

10:15 a.m.	Paul J. Fatseas, First National Bank, and Jane Allerton,	24
	Vice President, Finance. Discuss details of financing new bonds.	37
12:15 p.m.	American Manufacturing Council. Luncheon meeting at	50
	Copley Hotel.	53
2:00 p.m.	Janet Mitchell, Mitchell Advertising Agency. Discuss adver-	67
	tising campaign for next year.	73
3:00 p.m.	Arthur Cooper, Vice President, Manufacturing. Discuss pro-	86
	duction schedules for next fiscal year and the staffing	97
	plan.	98
5:00 p.m.	Lupita Diaz, Vice President, Research and Development. Dis-	112
	cuss topic for speech at next month's luncheon meeting.	123

68

68a ▶ 5

Preparatory practice

each line 3 times SS (slowly, faster, slowly); DS between 3-line groups; repeat selected lines as time permits

alphabet 1 Five zebras will quietly make appearances in this dark, exotic jungle.

figures 2 Crowds of 98,194, 94,785, and 97,360 totaled a record high of 290,339.

fig/sym 3 Invoices 5423-9 and 5680-1 totaled $709.13 and were paid by Ford & Co.

fluency 4 The workbox with the worn handle is also on the big chair by the girl.

| 1 | 2 | 3 | 4 | 5 | 6 | 7 | 8 | 9 | 10 | 11 | 12 | 13 | 14 |

68b ▶ 35

Format a news release and minutes of a meeting

plain sheets

Problem 1
News release

2" top margin; 1½" side margins; DS the body; indent ¶s

words

March 1, 19-- — 3
DS

FOR IMMEDIATE RELEASE — 7
TS

(Center) GENERAL PETROLEUM MAKES ACQUISITION — 14
TS

(¶ 1) The General Petroleum Company announced today that it had reached — 27
definitive terms to buy the American Oil Company of Texas for nearly $1.2 — 42
billion in cash and various securities. — 50

(¶ 2) Analysts estimate that General Petroleum will be buying American Oil — 64
Company's domestic oil and gas reserves for about $29 a barrel, or roughly 40 — 79
percent less than the cost of drilling for it. — 88

(¶ 3) The complex provisions of the deal call for General Petroleum, the nation's — 103
second-largest oil company, to pay an average of $45 a share for the 25.4 million — 119
shares of American Oil, a small oil and gas company. According to Mickey M. — 134
Phillips, President of General Petroleum, the transaction is in keeping with the — 150
long-term objectives of the company because it improves the company's — 164
reserves and production position in the United States. — 175
DS

(Center) ### — 176

76c, continued

Problem 3
3-column table

full sheet; reading position; DS body of table; 12 spaces between Columns 1 and 2 and 6 spaces be–tween Columns 2 and 3

Recall: SS above the 1½″ divider line and DS below it.

TEMPERATURES FOR SELECTED CITIES			7
November 14, 19--			10
City	High	Low	15
Anchorage	40	31	18
Baltimore	48	36	22
Des Moines	30	11	25
Miami	83	70	27
			31
Source: United Press International.			38

77a ▶ 5
Preparatory practice

each line 3 times SS (slowly, faster, slowly); DS between 3-line groups; repeat selected lines as time permits

alphabet	1	Max Jarwoski quickly asked if the bank gives to every organized group.
figure	2	Our company printed 6,537,318 books in 1940 and 1,264,827,302 in 1985.
shift lock	3	Do ANACOM and AMS exhibit at either the N-CBEA or the NBEA convention?
fluency	4	Susie and Alan spent their profit on a field and may dig a lake on it.

| 1 | 2 | 3 | 4 | 5 | 6 | 7 | 8 | 9 | 10 | 11 | 12 | 13 | 14 |

77b ▶ 10
Preapplication drill: use dollar signs

Format the drill on a half sheet, long side up, according to the instructions given at the right; leave a 1″ top margin; 12 spaces between columns; DS column entries.

If time permits, space down 4 lines and repeat the drill with 8 spaces between columns.

Placing dollar signs and totals

Place a dollar sign before the first amount in a column and before the total. Align the dollar sign 1 space to the left of the longest amount in the column. Indicate a total with a line under the column. DS above the total figure. Indent the word "Total" 5 spaces from the left margin.

Drill

Flight costs	$ 685.67
Per diem allowance	1,021.34
Other expenses	196.20
Total	$1,903.21

77c ▶ 35
Prepare documents

Problem 1
3-column table

half sheet, long side up; DS body of table; 14 spaces be–tween columns

RESIDENTIAL SALES			4
MARCH 3-10, 19--			7
Listing Agent	Seling Agent	Price	19
Burge	Hutto	$85,900	23
Davis	Welch	104,575	27
Jeansonne	Parker	97,800	31
Le Beau	Willis	72,580	35

---

words

Problem 2
Minutes of a meeting

1½″ top margin; 1″ side
margins; SS; indented ¶s

Indent listed data 5 spaces
from left margin.

SPECIAL MEETING OF BOARD OF DIRECTORS   8
BAY STATE TECHNICAL CORPORATION   14
DS

June 30, 19--   17
TS

Those present, being all of the Directors of Bay State Technical Corpora-   31
tion, today formally waived notice of the special meeting to be held June 30 and   47
by their action acknowledged the following votes as and for the action of the   63
Board of Directors of the Corporation: 71
DS

Upon motion duly made and seconded, it was unanimously   82

VOTED: To accept today the resignation of Sam Najjar as Director of said   98
corporation.   100

VOTED: That the President and Treasurer have the authority to execute   115
a lease for the premises at 688 Highland Avenue in Needham,   127
Massachusetts, for the continued operation of the corporation.   139
DS

There being no further business to accomplish, it was then unanimously   153
DS

VOTED: To adjourn.   158
Adjourned accordingly.   163
A true record.   166

(Return 4 times. Begin at center.)

170

Gerald J. Johnson, President   176

68c ▶ 10

Check communication skills

full sheet; 1″ top margin;
74-space line

1 Cover the answer key below.
Check your answers when you
have finished the exercise.

2 Read the sentences at the right,
noting errors in hyphen, comma,
and semicolon usage.

3 Format and type the sentences
as directed on p. 129.

Key: 1. spelling, pronunciation, **2.**
December; **3.** COMPUTERS, Scheid,
4. over–the–counter **5.** 1984, **6.**
state–of–the–art **7.** late; however,
15– 20–minute **8.** people, passion;

1. Use your dictionary for spelling pronunciation and definitions.
2. Her first payment was made in December the second payment is late.
3. PERSONAL COMPUTERS written by Sue Scheid is now in the bookstore.
4. The over the counter cough syrup provided relief for my cold.
5. In 1984 45 students were enrolled in this microcomputer course.
6. The course on microcomputers had state of the art equipment.
7. I was late however I still had a 15 to 20 minute wait in line.
8. To some people football is a passion and Hal is one of those people.

69a ▶ 5

Preparatory practice

each line 3 times SS
(slowly, faster,
slowly); DS between
3-line groups; repeat
selected lines as time
permits

alphabet   1   The five dozen quarts of blackberry and grape juice mixture were mine.

fig/sym   2   Terms of 2/10, n/30 were listed on Invoice #416-9758 from Moore & Son.

long words   3   Marianne, Constantine, and Bernadette are outstanding representatives.

fluency   4   The theory may make big problems if they both fight for the amendment.

| 1 | 2 | 3 | 4 | 5 | 6 | 7 | 8 | 9 | 10 | 11 | 12 | 13 | 14 |

69

Preapplication drill: center columns

Format the drill on a half sheet, long side up, according to the instructions given above the drill; leave 1″ top margin; 12 spaces between Columns 1 and 2 and 8 spaces between Columns 2 and

If time permits, space down 4 times on the same sheet and repeat the drill.

Varying intercolumn space

Tables with long description columns look better if more space is left between the description column and the next column than between the remaining columns. If a description item is exceptionally long, break it into 2 or more lines, indenting the second and subsequent lines of the entry 3 spaces. SS these lines. To determine placement of the tables, count the spaces in the longest line of the column, whether that line is the first line of an entry or any subsequent line of the entry, including 3 spaces for indention. To center column headings, choose the longest line in each column, as you have done for single-line entries.

Drill					
Effective Writing Techniques for Executive Secretaries SS			165		92%
Productivity Under Pressure DS	12 spaces		115	8 spaces	64%
Women in Management DS			131		73%

Prepare documents

Problem 1
3-column table

full sheet; exact vertical center; DS body of table; 16 spaces between Columns 1 and 2 and 10 spaces between Columns 2 and 3

LEAGUE ATTENDANCE RECORD

19-- Season

Team	Average	Highest	words
			5
			7
			14
Bay City Badgers	28,321	31,895	20
Big Apple City Slickers	29,174	32,386	27
Crawfish Country Cajuns	38,762	46,971	34
Everglades Froggers	39,383	42,645	40
Mississippi River Rats	31,673	32,347	47
Wild West Indians	30,694	40,765	53

Problem 2
3-column table

full sheet; exact vertical center; DS body of table; 12 spaces between Columns 1 and 2 and 8 spaces between Columns 2 and 3

FUNVISION VIDEO GAMES
(Games Scheduled for Release in October)

Game	Stock Number	Release Date	words
			4
			12
			23
Big Bad BG	HV7624	October 23	28
Bronco Bull Riding	HV6187	October 15	35
Night Flier	HV9080	October 2	40
Outer Space Satellite			44
Launch and Track	HV2013	October 29	50
Weeping Weirdos	HV5189	October 17	56
Zaparoo	HV8765	October 8	60

69b ▶ 45

Format an itinerary and a speech

plain sheets

Problem 1
Itinerary

center vertically and horizontally; DS body; 4 spaces between
columns

ITINERARY FOR WILMA JACKSON
June 10 to June 28

DATE	FROM	DEPART	FLIGHT	TO	ARRIVE
6/10	Boston	8:00 a.m.	AA/147*	Pittsburgh	9:33 a.m.
6/12	Pittsburgh	3:30 p.m.	AL/189	Philadelphia	4:32 p.m.
6/13	Philadelphia	5:00 p.m.	AL/204**	Chicago	6:05 p.m.
6/15	Chicago	8:30 a.m.	DL/23*	Cincinnati	10:36 a.m.
6/17	Cincinnati	11:00 a.m.	DL/190	St. Louis	11:10 a.m.
6/18	St. Louis	4:15 p.m.	UN/132**	Houston	6:05 p.m.
6/19	Houston	6:00 p.m.	EA/183**	New Orleans	7:03 p.m.
6/20	New Orleans	4:25 p.m.	EA/153**	Miami	7:04 p.m.
6/21	Miami	5:15 p.m.	DL/125**	Washington	7:26 p.m.
6/22	Washington	8:00 p.m.	EA/241	New York	8:45 p.m.
6/24	New York	7:30 a.m.	AA/162*	Atlanta	9:35 a.m.
6/26	Atlanta	11:45 a.m.	DL/127	Denver	12:35 p.m.
6/27	Denver	10:45 a.m.	CO/320	Kansas City	1:09 p.m.
6/28	Kansas City	3:50 p.m.	AL/124**	Boston	9:50 p.m.

*Breakfast flight
**Dinner flight

words

	words
ITINERARY FOR WILLMA JACKSON	5
June 10 to June 18	9
DATE FROM DEPART FLIGHT TO ARRIVE	22
6/10 Boston 8:00 a.m. AA/147* Pittsburg 9:33 a.m.	31
6/12 Pittsburg 3:30 p.m. AL/189 Phila 4:32 p.m.	41
6/13 Phila 5:00 p.m. AL/204** Chicago 6:05 p.m.	51
6/15 Chicago 8:30 p.m. DL/23* Cincinati 10:36 a.m.	61
6/17 Cincinati 11:00 a.m. DL/190 St. Louis 11:10 a.m.	71
6/18 St. Louis 4:15 p.m. UN/132** Houston 6:05 p.m.	81
6/19 Houston 6:00 p.m. EA/183** N Orleans 7:03 p.m.	91
6/20 N Orleans 4:24 p.m. EA/153** Miami 7:04 p.m.	101
6/21 Miami 5:15 p.m. DL/126** Washington 7:26 p.m.	110
6/22 Washington 8:00 p.m. EA/241 New York 8:45 a.m.	119
6/24 New York 7:30 a.m. AA/162** Atlanta 9:35 a.m.	128
6/26 Atlanta 11:45 a.m. DL/127 Denver 12:35 p.m.	137
6/27 Denver 10:45 a.m. CO/230 Kans City 1:09 p.m.	147
6/28 Kans City 3:50 p.m. AL/124** Boston 9:50 p.m.	157
*Breakfast flight	160
**Dinner flight	163

Problem 2
2-column table with main and column headings

half sheet, long side up; DS body of table; 16 spaces between col–umns

		words
TELEPHONE DIRECTORY CHANGES		6
	TS	
Employee	Telephone Number	16
	DS	
David Yoshino	787-4390	20
Maria LaGanga	251-6049	24
Jack Ruthowsky	384-5107	29
Anna Sedgwick	292-4087	34
Diane Wilson	318-6569	38

Problem 3
3-column table with main, sec-ondary, and column headings

full sheet; reading position; DS body of table; 10 spaces between columns

Note: To find reading position, find the top margin for exact center. Then subtract two lines.

			words
AVOYELLES PARISH OIL DISCOVERY			6
	DS		
November, 19--			9
	TS		
Company	Location	Depth	17
		DS	
Gravel Operations	Sec. 30-4N-4E	6,801	24
Jeffco Exploration	Sec. 22-1N-2W	5,985	31
Martin and Martin, Inc.	Sec. 20-2N-6E	7,448	39
Smith and Associates	Sec. 11-4N-3E	6,495	47
Long and Davis	Sec. 16-5N-3E	5,848	53
Multi-Service Drilling	Sec. 29-5N-3E	7,510	61

76a ▶ 5

Preparatory practice

each line 3 times SS (slowly, faster, slowly); DS between 3-line groups; repeat selected lines as time permits

alphabet 1 Janice was amazed at how quickly both experts verified the gains made.

figure 2 Please dial 253-8901 and ask for Extension 476 before 10:45 on May 23.

space bar 3 Jan may cut work and go down to the big city to fix the auto for them.

fluency 4 The town may risk an audit if it spent the profit on a social problem.

| 1 | 2 | 3 | 4 | 5 | 6 | 7 | 8 | 9 | 10 | 11 | 12 | 13 | 14 |

69b, continued

Problem 2
Speech

1½″ top and side margins; DS the ¶s; DS twice between ¶s; indent ¶s 5 spaces

1 Place the title **RESULTS OF THIS YEAR'S OPERATIONS** a TS above the text.

2 Number the second page on Line 4 at the right margin and start the text for that page on Line 7.

3 Correct errors as you work.

words
in heading 7

Thanks for coming to this annual stockholder's meeting
you attending *a* 19

of Apex Manufacturing Co. I'm going to speak very briefly
(sp) *am* *a* 32

about the results of some of the inroads we've made in the
that our company has 46

passed 12 months.
past 49

Durring this year, advances in technology have gone
continued 60

at a rabid pace, so that we can offer to our clients greater
with the result that we are able to 76

in productivity at smaller cost. This trend has led to
lower 87

some expansion of our customers despite a general down-
substantial *base,* 100

turn in the economy.
104

But, this economic worry very likely will keep on.
However, *uncertainty* *persist.* 116

One factor in it is sharp changes in foriegn currance rates.
this uncertainty 130

Our gross income from rentals has been affected by the pres-
adversely 145

ent exchange rates, but still we have not benefited from
and yet 156

depreciaiton because it's figured at historiacal exchange
that is 168

rates. In addition, gross profit margins on both sales and
180

rentals of our products somewhat have been eroded by our
191

big expenditures for manufacturing faculties.
major *facilities.* 201

But then, our big investment in additional items and
On the other hand, our substantial *capacity* 216

our development of several new chanels of distrabution let
allow 228

the company meet the needs of its consumers more quickly.
to *customers* *efficiently.* 242

This ability to provide greater client satisfaction
254

will cause an enduring trend of much growth in business vol-
assure *steady improvement* 264

ume and financial performance in the comming year.
274
DS twice

Thank you for your attention. And now, Jane
283

Allerton, Vice President for Finance, will speak to you
294

about the financial outlook of Apex Manufacturing.
314

LEVEL FOUR
Formatting/typing tables, forms, and reports

In Level 4, you will continue to build skill in keyboarding and in formatting communications. Emphasis is placed on communications containing statistical copy. You will learn to prepare tables with special features; frequently used business forms, including purchase requisitions, purchase orders, invoices, inventory forms, and statements of account; technical reports; and employment communications.

In addition, you will continue to improve your communication skills and your ability to type from straight-copy, script, rough-draft, and statistical copy.

It is especially important that you learn to design and format many different kinds of business communications and that you learn to use your judgment when you are not given specific directions. In the next level, you will be asked to apply these skills in a variety of office situations.

Measure skill on administrative communications

Time schedule:

		words
Assembling materials ...	3'	
Timed production	25'	
Final check; compute		
n-pram	7'	

Problem 1
Executive-size letter
(LM p. 149)

block style, open punctuation; date on Line 16; 1" side margins; proofread; correct errors

	words
June 30, 19-- | Ms. Dee Norton | 514 Culver Hill Drive | St. Louis, MO 63119-5768 |	16
Dear Ms. Norton	21
(¶ 1) Your "Ticket to Progress" is enclosed! Please use this ticket to attend	36
Multimedia Corporation's First Annual Computer Show to be held at St. Louis	51
Civic Auditorium. We have scheduled presentations on computer applications	66
for small businesses, exhibits and displays, and even opportunities to operate	82
the latest equipment.	86
(¶ 2) Do plan to attend the Computer Show--it's the entertaining, informative	100
way to learn more about the small business computers that will increase your	115
efficiency.	117
(¶ 3) See you at the Show!	121
Sincerely | Dan Kelly | Director, New Business Programs | xx | Enclosure	135

Problem 2
Simplified memo

plain sheet; 1½" top margin; 1" side margins

Format/type the copy shown at the right as a simplified memo from **Eric Shimmel, Training Supervisor**. Date the memo **June 30**; direct it to **Janice Fox, Word Processing Supervisor**; use **SEMINAR/DEMONSTRATION FOR WORD PROCESSING STAFF** as the subject. Proofread; correct errors.

	words
heading	20
(¶ 1) Midwest Electronics has agreed to conduct a seminar for all members of	34
our word processing staff. The seminar will be presented twice: once on	49
July 14 at 1:30 p.m.; again on July 21 at 9:30 a.m.	59
(¶ 2) New equipment and new software packages for the processing of informa-	73
tion will be demonstrated, and new automated systems will be presented and	88
analyzed in terms of our current and future word processing needs.	101
(¶ 3) You should divide your work force into two groups and assign one group to	116
the July 14 session; the other group, to the July 21 session. In this way, total	132
work stoppage in your unit can be avoided.	140
closing lines	147

Problem 3
Night letter

plain sheet; proofread; correct errors

	words
NIGHT LETTER | Night Letter | November 28, 19--, 7:45 p.m. | Mr. Elbert L. Cox |	15
325 Cameron Road | Willow Grove, PA 19090-2372	24
If you act quickly, you can receive a complimentary copy of our booklet FINAN-	39
CIAL ALTERNATIVES FOR TODAY. As an investor, you will be interested in	53
finding out what we at Ferrier, McAdoo & Hancock think are timely investment	68
opportunities. We have 25 years of expertise in all areas of finance, and we	84
would like to share this knowledge with you. Call 800-555-7300 to receive this	100
important information.	104
Miss Stephanie Gutierrez, Investment Counselor | Ferrier, McAdoo & Hancock |	119
xx	120

74c, continued

Problem 1
Letter with subject line
(LM p. 169)

modified block, mixed punctuation; indented ¶s; center subject
line; address envelope

September 15, 19-- | Mr. Robert Kelsey | 300 East Joppa Road | Towson, MD   14

21204-5798 | Dear Mr. Kelsey: | WELCOME RECEPTION FOR NEW MEMBERS   27

(¶ 1) The Community Action Association of Towson is pleased to invite you, as a   42
nominee, to our reception for new members. The reception will be held at the   58
Meridian Hotel at 5:30 p.m. on Thursday, October 9. This function will give you   74
an orientation to the club as well as an opportunity to meet other new members.   90

(¶ 2) We are enclosing a reply card on which you may indicate whether you will   105
attend. Our President, Marie Carpenter, joins me in urging you to come to this   121
important gathering. (97)   125

Very sincerely, | Richard Johnson | Membership Director | xx | Enclosure   139/**151**

Problem 2
Agenda for Meeting

plain sheet; 1½" top margin; 1"
side margins

NATIONAL PUBLICATIONS COMPANY   6

Agenda for Meeting of Board of Directors   14

Current date   17

1. Call to Order . . . . Nicholas E. Spitznagel   30

2. Reading and Approval of Minutes . . . . James C. Weber   42

3. Reports of Officers
    President . . . . Nicholas E. Spitznagel   58
    Vice President, Publications . . . . Marie Ann Ford   68
    Vice President, Marketing . . . . Charles Sauder   79
    Vice President, Finance . . . . Virginia L. Reed   89

4. Adjournment . . . . Nicholas E. Spitznagel   102

Problem 3
Half-page memorandum
(LM p. 171)

If a form is not available, prepare
the memo on a plain half sheet.

TO: Marsha Kendall FROM: Gerald Fitzsimmons DATE: August 26, 19-- SUB-   10
JECT: Author Conference Travel Plans   16

(¶) My travel plans are to arrive in Columbus at 6:30 p.m. on Sunday, October   31
2. My departure time is 2:20 p.m. on October 5.   41

(¶) I could save $115 by arriving on Saturday instead of Sunday (on the airfare,   56
that is); however, the extra lodging and meals would probably cost at least   71
half of that. I'm not aware of any reason that an extra day there would be   86
beneficial, particularly on a weekend.   94

(¶) I look forward to seeing you and the other authors. We have many new   108
challenges to face in the development of our new edition. xx   120

Problem 4
Business letter

plain paper; block style, open
punctuation

Reformat the letter in Problem 1.
Make the changes given at the right.
Total words: 129

1 Omit the subject line.
2 The meeting will be held on **Wednesday, October 15.**
3 The president of the club is **Howard Wilson.**
4 Miss Kay Boswell is **Membership Director.**

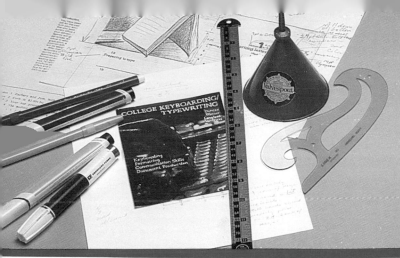

Learning goals

1 To increase basic skill on straight, rough–draft, and script copy.

2 To improve ability to punctuate copy correctly.

3 To refine keyboarding techniques.

Machine adjustments

1 Paper guide at 0.

2 Margins: 70–space line for drills and ¶ writings; as directed for problems.

3 Spacing: SS drills; DS ¶ writings; as directed for problems.

4 Indention: 5 spaces for ¶ writings; as appropriate for problems.

71a ▶ 5

Preparatory practice

each line 3 times SS (slowly, faster, slowly); DS between 3-line groups; repeat selected lines as time permits

For Line 3, beginning at the left margin, set 6 tab stops 10 spaces apart.

alphabet	1	Jagged wreckage will zoom into view quickly before the next stop sign.
fig/sym	2	Order #7066 (shipped July 31) totaled $2,985.40 (with a 9% sales tax).
tab/cap	3	Holly Teddy Carla Flynn Emily Abbot Bernadette
fluency	4	The busy auditor for the eight firms may also handle the formal visit.

| 1 | 2 | 3 | 4 | 5 | 6 | 7 | 8 | 9 | 10 | 11 | 12 | 13 | 14 |

71b ▶ 10

Build speed/ control

1 One 1' writing on the ¶; determine *gwam*.

2 Add 4 *gwam* to your *gwam* in Step 1 for a goal rate. Take another 1' writing on the ¶, try–ing to equal your goal rate.

3 Two 2' writings for speed; determine *gwam*.

4 One 2' writing at this new rate for control; circle errors. Goal: 2 errors or fewer.

Difficulty index

all letters used | Λ | 1.5 si | 5.7 awl | 80% hfw |

	gwam 1'	2'
More people are occupied today with information science than are	13	7	58
working in the huge fields of mining, production, farming, and per-	26	13	65
sonal services. This new job area is based on the creation, movement,	40	20	72
and storage of data. The vast expansion in this field in just the past	55	27	79
ten years has been quite remarkable, and this new growth will bring	68	34	86
about amazing change. We are now in an age in which the ways of com-	82	41	93
municating and learning are changing at a dizzying rate. Astute people	97	48	100
will keep up with this advance.	103	52	103

gwam 1' | 1 | 2 | 3 | 4 | 5 | 6 | 7 | 8 | 9 | 10 | 11 | 12 | 13 | 14 |
2' | 1 | 2 | 3 | 4 | 5 | 6 | 7 |

71c ▶ 9

Improve keyboarding technique

each pair of lines 3 times SS at a controlled rate; DS between 6-line groups

adjacent reaches	1	We quickly realized the proposed posting methods were quite effective.
	2	There are several additional copies of the weekly government booklets.
direct reaches	3	Their branch library must obtain my technical consumer service manual.
	4	My large payment for their many great services was unfortunately lost.
double letters	5	The school committee recommended that my books be shipped immediately.
	6	I am sorry your attached bill was addressed to their account in error.
long words	7	Forty representatives recommended appropriate specifications be added.
	8	We developed additional recommendations on transportation legislation.

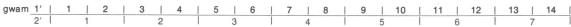

| 1 | 2 | 3 | 4 | 5 | 6 | 7 | 8 | 9 | 10 | 11 | 12 | 13 | 14 |

74a ▶ 5
Preparatory practice

each line 3 times SS (slowly, faster, slowly); DS between 3-line groups; repeat selected lines as time permits

alphabet	1	We will fight to save the complex project and raze the bridge quickly.
fig/sym	2	The last 467 units were reduced 30% ($1,089) and were sold in 25 days.
double letters	3	I recommend a committee meet this summer to take all necessary action.
fluency	4	I may handle the usual forms for the neighbor when he signs the title.

| 1 | 2 | 3 | 4 | 5 | 6 | 7 | 8 | 9 | 10 | 11 | 12 | 13 | 14 |

74b ▶ 10
Measure straight-copy skill

a 5' writing on all ¶s; circle errors; determine *gwam*

Difficulty index

all letters used	A	1.5 si	5.7 awl	80% hfw

gwam 1' | 5'

Managers are necessary in all types of companies. These important · 13 | 3 | 56
positions vary from the operator of a small candy store to the head of · 28 | 6 | 59
the largest manufacturing firm. But managers have many tasks in common. · 42 | 8 | 62
They must plan, organize, direct, control, and coordinate the work of · 56 | 11 | 65
their group. Managers must be able to train people so that they can do · 71 | 14 | 68
their jobs and to motivate them so that they will want to be successful. · 85 | 17 | 71

Of course, in order to do these tasks, managers must have certain · 13 | 20 | 73
skills. Some skills are acquired, and others are a result of natural · 27 | 23 | 76
talent; but all skills are better used once a manager has gotten some · 41 | 25 | 79
experience. Conceptual skills include the ability to see how all the · 55 | 28 | 82
parts of a situation fit together to form a whole. A good manager can · 69 | 31 | 84
mix conceptual skills with technical knowledge related to the work of · 83 | 34 | 87
the specific department. · 88 | 35 | 88

Two other vital areas that a manager must master are human rela- · 13 | 37 | 91
tions and communications. Human relations skill is the ability to inter- · 27 | 40 | 94
act with people. And this job may best be done through the use of good · 42 | 43 | 97
communication skills. All managers must relate to people; and, in trying · 57 | 46 | 100
to get things done through others, they must be able to communicate. · 71 | 49 | 102
The success or failure of managers is affected by their ability to use · 85 | 52 | 105
these skills in daily tasks on the job. · 93 | 53 | 107

gwam 1' | 1 | 2 | 3 | 4 | 5 | 6 | 7 | 8 | 9 | 10 | 11 | 12 | 13 | 14 |
5' | 1 | 2 | 3 |

74c ▶ 35
Measure production on administrative communications

Time schedule

Assembling materials ...... 3'
Timed production .... 25'
Final check; compute
n-pram .... 7'

1 Follow the schedule shown at the left.
2 Arrange the letterhead and memo (LM pp. 169–171), plain sheets, and other supplies for easy handling.
3 When directed to begin, format

and type the problems on page 160 for 25'. Correct errors neatly as you type. Address an envelope for the letter in Problem 1.
4 Proofread and circle uncorrected errors found in final check.
5 Compute n-pram.

71d ▶ 7
Improve skill transfer

a 1' writing on each line; additional 1' writings on each line for which your *gwam* was less than on Line 1

straight copy	1	They must unite many elements to form the right combination.	12
script	2	*Our main objective is to complete the entire job by tonight.*	12
statistical	3	My band includes 97 girls, 168 boys, 350 women, and 294 men.	12
rough draft	4	if we ~~don't try~~ risks we ~~won't get any great~~ opportunities.	12

(Line 4 edits: *seldom take* above "don't try"; *will avoid useful* above "won't get any great")

71e ▶ 7
Improve keyboarding technique

each pair of lines 3 times SS at a controlled rate; DS between 6-line groups

letter response	1	Only after you started as a union steward were you regarded as a czar.
	2	As you see, a water pump you gave him was set up at a site in my area.
word response	3	The problem they wish the formal panel to handle is the key amendment.
	4	I may make a profit when I rush the eighty bushels of rye to the firm.
combi-nation	5	My field of work may entitle me to start to save wages and halt risks.
	6	The rate panel may decree an award when they visit a few of the towns.

| 1 | 2 | 3 | 4 | 5 | 6 | 7 | 8 | 9 | 10 | 11 | 12 | 13 | 14 |

71f ▶ 12
Build script-copy skill

1 One 1' writing on each ¶; circle errors; determine *gwam*.
2 One 5' writing on all ¶s; circle errors; determine *gwam*; compare results with 1' writings.

Difficulty index

all letters used	A	1.5 si	5.7 awl	80% hfw

	gwam 1'	5'

Many of us frequently go through the routine process of driv- — 12 | 2 | 42
ing up to a computerized teller to pick up some extra cash from — 25 | 5 | 45
our neighborhood bank. This phenomenon, a highly innovative — 37 | 7 | 47
feature several years ago, has become a way of life. But it is — 50 | 10 | 50
just one of many interesting banking features that are now — 62 | 12 | 52
being developed. — 65 | 13 | 53

All sorts of new programs are being set up that will allow — 11 | 15 | 55
us to make contact with the electronic transfer system at the — 23 | 18 | 58
bank without our even leaving home. For example, it is now — 35 | 20 | 60
possible by dialing our telephones to transfer funds quickly — 48 | 23 | 62
via a computer. We can also cause financial data and — 59 | 25 | 65
banking instructions to show on our television screens. — 70 | 27 | 67

The development of these new banking features will bring — 11 | 29 | 69
about a great deal of competition among banks to lure us — 23 | 32 | 71
consumers. And the new technology will probably help us in — 35 | 34 | 74
making the choice. We will no doubt be able to adjust our — 47 | 36 | 76
television screens to tell us which bank offers the — 57 | 38 | 78
highest interest rate for savings. — 64 | 40 | 80

73c ▶ 35
Measure production on administrative communications

Time schedule

Assembling materials ...... 3'
Timed production .... 25'
Final check; compute
   n–pram .... 7'

Problem 1
Simplified memo

plain sheet; 1½" top margin, 1" side margins

1 Follow the schedule shown at the left.

2 Arrange the executive–size letterhead (LM p. 167), plain sheets, and other supplies for easy handling.

3 When directed to begin, format and type the problems below for 25'. Correct errors neatly as you type. Address an executive–size envelope.

4 Proofread and circle uncorrected errors found in final check.

5 Compute *n–pram*.

        words

June 15, 19-- | All Employees | RETIREMENT OF ROBERT CARY   11

On June 30, Bob Cary will retire after nearly 45 years of service. For more than   23
25 of those years, Bob has been our Director of Staff Services. Few employees   39
have contributed to our firm in so many varied ways. In recognition of   53
his contributions to the company and his unlimited assistance to so many   68
of us, an informal reception will be held on June 30 at 3:00 p.m. in the main   84
dining room. | J. D. BOBKINS, PERSONNEL DIRECTOR | xx | pc Diana Wash-   98
ington, President   100

Problem 2
Executive-size letter

(LM p. 167) or plain paper cut to size

modified block style; mixed punctuation; address envelope

Current date | Mr. Victor J. Goldberg | 505 King Avenue | Columbus, OH 43201-   16
7528 | Dear Mr. Goldberg: 21

(¶ 1) At Boyd Investment Service, we believe that your retirement should be   35
something you look forward to and not something you worry about. That is why   50
I would like to discuss with you our IRA, Keogh, and Simplified Employee   60
Pension retirement plans.   65

(¶ 2) Now that the tax laws have been changed, almost everyone who has earned   79
income is eligible for one or more of the IRS-approved, tax-deferred retirement   95
plans.   96

(¶ 3) An informative brochure has been mailed to you to acquaint you with the   110
basic facts about our flexible retirement plans. I will contact you after you   126
have had a chance to review the brochure so that we may discuss how you may   141
receive tax relief now and financial security later. (137)   151

Sincerely, | John J. Vanderson | Senior Account Executive | xx   163/175

Problem 3
Minutes of Meeting

plain sheet; 1½" top margin; 1" side margins; use the heading:
  MINUTES OF THE MEETING
OF THE BOARD OF DIRECTORS
        OF
BOSTON BUSINESS COLLEGE

   December 15, 19--

Problem 4
Business letter

Reformat Problem 2 above on a plain full sheet. Use block style and open punctuation.

      in heading   18

    The Thirty-fifth Annual Meeting of the Corporate Members of Boston   21
Business College was held at 3:00 p.m. on Monday, September 28, 19--.   35

    The first order of business for the Corporate Meeting was the election of   50
a Director of the Corporation. Upon motion duly made and seconded, it was   65
unanimously voted: To instruct the Clerk to cast one ballot for the nominated   81
Director, Louis F. Musco, Jr.   87

    The financial reports were discussed, with action delayed until additional   102
information could be made available. There being no further business, the   117
meeting was adjourned at 4:00 p.m.   124

        Respectfully submitted   128

                          135

        Manuel Aguilar, Secretary   140

72a ▶ 5
Preparatory practice

each line 3 times SS (slowly, faster, slowly); DS between 3-line groups; repeat selected lines as time permits

alphabet	1	Haywood may quiz eighty executives on kickbacks from false job prices.
fig/sym	2	Their Policy #856-02 is with Lee & May; wc will be reimbursed $19,437.
adjacent reaches	3	A few new buyers with deposits appeared quickly when the store opened.
fluency	4	A giant penalty may make the firm dismantle the big sign in the field.

| 1 | 2 | 3 | 4 | 5 | 6 | 7 | 8 | 9 | 10 | 11 | 12 | 13 | 14 |

72b ▶ 12
Build straight-copy skill

1 One 1' writing on each ¶; circle errors; determine *gwam*.
2 One 5' writing on all ¶s; circle errors; determine *gwam*; compare results with 1' writings.

Difficulty index

all letters used	A	1.5 si	5.7 awl	80% hfw

gwam 1' | 5'

Owning a home is a goal of many people in our nation today. A com- 13 | 3 | 55
fortable, attractive house is a source of pride and a good investment. 27 | 6 | 58
But home ownership can also be a source of many financial worries. In 41 | 8 | 61
order to make a thoughtful decision about buying a house, you should 55 | 11 | 63
first make a conservative estimate of your dependable monthly income and 70 | 14 | 66
then invest accordingly. 75 | 15 | 67

In selecting a house, as in buying any item that has an extended 13 | 18 | 70
life expectancy, you can choose among older and newer models. In many 27 | 21 | 73
cases, an older house may make more sense. Old residences often pro- 41 | 23 | 75
vide more living space for the same money than newer residences offer. 55 | 26 | 78
On the other hand, a new house generally has fewer big maintenance prob- 69 | 29 | 81
lems than does a house built long ago. It is important to have your 83 | 32 | 84
future home checked by an inspection service before you commit to it. 97 | 35 | 87

But even before you start looking for a house to buy, you must 13 | 37 | 89
first wander through a maze of questions. For example, what is an ac- 27 | 40 | 92
ceptable distance to commute to your job? Is there good transportation 41 | 43 | 95
by bus, train, or a freeway that is not congested at peak hours? Rea- 55 | 46 | 98
sonable property taxes, quality schools, pleasurable shopping, and a low 69 | 49 | 101
crime rate are only a few of the things that you must consider in your 83 | 51 | 104
ultimate decision. 87 | 52 | 104

gwam 1' | 1 | 2 | 3 | 4 | 5 | 6 | 7 | 8 | 9 | 10 | 11 | 12 | 13 | 14 |
5' | 1 | 2 | 3 |

72c ▶ 11
Improve keyboarding technique

each pair of lines 3 times SS at a controlled rate; DS between 6-line groups

adjacent reach	1	We were assured many election polls would open quickly for all voters.
	2	The popular poplar tree was an excellent stop to build a nest quickly.
shift key	3	The Spencer Corporation is now located on South Worthington Boulevard.
	4	The Boston Red Sox will play the New York Yankees in June and October.
direct reach	5	Why must a county library go to a great expense to receive my records?
	6	Why are my treasury funds with minimum account balances charged extra?

| 1 | 2 | 3 | 4 | 5 | 6 | 7 | 8 | 9 | 10 | 11 | 12 | 13 | 14 |

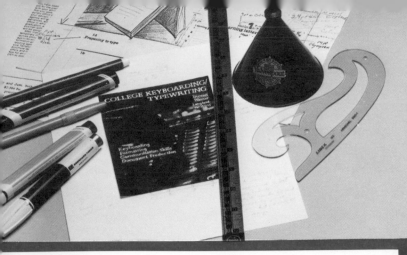

Measurement goals

1 To measure basic skill on straight copy.
2 To measure skill and under–standing in producing business letters, simplified com–munications, and administrative communications covered in lessons of Level 3.

Machine adjustments

1 Paper guide at 0.
2 Margins: 70–space line for drills and ¶ writings; as directed for problems.
3 Spacing: SS drills; DS ¶ writ–ings; as directed for problems.
4 Indention: 5 spaces for ¶ writ–ings; as appropriate for problems.

73a ▶ 5
Preparatory practice

each line 3 times SS (slowly, faster, slowly); DS between 3-line groups; repeat selected lines as time permits

alphabet	1	Karl expects the music for the group's dance review to be quite jazzy.
fig/sym	2	The 5% discount on Invoice #394-86 amounted to a savings of $1,720.36.
direct reach	3	Why must I obtain a maximum-length mortgage and make my interest more?
fluency	4	The firm may pay eight men to cut the hay in a field down by the lake.

| 1 | 2 | 3 | 4 | 5 | 6 | 7 | 8 | 9 | 10 | 11 | 12 | 13 | 14 |

73b ▶ 10
Measure straight-copy skill

a 5' writing on all ¶s; circle errors; de-termine *gwam*

Difficulty index

all letters used	A	1.5 si	5.7 awl	80% hfw

	gwam 1'	5'
Many small businesses fail. Surprisingly, though, many people are	13	3 · 59
still willing to take a chance on starting one of their own. A person	27	5 · 62
who is willing to take the risks necessary to manage a business in order	42	8 · 65
to receive the potential rewards is called an entrepreneur. In a sense,	57	11 · 68
such individuals are pioneers who enjoy each step on the way to achieve-	71	14 · 71
ing objectives that they have determined to be important. This type of	85	17 · 74
person has had a profound impact on shaping our economy and our quality	100	20 · 77
of life.	101	21 · 77
What does it take to start a business venture, and what kinds of	13	23 · 80
people make it work? Obviously, the desire to make money and to be	27	26 · 82
one's own boss are two basic incentives; but these alone are not enough	41	29 · 85
to guarantee success. Two qualifications common to most successful	55	31 · 88
entrepreneurs, whatever field they are in, are an attentiveness to de-	69	34 · 91
tail and a knack for solving day-to-day problems without losing sight	83	37 · 94
of long-range goals.	87	38 · 94
While there is a high risk in organizing any new business, the	13	40 · 97
entrepreneur who is successful is seldom someone who could be con-	26	43 · 100
sidered a gambler. Most gamblers expect to have the odds against them.	40	46 · 103
On the other hand, a clever businessperson sees to it that the odds are	55	49 · 105
as good as possible by getting all of the facts and planning carefully	69	52 · 108
before going ahead. Luck helps, to be sure; but a new business enter-	83	54 · 111
prise depends far more on good ideas and detailed plans.	94	57 · 113

gwam 1' | 1 | 2 | 3 | 4 | 5 | 6 | 7 | 8 | 9 | 10 | 11 | 12 | 13 | 14 |
     5' | 1 | 2 | 3 |

Build rough-draft skill

1 One 1' writing on each ¶; circle errors; determine *gwam*.

2 One 5' writing on both ¶s; circle errors; determine *gwam*; compare results with 1' writings.

Difficulty index

| all letters used | A | 1.5 si | 5.7 awl | 80% hfw |

| | gwam 1' | | 5' |

It could come as a surprize to noone that we inhabit, an — 13 | 3 | 46

age of computers. These mechanisms keep track of the flow of — 25 | 5 | 48

electrical that feeds our cities, the paterns that our air- — 38 | 8 | 51

planes fly, the amount of credit we get, and the balance in — 52 | 10 | 54

our bank account. Of course, no computer does this alone, — 64 | 13 | 56

computers are controlled by people. But not very many people — 75 | 15 | 58

outside of the automation industry have any real understanding — 87 | 17 | 61

of how even the most simple computer works. Most people's — 99 | 20 | 63

familiarity is limited to the face that they should not fold, — 111 | 22 | 66

spendle, or mutillate there bills monthly. — 119 | 24 | 67

Of course, computers have come to play a big role in the opera- — 13 | 27 | 70

tions of government and business. But presently computers are — 26 | 29 | 72

helping some of the most basic machines that fulfill our per- — 38 | 31 | 75

sonal needs. For one thing, the engines in several of the — 49 | 34 | 77

newer cars are equiped with tiny computers that control speed, — 63 | 36 | 80

temprature, and other factures, and then ajust the spark to — 74 | 39 | 82

get the best possibel millage for us. And we can be certain — 86 | 41 | 85

that more and more uses will be found for these things. — 98 | 44 | 87

Review/apply communication skills: punctuation

full sheet; 1″ top margin; 74-space line

Keyboard and format as directed on p. 129.

Key: 1b. (Saturday) 4c. (1783–1859) 5b. ($2,000)

Use parentheses

1. To enclose nonessential, parenthetical, or explanatory information.
2. To enclose numbers or letters which identify certain sections of an outline.
3. To enclose identifying letters or figures in lists.
4. To enclose nonessential dates, times, amounts, and references.
5. To enclose figures that follow spelled amounts.

review 1a. I said I was disappointed (not crestfallen) with your decision.
apply b. Call me tomorrow Saturday during the morning.

review 2a. Rank the items in an outline I., A., 1., a., (1), (a), 1), a).

review 3a. Follow these steps: (1) Press the enter key; (2) keyboard the name.

review 4a. In the year of the merger (1972), both firms agreed to relocate.
review b. They paid the bill ($47) on Tuesday (see Invoice #22783).
apply c. Washington Irving 1783-1859 was one of America's great writers.

review 5a. Seventy-seven (77) boxes arrived at the loading dock on Friday.
apply b. The antique show nets two thousand dollars $2,000 each year.

Checkup 1
Express numbers correctly

plain sheet; 70–space line; 1½" top margin; DS; correct errors as you keyboard

The Animal Welfare Association, located at 1 Fifty-second Street, reached its annual goal of $1,000,000 dollars. Nearly 40% of the funds came from private citizens. 50% of the donations were contributed by businesses, and the remaining ten percent came from miscellaneous donors.

Only 10¢ out of every dollar goes to administrative costs. This ensures a better life for three out of every 10 domestic animals that are homeless.

All contributions received after the 1:00 p.m., April 14th deadline are added to next year's goal.

Checkup 2
Capitalize correctly

plain sheet; block style letter, open punctuation; 1½" side margins, begin on Line 16; correct errors as you keyboard

january 7, 19-- | mr. Dwight jacobs, jr. | 3867 cromwell street | independence, mo 64055-2113 | dear mr. jacobs

(¶) the annual sales meeting of hatco, inc., will be held at the congress hotel, suite 207, in st. joseph, missouri, on March 24 and 25.

(¶) because you, mr. jacobs, are one of our top sales leaders in the missouri valley district, i am asking you to participate in a panel discussion which will be presented the thursday of our conference. Panel members will discuss the topic "self-confidence and increased sales." I am enclosing a program of the conference.

(¶) barbara ellis, who is a panel member from the detroit office, will contact you regarding this presentation. miss ellis has agreed to coordinate the panel's efforts.

(¶) i hope you will accept this challenge. our sales force could benefit from your vast knowledge and experience.

sincerely yours | jason v. morrison | sales manager | xx | enclosure

---

Checkup 3
Punctuate correctly

plain sheet; 74–space line; 1½" top margin; type the line number before each sentence; DS between the sentences; correct errors as you keyboard

1. Was it a home run Was it fair Was it foul Who called the play?
2. J A Anderson collected forty-seven dollars $47 for the charity.
3. Hurry. You will miss the kick-off
4. The high level meeting was held March 12th 1985.
5. May we go to the opera La Boheme, Sue asked.
6. Ms Rose's fragile package arrived today in first rate condition.
7. These hinges are too loose therefore the barn door will not close.
8. If they accept the contract we'll make delivery early next week.
9. I plan to read "War and Peace" next summer, he will read Moby Dick.
10. Wait for the wisest of all counselors, Time. Pericles

Punctuation

full sheet; 1″ top margin
74-space line

Keyboard and format as directed on p. 129.

Key: 1b. "The . . . stand,"
2c. "Robots in the Office."
3c. "stoops"

Use quotation marks

1. To enclose a direct quotation.
2. To identify titles of articles and other parts of complete publications, short poems, song titles, television programs, and unpublished works such as theses and dissertations.
3. To enclose translations of foreign words, formal definitions, technical terms, coined words, humorous and ironic expressions, and purposely ungrammatical constructions.

review 1a. "To err is human, to forgive divine," said Alexander Pope.
apply b. The defendant will stand, said Judge Hensley.

review 2a. "Fog" by Carl Sandburg is filled with imagery.
review b. Judy Garland sang "Somewhere Over the Rainbow" in The Wizard of Oz.
apply c. I read an interesting article, Robots in the Office.

review 3a. We made a faux pas, a "false step," when we met the ambassador.
review b. The president "interfaced" with the rest of the management team.
apply c. A falcon stoops when it dives to attack its prey.

Keyboard and format as directed on p. 129.

Key: 1b. Ethan Frome 2b. and's, but's 3b. carpe diem

Use an underline

1. With the titles of complete literary works such as books, magazines, and newspapers. Such titles may be typed in ALL CAPS without the underline.
2. To give special emphasis to words or expressions. Use an unbroken line unless each word is to be considered separately.
3. To set off a word being defined in a formal definition or to set off a foreign expression that is not part of the English language.

review 1a. I read the New York Times; she read the BOSTON GLOBE.
apply b. Ethan Frome is one of my favorite novels by Edith Wharton.

review 2a. Insert a comma before and after an appositive.
apply b. Omit the semicolons and add a few and's or but's.

review 3a. The term wright was used to describe someone "who worked in wood."
apply b. The term carpe diem literally means "seize the day."

Keyboard and format as directed on p. 129.

Key: 1c. reported: 2c. re—port: 3c. 2:45

Use a colon

1. Following an introductory statement which causes the reader to anticipate a list, enumeration, explanation, or illustration.
2. To introduce a statement, question, or long direct quotation.
3. To separate hours and minutes when time is expressed in figures, or between numbers when used to express proportions.

review 1a. He had three books: a dictionary, a thesaurus, and a cookbook.
review b. Only one question remains to be answered: Who pays the bill?
apply c. The following students reported A. Grimley, J. Zwick, and S. Yi.

review 2a. He suddenly exclaimed: "We are out of our flight path!"
review b. This is an important question: Who will take care of the animals?
apply c. The aide gave her report "The panel will be dissolved tomorrow."

review 3a. The plane left at 12:32 a.m. and arrived in Sao Paulo at 9:15 p.m.
review b. The top lawyer won the judgeship by a 2:1 margin over her opponent.
apply c. The employees evacuated the building at 2 45 p.m.

Punctuation

full sheet; 1″ top margin;
74-space line

Keyboard and format as
directed on p. 129.

Key: 1b. 4′ 2b. wasn't,
o'clock 3b. i's, s's 3d. 4s
4c. dog's, nails 5c. fox's
6c. Feldcress', students'
7b. Marjorie's 7d. Alison's,
Jean's

Use an apostrophe

1. As a symbol to signify feet in billings or tabulations and as a symbol for minutes.
2. To show omission of letters or figures.
3. To form the plural of most figures, numbers written as words, and letters of the alphabet using the apostrophe followed by s ('s). In market quotations, only the s is added to the figure to form the plural (5s).
4. To show possession by nouns not ending in the s or z sound by adding an apostrophe and an s ('s).
5. To show possession by singular nouns ending in the s or z sound by adding the apostrophe and s ('s) to words of one syllable and an apostrophe (') only to words of more than one syllable. Some writers use an apostrophe and s ('s) to form the possessive of a multi-syllable singular noun ending in s or z if a new syllable is formed by the pronunciation of the possessive (witness's).
6. To show possession of plural nouns or proper nouns of more than one syllable ending in the s or z sound by adding the apostrophe (') only.
7. To show joint ownership or possession after the last noun in a series of two or more persons or to indicate separate ownership after each of the nouns.

review 1a. A 20′ extension ladder will be necessary to paint the house.
apply   b. The dimensions of the cabinet are 6′ × 4 × 1′.

review 2a. Aren't you a member of the Class of '85?
apply   b. She wasnt in the office at one oclock.

review 3a. The 2's and the e's on this page are unclear.
apply   b. How many i s and s s are in the word Mississippi?
review   c. Globe Fund 3s were quoted at 19 and sold for 17 1/2.
apply   d. Hershel Fund 4's sold for more than anyone anticipated.

review 4a. The car's lights reflected off the metal street sign.
review   b. The children's toy box was full of broken toys.
apply   c. The dogs coat was shiny, but her nail's needed to be trimmed.

review 5a. Gus's baseball bat shattered as he slammed the ball.
review   b. For old times' sake, the alumnus' speech was read at the reunion.
apply   c. The fox' copper coat reflected against the autumn sky.

review 6a. The babies' rattles are located in the last aisle of the store.
review   b. Cornelius' party was held at the Clingenshears' home.
apply   c. Mrs. Feldcress grade book is with the students tests.

review 7a. Miss Whitney and Mr. Rainsford's book order has arrived in time.
apply   b. Ruth and Marjories report was informative.
review   c. Peter's and Howard's motorcycles are both red.
apply   d. Both Alisons and Jeans rooms will be painted this fall.

Keyboard and format as
directed on p. 129.

Key: 1b. volunteers—,
Ohio— 2c. problem— 3b.
age.—

Use a dash

1. To indicate a break or change in thought.
2. To indicate dramatic emphasis or pauses or hesitations in written dialogue.
3. To indicate the source of a quotation.

review 1a. I decided--the choice still surprises me--to become a chemist.
apply   b. The volunteers the five were from Ohio worked through the night.

review 2a. Money--that is what they want!
review   b. She will complete the essay--well, almost finish it--by 2:30 p.m.
apply   c. There is one way to solve that problem try harder.

review 3a. Happy is the house that shelters a friend.--Ralph Waldo Emerson
apply   b. Education is the best provision for old age. Aristotle

Capitalize

1 The first word of a complete sentence.

I have the final page of the report.

2 The first word of a direct quotation.

She said, "Let's work together."

3 The first and main words in titles or headings in books, poems, reports, songs, etc.

I read portions of <u>Leaves of Grass</u>.

4 Titles that precede personal names.

I met Major Busby and Mayor Lopez.

5 Titles of distinction that follow a personal name.

Ms. Chu is a U.S. Senator from Idaho.

6 Names of specific persons and places.

My friend Larry lives in Baltimore.

7 Words derived from the names of specific persons and places.

Barry, a Scot, wore an Edwardian costume.

8 Names of weekdays, months, holidays, and historic periods.

Thursday, November 27, is Thanksgiving.

9 Most nouns followed by identifying numbers.

Issue Check #7813 to pay Invoice 785-J.

10 The first word after a colon if it begins a complete sentence.

Notice: No running is permitted.

11 Seasons of the year if they are personified, and compass points if they designate definite regions.

The icy breath of Winter chilled the Midwest.

12 Trademarks, brand names, and names of commercial products.

My Peerless radio uses Rayovac batteries.

Do not capitalize

1 Compass points when they indicate direction.

We drove north to South Brunswick.

2 *Page* and *verse*, even when followed by a number.

The quotation is in verse 72 on page 512.

3 A title following a name that is not a title of distinction.

Rana was elected secretary of our club.

4 Commonly accepted derivatives of proper nouns.

Why not go dutch treat tonight?

5 The common noun following the name of a product.

I have a Silvertone radio; Jan has an SRE tape deck.

6 Generic terms when they appear in the plural to describe two or more names.

Meet me where Oak and Maple roads cross.

See also pages 65 and 129 of the textbook.

Numbers: Type as words

1 A figure that begins a sentence.

Three of the runners were disqualified.

2 Numbers ten and lower, unless used as part of a series of figures, some of which are above ten.

I carried five books with me today.
Only 9 of the 27 ducks had been banded.

3 Expressions of time with the word *o'clock*.

Dinner will be served at seven o'clock.

4 The smaller of two numbers used together.

Buy two 5-gallon containers of gasoline.

5 Isolated fractions or indefinite amounts.

Only one third of almost six hundred members attended.

6 Names of small-numbered (ten and under) streets.

He moved from First Street to Seventh Avenue.

7 Large even numbers.

My chances of winning are one in a million.

Numbers: Type as figures

1 Numbers preceded by most nouns.

Check Column 3 of the Volume 2 appendix.

2 Expressions of time followed by *a.m.* or *p.m.* and days and years used as part of a date.

We will meet again at 2 p.m., May 5, 1989.

3 House numbers (except One) and high-numbered street names (with *d* and *th*).

Deliver the flowers to 45 East 72d Street.
My temporary address is 340--39th Street.

4 Numbers used with abbreviations, symbols, or dimensions.

For a 2% solution, add 4 tsp. salt to 4 qts. of water.

5 Dates (with *d* and *th*) that precede the month and are separated from it by words.

We signed a lease on the 23d or 24th of April.

See also pages 77-78 of the textbook.

Use an apostrophe (followed by a single space unless a letter, figure, or mark of punctuation immediately follows it)

1 As a symbol for feet and minutes.
Take a 3' writing.
The crate measured 2' by 2' by 6'.

2 With s to form the plural of most figures, figures written as words, and letters. In market quotations, the apostrophe is not used.
2's two's C's Fourstar Fund 8s

3 To show omission of letters or figures.
Rob't Sec'y Class of '89

4 To show possession: Add the apostrophe and s to a singular noun not ending in s. If a singular noun ends in an s or z sound, add 's to form the possessive if the ending s is to be pronounced as a syllable; add the apostrophe only if the ending s would be awkward to pronounce.
book's cover horse's hoof Bess's crown
box's lid species' peculiarities

5 To show possession: Add the apostrophe and s to a plural noun that does not end in s.
men's hats women's coats children's toys

6 To show possession: Add only the apostrophe after (a) plural nouns ending in s and (b) a proper noun of more than one syllable ending in s or z.
workers' cards Cortez' trip Lois' wish

7 To show possession: Add 's after the last noun in a series to indicate joint or common possession of two or more persons; however, show separate possession of two or more persons by adding 's to each noun.
Alice and Bill's anniversary
Rita's and Trevor's birthdays

See also page 155 of the textbook.

Use an exclamation point (followed by 2 spaces)

1 After emotional words or phrases.
Wow! Watch it! Hurray! Look out!

2 After exclamatory sentences.
You spilled the chemicals!

See also pages 51 and 130 of the textbook.

Use a comma (followed by a single space, unless it is used internally in a large figure)

1 After introductory words, phrases, or dependent clauses.
If you don't answer, we may miss a call.
No, I cannot answer the phone now.

2 Between words or groups of words that comprise a series.
The flag is red, white, and blue.
We left home, drove to town, and saw a show.

3 To set off explanatory and descriptive words, phrases, and clauses used in a sentence.
Today, Friday, is my day off.
You did not, I know, leave early.

4 To set off words in direct address.
If you can, Betsy, write to Joan tonight.

5 To set off nonrestrictive adjective clauses (not necessary to the meaning of the sentence), but not restrictive adjective clauses (needed for meaning).
The books, some of which I read, are missing.
The guests who were late missed dinner.

6 To set off (a) a year that is used as part of a date and (b) the state when it follows a city.
On July 4, 1985, I left for Richmond, Virginia.
I saw her in Topeka, Kansas, on May 1, 1986.

7 To separate two or more parallel adjectives (adjectives that could be separated by the word and instead of the comma). Do not use commas to separate adjectives so closely related that they appear to form a single element with the noun they modify.
It was a frosty, windy day in March.
She sat under a green linden tree.

8 To separate (a) unrelated groups of figures that come together and (b) whole numbers into groups of three digits each (however, numbers that identify rather than enumerate are usually typed without commas).
At 5:15, 1,250 papers were sent to Room 4085.

9 To set off contrasting phrases and clauses.
People, not machines, make decisions.

See also page 131 of the textbook.

Use a hyphen (with no space before or after it)

1 To join compound numbers typed as words.

sixty-two forty-eight two hundred fifty-six

2 To join compound adjectives written *before* a noun they modify as a unit.

first-rate lunch up-to-date information

3 After words or figures in a series that have a common ending (suspended hyphenation).

two-, three-, and five-minute writings

See also pages 38 and 141 of the textbook.

Use a dash (two consecutive hyphens with no space before or after them)

1 For emphasis, clarity, or change of thought.

The trees--very large trees--loomed ahead.
The trip--it was my idea--was great fun.

2 To show the source of a direct quotation.

A dash separates; a hyphen joins.--Anonymous

3 To indicate in written form verbal pauses.

Yes--er--no--oh, I don't know!

See also pages 38 and 155 of the textbook.

Use parentheses (with no space between them and the data they enclose)

1 To enclose explanatory, parenthetical, or nonessential material.

My roommate (my older sister) owns the car.

2 To enclose letters or figures in a listing.

Show your (a) name, (b) address, and (c) age.

3 To enclose figures that follow spelled-out amounts to give clarity or emphasis.

You must pay fifty dollars ($50) now.

See also page 153 of the textbook.

Use a colon (followed by two spaces unless it is used with integrated figures)

1 To introduce a statement or listing.

Order these items: a lamp, a cord, and a plug.
This is the question: Where is Dan?

2 To separate integrated figures.

3:1 odds 2:45 a.m. ratio of 5:2

See also page 154 of the textbook.

Use a semicolon (followed by one space)

1 To separate two or more independent clauses in a compound sentence when the conjunction is omitted.

I came; I saw; I conquered.

2 To separate independent clauses joined by a conjunctive adverb (however, therefore, etc.).

He knows me well; however, we do not correspond.

3 To separate a series of word or figure groups if one or more of the groups contains a comma.

Bring a ball; a bat; and, of course, your mitt.

4 To precede an abbreviation or word(s) that introduce further explanation.

Myra was here; that is, I saw her earlier.

See also page 138 of the textbook.

Use an underline (continuously, unless each word is to be considered separately)

1 With titles of complete literary works.

<u>Hamlet</u> <u>The Daily News</u> <u>New England Magazine</u>

2 To emphasize special words or phrases.

Can he spell <u>convenience</u>? I know he <u>can</u>.

See also page 154 of the textbook.

Use a period (followed by two spaces if it ends a sentence, one space if it ends an abbreviation)

1 To end a declaratory sentence or a request.

It is raining. Will you hand me my umbrella.

2 With a variety of abbreviations.

Mr. R. E. Riaz, a CPA, called at 2 p.m.

See also pages 91 and 130 of the textbook.

Use quotation marks (after a comma or period, before a semicolon or colon, and after a question mark only if the quotation itself is a question)

1 To enclose a direct quotation.

She asked, "Who is in charge here?"
Did you hear her say, "Lex is a Gemini"?

2 To enclose titles and parts of publications.

"Storm Strikes Area" "The Mikado" "Trees"

3 To enclose special or coined words.

The child said he saw a "wabbit."

4 As a symbol for inches and seconds.

The board is 9″ long.
The timer is set for 45″.

See also page 154 of the textbook.

Word-division guides

A word may correctly be divided between syllables as defined in a dictionary or word-division manual. In special cases, the guidelines below will be helpful.

Short words. Do not divide words of five or fewer letters, even if they have two or more syllables.

area bonus alien aroma truth ideal

Double consonants. Divide between double consonants un-less the division involves a word that ends in double con-sonants.

excel-lent call-ing win-ner add-ing

One- or two-letter syllables. Do not divide a one-letter sylla-ble at the beginning of a word.

enough ideal opened aboard ozone

Do not separate a two-letter syllable at the end of a word.

friendly shaker nickel groggy fluid

Divide after a one-letter syllable within a word; if two single-letter syllables occur together, divide between them.

tele-vision ele-ment gradu-ation idi-omatic

Hyphenated words. Divide at the hyphens only.

self-centered off-white soft-spoken

Figures. Do not divide figures presented as a unit.

2,785,321 127,100 #3290533 150/371

Avoid if possible. Try to avoid dividing proper names, dates, and the last word on a page.

ZIP Code abbreviations

Alabama, AL	Kentucky, KY	Ohio, OH
Alaska, AK	Louisiana, LA	Oklahoma, OK
Arizona, AZ	Maine, ME	Oregon, OR
Arkansas, AR	Maryland, MD	Pennsylvania, PA
California, CA	Massachusetts, MA	Puerto Rico, PR
Colorado, CO	Michigan, MI	Rhode Island, RI
Connecticut, CT	Minnesota, MN	South Carolina, SC
Delaware, DE	Mississippi, MS	South Dakota, SD
District of Columbia, DC	Missouri, MO	Tennessee, TN
Florida, FL	Montana, MT	Texas, TX
Georgia, GA	Nebraska, NE	Utah, UT
Guam, GU	Nevada, NV	Vermont, VT
Hawaii, HI	New Hampshire, NH	Virgin Islands, VI
Idaho, ID	New Jersey, NJ	Virginia, VA
Illinois, IL	New Mexico, NM	Washington, WA
Indiana, IN	New York, NY	West Virginia, WV
Iowa, IA	North Carolina, NC	Wisconsin, WI
Kansas, KS	North Dakota, ND	Wyoming, WY

See also page 43 of the textbook.

Margins/Date Placement. The average letter, business or per-sonal, fits well on an 8½" × 11" page if 1½" side margins are used. When letterhead paper is not used, type a return address on Lines 14 and 15. Type the date on Line 16, just below the return ad-dress (or alone on letterhead paper). With a short or long letter, adjust the margins in or out ½"; lower or raise the return address and date as needed. (See also let-ter placement table on page 117.)

Horizontal placement of the date varies according to letter style. In block and AMS Simplified styles, type the date at left margin; in modified block style, begin the date at center point. Other letter parts, when they are used, are formatted at left margin, unless otherwise noted.

Mailing notation: on the second line space between the date and letter address. See Letter 2 below.

Letter address: on the fourth line space below the date. Type any official title on the same line as the name or below it, whichever gives better balance. A personal title (as *Ms.* or *Mr.*) precedes an individu-al's name.

Attention line: as the second line of the letter address. The saluta-tion corresponds with the letter address, not the attention line. See Letter 1 below.

Subject line: a double space below the salutation. An introduc-tion such as *Re.* or *SUBJECT:* is optional. See Letter 3 below.

Salutation: a double space below letter address or subject line. The salutation corresponds with the first line of the letter address. If the first line has no gender, use *Ladies and Gentlemen* or *Dear Sir or Madam.* See Letters 1 and 3 be-low.

Company name in closing: on the second line space below the complimentary close, in ALL CAPS, at center point for modified block style. See Letter 2 below.

Writer's typed name/official title: on the fourth line space below the complimentary close or company name. With the exception of the AMS style, the writer's title may go on either the same line as the name or below it—whichever gives better balance. A female sig-natory may indicate personal title preference; a male does not, as *Mr.* is always acceptable. See Let-ters 1–4 below.

Reference initials: a double space below the name and official title in lower case. See Letters 1–4 below.

Enclosure notation: a double space below the reference initials. See Letters 1 and 2 below.

Copy notation (cc, bcc, pc): a double space below the reference initials or enclosure notation, fol-lowed by the recipient's name. See Letter 1 below.

Postscript: a double space below the last letter item, in the same style as was used for other para-graphs. The letters P.S. are rarely used. See Letter 3 below.

Multiple pages: If a letter is too long for one page, at least 2 lines of the body of the letter should be carried to the second page. Begin the sec-ond and subsequent pages on Line 7; leave two blank line spaces below page headings. Use the same side margins as the first page.

Second-page headings

block form

```
Leslie Moll, Inc.
Page 2
October 23, 19--
                                              1"
TS
and it would seem appropriate for the remainder of the shipment
to be kept in storage at the Dubuque depot until the conditions
```

horizontal form

```
Leslie Moll, Inc.          2          October 23, 19--
                                              1"
TS
and it would seem appropriate for the remainder of the shipment
to be kept in storage at the Dubuque depot until the conditions
```

Communications Design Associates

348 INDIANA AVENUE
WASHINGTON, DC 20001-1438
Tel: 1-800-432-5739

February 14, 19--

Sunstructures, Inc.
Attention Mr. Harvey Bell
2214 Brantford Place
Buffalo, NY 14222-5147

Ladies and Gentlemen

This letter is written in what is called "block style."
It is the style we recommend for use in your business
office for reasons detailed in the following paragraphs.

First, the style is a very efficient one. All lines
(including date) begin at the left margin, and time is
not consumed in positioning special parts of letters.

Second, the style is easy to learn. New employees will
have little difficulty learning it, and your present
staff can adjust to it without unnecessary confusion.

Third, the style is sufficiently different from most
other styles that it can suggest to clients that your
company is creative. The style gains attention.

At the request of Thomas Wray, I am enclosing his booklet about business letter styles and special features.

Sincerely

Kathryn E. Bowers

Ms. Kathryn E. Bowers
Senior Consultant

xx

Enclosure

pc Mr. Thomas Wray

1 Block, open

Communications Design Associates

348 INDIANA AVENUE
WASHINGTON, DC 20001-1438
Tel: 1-800-432-5739

November 28, 19--

SPECIAL DELIVERY

Mr. Otto B. Bates, President
Third Bank and Trust Company
9080 Reservoir Avenue
New Brunswick, NJ 90901-4476

Dear Mr. Bates

This letter is written in the "modified block style."
It is the style we recommend for use in your office for
reasons detailed for you in the paragraphs below.

First, the style is an efficient one that requires only
one tab setting--at center point--for positioning the
date, complimentary close, and typed signature lines.

Second, the style is easy to learn. New employees will
have little difficulty learning it, and your present
staff can adjust to it without unnecessary confusion.

Third, the style is a familiar one; it is used by more
business firms than any other. It is conservative, and
customers and companies alike feel comfortable with it.

A booklet about business letter styles and special features is enclosed. Use the reply card, also enclosed,
if you need additional information.

Sincerely yours

COMMUNICATIONS DESIGN ASSOCIATES

Kathryn E. Bowers

Ms. Kathryn E. Bowers
Senior Consultant

xx

Enclosures: 2

2 Modified block, open

Communications Design Associates

348 INDIANA AVENUE
WASHINGTON, DC 20001-1438
Tel: 1-800-432-5739

November 2, 19--

Office Manager
Ramsey Engineering, Inc.
4799 Hamner Drive
Amarillo, TX 79107-6359

Dear Sir or Madam:

MODIFIED BLOCK STYLE LETTER

I am pleased to answer your letter. As you can
see, we use the modified block style, indented paragraphs, and mixed punctuation in our correspondence.
It is the style used in this letter.

The spacing from the top of the page to the date
varies with the length of the letter. Other spacing in
the letter is standard. The date, complimentary close,
and name and official title of the writer are begun at
horizontal center.

Please write to me again if I can help further.

Very truly yours,

Allen M Woodside

Allen M. Woodside
Marketing Manager

xx

Our new LETTER STYLE GUIDE will be sent to you as
soon as it comes from the printer.

3 Modified block, indented ¶s, mixed

Communications Design Associates

348 INDIANA AVENUE
WASHINGTON, DC 20001-1438
Tel: 1-800-432-5739

May 9, 19--

Dr. William S. Rapp
Rapp, Hedgson, & Emblatt
98 Clutter Mill Road
Great Neck, NY 11021-4527

AMS SIMPLIFIED LETTER STYLE

This letter is typed in the simplified style that is
recommended by the Administrative Management Society.
The letter features the following points which are designed to save time:

1. Block format is used.

2. Salutation and complimentary close are omitted.

3. A subject heading is typed in ALL CAPS a triple
    space below the address; the first line of the body
    is typed a TS below the subject line.

4. Enumerated items begin flush with the left margin;
    unnumbered items are indented five spaces.

5. The writer's name and title are typed in ALL CAPS
    on the 4th line space below the last line of the
    body of the letter.

6. The reference initials (typist's only) are typed a
    double space below the writer's name.

Correspondents in your company may like the AMS Simplified letter style both for its eye appeal and for its
potential reduction in letter-writing costs.

Luella E. Draper

MRS. LUELLA E. DRAPER, PRESIDENT

xx

4 AMS Simplified

Reference guide: letter styles

1 Interoffice memorandum

Ergonomics Consultants, Inc.

INTEROFFICE COMMUNICATION

TO: All Communication Processors

DATE: June 13, 19--

FROM: Rachel Darboro, Director

SUBJECT: Interoffice Memoranda

The exchange of information within a company is frequently typed on interoffice forms, either half or full sheets, depending upon the length of the message. The following points describe unique features of this form of memorandum.

1. Space twice after a printed heading; set the left margin stop for typing heading items and the body. Set the right margin stop an equal distance from the right edge. These margin adjustments will usually provide side margins of 1 inch.

2. Full addresses, the salutation, the complimentary close, and the signature are omitted.

3. Personal titles, such as Mr., are usually omitted from the memo heading. They are included on the envelope, however.

4. TS between the heading and the message; SS the paragraphs, but DS between them.

5. Reference initials, enclosure notation, and carbon copy notation are included if needed.

Special colored envelopes are often used for interoffice memos. Type the addressee's personal title, name, and business title or name of department for the address. TYPE COMPANY MAIL (in caps) in the postage location.

xx

pc Paul Glass, Assistant to the President

2 Personal letter on Monarch paper

4885 Crescent Avenue, N.
Chicago, IL 60656-3781
April 6, 19--

Ms. Alice Trent-Rocklet
Personnel Manager
Leisure Life Inns
1000 East Lynn Street
Seattle, WA 98102-4268

Dear Ms. Trent-Rocklet

The Placement Office at Great Lakes College tells me that your company has employment available this summer for students.

I am now in my junior year as an economics major. Although my educational background has been mostly in the liberal arts, I have learned to keyboard, and I have taken two accounting courses. In past summers I have worked successfully at a variety of jobs; in fact, I have accepted responsibility for most of my college expenses. I travel as much as I can; I like to meet new friends; and I have a friendly, outgoing personality.

Your interest in providing summer employment for students is much appreciated, Ms. Trent-Rocklet. I am sure I would enjoy working at Leisure Life Inns. May I send you a complete resume and a list of my references?

Sincerely yours

Lance J. Mykins

Lance J. Mykins

3 Message/reply form

Fairfield Manufacturing, Inc.

MESSAGE	REPLY
TO: Jonathan Kappel Director, Employee Development 126 Hancock Tower DATE: January 22, 19-- SUBJECT: Conference on Employee Development The attached brochure was received from the National Center for the Advancement of business practices. Since employee development will be a priority for us for some time, these conference topics may be relevant. Please let me know your opinion. SIGNED: Marla Gonzalez, Vice President	DATE: January 23, 19-- The topics listed are timely and relevant to our long-range plans. I suggest that I attend the conference in New York and make a formal proposal to the corporate officers by April 1. SIGNED: Jonathan Kappel

4 Half-page memo on plain paper

TO: Marilyn Williams, Personnel Director

FROM: Gerald Morris, Graphics Department

DATE: April 3, 19--

SUBJECT: Booklet on Fringe Benefits

Pages 1-10 of the booklet on fringe benefits for Reading employees are enclosed. The printer promises to have the rest of the booklet completed by the end of this week. I expect to receive the copy early next week.

I would appreciate receiving any corrections or suggestions you care to make on these first 10 pages as soon as possible.

xx
Enclosure

5 Personal data sheet

Sally Ann Dupois
123 Poinciana Road
Memphis, TN 38117-4121
(901-365-2775)

PRESENT CAREER OBJECTIVE

Eager to accept part-time position that provides opportunities for additional training and potential for full-time employment.

MAJOR QUALIFICATIONS

Knowledge of merchandising, management, inventory control, and related areas of a retail clothing store. Cheerful, outgoing personality and a dependable, cooperative worker.

EDUCATION

Junior at Memphis State University, Memphis, Tennessee, majoring in Marketing.

AA degree (associate degree/advertising; honors), State Technical Institute, Memphis, Tennessee.

Graduate (honors), East High School, Memphis, Tennessee.

EXPERIENCE

Assistant Manager, The Toggery, 100 Madison Avenue, Memphis, TN 38103-4219, June 1985 - Present.

Inventory Clerk and Cashier, Choble's, 1700 Poplar Avenue, Memphis, TN 38104-2176, June 1984 - September 1984.

Clerk and Assistant to the Buyer, Todds, 1450 Union Avenue, Memphis, TN 38104-5417, June 1983 - September 1983.

REFERENCES

Mrs. Evelyn J. Quinell Manager, Choble's 1700 Poplar Avenue Memphis, TN 38104-2176	Professor Aldo R. MacKenzie Marketing Department Memphis State University Memphis, TN 38114-3285
Ms. Lanya Roover The Toggery 100 Madison Avenue Memphis, TN 38103-4219	Mr. Robert E. Tindall, Jr. Attorney-at-law 1045 Quin Avenue Memphis, TN 38106-4792

Addressing procedure

Envelope address. Set a tab stop (or margin stop if a number of envelopes are to be addressed) 10 spaces left of center for a small envelope or 5 spaces for a large envelope. Start the address here on Line 12 from the top edge of a small envelope and on Line 14 of a large one.

Style. Type the address in *block style*, single-spaced. Type the city name, state name or abbreviation, and ZIP Code on the last address line. The ZIP Code is usually typed 2 spaces after the state name.

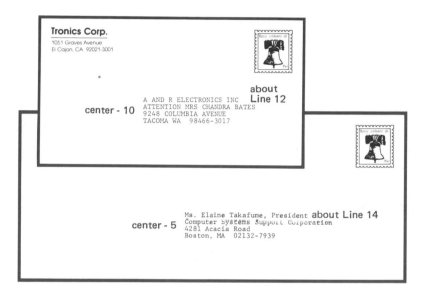

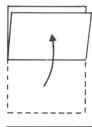

```
Tronics Corp.
1051 Graves Avenue
El Cajon, CA 92021-3001

                                              about
                  A AND R ELECTRONICS INC     Line 12
                  ATTENTION MRS CHANDRA BATES
   center - 10    9248 COLUMBIA AVENUE
                  TACOMA WA  98466-3017


                  Ms. Elaine Takafume, President  about Line 14
                  Computer Systems Support Corporation
   center - 5     4281 Acacia Road
                  Boston, MA  02132-7939
```

Addressee notations. Type addressee notations, such as *Hold for Arrival, Please Forward, Personal,* etc., a triple space below the return address and about 3 spaces from the left edge of the envelope. These notations may be underlined or typed in all capitals.

If an *attention line* is used, type it immediately below the company name in the address line.

Mailing notations. Type mailing notations, such as SPECIAL DELIVERY and REGISTERED, below the stamp and at least 3 line spaces above the envelope address. Type these notations in all capital letters.

```
Fairfield Manufacturing, Inc.
        4320 Aldine Drive
        San Diego, CA  92116-2307
   TS
HOLD FOR ARRIVAL

                                    SPECIAL DELIVERY

        Mr. Dennis Sukarski
        c/o E-Z Rest Motor Lodge
        352 Custer Court
        Modesto, CA  95351-4908
```

Folding and inserting procedure

Small envelopes (No. 6¾, 6¼)

Step 1
With letter face up, fold bottom up to ½ inch from top.

Step 2
Fold right third to left.

Step 3
Fold left third to ½ inch from last crease.

Step 4
Insert last creased edge first.

Large envelopes (No. 10, 9, 7¾)

Step 1
With letter face up, fold slightly less than ⅓ of sheet up toward top.

Step 2
Fold down top of sheet to within ½ inch of bottom fold.

Step 3
Insert letter into envelope with last crease toward bottom of envelope.

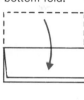 

Window envelopes (letter)

Step 1
With sheet face down, top toward you, fold upper third down.

Step 2
Fold lower third up so address is showing.

Step 3
Insert sheet into envelope with last crease at bottom.

Window envelopes (invoices and other forms)

Step 1
Place sheet face down, top toward you.

Step 2
Fold back top so address shows.

Step 3
Insert into envelope with crease at bottom.

  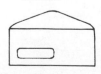

Formatting reports (See illustrations below)

Margins. Use 1" top, side, and bottom margins, except for the first page, which has a 1½" or 2" top margin.

Binding. Allow an extra ½" for side or top binding.

Spacing. Double spacing for the body of a report and 5-space paragraph indentions are usual.

Quotations. Single-space quotations of 4 or more lines and indent them 5 spaces from each margin; otherwise, enclose the quotations in quotation marks and include them double-spaced as part of the body of the report.

Ellipses. An ellipsis, an intentional omission of part of a quotation, is indicated by 3 periods with one space between each of the periods. If the omission ends a sentence, use 4 periods.

Leaders. If the report contains tabular copy, the columns may be separated by leaders. Leaders (spaced periods) can help a reader to move from one column to another. After typing the first item in the first column, space once and then alternate a period and a space to a point 2 or 3 spaces short of the next column. Note whether you type the periods on odd or even line-of-writing numbers; align subsequent rows by starting on an odd or even number as you did in the first line.

Justifying the right margin (manually). A preliminary copy must be typed to determine how many extra spaces must be added between words to insure an even right margin in a final copy. The normal procedure for the preliminary typing is to type as close to the end of each line as possible and then fill the remaining spaces with diagonals until the machine locks. Interpret diagonals as spaces to be added to each line in the final copy.

Footnotes. Footnotes may be placed at the end of a report, or they may be placed at the foot of the page on which reference to them is made.

Use a superior figure or symbol in the text of the report as reference to a footnote. Repeat the reference with the footnote.

Separate footnotes from the body of a report with a single underline 1½" long; single-space below the last line of the report to type the underline, type the underline, and double-space below the underline to begin the first line of the footnotes.

Single-space footnotes; double-space between them. Calculate footnote placement to insure a 1" bottom margin.

Formatting outlines

Data may be reduced to a more functional form through the use of an outline. Use the following suggestions.

Separate divisions and subdivisions of various orders with 4-space indentions.

Type first order divisions in ALL CAPS; capitalize main words only in second-order divisions; capitalize only the first word in third- and subsequent-order divisions.

Use the margin release and backspacer to type all Roman numerals other than I, V, and X.

The line length chosen must accommodate the longest line but must not exceed 70 spaces.

There must be at least two parts to any division.

```
                    HEADING

                      TS

     I.  FIRST-ORDER DIVISION

                      DS

         A.  Second-Order Division
         B.  Second-Order Division
             1.  Third-order division
             2.  Third-order division
         C.  Second-Order Division

                      DS

    II.  FIRST-ORDER DIVISION

                      DS

         A.  Second-Order Division
             1.  Third-order division
             2.  Third-order division
                 a.  Fourth-order division
                 b.  Fourth-order division
             3.  Third-order division
         B.  Second-Order Division
```

1 Unbound report, page 1

PREPARING REPORTS: THE PROFESSIONAL TOUCH

Both the writer and keyboard operator, or compositor, share
concern for the preparation and ultimate success of a report, but
usually the writer must accept final accountability. The compositor's contribution, however, is a vital one; and she or he should
proceed cautiously. For example, before starting to prepare a
final copy of a report, the compositor should determine

1. the specified purpose of the report and whether some
   particular format is required;
2. the number, kind, and grade of copies required;[1] and
3. deadlines for completion.

The keyboard operator should be prepared to work from script,
rough-draft, or printed copy and yet give the report a final presentation that is as professional as it is functional.

"Tricks of the Trade"

Those with experience in preparing reports have found that
there are special procedures they can use to simplify their tasks.
The following paragraphs contain samples of some procedures that
can be especially helpful to a person who has not previously keyboarded reports. (Anyone who plans to prepare more than a few
reports, however, should read several good books on the subject.)

Right margins. Attractive right margins result when good
judgment is exercised. Using the warning bell judiciously ensures
right margins that approximate left margins in width.

_____
[1]For further information, see The Chicago Manual of Style,
13th ed. (Chicago: The University of Chicago Press, 1982), p. 40.

2 Unbound report, page 2

2

Reference characters. To keystroke a superior figure, turn
the platen back a half line and type the figure. Asterisks and
other reference symbols require no such adjustment. Keyboards
with special symbol keys for report writing are available.

Page endings. A few simple guides become important whenever
a report has more than one page. For example, never end a page
with a hyphenated word. Further, do not leave a single line of a
paragraph at the bottom of a page or at the top of a page (unless
the paragraph has only one line, of course).

Footnote content. Underline titles of complete publications;
use quotation marks with parts of publications. Thus, the name of
a magazine will be underlined, but the title of an article within
the magazine will be placed in quotation marks. Months and loca-
tional words, such as volume and number, may be abbreviated.

Penciled guides. A light pencil mark can be helpful to mark
approximate page endings, planned placement of page numbers, and
potential footnote locations. When the report has been finished,
erase any visible pencil marks.

Conclusion

With patience and skill, the keyboard operator can give a
well-written report the professional appearance it deserves. Says
Lesikar[2],

Even with the best typewriter available, the finished work is no better than the efforts of the typist.
But this statement does not imply that only the most
skilled typist can turn out good work. Even the inexperienced typist can produce acceptable manuscripts
simply by exercising care.

_____
[2]Raymond V. Lesikar, Basic Business Communication (Homewood:
Richard D. Irwin, Inc., 1979), p. 364.

3 Title page

TRENDS IN OFFICE COMMUNICATION

Bernadette E. Blount
Northern Illinois University

January 11, 19--

4 Bibliography

BIBLIOGRAPHY

Blum, Lester. "Computer Generated Graphic Tutorials In Economics."
Collegiate Microcomputer 4 (Winter 1983): 289-97.

Crawford, T. James, et al. Basic Keyboarding and Typewriting Applications. Cincinnati: South-Western Publishing Co., 1983.

Hess, M. Elizabeth. Printing Manager, Effective Office Systems,
New Orleans, Louisiana. Interviewed by Lois Walker, March 20,
1985.

Ray, Patrick V. "Electronic Printing Applications." Class handout
in BADM 487. Central University, 1985.

Toffler, Alvin. The Third Wave. New York: William Morrow and Company, Inc., 1980.

LENDING POLICY FOR COUNTY BANK

Limits of Authority

The President of the bank is authorized to make loans up to $100,000 on a secured basis and up to $50,000 on an unsecured basis. Any request for a line of credit in excess of the limit specified for the President must be approved by at least two members of the Loan Committee other than the President. These lending limits are in agreement with recommended standards (Burge, 1985).

The President shall delegate authority to make loans to the senior officers of the bank. Senior officers may approve loans up to $50,000 on a secured basis and up to $25,000 on an unsecured basis. The President may delegate authority to make loans to other officers. Authority delegated to officers other than the senior officers shall not exceed $10,000 and shall be for secured loans only. This policy is based on recommended guides (White, 1985).

REFERENCES

Burge, S. Michael. "General Lending Policy," South-Western Banking Association Report. March 12, 1985, p. 8.

White, Deborah B. "Guides for Delegating Lending Authority." Class handout in Bankers' School, Central University, 1985.

1 Reference citations

TABLE OF CONTENTS

2 Table of contents

Cap or ≡	Capitalize
⌒	Close up
∮	Delete
∧	Insert
⌄	Insert comma
# or ⁄#	Insert space
⌄	Insert apostrophe
⌄ ⌄	Insert quotation marks
⊏⊐	Move right
⊏⊐	Move left
⊔	Move down; lower
⊓	Move up; raise
lc or /	Set in lowercase
¶	Paragraph
no new ¶	No new paragraph
‖	Set flush; align type
○ sp	Spell out
stet	Let it stand; ignore correction
∿ or *tr*	Transpose
___	Underline or italics

Proofreader's marks

Preliminary copy may be corrected with proofreader's marks. The typist must be able to interpret correctly these marks when retyping the corrected (rough-draft) copy. The most commonly used marks are shown above.

Correcting errors

There are several methods that can be used to correct errors, and they are explained below.

Correction paper ("white carbon")

1 Backspace to the error.

2 Place the correction paper in front of the error, coated side toward the paper.

3 Retype the error. The substance on the correction paper will cover the error.

4 Remove the correction paper; backspace; type the correction.

Rubber eraser

1 Use a plastic shield to protect surrounding and a typewriter (hard) eraser.

2 Turn the paper forward or backward in the machine to position the error for easier correction.

3 To keep bits of eraser out of the mechanism, move the carrier away from the error (or move carrier to the extreme left or right).

4 Move the eraser in one direction only to avoid cutting the paper.

Correction fluid ("liquid paper")

1 Be sure the color of the fluid matches the color of the paper.

2 Turn the paper forward or backward to ease the correction process.

3 Brush the fluid on sparingly; cover only the error, and it lightly.

4 The fluid dries quickly. Return to correction point and make the correction.

Automatic correction

If your machine is equipped with an automatic correcting ribbon, consult with your instructor or with the manufacturer's manual for operating instructions.

Horizontal centering

1 Move the margin stops to extreme ends of the scale.

2 Clear tab stops; then set a tab stop at center of paper.

3 Tabulate to the center of the paper.

4 From center, backspace once for each 2 letters, spaces, figures, or punctuation marks in the line.

5 Do not backspace for an odd or leftover stroke at the end of the line.

6 Begin to type where backspacing ends.

	Example
Scale reading at left edge of paper	0
+Scale reading at right edge of paper	102
Total ÷ 2 = Center point	102 ÷ 2 = 51

Spread headings

1 Backspace from center once for each letter, character, and space except the last letter or character in the heading. Start typing where the backspacing ends.

2 When typing a spread heading, space once after each letter or character and three times between words.

Vertical centering

Roll-back-from-center method

From vertical center of paper, roll platen (cylinder) back once for each 2 lines, 2 blank spaces, or line and blank line space. Ignore odd or leftover line.

Steps to follow:

1 To move paper to vertical center, start spacing down from top edge of paper:

  a half sheet
    down 6 TS (triple spaces)
      −1 SS (Line 17)

  b full sheet
    down 11 TS
      +1 SS (Line 34)

2 From vertical center:

  a half sheet, SS or DS; follow basic rule, back 1 for 2.

  b full sheet, SS or DS; follow basic rule, back 1 for 2; then back 2 SS for reading position.

Mathematical method

1 Count lines and blank line spaces needed to type problem.

2 Subtract lines to be used from lines available (66 for full sheet and 33 for half sheet).

3 Divide by 2 to get top and bottom margins. If fraction results, disregard it. Space down from top edge of paper 1 more than number of lines to be left in top margin.

For reading position, which is above exact vertical center, subtract 2 from exact top margin.

Formula for vertical mathematical placement:

$$\frac{\text{Lines available} - \text{lines used}}{2} = \text{top margin}$$

Prepare

1 Insert and align paper.
2 Clear margin stops by moving them to extreme ends of the scale.
3 Clear all tab stops.
4 Decide the number of spaces to be left between columns (for intercolumns).

Plan vertical placement

Follow either of the vertical centering methods explained on page xi.

Headings. Double-space (count 1 blank line space) between main and secondary headings, when both are used. Triple-space (count 2 blank line spaces) between the last heading (either main or secondary) and the first horizontal line of column items or column headings. Double-space between column headings (when used) and the first line of the columns.

Plan horizontal placement

Backspace from center of paper 1 space for each 2 letters, figures, symbols, and spaces in the *longest item* of each column and for each 2 spaces between columns. Set the left margin stop of the longest item when backspacing, carry it forward to the next column. Ignore an extra space at the end of the last column. (See illustration below).

An easy alternate method is to backspace for the longest item in each column first, *then* for the spaces to be left between columns.

Note. If a column heading is longer than the longest item in the column, it may be treated as the longest item in determining placement. The longest column item must then be centered under the heading, and the tab stop set accordingly.

Set tab stops. From the left margin stop, space forward 1 space for each letter, figure, symbol, and space in the longest item in the first column and for each space in the first intercolumn. Set a tab stop. Follow this procedure for each additional column to be typed.

To center column headings

Backspace-from-column-center method

From the point at which the column begins (tab or margin stop), space forward (→) once for each 2 letters, figures, or spaces in the longest item in the column. This leads to the column center point; from it, backspace ( ) once for each 2 spaces in the column heading. Ignore an odd or leftover space. Type the heading at this point; it will be centered over the column.

Mathematical method

1 To the number of the cylinder (platen) or line-of-writing scale immediately under the first letter, figure, or symbol of the longest item of the column, add the number shown under the space following the last stroke of the item. Divide this sum by 2; the result will be the center point of the column. From this point on the scale, backspace to center the column heading.

—or—

2 From the number of spaces in the longest item, subtract the number of spaces in the heading. Divide this number by 2; ignore fractions. Space forward this number from the tab or margin stop and type the heading.

To type horizontal lines

Depress the shift lock; strike the underline key.

To draw vertical lines

Operate the automatic line finder. Place a pencil or pen point through the cardholder (or the type bar guide above the ribbon or carrier). Roll the paper up until you have a line of the desired length. Remove the pencil or pen and reset the line finder.

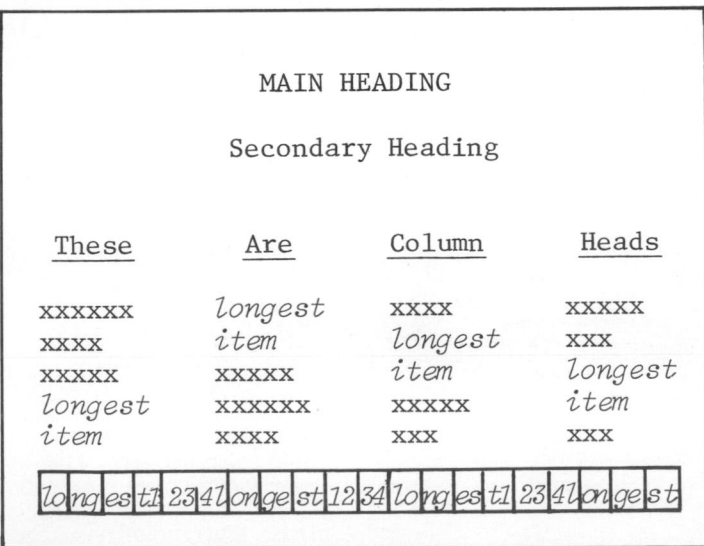